# A CENTURY OF

# WORLD COMMUNISM

## A SELECTIVE CHRONOLOGICAL OUTLINE

Gloria M. Barron Editions.

Books bearing this imprint represent
a distinguished contribution to
scholarship and to world understanding.
Their purpose is to help people learn
to live together in peace.

# A CENTURY OF
# WORLD COMMUNISM

## A SELECTIVE CHRONOLOGICAL OUTLINE

**GEORGE J. PRPIC**

Professor of History
Institute for Soviet Studies
John Carroll University

*Ref.*
*HX*
*36*
*P76*

*123865*

Barron's Educational Series, Inc.
Woodbury, New York

# Acknowledgment

The author and the publisher, *Barron's Educational Series, Inc.*, of *A Century of World Communism* acknowledge with thanks permission granted by the following publishers to quote from books named and maps listed:

Institute for Soviet and East European Studies, Ohio, 1967 for George J. Prpic. *Fifty Years of World Communism* (September 1967).

Institute for Soviet and East European Studies, Ohio for George J. Prpic. *World Communism.*

© 1961 by The New York Times Company, New York. Reprinted by permission, four maps of *Major Goals of Soviet Policy Today.*

Charles Scribner's Sons, New York, 1965, for Basil Dmytryshyn, *USSR: A Concise History.*

Frontispiece — Lenin — *Radio Times*

All inquiries should be addressed to:
Barron's Educational Series, Inc.
113 Crossways Park Drive
Woodbury, New York 11797

Library of Congress Catalog Card No. 71-75835

PRINTED IN THE UNITED STATES OF AMERICA

# *Preface*

It is a well-established fact that the basic reason for impressive Communist victories during the past fifty years was lack of knowledge of the nature of Communism, its ideology, its operational strategy and history.

Knowing exactly what they want gives the Communist strategists the extraordinary advantage in many situations. As a result, they created an illusion of being ten feet tall; and they insist no force in the world could prevent their victories through expansion.

Even the existing diversity in the Communist world does not hinder Moscow and Peiping in the direction of East Central Europe, Latin America, Middle East, Asia and Africa.

The Institute for Soviet and East European Studies at John Carroll University is primarily concerned with objective analysis and information for students and community about the developments in the Communist world; and for this purpose, it has a special program of training high school teachers in the area of "Democracy Versus Communism." The Graduate students and teachers enrolled in the Department of History with orientation toward the general area of World Communism and particularly East Central Europe receive a Certificate of Competence after earning fifteen graduate credit hours.

The faculty members of the Institute offering undergraduate and graduate courses in the field of Soviet and East European Studies greatly appreciate the publication of articles, monographs, and books in this area by leading specialists; but all of us felt the need for an objective, concise, chronological account of the development of World Communism. The other scholarly works in most cases reflect the opinion of authors in their evaluation of the causes for communist successes or failures.

Dr. George J. Prpic, Professor of History and member of the Institute for Soviet Studies, John Carroll University, has written for the use of teachers, students, and other interested individuals the chronological record of the World Communist movement.

Our students at John Carroll University, accepted this type of chronological account with great enthusiasm, since it gives them an opportunity to learn the historical facts without being required to accept an opinion of the author.

I am certain that thousands of students interested in Soviet and East Central European History will welcome this new work and will be grateful to the author for taking time out to prepare it.

The chronological record of the World Communist movement will serve a good purpose. It will remind readers of past Communist involvements in world affairs. It will give us an insight into the recent history of developments and deceptions in totalitarian dictatorships.

The wishful thinking of so many individuals in the academic profession in the United States who insist that Communists will give up their long-range objectives of dominating other nations by force was frustrated by the brutal invasion of Czechoslovakia in August, 1968.

The sympathizers of Communism hopefully will take notice that the Soviet declaration of the rights of nations to self-determination is meaningless and serves only as camouflage for Communist agression and conquest everywhere.

The Czechoslovakian tragedy should also serve as a warning that individual liberty under Communist regime, no matter how limited in scope, is impossible. The Communist dictators cannot feel secure when a man has a free choice.

Once again, we are thankful to Dr. Prpic for presenting this systematic and chronological account of past Communist behavior in the world community to teachers and students and indeed all interested individuals in our society who desire to learn about the factual reality of world communism.

MICHAEL S. PAP, Ph.D.
*Professor of History*
*Director, Institute for Soviet*
*and East European Studies*
*John Carroll University*

*To my brother, Ivan Prpić,
who at the age of twenty-three
lost his life – along with
many of his relatives, friends
and compatriots in the
tragic spring of the year 1945*

# Introduction

In 1967 the fiftieth anniversary of the Bolshevik Revolution was celebrated. In 1968, the Marxist Socialists and Communists all over the world celebrated the 150 th anniversary of Karl Marx's birthday. Exactly one hundred and twenty years before, in the revolutionary year of 1848, the most powerful, propagandistic, and the most revolutionary document of modern Communism — *The Communist Manifesto* — was published. A few weeks ago the centenary of Lenin's birth was observed.

This chronology resulted from an earlier more modest attempt: *Fifty Years of World Communism: 1917-1967 — A Selective Chronology*, published by the Institute for Soviet and East European Studies at John Carroll University in Cleveland, Ohio in 1967. It, in turn, was derived from an earlier publication: *World Communism; Selective Chronology, 1917-1964*. Both of these were meant to be textbooks for students at John Carroll University and for others who take courses in East European and Communist Studies. Many of these students have expressed satisfaction with *Fifty Years of World Communism*; they found it useful in their studies. Many graduate students voiced the same opinion. The idea of illustrations also received a warm reception. Sometimes more can be said by adding a little drawing, a photograph or symbol than with the written word only.

Approached and encouraged by the Barron's Educational Series, I decided to expand this book to *A Century of World Communism*: A Selective Chronological Outline. Actually, this book in its new edition covers about a hundred and fifty years: from the birth of Karl Marx, the founder of modern Communism in 1818, all the way to the end of May of the year 1970. It discusses the time period "from Marx to Mao." However, the stress is on the last hundred years.

As is evident from the entries, the discussion here involves both *Socialism* and *Communism*. The term *Socialism* is still a somewhat ambiguous one, and to different people it presents different meanings. Even present-day Communist leaders in the Soviet Union maintain that they have not as yet reached the stage of Communism, that they are still in Socialism. Their state also is called the Union of Soviet *Socialist* Republics. Several other Communist states in East Europe call themselves *Socialist* republics.

There have been ever since the time of the French Revolution all kinds of Socialism. Roughly, they can be grouped and classified as 1) Utopian, and 2) Marxian or Scientific Socialism. Socialist movements after the 1860's were strong in countries with numerous industrial workers. For many years a typical workers' Socialist Party was the German Social Democratic Party before and after World War I. A majority of the German Socialists and many of their followers in other countries as well rejected the Marxian idea of a proletarian revolution. They wanted to achieve reforms to better the status of the working class by peaceful and parliamentary means. With the rise of "Socialist Revisionism" in Germany and France, international Socialism became divided. This became especially evident in the Russian Socialist movement with the split of 1903 and the subsequent rise of Bolshevism.

Following the Bolshevik Revolution of November, 1917, all left-wing and radical Socialists joined the Communist International and followed the leadership of Moscow, Lenin, and then Stalin.

This is a chronology dealing with the events, trends, ideas and peoples from the early times of Socialism, beginnings of Marxism and Communism until the start of '70's and the present state of Communism.

It discusses revolutions and revolutionaries, wars and tragedies that have taken place in various parts of the world. It does not treat exclusively Communism but also other trends, ideologies, and happenings that have been directly or indirectly interrelated with the rise and development of Communism and revolutionary Socialism.

A chronology is primarily a reference book; it is not a history book in the usual sense. As such, it measures or computes time by regular divisions or periods. It assigns to events and transactions their proper dates; it arranges data and events in the order of time occurance. The reader expects from such a book quick and condensed information – and such is the purpose of this book.

Our Chronology has been compiled from numerous books on the history of Socialism and Communism, on international relations and various ideological movements. Dates have been derived in many cases from original documents and primary sources. It was impossible to always go back to the primary sources; however, I have tried to avail myself of the best authorities. They are too numerous to be quoted here. Most of them are mentioned in my earlier book: *Eastern Europe and World Communism*: A Selective Annotated Bibliography (John Carroll University, The Institute for Soviet and East European Studies, 1966; pp. 148; L.C. catalog card 66-6452).

In the course of my research I have found that many books and publications contain false dates, contradictory data, distortions of facts, and mispelled names. At times it was difficult to verify the contradictory dates or to establish the credibility of the respective information. In many cases there were different interpretations of the exact meaning or significance of the events or individuals involved in them. Needless to say, historians have always differed in the periodization of certain events or chains of events. There are seldom in history clearcut divisions in time. Periodical border lines are often blurred or overlapping.

It is interesting to note that there were exactly one hundred years between the birth of Marx and the revolutionary events in Russia. Precisely one century after the birthday of the founder of modern Communism the birthday of the World Communist Revolution took place. Regardless of how we divide the eras of the Communist revolutionary movement, the great divide still remains the year of 1917. As subsequent landmarks in this kind of chronology could be regarded: the age after the death of Lenin;

Stalin's rise to absolute rule (1927-1928); the period until 1939 (including the Great Purges in Russia, the rise of Hitler, and the Spanish Civil War); the World War II years: 1939-1945. In 1948 Stalin expelled Tito from the Cominform. From that time on international Communism ceased to be monolithic. When Stalin died in 1953, a new era began in the history of Communism. The death of the dictator, the subsequently following revolts in 1953 in East Germany and 1956 in Poland and Hungary as well as the rise of Chinese Communism definitely established the polycentrism of Communism. Moscow ceased to be the only center of this world-wide revolutionary movement. New centers appeared in Peking, Belgrade, Warsaw, Bucharest, and most recently even in Prague. All these new centers claim to have their own and true "Way to Socialism and Communism."

Communism has lost some of its original fervor, but it still remains primarily a revolutionary movement. While it is debatable how much of the original Marxism-Leninism has remained in some of the East European Communist states – including the Soviet Union – the Chinese Communism and the regimes in North Korea, North Vietnam, and in Cuba, are still outspokenly militant and revolutionary movements. The Communist governments rule today over more than a billion people. The Soviet Union and Communist China alone – as the two largest Communist states – comprise an enormous geographic area of about 13,500,000 square miles. Their combined population amounts to well over a billion people. Since 1939 Communist regimes were imposed on more than 130,000,000 people in East Central Europe. Over 22,000,000 of them came under direct Soviet rule. There are presently fourteen states, large and small, whose destinies are controlled by Communism. These facts alone justify our interest in the history of international Communism. From a few thousand Bolsheviks – followers of Lenin – in 1917, the Communist movement in the world has grown to more than forty million members. The armed forces and militias of all Communist states also number many millions.

One of the best chronologies on the rise and development of Communism is *World Communist Movement: Selective Chronology, 1818-1957*. It was prepared by the Legislative Reference Service of the Library of Congress and printed for the Committee on Un-American Activities. Its first volume of some 230 pages covers the history of Communism from 1818 to 1945. It was printed by the U.S. Government Printing Office, Washington, D.C., 1960, and contains a wealth of useful information, but it is overloaded with direct quotations. Although it is a selective chronology, some important dates that should have been included were left out. Three more volumes were published afterwards.

There is presently an ever-increasing interest in the area of East European, Communist and Slavic Studies. Many American and Canadian colleges and universities offer courses in such areas and have established special institutes and departments dealing especially with the Soviet empire and the Communist world. At our school, John Carroll University, each semester over three hundred students take courses in East European and Soviet studies on undergraduate and graduate levels. Most of them are in History, but there are some in Political Science, Philosophy, Modern Languages, Economics, and Education. Some fifty Master's theses and essays dealing with a variety of such topics have been written so far in History alone. Hundreds of high school teachers have participated in our Summer School Workshop Seminars to get preparation for teaching on Communism and the Communist world. Many high schools in America are offering such courses.

A student and a teacher need a concise and practical, one-volume handbook containing only basic facts. This is why we have prepared this book. We sincerely hope it will serve its purpose. Because of the nature of this book, the author has not dealt extensively with Communist ideology and doctrine. Herein are included only brief explanations of the basic theories and ideas of Socialism and Communism between the early 1800's and the end of 1960's.

A chronology such as this does not in detail analyze and discuss the events. It is a brief summary of relevant or pertinent happenings of the past. It is in the very nature of history that any historian covers only a part of the events and personalities that make up the actuality of history. This applies even more to a chronologist. His work actually consists in condensation of the works and writings of other historians, observers, eyewitnesses, of documents, books, articles, newspaper reports and similar sources. One problem that inevitably turns up in this condensation is that of selection and proportion, and of course very frequently of relevance. There is no chronology that can please and satisfy everyone!

And of course, there are various types of chronologies. Some of them contain only the most basic dates and very brief data listed in separate parallel columns. They refer to personalities mostly by their last names. They contain no explanation at all. Ours is not this kind of chronology. We believe that our type of a chronological historical survey is more practical and helpful to the reader – and particularly to students and teachers – than the old, dry, unappealing, dull and cryptical chronologies.

This is more an historical outline than chronology in its strict sense of the term. To better illustrate or underline the significance of an event I have occasionally used short direct quotations. Those who have sufficient background knowledge will be able to use these historical sketches and glimpses as memory refreshers. I have been told by students that *Fifty Years of World Communism* was of great help to them in studying for examinations. Teachers told me that it helped them to organize their lectures and courses. This new book which is more extensive and more complete should then be of even greater help!

It is a customary in chronologies to relate events of the past in the historical present. Wherever I have used complete dates (day, month, year) I have used the historical present; otherwise I have used mostly the past tense.

Some fifteen years ago the Korean War Ended. In three years and one month the United States suffered in that involvement some 33,600 deaths. For more than eight and a half years we have been engaged in the longest war of our history, in Vietnam. As of April 1, 1970, more than 48,000 from the U.S. had died in that bloody and tragic conflict, a great majority of them having been killed in action. At present we have about 450,000 troops engaged on this Asiatic battlefront against Communists. Behind this conflict – which has cost us many thousands of casualties and many billions of dollars – looms the huge shadow of Communist China.

The war in Vietnam and recently in Cambodia has caused a great deal of controversy. While at present the peace talks are conducted in Paris, the war is still raging with all its tragic consequences. Many of our young soldiers have been killed by Soviet-made weapons. The war itself is the best proof that even if we would wish to avoid the issue and impact of international Communism, we cannot do so. Whether we support the war or oppose it, the fact is that the armed conflict in Asia and Communism as such are affecting our lives, our economy, and our politics.

long scholarly and boring *Das Kapital.* Editions of the *Manifesto* in other languages appeared later. It was to be published in *hundreds of millions of copies!* Marx and Engels gave in this document many lasting revolutionary slogans to the oppressed masses of the world. Calling on the masses to overthrow the capitalist society, they concluded their appeal with the words that have echoed throughout the world ever since: *"The Communists disdain to conceal their views and aims. They openly declare that their ends can be attained only by the forcible overthrow of all existing social conditions. Let the ruling classes tremble at a Communist Revolution. The proletarians have nothing to lose but their chains. They have a world to win. Workingmen of all countries, unite!"*

However, in 1848 and 1849 the proletarians of Europe were not ready yet to unite. In fact, at the end of October, 1848, the peasant soldiers in the Croatian army of General Josip Jelačić enthusiastically crushed the revolt of citizens of Vienna. Only a few months later the Habsburgs, who were saved by the Slavic soldiers of their provinces and armies of neighboring Russia, imposed a brutal absolutism on all Slavs. And Marx, terribly disappointed by the intervention of the Croatians and other Slavs, angrily denounced them in his writings lamenting the defeat of the 1848 liberal revolutions.

## 1849
In the course of the year the liberal and nationalistic revolutions were smashed by the united forces of conservatism, the *status quo* forces, the military and wealthy middle class. The deposed kings and princes return to their thrones. The revolutionaries face now the firing squads, go to the prisons, or — as the German "Forty-Eighters" — leave for America, the asylum of all the oppressed and persecuted people.

In the summer of 1849 some 150,000 Russian troops defeated the Hungarian rebels and saved the throne for young Emperor Francis Joseph, the last real Habsburg ruler in the multinational empire. The conservative reaction was thus victorious all over Central Europe.

After the failure of the revolution into which he put his high hopes, K. Marx settles down in England. *It is the beginning of his last and longest exile.* Had it not been for his rich and wealthy friend, F. Engels, he

would have starved to death. The historians accuse Marx that one of his children died on account of malnutrition. For the remainder of his life he lived, studied, and wrote in England. Here he was exposed to the effects of the British Industrial Revolution. Thousands of hours he spent in the British Museum doing research and writing. The influence of England will forever affect the Marxian doctrine. It was to become an ideology primarily suited for *industrial societies*, unlike Russia that still was predominantly an agricultural country. If the Russian radicals wanted to draw on the sources of Marxism they had to adapt it to their own needs and necessities. Marx had very few hopes for Russia and — as stated already — constantly denounced her imperialism.

## 1850
The Russian exile, Alexander Herzen publishes his book *From the Other Shore.* In it he expressed his disappointment with Western Europe and the revolutions of 1848-1849. Historians have called Herzen the noblest of all Russian radicals. While all other Russian radicals denied concessions to non-Russian nationalities, he was the only true liberal who thought that oppressed nationalities of the Russian Empire had the right for freedom and independence. Herzen was opposed to violence and revolution.

### January 6, 1850
Eduard Bernstein, the leader of Revisionist Socialism, is born in Berlin.

### November 7, 1851
German Marxist, Joseph Weydemeyer, arrives in New York. He and another "Forty-Eighter" — Friedrich A. Sorge — are pioneers of American Marxism. A month later Weydemeyer publishes the short-lived periodical *Die Revolution* (The Revolution). In American foreign-born proletariat the Germans are very strong, outnumbered only by the Irish. Many of the German immigrants are tradesmen and skilled workers interested in the cause of Socialism and radical ideologies of the proletariat.

## 1852
*The Eighteenth Brumaire of Louis Napoleon,* written by K. Marx, appears in a series of articles in a German monthly, *Die Revolution*, the German monthly in New York City. Marx denounces here the nephew of Napoleon, Louis Napoleon Bonaparte, who was elected President of the French Republic by the

French in December of 1848, established a dictatorship in December of 1851 and in 1852 founded the Second French Empire. Later on this Emperor will cause a lot of troubles during the 1860's to the United States engaged then in the crucial Civil War.

## 1852

A. Herzen, who loved the West and became very disappointed with it, settled in London, the same place where Marx lived. Here Herzen was to stay until 1865.

## October 4 – November 12, 1852

The historic "Cologne Communist Trial" is held. The accused were the members of the Central Board of the Communist League, located at Cologne. Arrested by the Prussian authorities, seven were sentenced to a term between three and six years. Afterwards the League was dissolved.

## December 14, 1852

Daniel De Leon, one of the American Socialist leaders, is born in the Dutch colony of Curacao, off the coast of Venezuela. He comes to the United States in 1872. Graduated in 1878 from the Columbia Law School, he entered politics in 1880's and became one of the builders of the labor movement.

## March 20, 1853

Under Weydemeyer's initiative, the German immigrants found in New York City the American Workers' League. (Later on, during the Civil War, Weydemeyer served as a colonel in the Union Army.)

## October 16, 1854

Karl J. Kautsky, a German Socialist leader, was born in Prague, Bohemia, Austria. He became a strict follower of Marx and Engels.

## 1857

A. Herzen starts to publish one of the most influential Russian radical papers, *Kolokol* (The Bell), in London. The paper never reached beyond 3,000 copies, but was smuggled into Russia, was avidly read by many — including Tsar Alexander II who liberated the serfs— and promoted the cause of liberalism and moderate Socialism in Russia. In 1863 Herzen lost support in Russia because he was in favor of the Poles who revolted in that year. In 1865 Herzen moved the paper to Geneva, Switzerland, the traditional place of refuge for many Russian radicals. Herzen was a liberal and Socialist who suggested that Russia might skip capitalism and move directly into Socialism, an idea that influenced some later Russian Socialists.

## October 25, 1857

Friedrich Sorge, Conrad Carl, and Siegfried Meyer — all of them German immigrants — form the Communist Club in New York. (It will join the First International in October of 1867.) However, all these organizations are still far from being mass movements of the proletariat.

## 1859

Marx publishes *The Critique of Political Economy*, where again he asserted his beliefs in the materialist interpretation of history. This is otherwise known as *historical materialism.* He believed that necessities of life, the modes of production and the economic interests of various classes determine the form of societal organizations as well as of political and intellectual history. There is a constant struggle between the exploiters and the exploited. This is only one of many writings that Marx produced while spending his drab exile life in industrial England.

## 1861

F. Lassalle, a man endowed with many talents, a romantic as well as a socialist reformer, published in Germany his *The System of Acquired Right*. It dealt with the nature and meaning of the property. It disagreed with some basic ideas of Marxism.

## 1862

F. Lassalle delivered his famous lecture on the "Workers' Program."

## 1863

F. Lassalle, one of the leading contemporary Socialists in Germany, founded at Leipzig, Saxony the Universal Workingmen's Association.

## 1863

The first Russian translation of the *Communist Manifesto*, which was made by M. Bakunin, is published in Geneva, Switzerland.

(Bakunin who participated first in the Czech revolt in Prague in 1848, fought a year later in Dresden, Saxony, Germany in another revolution; there he was arrested by the authorities, condemned to death, and after a while he was turned over to Austrian authorities. The Austrians, after sentencing him to death, turned him over to the Russians. After six years in prison in Russia he was exiled in 1857 to Siberia, from which he escaped. Through Japan and the United States where he spent some time he made his way to Europe in 1861. In 1863 during the great Polish uprising against Russia, Bakunin fought on the side of the Poles. After moving back to Switzerland he founded "Alliance of Socialist Democracy." It joined the First International. Major principles that he preached were: anarchism, revolutionary struggle against any established order, and pure atheism. He will become a great enemy of Marx.

## 1863

America is in the midst of the Civil War. In the same year the Russians are mercilessly crushing the Polish revolt. The Russian government is kindly disposed towards the United States. After Tsar Alexander II issued the edict of Emancipation to liberate all serfs on February 19, 1861, President Lincoln liberates the slaves by his Emancipation proclamation on January 1, 1863. *During the Civil War, Karl Marx supported in his writings the cause of the Union*, a fact that is little known in America.

## 1864

F. A. Bebel met in Leipzig Wilhelm Liebknecht (Father of Karl) a veteran German Socialist who won him over to Socialism.

In the meantime Karl Marx continued his activities in London. A poor provider for his family, he was until his death supported financially by his loyal friend F. Engels. Marx was a correspondent of the New York *Tribune*, edited by Horace Greeley, from 1852 to 1861. In 1857 and 1858 he wrote a number of articles for the *New American Cyclopedia*, edited jointly by Charles A. Dana and George Ripley.

## August 31, 1864

Ferdinand Lassalle, mortally wounded in a duel (over a love affair), dies in Geneva. Truly dedicated to the cause of the workers, partly influenced by Romanticism and Hegelian idealism, he always remained a moderate Socialist opposed to the idea of a proletarian revolution.

## September 28, 1864

After maintaining for years contacts with many revolutionary leaders, Marx founded with Engels the First International in St. Martin's Hall, London. It was called the International Workingmen's Association. Marx wrote the statutes of the International, delivered the inaugural address and with Engels controlled for years its General Council in London. A loose federation of many heterogeneous elements, it was originally formed by French, German, Italian, Swiss and Polish Socialists. The International pledged to destroy "the prevailing economic system." From 1866 to 1869 the First International held annual congresses either in Switzerland or in Belgium. Neither Marx nor Engels attended these congresses; they did not consider them as important as long as they controlled the General Council in London. Marx considered the International as a very important vehicle to carry out the forthcoming revolutions. The first congresses of this organization were thus held: in Geneva (1866); in Lausanne (1867); Brussels (1868); and in Basel (1869). The group of the French anarchist J. P. Proudhon was also in the International. Its influence was felt as far East as Poland and Hungary.

*August Bebel (1840-1913)* – Radio Times

# 2. From the First International to the Outbreak of the Bolshevik Revolution: 1864-1917

**1865**

W. Liebknecht, after attempting to convert to Socialism various labor groups, was compelled by authorities to leave Prussia.

**August 20, 1866**

On the same day when pioneer of Marxism in America – Weydemeyer – dies, another Marxist, William H. Sylis, founds the National Labor Union in Baltimore. Weydemeyer's son Otto was to be the first to translate *Das Kapital* into English.

**1867**

K. Marx published the first volume of *Das Kapital*. This is one of the most important works for the modern Communist doctrine. It is a systematic historical analysis of the capitalist system. Vols. 2 and 3 appeared after Marx's death.

**December 5, 1867**

Josef Pilsudski, the future leader of Polish Socialists and the founder of modern Poland, is born in Zulow near Vilna, in Russian Poland.

**March 28, 1868**

A. M. Peshkov, better known as Maksim Gorky, the great realist Russian Socialist writer is born in Nizhny Novgorod (now Gorky). He was one of the predecessors of the Russian Revolution.

**1869**

W. Liebknecht and F. A. Bebel found at Eisenach, Saxony the Social Democratic Workingmen's Party. It became affiliated with the First International.

**1869**

The First International has some 800,000 dues-paying members.

**1870's**

Populism, a peculiar brand of Russian agrarian socialism, was growing strong in the Russian Empire. Defeated in the Crimean War (1853-1856) the Empire was compelled to grant many major concessions during the 1860's. In February of 1861 Alexander II liberated the serfs, a fact that gradually brought about many social and economic changes within the country and was bound to affect the development of radical ideologies. Many other reforms – some more and some less successful – were inaugurated. They could hardly satisfy the rising radical groups of different brands and orientations. The growth of radical movements was facilitated by the existence of the *intelligentsia*, a class with a cause, a specifically Russian phenomenon that lacked analogy in any other country.

One of the ideologists of the Populists (in Russian "Narodniki") was Peter Lavrov (1823-1900) who in 1870 joined his exiled countrymen in Western Europe. He was the author of the *Historical Letters* (1868-1869). Populism was based on the theory that it was possible for Russia to bypass the capitalist development by utilizing the typical Russian village commune – the *mir*. Among those who influenced Russian Populism were also A. Herzen and M. Bakunin. As a movement it assumed some terroristic tendencies. Close to eighty per cent of the population in the Empire belonged to the peasant class. Russian Populists were familiar with the Marxist literature. As Marxism was geared primarily to the industrial workers it had to be adapted to the Russian needs. In 1870's many Populist activists undertook "Going to the People" campaign preaching their theories to the peasants.

*Professor Peter Lavrov, one of the Russian Populism*
– Radio Times

**January 21, 1870**
Alexander Herzen, after spending his last years in Switzerland and France, dies in Paris.

**April 22, 1870**
Vladimir Ilich Ulyanov, later known as Lenin, is born in Simbirsk (now Ulyanovsk) as son of a school inspector.

**September 4, 1870**
After the disastrous defeat of Emperor Louis Napoleon at Sedan, during the Franco-Prussian War, a republic is proclaimed in Paris. The French Socialism is on the rise again.

**December 14, 1870**
Karl Renner, one of the future leaders of Socialism in Austria, is born in Dólni Dunajovice, Moravia.

**December 25, 1870**
Rosa Luxemburg is born in Zamósc, Russian Poland. She became later one of the leading radical Socialists in Germany along with Karl Liebknecht.

**End of 1870**
Several sections of the First International, established mostly by foreign-born radicals, exist in the United States.

**January 18, 1871**
During the German siege of Paris, the German Empire (Reich) is proclaimed in the Hall of Mirrors at Versailles.

**March 18, 1871**
The Commune of Paris starts its existence. A majority of the Communards were followers of Louis Blanqui. Some were supporters of J. P. Proudhon. Many of them are members of the First International.

**April 2, 1871**
As French troops attack the Communards, fierce fighting begins in Paris.

**May 21-28, 1871**
The "Bloody Week" of the Communard uprising. Over 20,000 Parisians were slaughtered. The uprising of the proletariat was crushed by troops. While the historians differ in the evaluation of the Commune, Marx and his followers considered it *as the first real Communist revolt in modern history and the first dictatorship of organized proletariat.* Some points in the Bolshevik program during and after the Revolution of 1917 were taken from the ideas of the Commune. In 1871 Marx wrote his *Civil War in France* on these events. The Commune fell on May 28. The proletariat again lost a battle.

**August 13, 1871**
Karl Liebknecht (son of Wilhelm), later to become one of the foremost German Socialist leaders, is born in Leipzig, Germany.

**August 20, 1871**
One of the American Marxist leaders, Friedrich A. Sorge, writes to Marx that "American workingmen in general, even in spite of industrial development — are quite unconscious of their own position towards capital and slow to battle against their oppressors."

**1872**
A. Bebel and W. Liebknecht, two Socialist deputies in the German Reichstag (parliament), were imprisoned for alleged treason against the German Reich.

*Mikhail Bakunin, founder of Russian Nihilism* – Radio Times

### 1872
*Das Kapital* was legally published in Russia and sold well.

### 1872
An English translation of the *Communist Manifesto* was published in *Woodbull and Claflin's Weekly,* a radical publication in New York. With the rising tide of the immigration, the cosmopolitan city of New York will eventually become an important center of radical activities in America.

### May 10, 1872
Some five hundred radicals from twenty-two states meet in New York and form the short-lived Equal Rights Party.

### September 2, 1872
A congress of the First International starts at The Hague, Netherlands. Marx and Engels attend for fear that M. Bakunin is out to capture the International for Anarchists and the "Swiss Federation of the Jura." Marx is strongly opposed to Anarchism. He and Engels succeed in expelling Bakunin from the International. Bakunin's influence was still strong in the International. Therefore Marx carried a resulution transferring the headquarters of the International to the United States (New York). Bakunin subsequently founded his own International. The last congress of the First International was held in Philadelphia in 1876, whereupon the International expired. Actually, the First International was killed by the failure of the Paris Commune and Marx-Bakunin split.

### September 18, 1873
The failure of the banking house of Jay Cooke and Co. (as a result of over-speculation in railroads) causes a long economic depression in America. The worst time will be over by the end of 1878, but effects will be felt until 1896. The depression, labor unrest, and strikes will help the cause of American Socialism in the future.

### 1875
The Marxian Socialists of Bebel and Liebknecht following merged with the Socialist Labor Group (moderate Socialist reformers) that was founded in 1863 by F. Lassalle. This fusion took place in Gotha, Germany and thus the Social Democratic Party of Germany was founded. Bismarck, the Chancellor of Germany, shared in general European horror at the recent Paris Commune, and decided to suppress German Socialism.

### 1876
The Russian Populists founded in St. Petersburg a new organization that became known as "Land and Freedom." G. V. Plekhanov, the future Marxist leader, was one of its members.

### January 3, 1876
Wilhelm Pieck, the German Communist leader after World War II, is born in Guben, Brandenburg. He was to become the successor of Ernst Thaelmann as Secretary General of the German Communist Party. As a young man he was first a Social Democrat.

### June 13, 1876
M.A. Bakunin, Russian revolutionary and anarchist, dies in Bern, Switzerland.

### July 15, 1876
The First International holds its last meeting in Philadelphia. The existing Socialist groups are still very weak in America. Marxian Socialists are split with the Anarcho-Communists, who are the followers of M. Bakunin.

**1877**

The newly founded Social Democratic Party of Germany polled at the Reichstag – German Parliament – election about 500,000 votes. It sent 12 deputies to the Reichstag.

**December 1877**

The Workingmen's Party changes its name to the Socialist Labor Party of North America. Its leaders are F. A. Sorge and other German Marxists. In this year of labor unrest the Socialists do well in several municipal elections. Chicago is becoming the nerve center of American Socialism. Some German Socialists in America are followers of F. Lassalle.

**1878**

F. Engels published *Herr Duehring's Revolution in Science*. It became popularly known as *Anti-Duehring*. (Karl Eugen Duehring 1833-1921 was a German philosopher and economist who taught at the University of Berlin from 1864 until 1874.) Engels lived now in London and was still very active in international Socialist movement.

**1878 – 1890**

Scared by Socialist success Bismarck set out to exterminate German Socialism. Anti-Socialist laws prohibited Socialist press and meetings. For twelve years German Socialism is virtually driven underground. To attract the workers to the monarchy Bismarck will inaugurate extensive social legislation.

**January 1878**

Under the leadership of Uriah Stephen the American Knights of Labor are organized on a national basis.

**January 24, 1878**

Vera Zasulich, a young Russian revolutionary, attempts to assassinate the chief of St. Petersburg police, General F. F. Trepov. The jury acquitted her on April 1, 1878. In 1880 she fled to Switzerland. She translated some of the basic Marxian writings into Russian.

**March 3, 1878**

After a victorious war, Russia imposes on Turkey the Treaty of San Stefano creating a Great Bulgaria (including Macedonia). All great powers reacted against Russian expansionism in the Balkans and the Near East and convoke an international congress in Berlin in mid-June. By the Congress of Berlin and the Treaty of mid-July, 1878 Great Bulgaria was dissolved, Russian expansionism was blocked, and Turkey was put under the international guarantee. In many of his writings Marx commented on such political events and denounced the Russian imperialism.

**1879**

Jules Guèsde founded the French Labor Party. Marx drew its statutes. French Socialism is disunited.

**1879**

The Russian "Land and Liberty" organization split on the issue of terrorism. Plekhanov with his supporters formed the "Black Partition" which was opposed to terroristic methods. The radical group became known as "People's Will." It was a well organized and disciplined group that used assassination to achieve the overthrow of the autocratic regime.

**1879**

The Belgian Socialist Party was founded.

**November 7, 1879**

Leon Davidovich Bronstein, later known as Trotsky, is born in the village of Yanovka, near Kherson, Ukraine. He was to become one of the leaders of the Bolshevik Revolution.

**December 21, 1879**

Yossif (Joseph) Vissarionovich Dzhugashvili, later known as Stalin ("the Man of Steel"), is born in Gori, near Tiflis, Georgia in the Russian Empire. He was a Georgian by nationality and his father was a cobbler.

**1880's**

New Marxist Socialist Parties grew rapidly all over Europe. With social reforms in Germany and other states the revolutionary zeal of the Socialists was diminishing.

**January 1880**

G. V. Plekhanov came to the West and settled in Switzerland.

**November 6, 1880**

The organization "People's Will" of Russia sends an emissary to America addressing a letter to the American people. The Russian revolutionaries appeal to the liberal Americans for understanding of revolutionary struggle in Russia. The Russian emissary never returned but settled down in America as a peaceful immigrant.

### 1881
H. M. Hyndman founded in England the "Democratic Federation"; it became known in 1884 as the "Social Democratic Federation."

### 1881
In spite of persecutions by Bismarck, the Social Democrats sent again 12 of their deputies to the Reichstag after a new election.

### 1881 – 1890
E. Bernstein and A. J. Bebel edited jointly the newspaper *Sozialdemokrat* (The Social Democrat).

### 1881 – 1894
During the harsh rule of Tsar Alexander III revolutionary movements grew stronger in Russia. Prolonged persecutions forced millions of Jews and non-Russians to emigrate to America.

### February 16, 1881
Vera Zasulich addresses a letter to Karl Marx asking him about his attitude as to what should be the stand of Russian Socialists in regard to the Russian village community. In his reply Marx stated that "history, in different countries, assumes different aspects, and runs through its various phases in different orders of succession, and at different periods."

### February 25, 1881
William Z. Foster, who became one of the leading Communists in America after 1921, is born in Taunton, Mass.

### March 14, 1881
Tsar Alexander II, the liberator of serfs and a great reformer, is assassinated by the members of "People's Will." Five members of the group were later executed by the authorities.

### March 10, 1881
The Executive Committee of the "People's Will" issues a public letter addressed to the new Tsar, Alexander III. They enumerated the causes for the assassination of his father and demand radical reforms in Russia.

### September 10, 1881
The same Executive Committee addresses a letter of condolence to the American people on the occasion of the death of President A. Garfield.

### June 28, 1882
Georgi Dimitrov, the first Bulgarian Communist leader, who later gained international fame, is born in Radomir, Bulgaria.

### September 1882
First Labor Day celebration is held in New York City. (By Act of Congress in 1894, first Monday in September was made an annual legal holiday.)

### 1883
Karl Kautsky, a close collaborator of Marx and Engels, started to publish his review *Die Neue Zeit* in Stuttgart. Under his editorship it became the most respected Socialist publication in Europe. He published it in London between 1885 and 1888 while in exile there. Kautsky became one of the leading Socialist theoreticians of his time. First opposed to the revisionism of E. Bernstein, Kautsky too became in later years a Socialist revisionist.

### 1883
G. V. Plekhanov published in Geneva *Socialism and the Political Action*.

### March 14, 1883
Karl Marx dies in London and is buried in Highgate Cemetery. His grave becomes a place of pilgrimage for all visiting Socialist and Communist leaders.

### September 1883
A group of Russian Socialists – former Populists – found in Geneva the first Russian Marxist Socialist political organization. It is called the Emancipation of Labor. On September 25, they publish their program and announce their break with Populism. Leading among them was George V. Plekhanov (1856-1918), author of many books and pamphlets and their foremost theoretician. The cofounders were: P. B. Akselrod (Axelrod) (1850-1928); L. G. Deutsch (1855-1943); Vera Zasulich (1849-1919); and V. N. Ignatov. Later historians have called Plekhanov the "Father of Russian Socialism." As a former Populist he lost his faith in the revolutionary potential of the peasants and became convinced that the future social revolution would be carried by the

*Vera Figner, member of Executive Committee of Party "Will of the People"* – Radio Times

industrial workers. Although he dissociated himself from later Bolsheviks, *Bolshevism through Lenin descended from Plekhanov's organization.*

## 1884
Plekhanov publishes a polemical pamphlet *Our Differences.*

## 1884
F. Engels published *The Origin of the Family, Private Property and State.*

## January 4, 1884
The Fabian Society, an English moderate Socialist group, is founded. The Fabians were opposed to Marxist theories. Among their founders were Sidney Webb and George B. Shaw. They derived their name from an ancient Roman Consul, Fabius Cunctator (the Delayer).

## 1885
Second volume of *Das Kapital* by Marx is published. It was edited by Engels who composed it from rough drafts and notes left by Marx.

## 1885
George Kennan (1845-1924) visited Siberia as correspondent of the American *Century Magazine*. In 1891 he published a book about Siberia and the Russian exile system.

## 1886
The Knights of Labor reach the peak of their membership in America: over 700,000. The Socialists fail to capture this industrial union (including unskilled workers). The rapid decline of the Knights was partly due to several unsuccessful strikes.

## May 1, 1886
Knights-sponsored general strike for an 8-hour day starts in Chicago. It ends in failure.

## May 4, 1886
Haymarket Riots take place in Chicago after the police broke up an Anarchist meeting. Somebody throws a bomb at the police — who now open fire — and kill seven of them. The subsequent trial is held from June 19 to August 20; four of the arrested are executed on November 11, 1887.

## December 8, 1886
The American Federation of Labor is founded in Columbus, Ohio by twenty-five labor groups. Its President is Samuel Gompers who declares "war" on Knights of Labor.

## May 1887
Alexander I. Ulyanov, Lenin's older brother, was executed as a member of a revolutionary group that attempted assassination of Tsar Alexander III. This incident influenced the future Lenin's political development.

## June 1887
After attending the gymnasium in Simbirsk, Lenin moved with his family to Kazan. (In Simbirsk the director of the gymnasium was F. M. Kerensky, the father of Alexander Kerensky, the future leader of the Russian Provisional Government.)

## October 20, 1887
John S. Reed, the radical writer, one of the founders of the American Communist Party, is born in Portland, Oregon.

## December 1887
V. I. Lenin was expelled from the University of Kazan. Here he studied jurisprudence and was engaged in illegal activities against the regime. After spending some time in jail Lenin returned to Kazan in the fall of 1888.

## 1888
The Polish Socialist Party was founded.

## 1888
Forced by Bismark's persecution, E. Bernstein came to London to stay here until 1901. He came to know F. Engels but rejected his revolutionary teachings. Instead he started to develop his own Socialist revisionist ideas.

## January 4, 1888
F. Engels denounces in a published letter Russian imperialism toward Rumania. (Many years later, in 1965, during their controversy with the Russians, the Rumanian Communists reprint this letter.)

## December 31, 1888
The Social Democratic Party of Austria is founded. Supported by industrial workers of different nationalities it developed into a strong and effective party.

*General view of Paris in 1880's* — Radio Times

**July 1889**

Two Socialist congresses were meeting at Paris. One was attended by the Marxian Socialists, and the other by non-Marxists. Engels who was living in London did not participate directly but influenced considerably the fusion of these Socialist forces.

**July 14, 1889**

The Second International is formed of the two major Socialist groups. It was a loose federation of many Socialist parties of which the two strongest were those of Germany and France. Its headquarters were established in 1890 in Brussels. It formally adopted basic Marxian concepts and tried by all means to preserve the unity within its ranks. It held congresses up to 1914 every two or three years. Its prestige within the international Socialism was considerable until the outbreak of World War I.

**1890 (birthday not known)**

Ho Chi Minh, a pseudonym meaning "Ho the Enlighter", was born in Indo-China.

**1890**

This was an important year in the history of German Socialism.

**1890**

F. A. Bebel comes to Berlin, the German capital, to become a very effective Socialist orator and the most influential member of the German Social Democratic Party. He edited the Socialist organ *Vorwaerts* (Forward).

**1890**

In spite of persecutions the Social Democratic Party of Germany polled in the general elections almost 1,500,000 votes which sent 35 deputies to the Reichstag. By now the German Social Democratic Party was by far the largest labor party in Europe. Its leaders were regarded by all European and Russian Socialist with high respect. The German workers were also better off than workers in any other European country.

**March 20, 1890**

Chancellor Bismarck of Germany, now 75 years old, is dismissed by the new Emperor William II. This is a real break for Socialism in Germany.

At about the same time K. Kautsky continued to publish in Stuttgart his Socialist review, *Die Neue Zeit* (The New Time) earning additional reputation. He will do it so until 1917 when he first became one of the founders of the Independent Socialists. Soon afterwards he became a resolute enemy of Lenin and Bolsheviks. Before that Lenin had hailed him as the "only among the Western Socialists who really understood the Russian problems."

**1891**

The Fabian Society of England became affiliated with the Second Socialist International.

**1891**

Lenin passes the bar examination. He went to Samara to practice the law and to found a Marxist circle there.

**1891**

Second Congress of the Second International met at Brussels.

**1891**

The Socialist Labor Party of America has 100 sections and branches of which 88 are German. In its ranks De Leon works hard for 24 years to make the S.L.P. the spokesman for the labor class.

**May 1, 1891**

The first May First celebrations, the international holiday of all workers, is celebrated in St. Petersburg.

**May 25, 1891**

The papal encyclical on labor is issued, one in a series on social problems of the Christianity.

**1892**

De Leon publishes Engels' book *Socialism: Scientific and Utopian*. From 1892 until his death in 1914, De Leon is the editor of *The People*, the organ of the Socialist Labor Party.

**1892**

Jozef Pilsudski became the leader of the Polish Socialist Party. A revolutionary, he was destined to become the leader of the Polish nation after 1918.

**March 9, 1892**

Matyas Rakosi, one of the leading Hungarian (Magyar) Communists, is born in Ada, Hungary.

**March 30, 1892**
Sanzo Nozaka, one of the founders of the Japanese Communist Party, is born. He later was a university student in London and became a Marxist.

**May 25, 1892**
Josip Broz, the Croatian Communist leader later known as Tito, is born in the village of Kumrovec, near Zagreb, the capital of Croatia, then Austria–Hungary.

**July 6, 1892**
Homestead Massacre takes place. During a clash between the strikers at the Carnegie Steel Co. plant at Homestead, Pa. and 300 hired Pinkerton agents, seven are killed. State militia take over on July 12; the strike is broken by November 20. On July 23, Alexander Berkman, a Russian-born anarchist shoots and stabs Henry Clay Frick, company's general manager.

**December 12, 1892**
A Pan-Slav Congress opens at Cracow, the ancient Polish city, now under the rule of Austria.

**1893**
The Polish Socialist Party splits on the issue of nationalism. Rosa Luxemburg became the leader of the Polish Socialist Party that wanted to preserve the unity with the Russian Socialists. She was against the idea that there should be separate Socialist parties for different nationalities in the Russian Empire. Thus the Polish Social Democratic Party was separated from Pilsudski's Socialists. Two distinguished members of the Polish S. D. Party were: Karl Radek (1885–1947) and Feliks E. Dzerzhinsky who later figured as prominent Bolshevik leader.

**1893**
V. I. Lenin moved to St. Petersburg where he joined a Socialist group. By his conviction he was a revolutionary and a Socialist. A year later he met a young Socialist activist, Nadezhda Krupskaya, his future wife.

**March 26, 1893**
Palmiro Togliatti, the future leader of Italian Communism and one of the most colorful personalities of the Communist world, is born in Genoa, Italy.

**June 30, 1893**
Walter Ulbricht, who later after 1945 became the leader of Communist East Germany, is born in Leipzig, Germany as son of a Socialist tailor.

**December 26, 1893**
Mao Tse-tung, the future leader of Communist China, is born in a peasant family in the village of Shaoshan, Siangton County, Province of Hunan, in Central China. This is a fertile province that has given China bandits and very good soldiers.

**1894**
F. Engels as editor published the third volume of *Das Kapital* by Karl Marx.

**1894**
Lenin published his first major political work *Who Are the "Friends of the People" and How Do They Fight Against Social Democrats?*

**April 17, 1894**
Nikita Sergeyevich Khrushchev is born in Kalinovka, Kursk Province, Russia in the same year when Nicholas II, the last Romanov, started to rule.

**June 21 – July 20, 1894**
The Pullman Strike is organized in Midwest by the American Railway Union under Eugene V. Debs. President Cleveland sends in federal troops to intervene. Debs is sent to prison, while the strike is smashed by authorities.

**1895**
G. V. Plekhanov publishes *Development of the Monist View of History*. It exercised great influence in Marxist circles. He subsequently wrote many studies on materialist conception of history.

Nearly 7,000,000 workers were by now employed in German industry. Germany was the most industrialized European country with the largest number of Socialists.

The French General Confederation of Labor was founded as the main base of revolutionary syndicalism (a form of modern Anarchism). Its main theoretician was Georges Sorel (1847-1922).

## April 1895
Lenin traveled for the first time to Western Europe. In Switzerland he met G. V. Plekhanov whom he considered as his teacher.

## August 5, 1895
F. Engels, then the greatest ideologist of Scientific Socialism, dies in London. All his estate he has willed to the children of his late friend K. Marx.

## September 1895
Lenin returns to Russia. With Julius Martov (Tsederbaum) (1873-1923) he united some 20 different Marxist groups in St. Petersburg in a new organization, the "Fighting Union for the Liberation of the Working Class."

## November 25, 1895
Anastas Ivanovich Mikoyan, one of the future top Soviet leaders, is born in the village of Sinain, near Tiflis, as son of an Armenian carpenter.

## December 1895
Lenin's Socialist organization was discovered by the police. Its leaders, including Lenin, were arrested and he had to spend the following fourteen months in the prison of St. Petersburg.

## 1896
Several branches of the "Fighting Union for the Liberation of the Working Class" were established in Russian industrial centers. The Socialists were organizers of a series of major strikes in St. Petersburg and in other Russian cities in this year. By mid-year some 30,000 workers in the capital were on strike demanding a ten-hour working day, higher wages and more rights for the workers.

While the Russian workers were struggling for their basic rights, their fellow-workers were much better off in Western Europe.

## November 23, 1896
Klement Gottwald, the future leader of Communist Czechoslovakia, is born in Dedice, a village in Moravia, Austria.

## 1897
Various Jewish Socialist organizations formed in Vilna, Lithuania (Russian Empire) "The General Jewish Workers' Union" better known as the *Bund* (the Alliance). It was a Jewish Socialist and labor party in Russia, Poland and Lithuania. Its founders and leaders were: I. Aizenstadt, V. Kossovsky, and A. Kremer. It demanded equality for all the Jews in Russia and a federalization of the Russian Empire. For a long time it was the largest and best organized Socialist party in Russia. It was a spokesman for the Jewish workers in Russia.

## February 1897
After 14 months in prison Lenin was banished for three years to Siberia (the Yenissey Province). In 1898 Krupskaya joined him and they were married. (They had no children.) While in exile Lenin could maintain contact with many fellow-Socialists, studied and wrote extensively. In Siberia he wrote *The Tasks of Russian Social Democrats* (published in 1898) and his very important book *The Development of Capitalism in Russia* (published in 1899 in St. Petersburg under pen name of Ilyin.)

## 1898
Eduard Bernstein published his *Evolutionary Socialism,* an important study that inaugurated a new era in international Socialism. From his experience of the success of the German Social Democracy, Bernstein came to the conclusion that the working class could achieve a lot more by peaceful and democratic means, by participating in parliaments. Lenin and for a while Kautsky in Germany, termed this as "opportunism" and "betrayal of the workers' cause." In the long run Bernstein's ideas proved to be right and realistic.

De Leon publishes Marx' *Eighteenth Brumaire of Louis Bonaparte.* De Leon is a dogmatic Marxian theoretician. He had tried in vain to take the control of A.F.L. from Gompers; then in 1895 he organized his own Socialist Trade and Labor Alliance. Eugene V. Debs (born in 1855) became a convert to Socialism (after his imprisonment in 1894) and founded in 1897 his own Social Democratic Party of America. Because of his inflexible dogmatism, De Leon provokes a split in his Socialist Labor Party. His leadership is challenged by moderates.

**March 14, 1898**

The First Congress of the All-Russian Social Democratic (Labor) Party takes place in Minsk, Bielorussia.
It is attended by nine delegates representing the Bund
and other Socialist organizations. One of them was a
police spy. *This is the actual founding of the first
Russian Socialist Party from which later the Bolsheviks emerged.* The Congress recognized Plekhanov as
its spokesman abroad.

**July 3, 1898**

Ernst Fischer, the Austrian Communist leader who
returned to Austria in 1945 with the Soviet troops, is
born in Graz, Styria, an industrial center and a
stronghold of Socialism.

**1899**

*The Fabian Essays,* written by seven prominent
members of the Fabian movement, appears in England.
It helps to popularize the Fabian program in England.
Among their leaders are the writer and historian H. G.
Wells; K. Hardie, the principal founder of the
Independent Labour Party; and Ramsay MacDonald.

**January 1899**

Luis Carlos Prestes, the leader of Brazilian Communism, is born in a country that is stricken by many
social ills. With its size, tremendous resources, and
wide-spread discontent of its peasants Brazil has been
a fertile soil for Communist revolution.

*Founders of "Fighting Union for the Liberation of the Working Class." Lenin (seated right center), Y.A. Martov (seated right)*
– Radio Times

*Catherine Breshkovaskaya,*
*"Grandmother of the Russian Revolution"* — Radio Times

## 1900

To hide his identity Vladimir Ilich Ulyanov adopts the pseudonym Nikolai Lenin.

The Second International was continuing its activities; after its Congress in 1896 in London, it held a Congress this year in Paris. However, the forces of Revisionism were already at work. E. Bernstein in Germany and Jean Jaurès in France were its principal spokesmen.

*This year marks the beginning of the twentieth century, an era when international Communism will attain victories all over the world.*

## 1900's

These years witnessed the rise of the Russian Socialist Revolutionaries that had gradually developed from former Populists and many revolutionary groups. The "S.R.'s" as they were popularly known in Russia were mostly active among the peasant masses of Russia. Their leaders were Catherine Breshkovskaya (the "Grandmother of the Russian Revolution"), G. Gershuni, A. Argunov, and V.M. Chernov. Gershuni became the chief of its terroristic section as the S.R.'s believed (like their predecessors in the "People's Will") that assassination was the most effective means for achieving the ultimate goals. Chernov was the main theoretician. Yevno Azev, a prominent member, was at the same time a police informer. In early 1900's the S.R.'s executed a large number of the prominent representatives of the Tsarist regime.

### February 27, 1900

British Socialists and labor leaders create a "Labor Representative Committee;" six years later, in February of 1906 the Committee decides to found the Labour Party. It is moderately Socialist.

### March 15, 1900

Luigi Longo, successor to Palmiro Togliatti, is born at Fubine Monferrato, Piedmont, Italy of peasant parents.

### July 1900

After serving his sentence in Siberia, Lenin arrives in W. Europe.

### July 20, 1900

Maurice Thorez, the forceful leader of the French Communist, is born in Pas-de-Calais, France.

### August 18, 1900

This is the birth of Tsola Dragoitcheva, the leading Bulgarian Communist woman leader. A real Balkan revolutionary she spent later in her life about nine years in prison. Bulgaria was predominantly an agricultural country and the sympathies for Communism were based on the traditional Bulgarian sympathy for "Mother Russia" which liberated Bulgaria from the Turkish yoke in 1878.

### November 6, 1900

Eugene Debs and Job Harriman receive almost 95,000 votes in the Presidential election as candidates of the Social Democratic Party. (Four years later in 1904 election, Debs as a candidate of the new Socialist Party receives 402,000 votes; in 1908 he wins 421,000, in 1912, 897,000. It should be noted that paid-up membership of the Socialist Party in 1908 was only 41,751.)

*Josif Stalin photos found in the files of the Tsarist Police* — Radio Times

**December 24, 1900**

The first number of the Russian Socialist paper *Iskra* (the Spark) appears in Stuttgart, Germany. Instrumental in publishing it were: G.V. Plekhanov, J. Martov, A. Potresov, and V. I. Lenin. The slogan of the paper was: "From Spark to Conflagration." The board of editors included Akselrod, Plekhanov, Zasulich, and Trotsky for a while. *Iskra* moved subsequently to Munich, then London, and finally to Geneva. From November 7, 1903 until October of 1905 *Iskra* was edited by the Plekhanov group without Lenin. The *Iskra* group was instrumental in forming the future Russian Social Democratic Party, which eventually split into Mensheviks and Bolsheviks.

**April 1, 1901**

Whittaker Chambers, an American prominent Communist and underground worker — who later defected from Communism — is born in Philadelphia.

**Late July, 1901**

At the Unity Convention of American Socialism, the Socialist Party of America was founded in Indianapolis; E. Debs' Social Democratic Party and Morris Hillquit's wing of the Socialist Labor Party of De Leon unite to form one party. They include an important group of Jewish Socialists from New York City who since 1897 have published the *Jewish Daily Forward*. (It should be noted that after a careful examination of many sources this author was unable to detect the exact date of the founding of the Socialist Party of America. . .)

**1902**

J. Stalin, who joined the Russian S. D. Party in 1898, was arrested by Tsarist authorities in Batum and exiled to Siberia.

The Socialist Revolutionary, S. Balmashov killed the minister of the interior, Sipyagin; in the previous year the S. R.'s had assassinated the minister of education; in the next year (1903) two provincial governors will be killed by the members of the same organization.

There are now factional struggles among the Russian Socialists. Lenin now published his treatise *What Is to Be Done?* He argued for a strongly centralized and well-disciplined party. His opponents denounced him for his personal lust for power.

**July 30 – August 23, 1903**
Called by the *Iskra* group, the Second Congress of the Russian S. D. L. P. convenes at Brussels. Forty-three delegates represented 26 organizations including the Jewish Bund. Forced by the Belgian authorities the Congress moved to London where it argued many problems. The present delegates split. The big issue was Socialist Revisionism. The Bund delegates left the Congress after it moved to London. Plekhanov and Lenin won majority and thus became known as *Bolsheviks* (*bolshinstvo* means in Russian "majority"). Their opponents led by Martov and Trotsky were called the *Mensheviks* (*menshinstvo* meaning "minority"). After the Congress Plekhanov broke with Lenin, who actually led only the minority in the S. D. Party but continued to claim that his group represented the orthodox wing of the Party and its "majority." While the Mensheviks favored a mass party, Lenin continued to adhere to his ideas that the party should be a well-knit organization of a revolutionary elite with strict discipline and a central committee. K. Kautsky, then a leading Socialist ideologist who was well acquainted with the Russian situation (and whom even Lenin held first in high esteem), accused Lenin for having caused the split within the Russian S. D. Party, a split that never healed.

**1904**
The Second International that abhorred the split within the Russian S. D. Party convened at Amsterdam; in view of the Russo-Japanese war, the Socialists denounced all wars as detrimental to the working class.

Young Georgi Dimitrov became secretary of the General Workers' Union of Bulgaria.

The revisionist split in Socialism grew stronger. Karl Kautsky as opponent of revisionism and "opportunism" prevailed in the Second International to condemn the French Socialist Alexandre Millerand who had accepted ministerial post in the French Cabinet.

Lenin published his treatise *One Step Forward, Two Steps Backward*. He discussed here some of the basic ideas of Bolshevism.

**January 1904**
J. Stalin escaped from Eastern Siberia and made his way to Tiflis, Georgia. He became one of the leaders of Transcaucasian Bolsheviks.

**February 20, 1904**
Alexei Nikolayevich Kosygin, the future Soviet leader, is born in a poor workers' family in St. Petersburg.

**July 28, 1904**
Y. Sazonov, a Russian Socialist Revolutionary, kills the minister of the interior, V. K. Plehve. Losing the war with Japan, Russia is facing a very critical internal crisis. The country is moving toward a revolution.

**December 1904**
Representatives of the S.R.'s, liberals and nationality parties meet in Paris to discuss future action in Russia.

**1905**
The French Socialists consolidate into one party under the leadership of Jean Jaurès and Jules Guesde. Jaurès was the leader of the Socialists in the Chamber of Deputies. (In 1904 Jaurès and Aristide Briand had founded the Socialist paper *L'Humanité*. Jaurès edited it until his death in 1914 when he was assassinated by a fanatic.)

**1905 – 1910**
Karl J. Kautsky published his great contribution to Marxism, *Theories of Surplus Value*. It consists of four volumes and is based on manuscripts and notes left by K. Marx. Marx originally intended it for his fourth volume of *Das Kapital*. In 1910 Kautsky published his own book *The Social Revolution*.

**January 1905**
V. I. Lenin starts to publish his own Bolshevik paper *Vpered* (Forward) in Geneva, after *Iskra* was taken over by Plekhanov and the Mensheviks.

**January 20, 1905**
Some 250,000 workers are on strike in St. Petersburg. Within a year over 2,500,000 workers all over the Empire were on strike and in support of the revolution.

**January 22, 1905**
The "Bloody Sunday" takes place in the Russian capital. Massive peaceful demonstrations were organized by Rev. G. Gapon who led the marchers to the Winter Palace to petition Nicholas II for minor concessions. The Tsar had fled the palace and his troops fired at peaceful demonstrators. Probably

29                                                                                   1905

*"The Bloody Sunday" – Gapon and his followers faced suddenly by troops* – Radio Times

about five hundred people were killed. Thus Gapon triggered the Revolution of 1905. All over the Empire social and national revolutions broke out. This was the hour of decision for Russia.

**February 5, 1905**
Wladyslaw Gomulka, the leader of Communist Poland, is born in Krosno, South-East Poland.

**February 17, 1905**
I. Kalyayev, a member of the Socialist Revolutionaries, kills the Grand Duke Sergei, the uncle of Tsar Nicholas II.

**April 25 – May 10, 1905**
Third (Bolshevik) Congress of the R.S.L.D.P. is convened in London.

**June 1905**
The Industrial Workers of the World are founded in Chicago by union members of forty different trades. One of the organizations that joined was De Leon's Socialist Trade and Labor Alliance. The members of the I.W.W. were later called "Wobblies." Its foremost leader was William S. Haywood, a radical labor leader from the West (born in 1860 near Salt Lake City, Utah.) He became known as "Big Bill." I.W.W. was strongly against A.F.L. It advocated strict Marxism, class and revolutionary struggle. ("Arise slaves of the World! No God! No master!") Before World War I I.W.W. organized a series of violent strikes and after 1914 it opposed our participation in the war. Around 1912 the Wobblies numbered about 100,000 – this was their peak. After 1918 and 1941 many Wobblies were active Communists.

**June 14-24, 1905**
The crew of the Russian battleship *Potyemkin* mutinies. They killed their most hated officers and found asylum in the Rumanian port of Constanza.

**September 1, 1905**
In the midst of the Revolution, Lenin writes from Switzerland: "With all our strength we shall help the peasantry to make the democratic revolution, and thus it will be easier for us, the Party of the Proletariat, to pass over as quickly as possible to the new and higher task of the Socialist Revolution." Again he is adapting Marxism to the needs of an agricultural country.

**September 5, 1905**
Russia signed in Portsmouth, N. H. the peace treaty with Japan. The head of the Russian delegation was S. Witte.

After a humiliating peace treaty the Tsarist regime will be compelled to grant major concessions to the masses of the people. In the same month a general strike broke out in Moscow.

**October 26, 1905**
As a mutiny rages in the Kronstadt naval base and revolutionary flame engulfs the Empire, the first Soviet of Workers' Deputies, a miniature revolutionary government, is set up by L. Trotsky and the Mensheviks. Four days later the Soviet published the first issue of its organ the *Izvestia* (The News). The Soviet, a precursor of the later Soviet regime, organized armed workers' brigades. It continued to exist for seven weeks. This was the high tide of the Revolution of 1905.

**October 30, 1905**
At the height of the crisis, as the uprisings rage throughout the Empire, Nicholas II signs his October Manifesto written by Count Witte. He promises full civil freedom and a State Duma as a legislative body. The Bolsheviks opposed participation in the Duma elections.

At a Bolshevik meeting in Tiflis Stalin declares: "What do we need in order to really win? We need three things: first – arms, second,– arms, third – arms and arms again."

**November 1905**
The entire leadership of the Peasants' Union, controlled by the Socialist Revolutionaries, was arrested by the authorities. The peasant revolts all over the country were gradually suppressed by punitive military expeditions.

Lenin returned to St. Petersburg to join the Revolution. He considered the First Soviet of Workers' Deputies (in which the Bolsheviks were a minority) as a provisional revolutionary government. Its military arm was the Fighting Organization.

**December 20, 1905**
The Soviet of Moscow composed of various Socialist groups but dominated by Bolsheviks calls for a general strike and an armed uprising. Prolonged street fighting breaks out.

*Sergius Witte, Russian Statesman* — Radio Times

### December 25-30, 1905
The first official conference of the R.S.D.L.P. is held in Tammersfors, autonomous Grand Duchy of Finland. Stalin, as a delegate of the Transcaucasian Bolsheviks attended it and met Lenin (who presided over the conference) for the first time.

### December 29, 1905
L. Trotsky is arrested as the virtual head of the Soviet in the capital. Shortly afterwards he was publicly tried and sentenced to life banishment in Siberia. However, he will manage to escape before reaching destination. He will come to Vienna to continue his struggle as one of the leading Mensheviks.

### December 29, 1905 – January 4, 1906
The First Congress of the Socialist Revolutionary Party takes place in Finland. The S.R.'s participate in the Revolution and in the First Soviet. Here at the Congress they adopt a party program drawn up by V. M. Chernov. They want a democratic republic with radical agrarian and social reforms and a federated Russia. The party split into two wings. The moderate elements opposed terrorism. The "Maximalists" were much more radical.

### End of 1905
The Revolution had spent itself. But in many parts of the Empire the national uprisings continued.

### 1906
During early 1906 most of the revolts were suppressed by brute force. Thousands of people lost their lives. All segments of the population are now hostile to the autocratic regime. As most problems remained unsolved the revolutionary forces will continue their activities. The regime gave concessions and many promises that it did not want to fulfill.

International Socialism was affected by the Russian Revolution of 1905-1906. In German Social Democracy it caused the parting of the ways. Appalled by the tragedy of the Russian proletarians, the German Socialists were now even more opposed to revolutionary means. In the course of 1906 even Karl Kautsky, who had opposed Revisionism, suggested the necessity of a change of tactics within the S.D. Party. Workers should in the future avoid such tragedies. As a result of such thinking the German Socialists split into three groups. The reformist right wing was controlled by the followers of E. Bernstein. The center was led by Bebel and later joined by Kautsky. The Marxist left wing was guided by R. Luxemburg and K. Liebknecht.

### January 2, 1906
The bloody Moscow uprising is ended by loyal Tsarist troops. A Bolshevik conference met to draw some conclusions from the revolution. 41 delegates represented 26 organizations with some 4,000 members.

### April 23 – May 8, 1906
The Fourth Congress, the Unification Congress, of the R.S.D.L.P. convenes in Stockholm, the Swedish capital. Of 113 delegates a majority were Mensheviks. The Bund was readmitted. In the newly formed Central Committee the Mensheviks had a majority. The Congress was under the impact of the recent revolution. Both Lenin and Plekhanov agreed that in view of recent events, more attention should be paid to the participation of the peasants in the future revolutionary activities. The unity was nominally restored. Lenin, however, cared only for the interests of his Bolshevik faction.

According to some sources, the Bolsheviks at this time numbered at the most 14,000; the Bund had about 33,000 members; the Polish Social Democrats were 28,000 strong; the strongest group of the Social Democrats belonged to the Mensheviks. Some sources maintained that there were now altogether about 70,000 members of the R.S.D.L.P.

### May 10, 1906
The First Duma, the first legislative representative body in the Russian history, convenes. Of 524 deputies there were: 178 Constitutional Democrats – "Kadets"; 94 radical peasants; 32 Polish Nationalists; 18 Mensheviks; and 44 right-wing pro-government elements. The Bolsheviks boycotted the elections and will soon regret it.

### July 22, 1906
The First Duma was too "radical" for the regime. By the orders of the Tsar it is dissolved.

### Fall of 1906
Lenin moves to Finland. The next year he went to Switzerland. He and his followers were now using all means to discredit the new leadership of the R.S.D.L.P. and to win the majority for the Bolsheviks.

*Karl Kautsky, one of the greatest expounders of Scientific Socialism, edited a magazine called "Neue Zeit"* — Culver Pictures

**November 16-20, 1906**
The Second Conference of the R.S.D.L.P. is held at Tammersfors, Finland.

**November 22, 1906**
The Russian government abolishes the village communes (*mir*), a peculiar Russian institution.

**November 29 – December 5, 1906**
Military and Fighting Organization of the R.S.D.L.P. holds its first conference at Tammersfors.

**1907**
K. J. Kautsky published his book *Ethics and the Materialist Conception of History*.

Maxim Gorky (Alexis Peshkov) (1868-1936) the great Russian Socialist writer published his famous book *Mother*.

Karl Renner, the leading Austrian Socialist, was elected to the Reichsrat (parliament) in Vienna. Never an orthodox Marxist, Renner soon became the leader of the Austrian Social Democrats. However, his leadership was challenged by the more radical Socialist Otto Bauer.

After recognizing their mistake in boycotting the Duma elections, the Bolsheviks did participate in 1907 elections. Of the 518 elected deputies 65 belonged to the R.S.D.L.P.

**1907**
Is a significant year for the Austrian Socialists; the Social Democratic Party wins in the first elections with universal manhood suffrage over 1,000,000 votes, sends 82 deputies to the parliament in Vienna and wins a majority in the Vienna municipal government.

**March 5, 1907**
The Second Duma convenes. It will be dissolved on June 16 by the Tsar.

**May 13 – June 1, 1907**
The Fifth Congress of the R.S.D.L.P. meets in London. A deep division still exists between the Mensheviks and Bolsheviks. Younger Bolsheviks now make a showing: G. Zinoviev, L. Kamenev, N. Bukharin, and K. Voroshilov. Trotsky represents the Mensheviks and is strongly opposed to Lenin. However, the Bolsheviks secured a decisive position in the new Central Committee, the most important part of the Party.

**June 25, 1907**
Under Stalin's management the Bolsheviks undertake a daring bank robbery at a square in Tiflis. This "expropriation" brought some 340,000 rubles to the Bolshevik funds. Plekhanov, all leading Socialists and the European public opinion deplore such tactics which only contributed to the Bolshevik decline during these years. (In September Stalin left Russia. In November he was arrested in Berlin and faked insanity, was extradited to Russia by German authorities, subsequently locked up by the Russians in an insane asylum. Then he escaped and was again arrested.)

**August 3-5, 1907**
Third Conference (Second All-Russian Conference) of the R.S.D.L.P. is meeting in Helsinki, Finland.

**August 18-24, 1907**
The Congress of the Second International meets in Stuttgart, Germany. Lenin was present there but enjoyed little prestige among the German Socialists because he is an obstacle to the unity of the Russian Socialists.

**November 14, 1907**
The Third Duma convenes in St. Petersburg. Of 18 Social Democrats only five were Bolsheviks.

**November 18-25, 1907**
The Fourth Conference of the R.S.D.L.P. gathers the leaders of the Russian Marxian Socialism.

**1908**
This year is rich in diplomatic perturbances. It brings Europe to the brink of war. However it is a bad year for revolutionary activities.

**January 3-9, 1908**
The Fifth Conference of the R.S.D.L.P.

**February 1908**
As the quarrels between the Russian Socialists continued, the Mensheviks started to publish their paper *Golos Sotsial-Demokrata* (The Voice of the Social-Democrat); they urged complete break with Lenin.

**April 1908**

Stalin was arrested, kept in prison for eight months and then exiled. Three years later he returned to St. Petersburg.

**July 1908**

The Pan-Slav Congress convenes in Prague.

**July 24, 1908**

The rising of Young Turks, a nationalist movement, takes place in Turkey. It resulted in many important events in the Balkans.

**October 5, 1908**

Austria-Hungary annexes Bosnia-Herzegovina. A serious international crisis broke out and war threatened Europe.

**1909**

Lenin moved from Geneva to Paris where he lived with Zinovievs. (In 1912 he and Zinoviev will move to Cracow in Austria.)

A prolific writer, Lenin published in the same year *Attitude of Workers' Party Towards Religion*. He stated: "Marxism is materialism . . . we must combat religion." The Bolshevik propaganda revolutionary activities, and the living expenses of their leaders were financed by bank robberies and contributions from wealthy donors.

**Summer 1909**

The Bolshevik membership in Russia is drastically reduced as result of the party strife and constant persecutions by the Russian government.

**November 23, 1909**

A South Slav Socialist Conference meets in Ljubljana, Slovenia (under Austrian rule). There were representatives from all the Habsburg provinces and from the Balkan states. Austrian Social Democracy, then a powerful movement, was represented by Drs. Victor Adler and Karl Renner.

**1910**

At the Budapest Anarchist Conference an American delegate participates. His name was W. Z. Foster. He later founded the Syndicalist League of America.

**January 1910**

A plenum of the Central Committee of the R.S.D.L.P. meets in Paris, the favorite spot of many revolutionaries. Russian Socialism was still split between Mensheviks and Bolsheviks. Lenin's faction has a minority.

**January 7-9, 1910**

The First Balkan Socialist Conference meets in Belgrade, the capital of the little Kingdom of Serbia which had very few workers. But Serbia had big plans for reuniting all the South Slav countries and even Socialists of Serbia served that chauvinistic scheme: to create a Greater Serbia (it later became known as Yugoslavia.) The first Balkan Socialist leader was Svetozar Marković, a Serb.

**August 28 – September 3, 1910**

A Congress of the Second International is held in Copenhagen, the capital of Denmark. Lenin, who was destroying the unity of the R.S.D.L.P., tried here to unify the ranks.

**1911**

Ho Chi Minh, the future Communist leader of Vietnam, visited France. He published for a while in Paris a radical magazine, *The Pariah*. He collaborated with the French Socialists who were strong critics of French colonialism.

**September 14, 1911**

The Russian premier, P. A. Stolypin, who with his reforms tried to save the Empire, is assassinated in the Kiev opera house – in the presence of the Tsar – by Dimitry Bogrov, a revolutionary and – an agent of the secret police.

**1912**

In the Reichstag elections the German Social Democratic Party scored over 4,250,000 votes and 110 deputies in the Reichstag. It was the largest single party in the German Empire.

Karl Liebknecht, the radical German Socialist, was elected to the Reichstag. He opposed the war preparations of Germany.

The Socialist Party of the United States (founded in 1901 with an original membership of some 10,000) numbered about 150,000 members. Many Socialists in this country were immigrants. The foreign language Socialist press was strong and active. The Socialists were organizers of many labor unions and in many instances spokesmen for various nationality groups.

They strove for many improvements in the lot of the workingman. American Socialists were influenced by German Social Democracy. They also watched with interest the development of Socialism in Russia and lent support to the Mensheviks. American Jewish Socialist and other organizations often intervened on behalf of their persecuted brethren in Russia.

### January 18-30, 1912

The Sixth Conference of the R.S.D.L.P. meets at Prague. Lenin and fifteen of his followers – the hand-picked "Rump Parliament" –constituted itself as a party conference. It elected an all-Bolshevik Central Committee that replaced the old one elected at the Fifth Party Congress.

The new C.C. included: Lenin, Zinoviev, Ordzhonikidze, Spandaryan, and Malinovsky (an agent of the secret police). Stalin who did not attend the conference was soon afterwards taken into C.C. *This was the final split between the Bolsheviks and Mensheviks;* for all practical purposes, from now on, the Bolsheviks existed as a separate party.

### February 12, 1912

China is proclaimed a republic as result of a revolution that still goes on. The main republican leader was Dr. Sun Yat-sen. After returning from the United States he was elected as the President of the Provisional Government of the Chinese Republic in Nanking. From 1912 until 1917 Mao Tse-tung attended the First Normal School.

### April 4, 1912

Russian Imperial troops fire at striking miners in the Lena gold fields in northern Siberia. Many workers were shot. In European Russia thousands of workers walked out from their jobs; more than 250,000 of them struck.

### April 15, 1912

Kim Il Sung, who later became the Communist leader of North Korea, is born in a poor family in Mankyungdal, near Pyoungyang, Korea, then under the Japanese rule.

### May 18, 1912

The first issue of *Pravda* (the Truth), a Bolshevik daily newspaper, appears in St. Petersburg. The publisher was Roman Malinovsky. Lenin determined the editorial policies. He stole the name *Pravda* from Trotsky who had published such a Menshevik paper

in Vienna. The Bolshevik *Pravda* was addressed primarily to the workers and it became very successful. Its publication was made possible through the generous contribution of the Russian millionaire Tikhomirov.

### July 1912

Lenin, Zinoviev, and Kamenev moved from Paris to Cracow, Galicia, Austria in order to be close to the Russian border, to facilitate the publication of the *Pravda*, and to direct Bolshevik activities in Russia. Lenin spent summers in Zakopane, a resort in the Tatra Mountains, meeting the Bolshevik delegates who were coming from Russia to visit him.

### September 1912

The Mensheviks started to publish their paper *Luch (The Light).*

### October 17 – December 3, 1912

The First Balkan War starts. The Balkan League, encouraged by Russian support, fought the Ottoman Turks. Within a few weeks the Turks lost most of their European territories. The war inaugurated a series of wars, upheavals and revolutions that will last for more than a decade.

### November 24-25, 1912

In the midst of this serious crisis a special Congress of the Second International convenes at Basel, Switzerland. The present Socialist delegates vigorously denounce the war. This was the last meeting of the International before the outbreak of World War I.

### November 1912

The Socialist Party of the United States polled 897,000 votes in presidential elections (6 per cent of the total vote.) Eugene V. Debs, the Socialist leader, was a powerful speaker who could really stir his audience. The American Socialist, were split in two wings: right and left.

### November – December 1912

Stalin made visits to Lenin in Cracow. Under Lenin's guidance he wrote *Marxism and the National Question.* In Bolshevik ranks Stalin is thus emerging as an expert on the national question.

### December 1912

A Party council met in Lenin's residence in Cracow to discuss the current problems. Bolsheviks are plagued

*Sun Yat-sen, Chinese Revolutionary leader* – Radio Times

*Josif Stalin. Card from the Register of the Tsarist Secret police of St. Petersburg* — Radio Times

with many difficulties. One of them was that many leading Bolsheviks were secretly working for the Russian police. In the Fourth Duma that convened in late 1912, there were 7 Mensheviks and 6 Bolsheviks (one of them was Malinovsky who was betraying the Bolshevik leaders to the secret police.)

## 1913
Georgi Dimitrov, the Bulgarian Communist, was elected as a deputy to the *Sobranie* (parliament) in Sofia.

## February 3 — April 23, 1913
Bulgaria and Turkey are at war again.

## March 1913
Living illegally under the name of Ivanov in St. Petersburg, Stalin was betrayed to the police by his fellow-Bolshevik, R. Malinovsky, arrested and deported to Kureika in the Arctic Circle. Here he stayed until the Revolution of March 1917. However, an amnesty granted in February of 1913 brought from exile many Russian revolutionaries.

## April 1913
Lenin lectured in Leipzig on Russian problems.

## June 29 — August 10, 1913
The Second Balkan War; this time it was between Bulgaria and her former allies. The main reason was the division of spoils between the Balkan states, notably of Macedonia. Bulgaria was defeated.

## August 10, 1913
By the Treaty of Bucharest the Balkan Wars are terminated. Serbia and Greece received most of Macedonia while Bulgaria was given only a small part of it. Turkey retained only E. Thrace with Constantinople. The international tensions and war threats continued.

## August 1913
Twenty-two Bolshevik delegates (including five police spies) met for a conference of the Central Committee with Lenin in a village near Zakopane, Austrian Poland.

## August 13, 1913
F. A. Bebel, the famous German Socialist, dies in Passugg, Switzerland. At that time (July — August) Lenin was lecturing in Switzerland on nationality

*August Bebel, for many years leader of the German Socialists.* – Culver Pictures

question in Russia. (His wife was then recovering in Switzerland from an operation.)

## End of August 1913

Six Bolshevik deputies in the Duma presented the seven Menshevik deputies with an ultimatum to accept Lenin's program. Mensheviks refused. *Pravda* now started a new campaign to discredit the Mensheviks. However, the Menshevik organ *Luch* became a serious competitor of *Pravda*, which was in financial trouble.

## October 1913

Lenin published *Critical Remarks on National Question*. In view of the Russian oppression of many nationalities, Lenin realized the potential of the unsolved national question as a means in Socialist revolutionary struggle. Now and repeatedly in the future, Lenin appeals to various peoples by promising them self-determination. However, he stressed in all his writings that in the future the barriers between nations would break down and there will be international unity under Communist leadership. Many Russian Socialists did not share Lenin's view on the national question.

## 1914

An historic year for the entire world and equally for international Socialism. The events that took place in the summer of this year were only a culmination of many years of international tensions, crises, colonialism, imperialism, clash between the Russian and German interests in the Balkans, and division of European powers in two major diplomatic camps: Triple Alliance and the Triple Entente. For a century Europe was without a major war. Now the Long Peace was over. A new era will result from this conflagration. For several empires the war will prove fatal. And it will facilitate the rise of revolutions and of Communism.

## May 7, 1914

Alexander Kerensky, a member of the Socialist Revolutionaries and of the Labor Group in the Duma (since 1912), reads in the Duma a statement on behalf of the entire Left, condemning the government.

## June 1914

The Bolshevik Central Committee meets in Cracow to discuss the future actions.

## June 28, 1914

Gavrilo Princip, a Serbian nationalist, assassinates in Sarajevo, Bosnia (an Austro-Hungarian province) the heir to the Habsburg throne the Archduke Francis Ferdinand and his wife. Four weeks later Austria attacks Serbia whose authorities were involved in the preparation of the assassination. Some of the young revolutionaries, active in Bosnia, were influenced by Socialist and Anarchistic ideas.

## July 29-30, 1914

In the midst of the great crisis the International Socialist Bureau meets in Brussels, Belgium. Karl Kautsky was present. The Socialists undertook everything to prevent the war. (Only four days earlier, on July 25 the Executive Committee of the German Social Democratic Party had issued a call to all workers of the world to protest against the war.) At this meeting the present delegates also discuss the problem of disunity within the Russian Socialist movement. Present were leading Mensheviks: Plekhanov, Axelrod, Martov, Trotsky (who will go afterwards to Paris and America), and Rosa Luxemburg. The Bolsheviks were conspicuously absent.

## August 1, 1914

*World War I begins* and throws the world into a chaos. What was to be a localized war between Austria-Hungary and little Serbia developed into a *world war* because of the alignment systems. All major powers enter the war.

The Socialist parties of various nations split on the issue of war. A majority of the Social Democrats in Germany came out in support of the German war effort, a fact that shocked Lenin, who with other "internationalists" — as the enemies of the war were named — vehemently denounced the war as imperialist. In his opinion German, French and other Socialists had betrayed the cause of the world revolution. Apparently nationalism of the workers was stronger than their international proletarian solidarity. Kautsky later admitted that "the majority of the proletariat had succumbed to the war fever." Even Mensheviks and Socialist Revolutionaries became divided on the war support. Trotsky became an "internationalist." G. V. Plekhanov demanded repeatedly that Socialists everywhere should support the Allies.

From now on Lenin appealed to all revolutionary Socialists to help transform an imperialist war into a revolution, and that in Russia the Socialists should do the same! This defeatist attitude by Lenin hurt Bolshevik cause in Russia.

The decision of the German Socialist majority to support the war just about killed the Second International. The International completely lost prestige. (After World War I it was revived and its headquarters were moved to London. A new name was adopted: the Labor and Socialist International. It excluded all Communists. The last congress of the L.S.I. was held in 1931.)

**August 8, 1914**
Lenin is arrested by Austrian authorities in Poland. On the 19th he was permitted to leave for Switzerland.

**August 17, 1914**
A large scale Russian offensive starts with the Russian invasion of East Prussia. At the battle of Tannenberg the Russians were defeated by generals Hindenburg and Ludendorff. By mid-September the disastrous defeat of the Russian armies was completed.

**August 18, 1914**
The Russian offensive against Galicia in Austria begins and is very successful. With Austrian permission the Socialist Jozef Pilsudski organized a Polish Legion to fight against the Russians.

**September 5, 1914**
Lenin arrives in Bern, Switzerland; immediately he formulated a document on "The Tasks of the Revolutionary Social Democracy in the European War." It was later used in Russia as anti-war propaganda.

**December 2, 1914**
Karl Liebknecht, as the leader of the anti-war Socialists, votes in the German Reichstag against war credits.

**1915**
As war fever is rising in America, the left wing of the Socialist Party secedes and embarks on a vigorous anti-war campaign.

*Karl Radek, one of the ablest Bolshevik spokesmen against the war* – Radio Times

**March 1915**
The Russians renew successful offensive in Galicia. They took many prisoners. One of the captured Austrian soldiers was a Croatian, Josip Broz (later named Tito), who was wounded at the Carpathian front. Subsequently he spent 13 months in a hospital and learned Russian. As a left Socialist he later joined the Bolsheviks during the Revolution.

**May 1, 1915,**
Austro-German offensive against the Russians in Galicia results in a major military disaster for the Russians. During this summer the Germans take Warsaw and are still advancing. Continued military defeats of the army cause serious repercussions and increased internal crisis in Russia.

**June 19, 1915**
Military defeat in Galicia forces the Russian government to convoke the Duma – the parliament. After it was reconvened, it became obvious that many members of the opposition were very critical of the policies of the government. On September 3, Duma was adjourned again.

**September 5-8, 1915**
Thirty-eight left-wing Socialists from eleven countries meet in the Swiss town of Zimmerwald. These were "internationalists" opposing the war. Already earlier in Berne during a conference of leading Bolsheviks in Switzerland (February 20 to March 3) Lenin had proposed creation of a new proletarian International to replace the compromised Second (Socialist) International. At Zimmerwald Lenin and Zinoviev represent the Bolsheviks; Axelrod and Martov represent the Mensheviks. The followers of Karl Liebknecht side with Lenin, and although his faction is in a minority, he exercises a very strong influence at Zimmerwald conference. Here is the embryo of the future Third International. Lenin attacks the war stand of the Second International. The majority statement condemns the war and calls for a struggle against the war and for Socialism. The Bolsheviks demand open civil war and establishment of a new International. At the end the so-called Zimmerwald Union emerges. It is a loose organization of the anti-war Socialist parties that will exist until the establishment of the Third International by Lenin.

**End of 1915**
Russian losses during the year are 2,000,000 casualties. There are 3,000,000 refugees from the Western parts of the Empire.

**January 1916**
As his funds run out, Lenin and his wife move to Zurich, Switzerland where they live in poverty. Here Lenin is very isolated from the events in Russia.

**January 27, 1916**
The Spartacus Group, led by Rosa Luxemburg and Karl Liebknecht, left radical Socialists, is founded in Berlin.

**March 24, 1916**
The split in the German Social Democratic Party is final. K. Liebknecht is expelled from the S.D. Party. (During the war E. Bernstein is the leader of the Independent Socialists. Later he rejoined the majority Socialists.)

**April 23, 1916**
The Irish Easter Rebellion against England begins. Democratic England butchers in cold blood the Irish revolutionaries.

*Rosa Luxembourg, German* – Radio Times

**April 24-30, 1916**
The anti-war Socialists meet in the Swiss village of Kienthal. Lenin again denounces the war and the Second International. He wants immediate peace without indemnities and annexations. Lenin and his supporters are outvoted. This marked the definitive split between the moderate Socialists of Europe and the extreme radical wing led by Lenin, a very unpopular man in international Socialist circles.

**May 1, 1916**
In his May Day (the holiday of all European workers) speech, Karl Liebknecht violently denounces the war. Immediately he is arrested and imprisoned for high treason by German authorities.

**June 28, 1916**
First "political" strike breaks out in Berlin.

**Summer of 1916**
Fierce battles rage on all fronts. The war inflicts immeasurable suffering on the masses of the European peoples. The list of battles on all fronts is too long to be enumerated here. On all fronts the Central

Powers (Germany, Austria-Hungary, Bulgaria, and Turkey) still have the upper hand. America, whose President Wilson was to be re-elected in November of 1916, because "he kept us out of war" is still officially "neutral." In the summer of 1916 the Russians undertake a huge offensive under the command of General Alexander Brussilov. They lost a million of best troops.

### July 2, 1916
Lenin publishes *Imperialism, the Highest Stage of Capitalism.*

### October 21, 1916
Friedrich Adler, an Austrian Socialist and a son of the famous Austrian Socialist leader, Victor Adler, assassinates the Austrian foreign minister Stuergkh. Lenin's reaction to this was: "Adler committed a foolish act."

### November 21, 1916
Emperor Francis Joseph of Austria-Hungary dies. (He started to rule in 1848 and was contemporary of many revolutionary events and wars.) The last of the great Habsburg rulers did not live to see two years later the disintegration of his multi-national empire.

### December 6, 1916
The armies of Central Powers enter Bucharest, the capital of Rumania.

### December 20, 1916
G.Y. Rasputin, a fake monk and an evil advisor of the Tsar, is assassinated; but this act did not solve the internal crisis in Russia which was drifting towards the final disaster.

### The end of 1916
Lenin's fortunes are at a low ebb. He is isolated from Russia and deserted by most of his former friends. Most of the Socialist leaders regard him now as a crackpot. He and his heroic wife are struggling with poverty. The future seems uncertain and bleak. However, his greatest hope — of which he was not aware at the time — was in the fact that Russia was tired of war and on the verge of collapse.

*Rasputin* – Culver Pictures

# 3. *1917: The Year of the Great Revolutions*

## 1917

This is the fateful year of the two great revolutions in the Russian Empire. The first one – in March, according to our calendar – was a more moderate, liberal and democratic. The second revolution was the Bolshevik Revolution, violent, led by radical Socialists and Communists under Lenin. In a sense the Bolshevik November Revolution was only the *beginning* of a long revolution.

## January 1917

Lenin's name was still only vaguely known in Russia.

Lenin delivers a lecture to the young Socialists in Zurich, Switzerland, on the twelfth anniversary of the "Bloody Sunday." In it he states: "We of the older generation may not live to see the decisive battles of this coming revolution."

## February 13, 1917

As Russia was undergoing serious crisis and losing the war against the Central Powers the workers begin strikes in a number of Petrograd factories. (After the beginning of the war, St. Petersburg was renamed Petrograd.)

## February 15, 1917

Michael Rodzianko, the President of the Duma, warns the Tsar, Nicholas II, that the country is on the brink of the revolution. He demands radical changes and reforms. The Tsar threatens reprisals.

## February 27, 1917

The Russian Duma resumes sessions. Demonstrations break out in many cities. The revolutionary spirit is mounting.

## March 3, 1917

A strike breaks out in Putilov factories in the capital of Russia. Some 90,000 workers join the strike. Most of them are Mensheviks and S.R.'s. There is shortage of bread. Angry women contribute to the rising revolutionary mood of the masses.

## March 8, 1917

On the "Day of Female Worker" the scheduled demonstrations take place. In the capital the demonstrators clash with the police. The number of strikers increases. Many members of the government are dissatisfied with Nicholas II and the ruling clique. The Tsar is in Mogilev—the military headquarters. The armed forces are tired of war. Many soldiers leave the front and desert to the cities to contribute to the revolution.

## March 10, 1917

General Khabalov, commander of the Petrograd garrison, sends message to the Tsar that the situation is critical. A general strike breaks out in Petrograd. There is shooting all over the city. First elections to the Petrograd Soviet of Workers' and Soldiers' Deputies are held. The Duma demands freedom of speech and press. The Tsar decrees dismissal of the Duma and thus contributes to the increasing tensions.

## March 11, 1917

Strikes spread in Moscow and all major cities. The Volyn Guard regiment, composed mostly of Ukrainians, joins the revolutionary forces in the capital. *This is a real revolution.* The Central Committee of the Russian Social Democratic Labor Party (Mensheviks) issues a manifesto calling for formation of a "provisional revolutionary government."

While the Empress was sending the Tsar the letters of comfort, Rodzianko sends him a wire: "The situation is serious. The capital is in a state of anarchy.... There is wild shooting in the streets; troops are firing at each other."

**March 12, 1917**
The Tsar replies to Rodzianko, the President of the Duma: "Dissolve the Duma." By this order Nicholas II sets the revolution loose. Chaos spreads in the army. The troops revolt and kill many of their officers. In the capital the soldiers, Cossacks, and sailors join the revolution and fraternize with the people. The Council of Ministers resigns. The Provisional Committee of the Duma announces it has taken over the affairs of the state. The Petrograd Soviet elects as its chairman N. S. Chkheidze, leader of the Social Democratic Duma delegation; A. Kerensky becomes the vice-chairman. By now the Soviet in Moscow is also set up. The revolution spreads all over the Empire and there is no force that can stop it.

**March 14, 1917**
The First Provisional Government is formed under premiership of Prince George Lvov, a liberal and progressive reformer. P. N. Milyukov, a Constitutional Democrat, is Minister of Foreign Affairs. Kerensky, the leader of the non-Marxist Labor group in the last Duma, becomes the minister of justice. The new government promises democratization and restoration of all liberties as well as convocation of a Constituent Assembly. Soon a rift develops between the Petrograd Soviet and the Provisional Government.

**March 15, 1917**
The Soviet restores normal life in Petrograd by calling off the general strike. On this day Nicholas II signs the document of abdication—in favor of his brother Grand Duke Michael—in a train near Pskov. The 304-year long rule of the Romanov dynasty is thus ended.

A temporary Ukrainian national legislature under the name of Ukrainian Central Rada (Council) is formed in the capital of Ukraine, Kiev.

**March 16, 1917**
Grand Duke Michael issues a Manifesto to the peoples of Russia to support the Provisional Government until the election of a Constituent Assembly, when the future of monarchy would be decided.

**March 19, 1917**
General amnesty is declared. Autonomy of Finland is proclaimed. The Empire is disintegrating. Soviet commissars are appointed to all army units. The soldiers are in no mood to fight the war any longer.

The biggest worry of the Allies is to keep Russia in the war and by holding the German divisions on the Eastern Front to relieve the German pressure against the Allied troops on the Western Front.

**March 20, 1917**
President Wilson recognizes the Russian Provisional Government hoping that peoples of Russia would finally have a democratic government and that Russia would stay on the Allied side. However, the Petrograd Soviet appeals to the proletarians of the belligerent countries to strive for peace and stop the war.

**March 21, 1917**
Nicholas II is arrested by the Provisional Government. All properties of the imperial family are confiscated.

**March 25, 1917**
Stalin arrives in the capital from exile and as an obscure Bolshevik joins the revolutionary forces.

**April 6, 1917**
America declares war on Germany and thus she enters World War I on the Allied side. The Allies are at this time badly pressed on the Western Front while the

*Czar Nicholas II and family in Siberian exile*—Culver Pictures

Eastern Front is considerably weakened by the Russian Revolution.

### April 7, 1917
The Socialist Party of the U.S.A. starts convention in St. Louis; it appeals to the workers of the world to stop supporting their belligerent governments. It also denounces America's entry into the war.

### April 9, 1917
After prolonged negotiations with the German government, which agreed to permit the trip in a sealed car through German territory, Lenin, his wife, Zinoviev, Radek and about a dozen of other Bolsheviks and a few other revolutionaries embark in Zurich for return to Russia. It should be noted that the outbreak of the Revolution came as a surprise to Lenin and other Bolshevik leaders in exile. Trotsky and Bukharin were then in New York. Before leaving Switzerland Lenin issued a statement addressed to the Swiss workers, calling the revolution in Russia "bourgeois-democratic." In Lenin's opinion: "The German proletariat is the best and most reliable ally of the proletarian revolution in Russia and of the world revolution." German authorities, hoping that Bolsheviks—if they would take over the revolution—would get Russia out of war, transport Lenin and his group in a sealed railroad car.

### April 16, 1917
On this Monday, at 10:30 p.m. Lenin and his party arrive at Finland Station in Petrograd. They are greeted by a huge crowd of revolutionaries. In the name of the Soviet they are greeted by N. S. Chkheidze who expresses the hope that Lenin would not split the revolutionary ranks. However, in his fiery speeches on this very first day Lenin spoke of *another* revolution and to the masses he promised "Peace, Land, and Bread."

The entire Bolshevik organization at this time numbers only about 5,000 members, some 200 "cadres" of propagandists, and 30 members in the Petrograd Soviet. Soon the membership will climb to over 25,000; and yet, Lenin was acclaimed as "the leader of the Petrograd masses, workers, soldiers and sailors." In a few days Lenin attacked the policies of the Provisional Government and demanded "All power to the Soviets!" There should be only one government in Russia—that of the Soviets; the Bolsheviks should control the Soviets and thus take over the government!

### April 19 – 21, 1917
All-Ukrainian Congress, a national constituent assembly is held in Kiev.

### April 20, 1917
The Bolshevik paper *Pravda* publishes Lenin's "April Theses." He denounces the Provisional Government, wants to see the revolution transformed into a Communist revolution, and calls for "All power to the Soviets!" He drew many revolutionaries to his side.

### May 1917
At the first All-Russian Congress of the Peasant Soviets, out of a total of 1115 delegates only 14 were Bolsheviks. The great majority belong to the S.R.'s.

### May 1, 1917
Foreign Minister Paul Milyukov publishes a note addressed to the Allies. He states that Russia is determined to continue the war on the Allied side. The revolutionary masses protest in violent demonstrations on May 3 against such policies of the Provisional Government.

### May 7 – 12, 1917
Seventh All-Russian Conference of the Bolshevik Party meets in Petrograd. There are 133 delegates who claimed to represent some 80,000 party members. A majority sides with Lenin, although some Bolshevik leaders did not agree with his policies. He announces also self-determination of all non-Russians at the time when many nationalities were already seizing the opportunity and were cutting off the ties with Russia. This was the first legal gathering of Bolsheviks in Russia.

### May 17, 1917
After his sojourn in America where he worked during 1916–1917 for the *Novy Mir* in New York, and after British captivity in Halifax, Nova Scotia, Trotsky is released through the intervention of the Provisional Government. On May 17 he arrives in Petrograd; in July he formally joins the Bolsheviks and manages to become next to Lenin the most important leader of the Revolution.

That Spring and Summer "all roads led to Petrograd," the capital of the Revolution. As David Shub puts it in his biography of Lenin, "From all parts of Europe and America, from the wastelands of Siberia and

Asiatic Russia, all roads led to Petrograd in the spring of 1917." The returning exiles belong to all kinds of political groups; some were veterans of the 1905 revolution. Some were liberals; many were Socialists; a majority of them were opponents of Lenin. Among them were "idealists and shady adventurers, young men and old."

## May 18, 1917
As a result of the reaction to Milyukov's Note, a new coalition government was formed under the public pressure. Prince Lvov was still premier. The new cabinet consisted of ten non-Socialists, three S.R.'s, and two Mensheviks. Kerensky became the minister of war and navy. The government promised peace without annexations and indemnities.

## End of May, 1917
The Bolsheviks continued their opposition against the Provisional government. By now a majority of the workers' representatives in the Petrograd Soviet were on Lenin's side. Of 150,000 troops in the capital most units gradually go over to the Bolsheviks.

## June 13, 1917
The American Mission headed by Senator Elihu Root arrives in Petrograd. The Mission wants to find out whether Russia is capable and willing to continue the war on the Allied side. Root promises aid of America to preserve democracy in Russia. On the 15th of June Senator Root addresses the Council of Ministers of the Provisional Government.

## June 16, 1917
First All-Russian Congress of Soviets meets in Petrograd. Of about 1,000 delegates only 105 are Bolsheviks. Lenin addresses this assembly on the next day and demands that the Soviet take all power from the Provisional Government. This Congress takes place in the Tauride Palace, the seat of the Soviet. The present 285 S.R.'s and 248 Mensheviks outvote the Bolsheviks.

## June 23, 1917
The Ukrainian Council proclaims a broad autonomy of Ukraine: subsequently it became the National Government of Ukraine, the largest non-Russian territory within the former Empire.

## June 29, 1917
Kerensky as Minister of War calls on officers and soldiers to undertake a grand offensive against Germans.

## July 1, 1917
Under Kerensky's directives General Brusilov undertakes a major offensive on the Galician front. By July 19 the Germans regain their strength and are counter-attacking. The offensive was a failure and Kerensky thus had used up the last of best troops. His offensive was very unpopular among the revolutionaries of Petrograd.

Utilizing the general dissatisfaction with the government, the Bolsheviks stage large scale demonstrations in the capital. Subsequently the Bolsheviks start to organize an uprising against the government.

## July 15, 1917
The Central Committee of the Bolshevik Party decides to revolt against the government. They count on the support of the Kronstadt sailors, located in a naval base (an island) dominating the access to the capital.

## July 16 – 18, 1917
The Petrograd Bolshevik uprising against the Provisional Government is a failure. On the 17th the troops kill and wound some 400 Bolshevik demonstrators. To escape arrest, Lenin flees to Finland where he lives in hiding. There he finishes his *The State and Revolution* declaring the ultimate goals of Communism in Russia. He argues that it is possible for the Bolsheviks to seize the power.

## July 24, 1917
After resignation of Lvov, Kerensky forms the second coalition government. Kerensky is now the premier and the minister of war. The power of the Provisional Government is waning. More and more power comes into the hands of the Petrograd Soviet. This will facilitate the Bolshevik seizure of the government.

## August 8, 1917
The Sixth Congress of the Bolsheviks meets for eight days in Petrograd. They claim a membership of 240,000.

*Lenin. Forged passport with picture of himself in disguise enabled Lenin to escape to Finland in the fall of 1917.  Warrant for his arrest had been issued in July of that same year.* – Radio Times

### August 17, 1917

John Reed, the brilliant radical writer and a left Socialist, leaves America for Russia as correspondent of radical papers and periodicals. Late in August he arrives in Russia. There he became an eyewitness of the revolutionary events thereafter. In Petrograd he met quite a few returned exiles from America who became prominent in the forthcoming Bolshevik Revolution. He will meet Lenin, Trotsky and other leaders of the Revolution, collect the documents and write a famous book about the November Revolution: *Ten Days that Shook the World.*

### September 6 – 10, 1917

The revolt of General L. G. Kornilov against the regime in Petrograd (primarily the Soviet) is defeated by the Provisional Government. Kornilov had been commander-in-chief since July 18. During the revolt Kerensky distributed the arms to Petrograd workers many of whom were Bolsheviks; he now became the commander-in-chief. After taking over the Petrograd Soviet the Bolsheviks were increasing their power while the power of Kerensky's government was gradually disintegrating.

**September 14, 1917**
Russia is proclaimed a republic.

**October 7, 1917**
Kerensky forms third coalition government; there were two Socialists and six non-Socialists in the cabinet.

**October 20, 1917**
Lenin secretly returns from his hiding in Finland. After arriving in Petrograd he started to prepare for revolt against the government.

**October 23, 1917**
The Central Committee of the Bolsheviks meets secretly. Present are: Lenin, Trotsky, Stalin, Zinoviev, Kamenev, Sverdlov, Uritsky, Dzerzhinsky, Kollontai, Bubnov, Sokolnikov, and Lomov. Lenin wants an uprising before the convocation of the Constituent Assembly, which—he knows—will be against them. Lenin's proposal for an armed uprising was accepted. According to the Soviet sources, only Zinoviev and Kamenev voted against, while Trotsky later stated that more members of the C.C. were opposed.

*Guarding the Soviet (Council of Workmen's and Soldiers' Delegates) and the Peoples Commissaries at the Smolny Institute, Petrograd* – Radio Times

### November 5, 1917

The Bolsheviks elect a Political Bureau of seven to undertake the final preparations for the revolt. On Trotsky's initiative, a Military Revolutionary Committee—under the control of the Petrograd Soviet—is founded to carry out the revolt. The President of Petrograd Soviet, L. Trotsky is the main organizer of the revolt.

### November 7, 1917

On the night of this historic day the Bolsheviks storm the Winter Palace, the seat of the Provisional Government which was overthrown. Kerensky escaped. He had few troops at his disposal. The Bolsheviks had on their side most of the troops in Petrograd. This is the beginning of the Bolshevik Revolution. There was little bloodshed on this day. Life is normal in the capital and for a few days many people don't even know who is actually in power.

The first Soviet government, the Council of People's Commissars, is proclaimed. It is headed by Lenin. Trotsky is Commissar for Foreign Affairs; Commissar of the Interior is A. I. Rykov, while Stalin is in charge of Nationality Affairs.

### November 8, 1917

The rump Second All-Russian Congress of Soviets approves the Bolshevik seizure of power and Chairman Lenin's first two decrees: Decree on Peace (whereby Russia quit the war), and Decree on Land which seized over 360 million acres of land.

As civil war starts all over Russia, A. M. Kaledin, the Ataman of the Don Cossacks and former Tsarist general, issues an appeal to his armies to fight the Bolsheviks. He is the President of the Don Cossack Government which continued to fight against the Bolsheviks.

### November 9, 1917

Kerensky's troops take Gatchina, thirty miles southwest of Petrograd. They undertake an offensive against Petrograd and take Tsarskoe Selo. The capital of the revolution was defended after a desperate struggle by the proletarians and the Bolshevik army units. When the Red Guards took Tsarskoe Selo on the 12th they found in a house an old sick man: G. V. Plekhanov. He had returned after the spring revolutions and was welcomed by the Soviet. The next year (1918) he will die in Finland as a great opponent of the Bolsheviks.

### November 15, 1917

After the defeat of Kerensky (supported mostly by the Cossacks) the Bolsheviks are victorious in Moscow after fierce fighting. Although few people at that time believed that they would remain in power, these initial victories secured the victory of Lenin. In the subsequent civil war and chaotic conditions many non-Russian nationalities proclaimed their independence. For a few years civil war raged between the Baltic and the Pacific.

The Baltic country of Estonia proclaims independence from Russia. It is still far from being secured.

### November 17, 1917

Estonia's southern neighbor Latvia proclaims independence. Many struggles still lay ahead. Many Latvian Bolshevik soldiers fought on the side of Lenin during the revolution and the civil war.

### November 20, 1917

Ukrainian Rada-Assembly proclaims autonomous Ukrainian National Republic. Numerous Bolshevik forces are on the Ukrainian territory and struggles between the Reds and Whites will take place in many parts of Ukraine.

### November 22, 1917

Lenin orders General N. N. Dukhonin, the chief of staff, to start negotiations with the Germans. Dukhonin and the General Staff refused to obey the order of the Soviet Government. Dukhonin was dismissed and right away lynched in Moghilev by Red Soldiers. Immediately the Bolsheviks start negotiations for peace with Germany.

### November 25 – 27, 1917

Elections for the Constituent Assembly are held in what is left of the former Russian Empire. Over 41 million people voted in the first and last democratic election in the history of Russia. Socialist Revolutionaries scored almost 16 million votes; Mensheviks received about 1,300,000 votes; "Kadets" had almost 2 million votes; Cossacks scored almost 700,000; while the Bolshevik Party had almost ten million votes which was still less than 25 per cent of the total vote. This was really a victory of Democracy in Russia and the Bolsheviks were determined to prevent its establishment.

### December 1, 1917

Bolshevik delegates leave for Brest-Litovsk to negotiate armistice with Germany and the Central Powers. Lenin needed peace to consolidate the Revolution.

### December 6, 1917

The Finnish Diet proclaims complete independence of Finland.

**December 10, 1917**
A Crimean Tartar Republic is proclaimed by the Tartars.

**December 11, 1917**
The Bolshevik government outlaws the Constitutional Democratic Party (the "Kadets"); one party after another will be abolished by the Soviet regime.

**December 15, 1917**
An armistice is signed between the Bolsheviks and the Central Powers in Brest-Litovsk.

**December 17, 1917**
The First All-Bielorussian Congress, a constituent body, meets in Minsk, the capital of Bielorussia (White Ruthenia). It has 1,872 freely elected delegates. The Congress was dispersed by the Bolsheviks who, although they speak of self-determination of the peoples, want to bring them all under the rule of Russia.

**December 20, 1917**
The All-Russian Commission for Combatting the Counterrevolution—Cheka is founded by Lenin to organize the mass terror against the enemies of Bolshevism in Russia. F. E. Dzerzhinsky (1877–1926) was the head of this outfit. (In 1922 Cheka will be renamed OGPU. In 1920 he combined this post with that of the Commissar for the Interior. He helped Stalin to his rise to power.)

**December 25, 1917**
An Ukrainian Soviet Government is organized in Kharkov to challenge the authority of the national government, a real representative of the Ukrainian people, in Kiev.

**The End of 1917**
Austria-Hungary was in serious crisis on account of the nationality question. Otto Bauer, a leading Austrian Marxist Socialist (born in Vienna in February, 1881) was now in the capital of the Habsburg Empire as the leader of the radical wing of the Social Democratic Party. Like Lenin, he advocated the self-determination of all nationalities. He became famous for his book in German, *The Nationality Question and Austrian Social Democracy*.

*Leon Trotsky reviewing troops in Red Square* — Radio Times

# PART II:

# From Lenin to World War II: 1918-1939

The Period of War Communism, 1918–1922 ■ The Civil War and Foreign Intervention in Russia ■ The Famine ■ The Failure of the Revolution in Germany ■ Founding of the Comintern ■ Failure of Bolshevism in Hungary ■ The Repercussions of the Paris Peace Treaties ■ Red Scare in America ■ The Miracle on the Vistula River ■ Beginnings of Stalin's Climb ■ Rise of Fascism in Italy ■ Founding of the U.S.S.R. ■ Revolutionary China ■ Death of Lenin and Rise of Stalin ■ Trotsky is Eliminated ■ Disunity of American Communism ■ Congresses of the C.P.S.U. ■ The Political Struggle in Germany ■ Activities of the Comintern ■ Stalin vs. Trotsky ■ The New Economic Policy is Abolished ■ Liquidation of the "Kulaks" ■ Stalin Removes the Opposition ■ Great Depression in America and Europe ■ Temporary Failure of Communism in China ■ Republic in Spain ■ F.D.R. Starts the New Deal ■ Hitler's Rise to Power ■ Washington-Moscow Ties Re-established ■ The Popular Front Policy ■ Dictatorships in the Balkans ■ Germany Rearms ■ The Seventh Congress of the Comintern ■ Great Purges in the U.S.S.R. ■ Civil War in Spain ■ Gradual Rise of Mao Tse-tung ■ Japan's Aggression in Asia ■ Hitler Takes Saar and Austria ■ The Munich Agreement ■ Nazi Nightmare Hits Also Other Parts of Europe ■ Hitler Prepares Attack on Poland ■ Nazi-Soviet Agreement Makes Nazi Attack on Poland Possible ■ World War II Starts ■ The Soviets Expand in Poland and the Baltic ■ Finland Becomes Soviet Victim ■

52

*Josif Stalin in 1918* – Radio Times

In this period of some twenty years Communism asserted itself. This era embraces the time: from the most critical period of Soviet Communism to the outbreak of World War II. During the time of the Revolution the Russian Bolsheviks under the leadership of Lenin knew how to secure the power for themselves. Had it not been for the able leadership of Lenin, Trotsky and some of their collaborators, it is questionable whether they would have been victorious.

During these years the center of International Communism was in Russia, or as it was called after early 1920's, the Union of Soviet Socialist Republics. Russia was the Mother Country of Communism. Moscow was the new Third Rome of a radical international revolutionary ideology. However, Lenin died in early 1924, a fact that was regretted by many of his followers. These followers were scattered all over the world: in Russia, in the Russian Asiatic possessions, in the adjacent country of China, in Europe, North and South America. Communism bred on the ills of the old societies; it found a fertile ground wherever was discontent and opposition to the Old Order. The revolutionary masses were hoping that the *new societies* were going to be built on the foundations of Marx, Engels, Plekhanov, Trotsky, Lenin and Mao. If they were cheated, it was through the leaders of Communism who happened to be located in Russia: Leningrad, Moscow, and the Kremlin.

Marx himself had stated that he did not want to be a "Marxist." His teachings, all centered about the dialectics, were so flexible to many that today no one seems to be able to give an authoritative explanation of what it really is. Therefore, even today it is extremely difficult to explain *who* is the most legitimate interpreter of Marx. After Lenin's death Stalin imposed himself as his interpreter. After he — Stalin — took power during the 1920's, the U.S.S.R. underwent the most tragic period of bloodshed, genocide and extermination. At the same time Mao Tse-tung was building up Communism in China. He has claimed to this very day that he is the sole true interpreter of Marx-Engels-Lenin and that *his* is the only true version of international Communism.

Paradoxical as it may seem, in those countries that were close to the Soviet Union, all East European countries, the Soviet Communism has failed miserably. The East European peasantry especially, including all the *Slavic* peasants, has on the whole rejected the ideology of Marx-Engels-Lenin. Germany, the pivotal country in Lenin's strategy for the conquest of Europe, with the most advanced working class, with the most Socialist Party members, and the best grass-roots understanding of the problems of the Proletariat, went out of her way to denounce the Bolshevism of Lenin and his compatriots. Just as miserably Communism failed in Hungary, Bulgaria, and the South Slav State (Yugoslavia) — the countries where the Communists could claim great numbers of their members.

After the failure of the Revolution in Germany and in Central Europe, after the rejection of Communism in the Balkans, and the bloody suppression of it in Asia, it had to change its tactics. The Communist International was changing its rules of action, its tactics and revolutionary means from year to year. But all the time the Comintern remained what it was supposed to be from the time of its inception by its father, Vladimir I. U. Lenin, an arm of the Russian imperialism. This Russian chauvinism, illogical as it may seem within the context of Communist internationalism, caused the failure of Communism in China and India, and it explains why during the 1930's the Slavic Russian Communists finally found their most potent allies in German Nazis.

The 1930's were equally tragic in America and in Europe. By the default of the West, Hitler was able to gain power in Germany in January of 1933. In the same year when America was undertaking a social revolution under the leadership of Roosevelt, Europe was going through the social reforms of Stalin, Mussolini, and Hitler. No man is an island; and for that matter: no country is an island. Our destinies were intertwined and interrelated. What was happening in Europe and in China — where Japan was building an empire — was of extreme importance to all of us in this country.

One of the most tragic aspects of the history during the Thirties was the Great Purges in the Soviet Union. Through the whim of one single man, millions of people were doomed. They perished. They were massacred by the order of the man, whom Milovan Djilas, a former Montegrin Communist in Yugoslavia (and the former Vice-President of Yugoslavia) calls the greatest assassin of all times. During the 1930's many millions of innocent people, Russians and non-Russians alike, were exterminated by a regime that claimed to be the government of the people.

Thus the years between the end of the war that was supposed (according to W. Wilson) to "end all the wars" and the year of 1939, was an era of an uneasy peace. In fact it was not peace at all, judging from the records on all the continents. In China hundreds of thousands perished in a civil war between the Nationalists and Communists and the native Chinese and the Japanese occupiers. In the Soviet Union virtually millions were deprived of their utmost right: to live and exist. The Soviet-created famine in the Ukraine killed millions of the Ukrainians; and the starvation was so terrible that the people had to debase themselves to the level of cannibalism. In Spain, during the Civil War almost a million of good patriotic Spaniards on both sides perished in a most terrible fratricidal war.

England slept during those years as it was so vividly described by a Harvard student, a young man named John F. Kennedy, the son of the U.S. Ambassador in London, Joseph P. Kennedy. It was the time of appeasement. It was the time when Austria, Czechoslovakia and even Poland — the largest of the East Central European nations — were sold "down the river" by the West who did not care what was going to happen in Europe under the Nazis, Fascists and Bolsheviks; and what was going to happen to its six million Jews. . . .

What really happened in detail during those twenty-odd years is revealed in the next pages.

# 1. *Under Lenin's Leadership*

**1918 – 1922: The Period of War Communism**

The Civil War was fought in many parts of the former Russian Empire. Millions of people were killed by both sides. Several countries in the West of Russia: Finland, Estonia, Latvia, Lithuania, and Poland became independent while other countries like Bielorussia, Ukraine, the Cossack Don Republic, Georgia, Armenia, Azerbaijan and others were less fortunate.

Under the able leadership of Lenin who was more realistic than Trotsky, the first strategy of Bolsheviks was the immediate World Revolution. This was the period of "War Communism", of civil war and foreign intervention. Lenin's strategy to consolidate the revolution even at the price of a humiliating peace treaty, did materialize. But the struggle for Germany, in which Lenin had such high hopes, proved a failure. The Bolsheviks won because of Lenin's able leadership and Trotsky's genius as a military leader. The disunity among the White forces helped the Bolsheviks too. The anti-Communist Whites were all for the *status quo,* against the concessions to the non-Russian peoples. The Western Powers by their reluctance to help the anti-Communist forces only played into Lenin's hands.

**1918**

Everyone was tired of war. Former soldiers were mostly workers and even more peasants who were eager to go home. They came home with the ideas they picked up at the front or in P.W. camps; very often these ideas were Bolshevik.

The British Labor Party (formally founded in 1906) adopted a program embodying the essential ideas of Fabianism.

**January 1918**

Rumania by invitation occupies the Russian province of Bessarabia which wanted to escape Bolshevik rule. A Moldavian Republic had existed there since early December, 1917.

**January 14, 1918**

The Soviets introduce the new, Gregorian, calendar. (There is a difference of 13 days between the old Julian Calendar used by all Russian historians, and our Gregorian calendar. Thus the Bolshevik "October Revolution" is to us the "November Revolution".)

**January 18, 1918**

The long-awaited Constituent Assembly opens. This was supposed to be the beginning of the democratic rule in Russia. Bolsheviks and their stooges, including the left-wing S.R.'s, withdraw from the Assembly in which they have only a small minority. Lenin, opposed to any democracy, sent his Red troops to disperse this legally elected legislative body. *This is the death of democracy in Russia.*

**January 22, 1918**

Ukrainian Rada proclaims Ukraine an independent and sovereign state.

**January 28, 1918**

The Third All-Russian Congress of the Soviets resolves to establish a Russian Soviet Federal Republic. This is the nucleus around which the future U.S.S.R. will form.

**January 29, 1918**

A rival Communist government is formed in Finland. The country is fighting a civil war. At the same time the Soviet troops entered Kiev to crush the Ukrainian independence.

*General Petliura, ex-dictator of the Ukraine* – Radio Times

### February 9, 1918
The Ukrainians sign a separate peace treaty with Central Powers in Brest-Litovsk. In order to save and consolidate the revolution, Lenin – the master tactician of retreat – was for acceptance of harsh German terms. Trotsky, who now headed the Soviet delegation, was for the policy: "no war, no peace." Infuriated by the Ukrainian separate treaty, Trotsky broke off the negotiations.

### February 16, 1918
The Lithuanians proclaim their complete independence. The non-Russians are no longer content with mere autonomy within Russia.

### February 18, 1918
The Germans start their offensive against Petrograd. The Soviets realized the imminent danger – the loss of their capital, and accept Lenin's idea: sign the treaty with the Germans!

### February 25, 1918
Kaledin, the Cossack leader, had committed suicide. For a while Rostov on the Don was in the possession of the Cossacks. On the 25th the Communists capture the Cossack capital.

### March 3, 1918
The Bolsheviks sign the Peace Treaty of Brest-Litovsk. They give up the non-Russian territories in the West: parts of Poland, entire Finland, Estonia, Latvia, and Lithuania. They had to recognize independence of the Ukraine and Finland. The Russians lost their most industrialized parts. In addition they lost to Turkey: Kars, Batum and Ardagan. Historians have called this treaty a punitive treaty imposed by victorious Germans; it created a precedent for the forthcoming Treaty of Versailles. Actually all territories the Russians lost by Brest-Litovsk were non-Russian from ethnical standpoint.

### March 5, 1918
Some British troops land in Murmansk in Northern Russia to intervene against the Bolsheviks. It was the start of an ill-fated adventure.

### March 6 – 8, 1918
Hastily summoned by Lenin, the Seventh Congress of the Bolshevik Party convenes. In Moscow the party adopts its real name: the Communist Party. 340 delegates represent some 270,000 party members. (They will ratify the Treaty of Brest-Litovsk in spite of strong opposition by N. I. Bukharin and the left wing of Communists.)

### March 12, 1918
Moscow again becomes the capital of Russia. The Bolsheviks thus emphasized the Eurasian character of their state and reverse the decision of Peter the Great to have the capital in the most European of all Russian cities – Petrograd.

### March 15 – 16, 1918
The Fourth Congress of the Soviets ratifies the Treaty of Brest-Litovsk. The Bolsheviks still have to bring the civil war to a successful end – if they want to preserve their regime.

*Trotsky and the Russian delegation received at Brest-divorsk on January 7, 1918 by the German officers. Kamenev on left, Joffe center and Trotsky on right.* – Radio Times

## Spring 1918

Civil War was raging all over the territory of the former Russian Empire. The Bolsheviks were in the midst of their First Strategy: "Immediate World Revolution." They hoped it was "just around the corner." A Communist Party was founded in Netherlands by the left-wing Social Democrats. In Czechoslovakia this marked the beginning of a Communist Party. In the same year the Greek Communist Party was founded. Josip Broz Tito was fighting on the Bolshevik side in Russia. M. Rakosi, a Hungarian Communist, returned to his homeland from Russian captivity to found a Communist movement. Thousands of former Austro-Hungarian prisoners of war did return after 1917–1918 to their homelands as an avant-garde of of Soviet Communism. Some 15,000 Finnish Communists fought a civil war against the government in Helsinki.

## March 25, 1918

The Governing Council of Bielorussia, a former Russian province, proclaims independence of Bielorussia (White Ruthenia). Later on, the Bielorussian Democratic Republic was overrun by Bolshevik forces.

## April 5, 1918

The Japanese and British land at Vladivostok on the Russian Pacific Coast. The alleged purpose for this intervention was to save the 60,000 strong Czech Legion (who consisted of former Austrian prisoners of war in Russia) and to save great quantities of military supplies sent to Russia by former Allies.

## April 9, 1918

The union between Bessarabia and Rumania is proclaimed.

## April 14 – 30, 1918

The Don Cossacks stage a mass revolt against the Bolsheviks. However, many Cossacks fought on the Soviet side.

## April 15, 1918

The Turks seize Batum on the Black Sea coast of Georgia which was fighting for her independence against the Russians.

## April 22, 1918

The Transcaucasian Federation is founded. It consists of: Georgia, Armenia and Azerbaijan. Its head was Akaky Chkenkeli, who signed a separate peace treaty with the Germans.

## April 30, 1918

Hetman P. P. Skoropadsky (1873–1945), a former Tsarist general, becomes the head of the German-friendly Ukrainian government. The Germans are also in the Crimea and need the Ukraine as their "bread basket."

## May 14, 1918

The Czech anti-Soviet forces clash with the Bolsheviks in Cheliabinsk. They control the Trans-Siberian railroad and are advancing.

## May 16, 1918

Helsinki (Helsingfors), the capital of Finland, is liberated from the Bolshevik forces. G. C. Mannerheim (1869–1951), a former Tsarist general and later the marshal of Finland, was the leader of the Finnish struggle for independence.

On the same day P. N. Krasnov (1869–1947), also a former Tsarist general, is elected the Ataman—the supreme leader—of the Don Cossacks and continues the Cossack struggle against the Red forces. In October of the same year he will attempt to take Tsaritsyn (later Stalingrad) from the Bolsheviks. (After the collapse of the civil war he emigrated to Germany, fought on the German side during World War II, was captured by the Soviet troops and executed in Russia in 1947.) Mannerheim and Krasnov were two of many anti-Communist leaders who fought on the German side during the last war. The primary reason why they fought on the German side was: they wanted to fight against the Communist Russians whom they considered as their *main* enemies.

## May 25, 1918

A general uprising of the Czech troops starts against the Bolsheviks.

## May 26, 1918

Georgia, the native country of J. Stalin, proclaims independence. Georgians are not Slavs and they have always detested the Russian rule of their country.

## May 28, 1918

Armenia, an ancient Christian country in the Caucasus, for centuries oppressed by both Turks and

Russians, proclaims independence. For many decades the Armenians were massacred by the Turks. Thousands of them were saved by emigrating to America.

Azerbaijan, a country in Caucasus inhabited by Turkish people, proclaims her independence.

**June 5, 1918**
The Don Cossack region is proclaimed an independent country (Cossackia).

**June 10, 1918**
The Fifth All-Russian Congress of Soviets adopts a new Constitution for the Russian Soviet Federated Socialist Republic (R.S.F.S.R.).

The Red Army is founded. Its organizer and leader was Leon B. Trotsky, the Commissar for War. Most of the officers were former Tsarist officers and the first cadres were only 25 per cent Communist.

**June 25, 1918**
Under Soviet sponsorship, the Turkish Communist Party is founded in Baku, Azerbaijan.

**July 4, 1918**
Siberia is proclaimed an independent republic.

**July 6, 1918**
The German ambassador in Moscow, Count von Mirbach, is assassinated in Moscow by a left Socialist Revolutionary.

The American *Literary Digest*, reflecting the views of the entire American press, reports on British and Japanese landings in Vladivostok.

**July 7, 1918**
The Bolsheviks suppress a revolt of the Socialist Revolutionaries in Moscow.

**July 16 – 17, 1918**
As the White armies were approaching, Tsar Nicholas II and his entire family were liquidated by the Bolsheviks in Yekaterinburg. Their bodies were destroyed.

**July 17, 1918**
President Wilson issues an aide-memoire about the American decision to help the Czech Legion in Siberia. The Japanese eagerly respond by sending additional thousands of troops.

**July 19, 1918**
*The Outlook* in America urges recognition of Siberian independence.

**July 25, 1918**
The Czech anti-Communist forces capture Yekaterinburg. It is too late to save the Tsar's family.

**July 27, 1918**
The *Literary Digest* in America publishes a report of interview with A. I. Konovalov, the Minister of Trade and Industry in Kerensky's government. As he was visiting America he pleaded for American aid to the anti-Communist forces in Russia.

**August 2, 1918**
Additional Allied forces, including the Americans (who are already tired of war) land in Archangelsk in Northern Russia.

**August 3, 1918**
General W. S. Graves receives orders from Washington to lead the American forces of 7,000 men to Vladivostok.

**August 16, 1918**
Americans on board of three British ships (having embarked at the port of New Castle) land in Archangelsk. Most Americans are from Michigan and Wisconsin.

**August 30, 1918**
Dora Kaplan, a Socialist Revolutionary, attempts to kill Lenin. He was only wounded. Red and White terror rage throughout Soviet Russia.

**September 1, 1918**
General Graves with the American troops lands at Vladivostok. There were already some 70,000 Japanese in Siberia and Washington was worried about their presence there.

**September 8, 1918**
General Graves cables to Washington: "Practically all organized resistance in Siberia has disappeared." The Red Army was gaining momentum.

**September 8 – 23, 1918**
Anti-Bolshevik groups meet in a massive conference in Ufa and form an All-Russian Government. On the 23rd they adopted a Constitution and elected an All-Russian Provisional Government.

**September 23, 1918**

American newspapers publish the appeal of N. K. Tchaikovsky, the head of the North Russian Government (in Archangelsk), who pleads for more Allied aid.

**October 4, 1918**

After Lenin's appeal to prepare for a world revolution, the Bolsheviks pledge support to the German proletariat.

**November 1, 1918**

The Communist Party of Austria is founded. The Austro-Hungarian Monarchy had just ceased to exist and Austria is now a small republic with a huge capital, Vienna. It was undergoing chaotic conditions. The Social Democratic Party was the strongest political group.

**November 4, 1918**

The Communist Youth Organization (Komsomol) is founded in Soviet Russia.

**November 5, 1918**

Roman Malinovsky, the old Bolshevik and the accused spy for the Tsarist police, is put on one-day trial and sentenced to death.

**November 7, 1918**

In the midst of a civil war, the Bolsheviks celebrate the first anniversary of their revolution.

The Slavic Socialist Federations of Chicago form the Communist Propaganda League. About a week later the Lettish Federation in Boston issues the first number of its radical periodical, the *Revolutionary Age.*

**November 11, 1918**

The Armistice Day. The World War I ends; but the Civil War in Russia goes on.

In the first post-war revolutionary government in Austria, Otto Bauer, the leading Austrian Socialist, is the Secretary for Foreign Affairs.

**November 13, 1918**

After the downfall of Germany the Bolsheviks declare the Brest-Litovsk Treaty null and void.

**November 18, 1918**

Admiral A. V. Kolchak, who had established an anti-Soviet government in Omsk, Siberia, proclaims himself the "Supreme Ruler" of Russia. The main reason for the failure of the "Whites" was that they were not willing to give concessions to neither non-Russians nor to the peasants of Russia. It was a desperate struggle bound for failure.

**November 20, 1918**

Rumania forbids the Communist Party.

**November 27, 1918**

A Provisional Soviet Government is proclaimed in the Ukraine.

**December 1918**

The Communist Party of Poland is formed.

**December 1, 1918**

The Kingdom of Serbs, Croats, and Slovenes is proclaimed in Belgrade under the Karageorgevich dynasty. Created by the victorious Allies—as a result of the peace treaties—this multi-national state will become scene of bitter fight between: Macedonians, Montenegrins, Slovenes, and Croatians on one side and the Serbs, as the ruling nation, on the other side. The Bolsheviks saw here opportunity to utilize nationality question for spread of Communism.

**December 8, 1918**

The Soviets establish in Lithuania a Peasant Revolutionary (Communist) Government.

**December 14, 1918**

The fall of Hetman Skoropadsky in the Ukraine.

**December 17, 1918**

The Bolsheviks proclaim Latvia a Soviet republic.

**December 18, 1918**

The Bolsheviks proclaim the Ukrainian Soviet Republic. Kharkiv was the capital of this Bolshevik creation. Some Communist Ukrainians collaborated with the Russian Communists to bring about the downfall of independent Ukraine.

**December 31, 1918**

The Bolsheviks establish their own government in Bielorussia.

*Karl Radek, Russian Journalist* — Radio Times

The Communist Party of Germany is founded with Soviet support. Karl Radek was their best known expert in Germany. The C.P. of Germany was founded by the Spartacus group of Rosa Luxemburg and Karl Liebknecht. It became one of the best and most active European Communist Parties. Germany was Number One country in Lenin's strategy to capture Europe for Communism.

**January 1, 1919**
A Bielorussian Soviet Socialist Republic is proclaimed.

**January 5, 1919**
Led by Rosa Luxemburg and Karl Liebknecht the Spartacists revolt in Berlin. Within a few days the Communists were defeated by the military forces. On the 15th both leaders were arrested and liquidated by the soldiers.

**January 21, 1919**
The strike of 35,000 shipyard workers in Seattle, Wash. begins. By February 11 it is smashed by use of force: 3,000 troops and policemen called by Mayor Ole Hanson. There are throughout 1919 some 3,600 strikes involving more than 4,000,000 workers.

**January 29, 1919**
U.S. Senator from California, Hiram Johnson urges in a Senate speech withdrawal of American forces from Russia.

**February 4, 1919**
A short-lived Soviet Republic is proclaimed in Bremen, Germany.

**February 12, 1919**
Karl Radek is arrested in Berlin and is accused of having a draft for a general Communist revolution in Central Europe for early 1919.

**February 8, 1919**
The *Revolutionary Age* publishes its Manifesto and the Program of the Left Wing of the American Socialist Party. A week later the Left Wing Section of the Socialist Party was founded in New York City. (According to the Justice Department some 470 radical papers exist in the United States.)

**February 21, 1919**
Kurt Eisner, the leader of the Bavarian Soviet Republic is shot to death by anti-Communist forces.

**March 2 – 6, 1919**
The First Congress of the Communist International (Comintern) – or Third International – convenes in Moscow. The Comintern was formed under Lenin's initiative. G. Zinoviev was elected President of the International. The Russians, in spite of German opposition, held complete control of the organization that was supposed to replace the Second International.

**March 18 – 23, 1919**
The Eighth Congress of the Russian C.P., which has about 314,000 members, convenes. The reorganization of the C.P. was undertaken. The *Politburo* was reconstituted; it was to decide all important policy matters. An Organizational Bureau (*Orgburo*) and the Secretariat were established; all three were subject to the Central Committee; it consisted of 19 members at the time. A new party program was adopted. In the first large-scale purge many thousands of opportunists were expelled from the party.

**March 21, 1919**
Hungarian Communists led by Bela Kun overthrow the Socialist government, seize power and establish a Soviet Republic. It lasted 133 days.

## March 27, 1919

The Allied Supreme Council rejects the plan of French Marshal Ferdinand Foch for an anti-Communist crusade.

## April 1919

Left Wing Socialists start publishing the *New York Communist.* John Reed is its editor. The Old Guard Socialists start now their *New York Socialist.* They already have as their organ, the *Call.*

## April 9, 1919

American troops are leaving England for Archangelsk in Northern Russia. Their intervention is bound to failure.

## April 16, 1919

A Communist regime is established in Bavaria, Germany. (The first attempt took place in January, 1919.) After five days of fighting it was defeated by the government and the "Free Corps." This again was a blow to Lenin's and Comintern's designs.

## April 20–23, 1919

The Socialist Workers' Party of Yugoslavia (Communist) is founded in Belgrade. The Communists were skillfully utilizing the difficult nationality question of this multi-national state.

## May 1, 1919

The first issue of the *Communist International* appears in Moscow under Zinoviev's editorship.

## May 1, 1919

Anti-leftist May Day riots take place in Cleveland, Ohio during a parade led by radical Charles Ruthenberg.

## May 13, 1919

The "White" general N. N. Yudenich opens from Estonia an offensive against the Bolsheviks in Petrograd. The offensive failed after a few days.

## May 22, 1919

Riga, the capital of Latvia, is liberated from Bolshevik occupation.

## May 28, 1919

Armenia proclaims its independence.

*Kurt Eisner, German Socialist* – Radio Times

## June 12, 1919

G. Zinoviev, the chairman of the Comintern, states in a wire to Bela Kun that "before long the entire civilized world will become Communist."

## June 15, 1919

A Communist insurrection is prevented by the Austrian government.

## June 16, 1919

With the help of Bela Kun's Red Army a Slovak Soviet Republic is proclaimed in eastern parts of Czechoslovakia. It lasted only three weeks.

## June 21, 1919

The Left Wing Socialists (94 delegates from 20 states) open their National Conference in New York City.

## June 28, 1919

The Treaty of Versailles is signed between the Allies and Germany in the Hall of Mirrors. The dissatisfaction of all Germans with what they considered harsh and unjust stipulations will partly contribute to the rise of National Socialism during the 1920's and 1930's.

## July 1919
Many American newspapers report a mutiny of American troops in Archangelsk. The press urges the U.S. government to withdraw all troops from Russia.

## July 28, 1919
91 delegates from 14 European countries and the U.S., representing almost 18,000,000 trade unionists, meet in Amsterdam to form the International Federation of Trade Unions.

## August 2, 1919
After failure of his revolution, Bela Kun flees Hungary; with Matyas Rakosi, another Communist leader, he goes to Russia. Communism in Hungary was defeated by nationalist forces under Admiral N. Horthy and by Rumanian troops. On August 4 The Rumanians enter Budapest, the capital of Hungary.

## August 11, 1919
After many weeks of deliberations in the city of Weimar a democratic, liberal, republican constitution for Germany is adopted. The country, suffering from the defeat in the war, was now ruled by a coalition of Social Democrats (who were strongly anti-Bolshevik), Center Party (the Catholics), and Liberal Democrats. German republic between 1919 and 1933, when Hitler took over, was known as the Weimar Republic. In this highly democratic state all political parties enjoyed complete freedom, a fact that was fully utilized by the Communists.

## August 24, 1918
The Communists receive almost 120,000 votes in Bulgarian elections. Bulgaria was a monarchy under King Boris. There were few industrial workers in this predominantly agricultural country. The small C.P. under Dimitrov's leadership was active and militant. Many people sympathized with Communism because of their traditional attachment to Russia, the liberator and protector of Bulgarians in the past. Bulgaria was a typical Balkan peasant country; their leader at the time was Alexander Stambuliski (1879-1923).

## August 30, 1919
Left-wing Socialists and Communists convene in Chicago. There is a great split and division within American radical movements. It should be noted that this was the time of Red Scare in America. The U.S. Senate was investigating the Bolshevik activities in America, especially after the outbreak of a general strike in Seattle, Wash. (February 6, 1919). Rebuffed by the Communists the left-wing Socialists decide to act alone.

## August 31, 1919
These left-wing Socialists formed in Chicago the Communist Labor Party. One of its founders was John Reed, who had come back from Russia and had published his famous book on the Bolshevik Revolution, *Ten Days That Shook the World*, an eyewitness account. Reed was a friend of Lenin, Trotsky and many leading Bolsheviks.

## September 1, 1919
Other left-wing groups — meeting in Chicago — found the Communist Party of America. Charles E. Ruthenberg was named its National Secretary.

In late 1919 the Socialist Party of America has close to 40,000 members; the Communist Party of America between 30,000 and 60,000 active members; and the Communist Labor Party between 10,000 and 30,000.

## September 9, 1919
The famous Boston police strike starts.

## September 16, 1920
In the Wall Street bombing in New York City 29 persons are killed. The damage is about $2 million. This terror act stirs up the public even more against radicalism.

## September 20, 1919
G. Zinoviev in Petrograd hails the creation of the Communist Party of America as "the first swallow which foretells the coming of a worldwide Communist spring." The hopes of the Russians in American Communism were very high.

## September 22, 1919
In the wave of many strikes during 1919, a massive strike was declared against U.S. Steel. In the long strife eighteen strikers were killed. Federal and state troops were used. Under the instructions of the

president of the American Federation of Labor, Samuel Gompers, the drive was undertaken to organize the steel workers. William Z. Foster, then a left-wing syndicalist, was one of the principal leaders in the strike. In this crucial battle the workers lost the support of the public opinion that was under the impact of Bolshevik scare. In U.S. Steel some 340,000 workers struck; the strike spread to Bethlehem Steel too.

## October 1919
The "White" general A. I. Denikin (1872-1947) is defeated by the Bolsheviks and withdraws his forces to southern Russia. He had organized anti-Bolshevik forces in the Don region. Denikin's army included the Kuban and Don Cossacks under generals Shkuro and Krasnov. In the summer of 1919 these forces had taken Kharkov, Kiev, Voronezh and Orel before they were defeated by the Bolsheviks. (In the spring of 1920 many of Denikin's troops were placed under the command of the White general Wrangel.)

## October 6, 1919
The peasant leader of Bulgaria Alexander Stambuliski takes over the government and undertakes radical agrarian reforms. He had led in 1918 a peasant uprising, after Bulgaria's defeat in the war, against King Ferdinand and forced his resignation. Stambuliski became famous among all Balkan peasants and wanted to organize them in a Green International.

## November 1, 1919
*The Communist World,* the official organ of the Communist Party of America appears. They state: "Our object is ... the establishment of the Communist Commonwealth through the dictatorship of the proletariat."

## November 11, 1919
In Centralia, Wash. four W.W.I. veterans are shot to death in a fight with the local members of the I.W.W.

## November 14, 1919
The Red Army captures Omsk in Siberia. Admiral A. V. Kolchak (1873-1920) retreats to Irkutsk. Gradually, *the Bolsheviks are winning on all fronts. They are winning the Civil War!*

## December 2-4, 1919
The Russian Communist Party meets in its Eighth All-Russian Conference. As the tempo of the Civil

War was increasing, the drive for new members proved very successful. The party is regenerated and has some 500,000 vigorous members.

## December 10, 1919
Under the pressure of the Allies the Rumanians, old enemies of the Hungarians, are forced to evacuate Budapest after a generous plunder of the city.

East Central Europe, located between Soviet Russia and Western Europe, was at the time rich in events. Between the Baltic and the Adriatic, between Trieste and the Black Sea this was the time of transition. Many nationalities with too many problems figured high in Lenin's overall strategy to capture Europe for Bolshevism. (On September 10, 1919 the Treaty of Saint Germain between the Allies and defeated Austria was signed. Bulgaria signed the humiliating Treaty of Neuilly with the Allies on November 27, 1919. She was deprived of Macedonia.)

## December 21, 1919
The Red Scare was in full swing in America. Thousands of immigrants — some innocent and some with radical convictions — were given miserable treatment by the Department of Labor (which was then in charge of the Immigration and Naturalization Service) and by the Justice Department under the Attorney General A. Mitchell Palmer of Pennsylvania. The entire Federal Bureau of Investigation was set loose to catch all the alleged Bolsheviks and radicals of all colors. On December 22, 1919 some 250 known Russian and Ukrainian Communists, the residents of the United States, were shipped to Finland aboard the *Buford*. Among them were the Anarchists Emma Goldman and Alexander Berkman.

## End of 1919
America was withdrawing into isolation. New immigration laws to prevent the flood of the "New Immigrants" from southern and eastern parts of Europe were being prepared to close the gates of America. The organized labor was losing its battles everywhere in America. The civil liberties were violated in thousands of cases. At the same time V. I. Lenin wrote a Foreword to John Reed's book on the Russian Revolution of November 1917. Said Lenin: "Unreservedly do I recommend it to the workers of the world. Here is a book which I should like to see published in millions of copies and translated into all languages."

## January 1920
American Communists go underground because they are persecuted by the U.S. Government.

## January 1, 1920
On New Year's Day thousands of Federal agents undertake one of the biggest "Palmer's Raids" against the radical aliens. Some six thousand people, many of them U.S. citizens and non-Communists, were arrested and sent to jails and bull pens. Even foreign nationality wedding parties were raided in one of the largest discrimination manifestations against the foreign nationals in America. One-third of victims were released for lack of evidence. (556 aliens were eventually deported to Russia.)

## January 1, 1920
The Red Army, a creation of Trotsky and a powerful revolutionary machine, is 3,000,000 strong. Lenin has big plans for this year. Germany, the pivotal part of Europe, must be Bolshevized.

## January 4, 1920
Admiral Kolchak resigns as the leader of the White movement in Russia.

## January 10, 1920
The League of Nations, a pet idea of President Wilson, starts its official existence. From the very beginning it proved an impotent organization and was doomed to failure. The Soviets, isolated from the rest of the world, were now boycotting it.

The Red Army was now in the possession of Rostov on the Don. The American steel strike came to its unsuccessful end (on January 9).

## January 15, 1920
The Soviets liquidate the Eastern Front. They scored their victories with a tough and disciplined organization of their forces.

## January 28, 1920
The Albanian National Congress meets in Lushinja and decides on a general election. This is the smallest and most backward Balkan country with few prospects for Communism.

## February 2, 1920
Estonia, a small Baltic country of some 1,000,000 people – after successfully rejecting Communism – signs a peace treaty with the Bolsheviks in Dorpat, Estonia. Lenin intends to reverse this decision in the future.

## February 7, 1920
Admiral Kolchak, who was delivered to the Bolsheviks by the French, is executed by the Soviet authorities. The anti-Soviet resistance in Siberia collapsed completely.

## February 19, 1920
The anti-Communist Northern Government of Russia in Archangelsk is overthrown by the Bolsheviks.

## February 29, 1920
Under the Presidency of Thomas G. Masaryk, a friend of America (which helped to establish his country Czechoslovakia), the Czechoslovak National Assembly votes for a new democratic constitution.

## March 13, 1920
The Bolsheviks liquidate the Northern Front. Slowly they are consolidating their power in Russia in spite of general predictions that they were doomed.

## March 27, 1920
The Bolsheviks conquer Novorossisk. This is the end of Denikin's army.

## March 27, 1920
The Albanian National Legislative Assembly meets in Tirana, the capital of the small country with a million inhabitants.

## March 28, 1920
The Bulgarian Agrarians led by A. Stambuliski achieve great electoral victory in Bulgaria.

## March 29 – April 5, 1920
The Ninth Congress of the Bolshevik Party meets. The membership, replenished with new elements, is over 600,000. A Party Secretariat of three was named.

## April 4, 1920
General N. N. Wrangel takes over command of the White Army in the South.

## April 6, 1920
Far Eastern Republic is founded.

**April 25, 1920**

The Poles under Pilsudski launch a full scale offensive against the Bolsheviks after an agreement with Ukraine. Now two Soviet armies march towards East Prussia and Vistula.

**April 27, 1920**

Azerbaijan Soviet Government is founded.

**May 2, 1920**

The Communists win 182,000 votes in Bulgarian elections.

**May 7, 1920**

Polish and Ukrainian forces liberate Kiev from the Bolsheviks. Pilsudski marched into Ukraine after an agreement with S. V. Petlyura, the chief of Central Ukrainian Rada

**May 11, 1920**

Turkish National Assembly meets in Ankara.

**June 4, 1920**

The Treaty of Trianon is signed between the Allies and Hungary.

**June 20-24, 1920**

The Second Congress of the Socialist Workers' Party of Yugoslavia (Communists) meets in Vukovar, Croatia. The new name: the Communist Party of Yugoslavia is adopted; it joins the Comintern. There are at least 65,000 active Communists in Yugoslavia.

**July 6, 1920**

Two Bolshevik columns—one of them led by Budenny—start the offensive against Poles who were now retreating from the Ukraine. Lenin—in spite of warnings from German and Polish Communists—wants to conquer Poland and Germany and make them Soviet republics. During this Bolshevik drive, the British Foreign Secretary Lord Curzon proposed mediation and a line of demarcation between Poland and Soviet Russia. This is how the controversial "Curzon Line" originated. Lenin did not accept it.

**July 6, 1920**

The British troops evacuate Batum in Russia. Foreign intervention against the Bolsheviks is gradually breaking up.

**July 12, 1920**

During their march towards Poland the Soviets sign a peace treaty with Lithuania. The Lithuanians obtain Vilna, their ancient capital. Lithuania was opposed to the establishment of a Great Poland.

**July 19 – August 7, 1920**

Second Congress of the Comintern meets in Moscow after preliminary meetings in Petrograd. Left-Socialists and Communists from 37 countries were represented. John Reed represented the American Communists and was elected to the Executive Committee of the International. The Congress agreed on Conditions of Admissions to its ranks (21 Points formulated by Lenin). Its aim was to create a single Communist Party for the entire world (under Soviet leadership) and by armed struggle to overthrow the existing "international bourgeoisie" in order to create "an international Soviet Republic." The authority was vested in an Executive Committee. The Comintern had a large permanent staff. Later on the organization was run by regional secretariats under a presidium that was controlled by the Bolsheviks.

**July 31, 1920**

Having reached Polish territory, the Bolsheviks found a Polish Revolutionary Committee.

**July 31 – August 1, 1920**

The British Communist Party is founded in London. It claims a membership of 10,000.

**August 11, 1920**

Peace treaty with Latvia is signed by Bolsheviks.

**August 14, 1920**

Czechoslovakia and the Kingdom of Serbs, Croats and Slovenes sign a treaty of alliance. This is the beginning of the Little Entente joined by Rumania three days later.

**August 14-19, 1920**

Under leadership of their young generals: M. Tukhachevsky and S. Budenny the Red Army was at the gates of Warsaw. Poland was in a desperate situation. With little military aid and advice from the West by French General Maxime Weygand, Pilsudski pushed through the gap between the two Bolshevik armies and forced them to retreat. This was the "Miracle on the Vistula River." The serious military defeat upset Lenin's plans for conquest of central Europe. By late August the Bolsheviks retreated from Polish territories.

*New Monument of Marx and Engels in Moscow* — Radio Times

**September 1920**
Peace negotiations start between victorious Poland and the Soviet Russia. Poland was now striving for better boundaries than those proposed by Lord Curzon.

**September 2, 1920**
The Congress of the Peoples of the East opens in Baku under Comintern's sponsorship. Some 2,000 delegates were present. The Bolsheviks want to be quite active in many colonial territories.

**September 22-25, 1920**
Meeting of the Ninth All-Russian Conference of the Communist Party.

**October 1, 1920**
Austria receives a democratic constitution creating a federative republic.

**October 12, 1920**
Poles and Russians sign a preliminary peace treaty in Riga, Latvia.

**October 12, 1920**
A peace treaty is signed between Finland and Soviet Russia.

**October 19, 1920**
John Reed dies of typhus at the age of 33 in Moscow and was buried in the Kremlin.

**October 30, 1920**
The Communist Party of Australia is founded.

**November 14, 1920**
General Wrangel is forced to evacuate Crimea and to seek asylum in Constantinople. The Crimean front was thus liquidated by the Bolsheviks.

**November 26, 1920**
In a speech to the Communist functionaries in Moscow Lenin advises Communists to exploit the existing antagonisms between the world imperialists.

**November 28, 1920**
In the elections for the Constituent Assembly of Yugoslavia the Communists won over 198,000 votes and 58 of 419 deputies in the assembly. This was the only time that the C.P. enjoyed complete legality in Yugoslavia.

**December 1920**
The Communist Party of New Zealand was formed in Wellington.

**December 2, 1920**
By the Peace of Alexandropol, Armenia cedes a large part of her territory to Turkey. There was a revolutionary movement in Turkey under the leadership of an army general and nationalist Mustapha Kemal. His group rejected the peace treaty of Sèvres between the Allies and the government in Constantinople.

**December 28, 1920**
The Bolshevik forces finally gain their control over the Ukraine. The largest non-Russian territory, within the future Soviet Union, was now under the control of the Kremlin.

**December 29, 1920**
The government in Belgrade issues a special Law for the Defense of the State against Communist Party and all extreme movements. A reign of terror was inaugurated.

**1921**
Comintern inaugurated its "Second Strategy." As revolutions in Europe failed to materialize, the Communists will prefer agitation instead of direct revolt. The Soviet state had to be rebuilt and Communism consolidated there first, before it could be successfully exported.

**January 15, 1921**
The Seventeenth Congress of the Italian Socialist Party begins at Leghorn. The party is split between a Communist majority and a Socialist minority. Italy was now in turmoil. A former Socialist Benito Mussolini (1883-1945) founded in February of 1919 his fascist movement. The Leghorn congress was attended by Matyas Rakosi as Comintern's representative.

**February 1921**
The Transcaucasian Federation, which had in 1920 gained Allied and Soviet recognition, was now facing both Turkish and Soviet intervention.

**February 22, 1921**
The Soviets adopt the *Gosplan* (Economic Planning).

**February 23 – March 17, 1921**
The uprising of the Kronstadt sailors, the former avant garde of the Revolution. Under the slogan "The Soviets without Bolsheviks" the 14,000 rebels demanded radical concessions from the Soviet regime. The uprising was ruthlessly suppressed by the Red Army under Trotsky and Tukhachevsky. Lenin interpreted the uprising as a warning to inaugurate the New Economic Policy and other reforms.

**February 26, 1921**
The Bolsheviks sign a treaty with Persia.

**February 27, 1921**
Georgia is overpowered by the Bolsheviks. After Soviet troops took Tiflis, a Turkish-Soviet treaty established present borders in Caucasus area. The real ruler of Georgia became Sergo Ordzhonikidze, (1886-1937), the political commissar of the Eleventh Red Army and one of the famous Bolshevik leaders. A year later together with Stalin he forced the incorporation of Georgia and the rest of the Transcaucasian Federation into the U.S.S.R.

**March 1921**
Failure of Communist revolts in Germany, referred to as "Disaster of March 1921," compelled Comintern and Lenin to continued tactical changes. The failure of revolution in Germany and unwillingness of the German proletarians to support the Bolsheviks caused a great personal aggravation to Lenin. Now new peaceful tactics had to be applied all over the world.

**March 4, 1921**
Warren G. Harding, a Republican, becomes the twenty-ninth President of the United States.

**March 8-16, 1921**
The Tenth Congress of the Bolshevik Party is a turning point in the history of the party. The Kronstadt rebellion took place at this time. Lenin proposed the New Economic Policy, a partial return, to capitalism. It was a temporary retreat, a return to limited private enterprise. Party unity was strengthened. Stalin in his report discussed here "Marxism and National Question."

**March 16, 1921**
Treaty of friendship and peace is concluded between Turkey and the Soviet government. As they were almost completely isolated in the world of diplomacy, the Bolsheviks were very eager to conclude treaties and establish diplomatic relations with as many countries as possible.

**March 16, 1921**
The Soviets sign a trade agreement with Great Britain.

**March 18, 1921**
The Treaty of Riga is concluded between the Soviet and Polish governments terminating the war of 1920. Poland was given the non-Polish territories in the East (beyond the Curzon Line) with almost 4,000,000 Ukrainians and White Russians. The Poles also kept Vilna and eastern parts of Lithuania.

**March 21, 1921**
The New Economic Policy goes into effect.

**Spring of 1921**
*Mao Tse-tung considers himself a Marxist.* During the winter 1920-1921 he had read the *Communist Manifesto* in Chinese. This was the first Marxist book ever to be printed in China. Since spring of 1918 a Society for the Study of Marxism had existed at the University of Peking; Mao was one of its members.

*Leon Trotsky reviews Red Band* – Radio Times

**May 1921**

At a unity convention in Woodstock, New York, the United Communist Party and the Communist Party of America—under directions of Comintern—merge into a single Communist Party of America.

**May 8, 1921**

The Communist Party of Rumania is founded. The country has many proletarians, an impoverished peasantry, unsolved nationality problems, with a lot of economic, social and political problems.

**May 14, 1921**

The Communist Party of Czechoslovakia is formally founded.

**May 19, 1921**

Emergency Quota Immigration Act passed by America. The annual immigration was limited to 357,000. The law reflected the fear of the "New Immigration" and radicalism after the passing of the Red Scare.

**May 26-28, 1921**

The Tenth All-Russian Conference of the C.P. is held.

**May 31 – July 14, 1921**

The trial of Nicola Sacco and Bartolomeo Vanzetti, two Italian anarchists, in Boston for alleged holdup and murder in South Brantree, Mass. (They were arrested on May 5, 1920 in the midst of the Red Scare.) Sacco and Vanzetti were convicted and sentenced to death. Throughout America and Europe the leftist and liberal groups believed that they were not sentenced for murder but for the fact they were anarchists.

**June 1921**

Gregory Voitinsky, a Comintern agent, arrived in Peking and then went to Shanghai to prepare the First Congress of the Chinese Communist Party. (Mao stated that the party was founded in May; another Chinese source maintains it was formed in July.) Anyhow, the Chinese Communist Party—later to grow to the biggest Communist Party of the world—was organized by twelve delegates and fifty members in 1921.

**June 22 – July 12, 1921**

The Third Congress of the Comintern takes place. 509 delegates from 48 countries were compelled by the failure of the revolution in Germany and central Europe to reshape the policies of international Communism.

**July 1921**

Herbert Hoover, who was well known for his administration of the American relief to starving Belgium before U.S. entered the War, receives a letter from the famous Russian writer Maxim Gorky appealing to the American people for aid in the stupendous Russian famine that was a result of the Revolution.

**July 3, 1921**

The First Congress of the Red International of Labor Unions starts in Moscow. An American delegate, William Z. Foster made here his definitive conversion to Communism.

**July 17, 1921**

Important agrarian laws are passed in Rumania.

**August 20, 1921**

An agreement is reached between the American and Soviet governments on terms of relief. Over 100 Americans are released from Soviet prisons. Some 200 Americans go to Russia to perform and control the relief.

**September 21, 1921**

The activities of the American Relief services begin in Soviet Russia. The U.S. appropriated $20,000,000; $8,000,000 were spent in U.S. Army's medical supplies; many millions were spent by private agencies. In Hoover's own words: "In the acute period of the spring we were giving food to 18,000,000 persons." The acute crisis ended with the Russian harvest in 1922. The American Relief Administration brought in more than 700,000 tons of goods.

**November 5, 1921**

A treaty is signed between the Soviets and the Mongolian People's Republic. Formerly the center of the great Mongolian Empire, this will become an area of contest between the Russians and the Chinese.

**November 7, 1921**

The Bolsheviks celebrate the fourth anniversary of the Revolution.

**November 9, 1921**
A conference of the ambassadors votes for the reaffirmation of the Albanian frontiers in 1913. (Greece and Yugoslavia wanted to annex this little country.) Ahmed Zog will soon emerge as the leading politician, very much anti-Communist, in Albania.

**December 19-22, 1921**
The Eleventh All-Russian Party Congress is held.

**December 23, 1921**
A convention meets in New York City to organize the Workers' Party of America, a legal "above ground organization" that was suggested by Lenin and the Russian Bolsheviks, who thought that America as a capitalist country was very important for the success of the international Communist movement. (In November a Proletarian Party of America held its second convention. This leftist party was not recognized by the Comintern. It denounced the Socialist Party.)

**1922**
The Civil War was over. Communism was firmly established in Russia. While outside Russia Bolshevism failed, it was victorious in its own country. This was also Lenin's victory.

The Canadian Communists counted some 5,000 members, many of them of Slavic origin.

Bulgarian Communism was very weak because the Stambuliski regime attracted the peasants, who disliked Communism and composed almost 90 per cent of the Bulgarian population. Everywhere in the Balkans the peasants proved to be the most persistent opposition to Communism. There were about 40,000 Communists in Bulgaria at this time. G. Dimitrov was a very powerful Communist leader.

**January 21, 1922**
The Toilers of the Far East, a Communist Front organization, meets in Irkutsk, Siberia and then moves to Moscow.

**February 1922**
Cheka, the dreaded Soviet secret police that liquidated millions of people, took a new name – G.P.U.

*Gregory Zinoviev, Red orator (hatless), in Petrograd* – Radio Times

**February 2, 1922**
*The Worker,* a weekly of the Communist Party of America, publishes a special appeal of the Comintern to meet in Moscow on February 22.

**February 3, 1922**
The Workers' Defense Conference of New England issues a call for the convention to be held on February 28 in New York City. (This convention organized the United Toilers of America.)

**March 12, 1922**
The Soviet governments of Georgia, Armenia and Azerbaijan form the Transcaucasian Socialist Soviet Republic.

**March 27 – April 2, 1922**
The Eleventh Congress of the Russian C.P. convenes in Moscow. This was the last that Lenin attended.

**April 3, 1922**
Joseph Stalin becomes Secretary General of the Russian Communist Party. He will make his office the most important in the party and secure his own climb to power.

**April 16, 1922**
During the meeting of the International Conference in Genoa, Italy (April 4 – May 19) Soviet Russia and Germany sign the Treaty of Rapallo. It establishes friendly diplomatic and economic relations between the two countries. The treaty came as a great surprise to Western powers. An additional agreement signed on November 5, 1922 in Berlin extended the treaty to other Soviet republics.

**April 20, 1922**
At a secret convention the American Young Communist League is organized.

**May 13-15, 1922**
The Young Workers' League of America, a branch of the [Communist] Workers' Party of America, is founded.

**May 26, 1922**
Lenin suffers his first stroke.

**July 1922**
The Comintern sends to the United States three delegates to organize a strong and united Communist movement. In 1922 this movement consisted of a legal Workers' Party of America, a legal United Toilers Party, and two underground Communist organizations, of which one was split in two factions. The Comintern recommended that American Communist organize a legal party which would unite all the factions.

**July 1922**
The Chinese Communist Party held its Second Congress in Shanghai. It had now some three hundred members of whom ninety per cent were intellectuals. The party jointed the Comintern.

**July 5, 1922**
The Communist Party of Japan is founded.

**July 8, 1922**
The Dutch Communist Party receives some 54,000 votes in parliamentary elections: two Communist deputies enter parliament.

**July 15, 1922**
The Communist Party of Japan holds its first convention.

**Summer of 1922**
The Bolsheviks staged a public trial of leading Socialist Revolutionaries. Twelve members of the Central Committee of the S.R.'s were sentenced to death. The sentence was not carried out.

**August 4-7, 1922**
Twelfth All-Russian Conference of the C.P. is held.

**August 22, 1922**
U.S. government agents raid the secret Communist convention in a forest near Bridgman, Mich.

**September 10, 1922**
A commercial treaty is concluded between Soviet Russia and Great Britain.

**September 13, 1922**
Turkish forces under the leadership of Mustapha Kemal capture the Greek stronghold Smyrna in Asia Minor.

**October 28, 1922**

Mussolini's Italian Fascists undertake their March on Rome which resulted in Fascist take-over. The Executive Committee of the Italian Communist Party had issued already on October 11 instructions for underground activities in case of a Fascist dictatorship. However, within a few years Mussolini will almost completely wipe out Socialism and Communism in Italy.

**November 1, 1922**

Mustapha Kemal proclaims Turkish republic and launches many reforms. Although he maintained good relations with the Bolsheviks, Kemal suppressed all Communist activities in his own country.

**November 5 – December 5, 1922**

The Fourth Congress of the Comintern was attended by 408 delegates from 58 countries. Lenin spoke on the New Economic Policy and prospects of the world revolution.

**November 10, 1922**

The Bolsheviks annex the Far-Eastern Republic.

**December 1, 1922**

J. Pilsudski resigns as President of Poland.

**December 22, 1922**

After another stroke Lenin dicated his Testament to which he added a postscript on January 4, 1923 suggesting removal of Stalin as secretary general of the party. The Testament was never made public during Stalin's time, nor was the breach between Lenin and Stalin publicized.

**December 30, 1922**

The First Congress of Soviets of the Union of Soviet Socialist Republics opens in Moscow. This is the birth of the U.S.S.R. It adopts a declaration on the formation of the U.S.S.R. and a Treaty of Union. It elects a supreme legislative body – the Central Executive Committee of the U.S.S.R. Its chairman was M. I. Kalinin (1875-1946). Lenin, although ailing, became the Chairman of the Council of People's Commissars of the U.S.S.R. (equivalent to premier of a government).

Originally the U.S.S.R. included only four republics: the Russian S.F.S.R., the Ukrainian S.S.R., the White Russian S.S.R., and the Transcaucasian S.F.S.R. For

*Lenin and his wife, Nadezhda at his dacha in Gorki* — Radio Times

all practical purposes – in spite of the idea of federation – the Union has been dominated by the Russian S.F.S.R. for its mere size: some 6,5 million square miles has secured the domination of the Russian people over many non-Russian peoples. A year later, Uzbekistan and Turkmenia in Central Asia joined the Union. These were then followed by the adjacent nations – Tadjikistan, Kazakstan, and Kirghizia. At the same time Transcaucasia was divided into its three component republics: Georgia, Armenia, and Azerbaijan. By 1926 there were eleven republics in the U.S.S.R.

**December 30, 1922**
The First Union Congress of Soviets adopts the Articles of Confederation.

**January 1923**
The German Communist Party holds its Congress in Leipzig.

**January 1923**
In a wave of anti-Communist persecutions the Rumanian authorities arrested the leading Communist Anna Pauker.

**January 10, 1923**
The Lithuanians occupy Memel, their only access to the Baltic and a territory disputed between them and Germany.

**January 30, 1923**
At Lausanne, Switzerland where the Allies were negotiating a new peace treaty with Kemal's Turkey, an agreement is signed about compulsory exchange of Turks and Greeks. It resulted in an expulsion of 1,300,000 Greeks from Asia Minor to Greece, and some 400,000 Turks from Greece to Turkey.

**February 16, 1923**
The Allies assign the Memel Territory to Lithuania.

**March 4, 1923**
The *Pravda* publishes the last article by Lenin under the title "Better Less But Better" in which he denounced the Red bureaucracy. Five days later he had the last stroke from which he never recovered.

**March 14, 1923**
The Allies assign Vilna and Eastern Galicia to Poland, thus confirming the Treaty of Riga.

**April 7, 1923**
At a convention in New York City the American underground Communist organizations are dissolved and the legal Workers' Party of America became the Communist Party of America.

**April 17-25, 1923**
The Twelfth Congress of the Russian C.P. It was the first congress that was not attended by Lenin. The delegates at the congress did not know that already in March, before he suffered his third stroke, Lenin had broken with Stalin because of Stalin's treatment of Georgian Bolsheviks.

**May 10, 1923**
V. V. Vorovsky, a Bolshevik diplomat, is assassinated by a Russian exile in Lausanne, Switzerland.

**May 27, 1923**
The Second (Socialist) International is revived in a congress at Hamburg, Germany.

**June 1923**
The Third Congress of the Chinese C.P. was held in Canton.

**June 9, 1923**
Alexander Stambuliski, the Bulgarian agrarian premier, is overthrown by the military circles and Macedonian nationalists. The Communists remained neutral in this struggle and were subsequently rebuked by the Comintern. A new government was established under Alexander Tsankov.

**July 6, 1923**
The draft of a new constitution for the U.S.S.R. is finished. (It will be finally adopted on January 31, 1924.)

**July 10, 1923**
The President of the U.S.S.R. Kalinin sends a letter of thanks to Herbert Hoover "in the name of the millions of people who have been saved." Later on, the Soviet historians either ignored the American aid or described it as "imperialist activities" against the peoples of the Soviet Union.

**July 24, 1923**
A peace treaty between the Allies and Kemal's Turkey is signed in Lausanne, Switzerland.

At the same time the triumvirate: Zinoviev, Kamenev and Stalin were ruling the U.S.S.R.

*Kalinin, President of the Russian Union* – Radio Times

*Dr. Sun Yat-sen, Chinese revolutionary leader* — Radio Times

**August 1923**
The Chinese patriot Sun Yat-sen sent his general Chiang Kai-shek, who was his chief of staff (b. in 1886), to Moscow to negotiate with the Bolsheviks, to study the conditions in the Soviet state and to negotiate for Soviet aid. China still had two governments: one in Peking maintained by the military war-lords and one in the South led by revolutionary Kuomitang republican forces (then aided by the Communists). It should be noted that on January 26, 1923, the new Soviet representative in revolutionary China, Adolf Joffe, issued a statement to the effect that the Soviets would support Sun Yat-sen's group in China. In February of 1923 the militarists in Peking undertook wholesale massacres of Communists. In October of 1923 Michael Borodin came to Sun's forces as the new Soviet envoy. By late November, 1923, Sun openly sided with Russian Communism. All these development were important for the future of Chinese Communism.

**August 27, 1923**
Italian-Greek incident breaks out. The Italians occupy the strategic island of Corfu that guards the entrance to the Adriatic. On September 27, the Italians were forced to evacuate it.

**September 1923**
Lenin was recovering at Gorky, near Moscow, from his stroke.

**September 1923**
The Bulgarian Communists, few but powerful, attempt a revolt against the government of Prof. Tsankov. The revolt was crushed by the military which was loyal to the monarchy. Georgi Dimitrov and some 1,000 Communists left the country.

**October 5, 1923**
German Communists enter the provincial governments in Thuringia and Saxony. An unsuccessful Communist revolt was attempted in the city of Hamburg. The confusion precipitated by the Communists gave excuse to Adolph Hitler and the extreme Right to undertake future revolts.

**November 8, 1923**
A. Hitler undertakes his revolt in Munich. It fails.

## October – November, 1923
Communist riots in Germany fail.

In the winter of 1923-1924 all Communist efforts in Germany met with disaster. This was still more to affect the future tactics of the Comintern, which was an arm of the Russian Bolsheviks.

## December 30, 1923 – January 2, 1924
The Workers' Party of America holds its Third Convention in Chicago. W. Z. Foster and his group obtained a majority. But the American Communist movement remained still plagued by strife and factionalism.

## January 21, 1924
V. I. Lenin dies of his last stroke in Gorki, near Moscow. *A new era begins in the history of World Communism.*

Some realistic historians have noted that during Lenin's time about a million people were killed by the Bolshevik terror machine; that about five million Russians and non-Russians died through famine; and that several millions died in the course of Civil War; altogether Lenin's rule cost the Russians and non-Russians some ten million human lives.

In four days some 700,000 people marched past Lenin's body.

## January 23, 1924
The British Labor Party under Ramsey MacDonald takes over the British Government. These are Socialists, but not Marxists. However, many British believe that the Laborites are "too soft" to the Bolsheviks.

## January 25, 1924
Lenin is eulogized in the Bolshoi Theater in Moscow. One of the speakers is Joseph Stalin. He goes out of his way to praise Lenin, and vows that Russian Communist will continue to fight for the victory of the international proletariat.

France which dominates the diplomatic scene of East Central Europe in 1920's and early 1930's, concludes a Treaty of Alliance with Czechoslovakia. France is supporting weak states, especially those that were born on the ruins of the Habsburg Empire; she supports dictatorial regimes.

## January 27, 1924
In the evening Lenin is buried with all the pomp and almost immediately becomes a Communist deity. He lies in the Red Square and later a mausoleum will be built for his embalmed corpse. Trotsky happened to be away and Stalin tricked him into not coming to the funeral, a fact that helped him later to eliminate Trotsky.

*Lenin's Mausoleum* – Keystone

# 2. *From Lenin's Death to the Beginning of World War II: 1924-1939.*

**January 31, 1924**
The Federal Constitution of the U.S.S.R. is ratified by the Second Congress of the Soviets. The Congress meets during January 26 – February 2, 1924. (On the 26th of January the Congress renamed Petrograd into Leningrad – the City of Lenin.

**February 1, 1924**
Great Britain (ruled by the Labor Cabinet) recognizes the Soviet Government. A little later Italy, too, recognized the U.S.S.R.

**February 3, 1924**
Former President W. Wilson, the man who announced to all East European peoples the right of self-determination (later also repeated by Lenin), dies a broken man. His greatest disappointment was that his country did not want to enter the League of Nations which he originated. Wilson has been hailed in East Central Europe as a great man.

**March 3, 1924**
Kemal's Turkey abolishes the Caliphate.

**March 9, 1924**
The city of Fiume is annexed by Italy. (It was located in the Croatian part of the South Slav state, Yugoslavia.)

**April 1924**
Joseph Stalin publishes *The Foundations of Leninism*. Stalin wanted to emerge as the great successor of Lenin.

**April 6, 1924**
In Italian national elections, in spite of Fascist terror, the Communists win 18 seats in the Parliament.

**April 13, 1924**
Greeks vote in favor of establishing a republic. The politics of Greece have been a constant change between the monarchy and republic.

**May 1924**
The Chinese Whampoa Military Academy under the control of the Kuomitang Party in China was established. It was partly directed, staffed and supported by the Soviet Government which still believed in the Leninist principle that "road to Paris leads through Peking." Chiang Kai-shek was its commandant; Chou En-lai was the political (Communist) adviser.

**May 4, 1924**
The Communists are very successful in German elections. The Thirteenth Congress of the Russian C.P. meets. Stalin, hungry for power, emerged as a victor over L. Trotsky whose thesis was unanimously defeated by the Congress. Stalin advanced his own theory on "Socialism in One Country" against Trotsky's "Permanent Revolution." Stalin's idea was that before the Communist ideology could be exported to foreign countries, it had to be consolidated in Russia.

**May 31, 1924**
The U.S.S.R. and republican China establish diplomatic relations.

**June 10, 1924**
The Socialist deputy Mateotti is murdered by Fascists in Italy.

**June 17, 1924**
After overthrow of premier Ahmed Zog, the government of Dr. Noli takes over the affairs of little Albania.

*Part of Russian delegation at Communist International* – Radio Times

**June 17 – July 8, 1924**

The Comintern holds one of its most important congresses. On account of the German fiasco, the Comintern is forced to adopt new tactics. At the same congress the Bolsheviks denounced the chauvinistic tendencies of the Serbian Communists in the C.P. of Yugoslavia, the group led by a Serbian teacher Sima Marković. Stalin explicitly stated that Macedonia, Slovenia, and Croatia had the right of secession from the Yugoslav state.

**July 8-9, 1924**

The American Communists decide to run for the presidency in U.S. in the forthcoming elections. Foster will be the candidate for President and Gitlow for Vice-President. Most of the American Communists denounce the Trotsky faction in U.S.S.R. There are some 20,000 Communist party members in America at the time.

**August 1924**

Sam Carr, a Communist leader born in the Ukraine, arrives in Canada to organize a Communist movement.

**October 22, 1924**

The Norwegian Communists poll almost 60,000 votes in national elections.

**October 28, 1924**

France gives *de jure* recognition to the U.S.S.R.

**October 29, 1924**

The Labor Government of MacDonald in Great Britian – that was too "soft" (in British opinion) on the Bolsheviks and that had just concluded a trade agreement with the U.S.S.R., lost heavily in the elections. The victory of the Conservative Party was made possible primarily through the publication of a

*Sun Yat-sen, President of the southern government of China, photographed with Mrs. Sun Yat-sen and officers of the presidents army. From Whampoa Military Academy* – Radio Times

letter allegedly written by G. Zinoviev, the chairman of the Communist International, addressed to the British Communists and urging them to revolt. (The British Foreign Office obtained the letter on October 10; the letter – later proved to be a forgery – was subsequently printed by the *Daily Mail.*)

**November 4, 1924**
Calvin Coolidge is elected the President of the United States. The Communist candidate for the presidency W. Z. Foster received slightly over 33,000 votes. His running mate was Benjamin Gitlow, who later broke with the C.P. and stated that the Bolsheviks had furnished $50,000 for this campaign.

Renewed civil war breaks out in China.

**November 21, 1924**
The new Conservative Cabinet in Britain led by Stanley Baldwin denounces treaties with Russia that were previously concluded by the Labor Government.

**December 1, 1924**
The Communist coup in Tallinn, capital of Estonia, is organized by a few hundred Communists, organized by the Comintern. It was immediately crushed by the Estonian authorities.

**December 7, 1924**
Nationalists and Communists are defeated in German elections.

**December 14, 1924**
U.S.S.R. and China break off diplomatic relations. Chiang Kai-shek overthrows the government in Hankov.

**December 16, 1924**
Krupskaya, Lenin's widow, publishes a statement in *Pravda* about J. Reed's book *Ten Days That Shook the World*; she writes that it contains "legends and inaccuracies." (The first Russian edition was printed in 1923.)

**December 20, 1924**
Adolph Hitler is released from the Landsberg Prison in Bavaria where he served only eight months of his five-year term. While in jail he wrote *Mein Kampf.*

*Krupskaya, Lenin's wife in 1924* – Radio Times

**End of 1924**
The anti-Bolshevik uprising in Georgia that was led by H. Cholokashvili was completely liquidated by the Red Army.

**1925**
The number of the C.P. of the Soviet Union reached over 800,000. At the same time there were only some 4,000 organized Communists in America; about 93,000 C.P. members in Czechoslovakia; and some 83,000 in France.

During early 1925 leaders of various factions of American Communist movement paid visit to Moscow. Among them were: Ruthenberg, Lovestone, Foster, and Cannon.

During 1925 the Malayan Communist Party was founded but was forbidden by British authorities.

In the same year Communist activities were organized in many countries. Vienna in Austria became an important center especially for the activities in the Balkans. G. Dimitrov returned to Vienna from Moscow to organize activities in the Balkans. The increased activities were reported in France, Norway, Sweden, and Czechoslovakia. In Latin America Mexico was becoming a significant front for Communism.

## January 1925
Leon Trotsky, who was leading opposition against Stalin, Kamenev, and Zinoviev, was removed from his position as Commissar of War. Trotsky advocated the concept of the "permanent (world) revolution" against Stalin's policy of "Socialism in One Country."

## January 20, 1925
U.S.S.R. and Japan establish diplomatic relations. The northern part of Sakhalin Island is returned to the Russians.

## January 20, 1925
Anglo-Chinese treaty is signed with the Chinese government in Peking.

## January 31, 1925
Ahmed Zog is elected President of Albania.

## February 12, 1925
Estonia prohibits the Communist Party. The chances for Communism in the Baltic area remain very poor.

## February 28, 1925
Friedrich Ebert, the President of the German (Weimar) Republic dies. He was one of the leaders of the Social Democrats and was instrumental in 1919 in the suppression of the Spartacist revolt.

## March 12, 1925
Sun Yat-sen, the leader of modern republican China dies.

## March 22, 1925
Stalin states in the *Pravda* that Communist parties all over the world must support the Soviet Union.

## March 25, 1925
The *Communist International*, the organ of the Comintern praises the activities of Indonesian Communists. Two outstanding Communist leaders were Sardjano and Tan Malakka.

## March 30, 1925
Stalin denounces in a speech delivered at a session of the Yugoslav Commission of the Comintern the leader of the Yugoslav C.P. - Sima Marković. Stalin stated that non-Serbian nationalities have the right to "self-determination, including the right to secession." Croatians and Macedonians are entitled to this.

## April 14, 1925
General Konstantin Gheorgiev is assassinated by Bulgarian Communists.

## April 16, 1925
At funeral services for Gheorgiev in the cathedral of Sofia with the entire government present (King Boris was absent) a Communist-planted bomb exploded. It killed 128 innocent people. The plotters wanted to kill King Boris. Communists were discredited by this act of terror. Dimitrov was sentenced to death *in absentia*. The C.P. of Bulgaria was abolished and its deputies expelled from the parliament. The government of premier A. Tsankov subsequently undertook severe persecutions of Communists and liquidated at least 300 of them.

## April 17, 1925
Korean Communist Party is founded.

## April 26, 1925
Marshal Paul von Hindenburg, the hero of World War I, is elected the new German President.

## April 27-29, 1925
The Fourteenth Conference of the Russian Communist Party meets. Stalin advances his theory on "Socialism in One Country;" before it could be exported, Communism had to be consolidated in the Soviet Union first. Stalin also urged consolidation of Communism in colonial areas.

## May 9, 1925
Commenting on the last Conference of the Russian C.P. Stalin states that the conflict between capitalism and Communism is inevitable.

## May 30, 1925
The British police kill 12 Chinese demonstrators in Shanghai, China. This touched off strikes all over China. Communists and Kuomitang members alike, were killed by the military government in Peking.

## June 1925
As American Communists are still struggling among themselves, Comintern attempts again to end their disputes and create the unity.

**June 23, 1925**
In Canton, China the Shameen Massacre takes place. Mao, who was active in propaganda work, now decides to start organizing the peasants.

**August 21-30, 1925**
The American Workers' Party holds its Fourth Convention in Chicago and at the orders of the Comintern it became the Workers' (Communist) Party of America. Ruthenberg-Lovestone faction takes over. Foster was no longer party chairman; Ruthenberg became the General Secretary, which was a newly created office.

**September 26-28, 1925**
The Communist Party of Czechoslovakia holds its Third Congress. Klement Gottwald was elected to the Central Committee and the Polit-Bureau.

**October 5-16, 1925**
Locarno international conference meets. The Locarno treaties were signed in London on December 1.

**October 12, 1925**
A trade agreement is signed between Germany and the Soviet Union.

**October 12, 1925**
The French Communists organize a general strike in which a million workers participate. It was the first political strike undertaken by French Communists.

*Voroshilov, new head of the Soviet Armed Forces* – Radio Times

**November 26, 1925**

The American Proletarian Party holds its Fourth Convention in Detroit. This Communist group is not accepted by the Comintern, although at this convention its members express support for the policies of the Comintern.

**December 17, 1925**

Turkey and U.S.S.R. sign a Treaty of Friendship and Neutrality. Because of the Straits, the Bolsheviks are very interested in good relations with the Turks.

**December 18-31, 1925**

At the Fourteenth Party Congress Zinoviev and Kamenev with the Leningrad Party organization oppose the group: Stalin, Tomsky, Bukharin and Rykov. It was at this congress that the Russian Communist Party changed its name to the Communist Party of the Soviet Union — the C.P.S.U.

**December 1925**

S. M. Kirov becomes the Party Secretary in Leningrad, a very important post.

**1926**

The C.P. of the Soviet Union has more than 1,000,000 members.

**1926**

According to some estimates there were now about 1,250,000 organized and registered Communists all over the world. The members of left-oriented trade unions were not included here.

**1926**

The C.P. of Great Britain had some 10,000 members.

**1926**

The C.P. of France numbered some 65,000 members.

**1926**

The Czechoslovak C.P. numbered about 93,000 members.

**1926**

The Lenin University was established in Moscow to train activists and leaders of Communism all over the world.

**January 25, 1926**

Stalin's major work *Problems of Leninism* is published.

*Generalissimo Chiang Kai-shek* — Radio Times

**March 1926**

Chiang Kai-shek undertakes his first coup. He removed Communists from the Central Executive Committee of the Kuomitang. Mao Tse-tung then went to Shanghai to head the peasant department of the Chinese C.P.

**April 24, 1926**

A Treaty of Neutrality and Non-Aggression is signed between Germany and the Soviet Union.

**May 1927**

Fifth Conference of the Chinese C.P. convened in Wuhan. The Chinese Communist leadership was split on matters of revolutionary tactics. While one faction believed that revolution should be carried out primarily by the city proletarians, Mao emphasized the primary role of the peasants in the revolution.

**May 1, 1926**

The strike of British coal miners starts. It will last until November 27, 1926. The strike was endorsed by British Communists and their numbers were increased during 1926 in the mining areas. However, the greatest crisis in British labor history was the general strike of the same year that paralyzed the whole country.

**May 12, 1926**
J. Pilsudski with the help of the Polish army undertakes a coup against Polish government. His coup, in which he overthrew the cabinet of the peasant party leader W. Witos, was later legalized.

**May 25, 1926**
Symon Petlyura, former President of independent Ukraine and the Supreme Commander of the Ukrainian forces, is assassinated in Paris by a Soviet agent. Many of the exiled anti-Bolshevik leaders are disposed of by the long arm of the Soviet secret police.

**July — October, 1926**
Trotsky, Zinoviev, and Kamenev—the so-called "left opposition" in the Soviet Union—were defeated by the "right wing" of Stalin. Trotsky was removed from the Politburo. The struggle for power continued.

**July 2, 1926**
The anti-Church legislation is passed in Mexico. The Catholic Church underwent severe persecutions.

**August 22, 1926**
The dictatorship of general Theodore Pangalos is overthrown in Greece.

**September 8, 1926**
Germany becomes a member of the League of Nations. The Soviets whose foreign affairs are conducted by Georgy Chicherin are still not permitted to join the League. They denounce it as a capitalistic institution.

**September 16, 1926**
Fascist Italy and Rumania conclude a treaty of friendship. As Rumania is a Latin country and a

*Stalin, Rykoff, Kameneff and Sinorier* — Culver Pictures

neighbor of Communist Russia, Italy—because of her Latin culture—takes a special interest in the affairs of Rumania.

**September 25, 1926**
J. Pilsudski becomes premier of Poland.

**October 26 – November 3, 1926**
The Fifteenth All-Union Party Conference is held. A proposal for a Five-Year economic plan is adopted; Stalin attacked the "deviationists" in the Party. Trotsky and his group were opposed to Stalin's Five Year Plan.

**November 6, 1926**
The Fascist regime expels the Communist deputies from the Italian parliament.

**November 22 – December 16, 1926**
The Executive Committee of the Comintern is meeting in its Seventh Plenum. Here again in his speech on the 10th of December Stalin attacked Trotsky and his followers.

**December 17, 1926**
Alarmed by Communist propaganda a group of Lithuanian army officers disperses the parliament. President Anthony Smetona and premier Waldemaras introduce a sort of dictatorship to prevent the rise of Communism.

**1927**
The Workers' Communist Party of America numbered only about 3,000 members.

**1927**
The French C.P. numbered 56,000, while the well-organized C.P. of Czechoslovakia boasts of a membership of almost 140,000. The Secretary General of the Czechslovak C.P. became K. Gottwald. He was elected to the parliament. In spite of its deficiencies Czechoslovakia was the most democratic country in East Central Europe between the two Wars.

**1927**
The struggle still goes on in revolution-torn China, suffering under foreign domination and interventions. In this year the Chinese C.P. numbered about 58,000 militant members. The Communist-controlled trade unions had an impressive number of 3,000,000 members.

**January 1927**
The *Daily Worker*, the organ of the American Communists and one of the major means of their propaganda, was transferred from Chicago to New York.

**January 1, 1927**
A Chinese Nationalist Government is established in Hankow, China.

**January 31, 1927**
The Allied military control of Germany is ended.

**March 2, 1927**
Charles Ruthenberg, the American Communist leader dies. His ashes were buried in the Kremlin wall.

**April 9, 1927**
The Italian anarchist immigrants, Sacco and Vanzetti are sentenced to death in spite of world-wide protest. Socialists and humanitarians all over the world denounce the trial as a miscarriage of justice. They are of the opinion that regardless of the fact whether they were guilty or not, the two Italian immigrants should not have been executed after seven years of waiting for this sentence.

**April 12, 1927**
Chiang Kai-shek in China suddenly attacks the Communists in Shanghai, occupies the city, and liquidates some 4,000 Communists. The government in Wuhan then expelled him from Kuomitang.

**April 15, 1927**
Chiang Kai-shek organizes his government in Nanking.

Switzerland and the Soviet Union resume diplomatic relations.

**April 25, 1927**
In national election the Austrian Communists receive only 18,000 votes.

**May 13, 1927**
"Black Friday" in Germany. German economy suffers complete breakdown.

**May 24, 1927**
Stalin delivers before the Executive Committee of the Comintern his report "The Revolution in China and the Tasks of the Comintern."

**May 27, 1927**
Thomas G. Masaryk is re-elected President of Czechoslovakia.

**May 27, 1927**
On account of increased Communist activities, Britain breaks off diplomatic relations with the U.S.S.R. (They will be re-established in July of 1929.)

**July 15 – 16, 1927**
Socialist riots take place in Vienna. The Palace of Justice is burnt. The little republic of Austria is in a difficult economic and political situation.

**July 15, 1927**
The Wuhan Government in China breaks off with the Communists, outlaws the Communist Party and expells the Soviet representative from Nationalist China.

It was during these revolutionary events in 1927 that Ho Chi Minh, a Vietnamese Communist, appeared in China. He came from Moscow where he was staying between 1923 and 1927. Ho worked as a "translator" in the Soviet consulate in Canton. His real job was to assist Michael Borodin, the main Soviet representative in China, and to spread Communism in Asia. After the break between the Nationalists (Kuomitang and other groups) Ho Chi Minh fled Canton, went to Hong Kong and eventually returned to Moscow.

**July 20, 1927**
F. E. Dzerzhinsky, head of the dreaded Soviet secret police (G.P.U.), and a faithful supporter of Stalin, dies. He was succeeded by V. R. Menzhinsky who then remained in this most important position until his death in 1934. It was rumored that his successor Yagoda had secretly liquidated him.

**July 29 – August 9, 1927**
The session of a Joint Plenum of the Central Committee and the Central Control Commission of the C.P.S.U. discusses many current problems. The majority decides to issue only a strict warning and reprimand to Trotsky and Zinoviev instead of expelling them from the Party. In a speech on August 1 to the Plenum Stalin stated that Communists all over the world have a duty to defend the Soviet Union.

**August 5, 1927**
Bombings take place in New York, Philadelphia, and Baltimore as protest against the death sentence of Sacco and Vanzetti.

**August 7, 1927**
On advice from Moscow a special conference of the Chinese C.P. is held. Ch'en Tu-hsiu, the Secretary of the party, was removed on account of "right opportunism." It was decided to break permanently with the Nationalists. Mao was dismissed from the Politburo and sent to his native Hunan province to organize the peasants. This was the beginning of the "ten lean years" of Chinese Communism.

**August 22, 1927**
The Allied military control ceases in Hungary.

**August 23, 1927**
Sacco and Vanzetti are executed in Charleston State Prison. Demonstrations against America are held all over the world. The Soviet press publicized the case of the two condemned proletarians. The historians are still arguing over the Sacco-Vanzetti case.

**September 9, 1927**
Stalin declares to an American labor delegation that American Communists receive no orders from Moscow.

**October 1927**
The American Communists move their national headquarters from Chicago to 35 East 12th Street, New York City.

**October 1, 1927**
The Soviet Union signs a Neutrality Pact with Iran (Persia), a country that is the southern neighbor of the U.S.S.R.

**October 19, 1927**
The Communists poll only 40,000 votes in Norwegian national election. This was considered a big defeat in this Scandinavian country for the Communist movement.

**October 21–23, 1927**
Trotsky and Zinoviev are definitely removed from the Central Committee of the C.P.S.U. at a session of the Central Committee and the Central Control Commission. On October 23 Stalin delivered a report entitled "The Trotskyist Opposition Before and Now."

**November 7, 1927**
The Communists in Russia and all over the world celebrate the tenth anniversary of the successful Bolshevik Revolution. Trotsky leads a street demonstration against Stalin and his group.

**November 11, 1927**
Yugoslavia and France conclude a Treaty of Friendship. France was at the time exercising considerable control in Yugoslavia and in the chain of states between the Baltic and the Black Sea that served—according to the French policies—as a "cordon sanitaire" against the Soviet Union. Many thousands of White Russian exiles found asylum in Yugoslavia, whose dynasty (Karageorgevich) was related to and had many ties with the Romanovs.

**December 2, 1927**
The Fifteenth Congress of the C.P.S.U. meets in Moscow. In his speech on the first day Stalin stated that coexistence between Capitalism and Communism was possible. Such changes of policy were in accordance with flexible Leninist principles as long as they served the final goal of Communism.

**December 3, 1927**
In another speech during the Congress, Stalin emphasises the importance of the Revolution in China in regard to the conquest of Asia. Stalin also outlines the Soviet collectivization policy. (This was still the era of the New Economic Policy which a few months later was completely abolished by Stalin who actually adopted some ideas of the Trotsky faction.)

**December 11 – 14, 1927**
The Chinese Communists establish an unsuccessful Commune in Canton. Stalin had sent several European Communists (Joseph Pogany-Pepper, Gerhart Eisler, and Heinz Neumann) to help the activities of the Chinese Communists. The bloody revolt was smashed by Chiang's forces.

**December 17, 1927**
The Soviet Union breaks off diplomatic relations with China. The break will remain in effect until the month of December, 1929.

**December 17, 1927**
The U.S. Secretary of State, Frank B. Kellogg, suggests an international pact to renounce all the wars in the future.

**December 18, 1927**
This so-called "United Congress" expells from the C.P.S.U. Trotsky and 74 other leading Russian members of the "United Opposition". The Congress condemned all deviations from the general party line determined by Stalin. This was a complete victory for Stalin. Thus the real era of Stalinism began with the end of 1927 and the beginning of 1928. The followers of Trotsky were purged by the thousands. This had serious repercussions in many Communist parties abroad. Trotsky refused to meet the demands of this Congress and was then subsequently expelled to Alma-Ata, Kazakhstan. Zinoviev and Kamenev, in order to save their necks, recanted.

**1928**
The year 1928 marks the end of the New Economic Policy (N.E.P.) and the beginning of the First Five-Year Plan in U.S.S.R. This was a denial of Lenin by Stalin!

**1928**
Ten years after the end of World War I Europe and the rest of the world live in tension, plagued by many problems. Various "Isms" (Communism, Socialism, Fascism, etc.) are competing for the minds of men.

**1928**
While the C.P.S.U. has some 1,300,000 members, the French C.P. has about 53,000; and the C.P. of Czechoslovakia had roughly 150,000. In Italy the Communists engage only in underground activities. This and the next year were marked by Fascist terror against the Communists in Italy.

**April – October, 1928**
After the defeat of the "United Opposition" of Trotsky in December of 1927, Trotsky remained active even in his exile in Alma-Ata. He sent some eight hundred letters—of which some were long political discourses—and about 550 telegrams to his friends and followers. And he received many messages from his supporters. As Trotsky had many followers in various foreign Communist Parties—and in the Soviet Union—his presence here was dangerous to Stalin.

**May 1928**

Mao Tse-tung in China was joined in Hunan by Chu Teh (b. in 1886) and his forces. In an isolated mountain area, they both organized a well disciplined Red Army which in 1931 will amount to 60,000 soldiers.

**May 20, 1928**

In German election the Social Democrats receive 9,150,000 votes (152 deputies in the Reichstag); the Communists poll 3,600,000 votes (54 deputies); while the Nazis receive 4,700,000 votes with 78 deputies. This is a powerful turn to the left. Germany was heading for turbulent times.

**June 20, 1928**

Two Croatian Peasant Party deputies are shot to death in the Belgrade Parliament. The leader of the Croatian Peasant Party, Stjepan Radić is mortally wounded. He died two months later. In, widespread demonstration the Communists too participate to take advantage of Croatian nationalistic turmoil.

Radić had been well acquainted with Russia. He entertained ideas similar to those of the Bulgarian peasant leader Stambuliski. Radić organized the Croatian peasantry—and influenced the peasants all over the Balkans—with an ideology that was partly based on ideas of old Russian Populism. The 1920's and 1930's witness in many East European (especially Balkan) countries the rise of peasantry in politics. These peasants cared little for Communism although their ideologies were in fact equivalent of an agrarian Socialism. All over East Europe the Communists failed to attract the support of the peasant. (Later in 1940's and 1950's these peasants will present the main and the strongest opponent of Communism.)

**July 17 – September 1, 1928**

The Sixth Congress of the Comintern convenes. 532 delegates from 57 countries were present. They adopted the program drafted by Bukharin. This congress also fully implemented Stalin's ideas and stressed the line that U.S.S.R. was the main basis of the World Communism. Some new tactics, especially those to combat the Socialist parties, brought about disastrous results especially in Germany where Hitler took advantage of these circumstances. This congress inaugurated the so-called Third Strategy of the Comintern (it called for revolutionary extremism in defense of the Soviet Union). Important decisions were passed for Sovietization of China.

The Congress also discussed the Negro question in America. It had to be exploited to promote the cause of Communism. In addition, "Theses on Revolutionary Movement in Colonies" were adopted.

**September 1, 1928**

Program adopted by the Comintern calls for the creation of the World Union of Soviet Socialist Republics. It should be achieved through revolution. Full support should be given to the Soviet Union. A new era of Communist aggressivism begins.

In pursuing the Comintern directions, the American Communists use the campaign for presidential election propagating the "self-determination of Negroes."

**September 1, 1928**

Ahmed Zog becomes King of Albania, a country that cares little about Communism.

**October 1, 1928**

The Soviet Union launches officially the First Five Year Plan calling for massive industrialization and collectivization.

**October 27, 1928**

American Trotskyite group led by James P. Cannon is expelled from the Workers' Communist Party. Cannon's group was known as the Communist League of America. It started to publish its own organ, *The Militant*. Cannon was one of the founders of the Trotskyite Fourth International.

**November 7, 1928**

Herbert Hoover is elected the President of the United States.

**December 1928**

The G.P.U. gives Trotsky an ultimatum to relinquish the "direction of the opposition." Reprisals were undertaken against his relatives.

**December 12, 1928**

The National Peasant Party wins majority in the Rumanian election. Their leader J. Maniu forms the new cabinet. The party was strongly anti-Communist.

**1929**

All over the world the Communists were very active. In some countries they were severely persecuted. Josip Broz Tito was in jail in Yugoslavia. While in the

Soviet Union the membership of the C.P. kept rising, in many countries it was declining. In Czechoslovakia, for instance, the number of Communists was now only some 81,000 (a loss of about 70,000 from previous year.)

**1929 – 1931**
During the First Five Year Plan and its massive industrialization, the city of Magnitogorsk in Urals was founded. Many American engineers are employed (and well paid) by the Soviet government.

**1929 – 1931**
Liquidation of *kulaks* ("rich peasants" many of whom were now poor) took place. This mass terror was described by official Soviet history books as "transition from policy of restricting activities of *kulaks* to policy of abolishing them as a class on the basis of complete collectivization." 1929–1934 was the period of such complete collectivization of agriculture.

**January 6, 1929**
King Alexander proclaims dictatorship in Yugoslavia. Thousands of Communists and nationalists alike undergo terrible police brutality and are sent to long prison terms.

**January 18, 1929**
Stalin asks the Politburo to deport Trotsky from the Soviet Union.

**January 31, 1929**
Trotsky and family are expelled from the Soviet Union. He found first refuge in Constantinople. Afterwards he spent some time in Norway. Finally he found asylum in Mexico. Many Trotsky followers were now prosecuted by Stalin. As Stalin was now actually implementing some ideas of the Trotskyite opposition, many followers of Trotsky switched to Stalin.

**February 9, 1929**
The Eastern Pact is signed. It is also known as the Litvinov Protocol after the Soviet Deputy Commissar for Foreign Affairs, Maxim Litvinov who brought about the pact. It is a response to the Kellogg Pact in the West and likewise it denounces the war. The original signatories were: U.S.S.R., Poland, Rumania, Estonia, and Latvia.

**February 18, 1929**
The Czechoslovak C.P. holds its Fifth Congress. Under the leadership of K. Gottwald the party claims to be "the vanguard of the working class."

**February 27, 1929**
Turkey joins the Litvinov Protocol. All signatories were neighbors of the U.S.S.R.

**March 1 – 10, 1929**
At a convention in New York City, the Workers' Communist Party of America changed its name to the Communist Party of the United States of America—the C.P.U.S.A. In spite of the Comintern orders that Foster be the new secretary, the Lovestone group put in charge of the post of Secretary General Ben Gitlow. Soon they traveled to Moscow to discuss the problems of disunity with Stalin himself.

**March 4, 1929**
Herbert Hoover is inaugurated as the thirty-first President of the United States.

**March 18, 1929**
British authorities arrest thirty-one Communist leaders in India.

**April 3, 1929**
Persia joins the Litvinov Protocol.

**April 5, 1929**
Lithuania joins the Litvinov Protocol.

**April 23 – 29, 1929**
The Sixteenth Conference of the C.P.S.U. Subsequently Stalin gave directives to the present American Communists for their future activities. Said Stalin: "I consider the Communist Party of the United States one of the Communist Parties to which history has given decisive tasks from the point of view of the world revolutionary movement."

**May 6, 1929**
In his speech to the President of the Executive Committee of the Comintern Stalin states: "I think that the moment is not far off when a revolutionary crisis will develop in America. And when a revolutionary crisis develops in America, that will mean the end of the world capitalism as a whole."

**May 12, 1929**
The Lovestone group of the American Communists are told by Moscow that the future leader of American Communism was to be W. Z. Foster.

**May 20 – 28, 1929**
The Fifth Congress of the Soviets of U.S.S.R. approves the First Five Year Plan.

**May 30, 1929**
In the British General Election the Labor Party wins a great majority: 287 seats in the Parliament.

**June 1, 1929**
In the Finnish election the Communists win 23 seats out of 200 in the Parliament.

**July 3, 1929**
The Tenth Plenum of the Executive Committee of the Comintern removes N. I. Bukharin, the leader of the "rightist deviation," from the Comintern. He was one of the leading Bolsheviks in the Revolution of 1917.

**July 5, 1929**
The Dutch Communists win 37,000 votes and one seat in the Parliament.

**September 19, 1929**
The dictatorship of Woldemaras is overthrown in Lithuania.

**October 3, 1929**
Anglo-Soviet relations are resumed.

**October 28, 1929**
The Stock Exchange crash takes place in America and provokes a world-wide economic crisis. The coming of the great depression was welcomed by the Kremlin as an opportunity to further the Soviet goals. As a result of the American economic collapse, the European economy collapsed too. This helped the rise of Communist and Fascist ideologies.

**November 17, 1929**
Bukharin and his followers—all opponents of Stalin—are expelled from the C.P.S.U. Stalin was entrenching himself in the leadership of the Soviet state.

**December 1929**
It is reported that the Japanese C.P.—which operated underground—has a membership of only 3,000.

**December 1, 1929**
The rightist Lapua Movement in Finland demands total suppression of Communism.

**December 5, 1929**
The Russians establish the Tadzhik Soviet Socialist Republic in Central Asia.

**1930**
The C.P. of the Soviet Union numbered some 1,850,000 members after a purge of some 160,000 of Trotskyites.

**1930 – 1948**
According to the testimonies of W. Chambers, for years an active Soviet spy, the Communists and fellow travelers—and their dupes—are infiltrating the U. S. Government agencies and offices. They promote the triumph of Communism in China and thus "have decisively changed the history of Asia, of the United States, and therefore of the world." And "one of them was Alger Hiss." While Hiss never repented, General Walter Krivitsky, an underground Soviet agent did defect—like many of his fellow Communists—and later—under pressure—committed suicide. It must be recorded that in 1929 Ben Gitlow, a Stalinist, captured the C.P.U.S.A. It also should be remembered that John Pepper, alias Joseph Pogany (a Hungarian Communist of Bela Kun Revolution) was Comintern's secret representative in the C.P.U.S.A. For years the Soviet agents were very active in New York City and Washington, D.C.

**January 20, 1930**
A long war breaks out between Bolivia and Paraguay. Both South American countries were poor and backward. The whole of Latin America is a fertile ground for Communism.

**Janury 28, 1930**
The rightist dictatorship of Primo de Rivera ends in Spain. Torn by internal struggles, the country is getting ready for a long and terrible civil war.

**February 3, 1930**
The Indo-Chinese C.P., the Annam C.P., and the Indo-Chinese League merge into Vietnam C.P. and

later the Indo-Chinese C.P. Their leader is Moscow- and Chinese-trained Ho Chi Minh.

### March 6, 1930
Prompted by the Comintern, the American Communists stage mass demonstrations in New York and other cities against unemployment.

### March 12, 1930
Mahatma Gandhi, the great leader of the Indian independence movement—a convinced pacifist—opens civil disobedience drive against the British rule in India. The subcontinent of India with all its problems was an area coveted by the Comintern. In spite of all efforts it accomplished there very little.

### April 3, 1930
J. Stalin formally declares war on *kulaks* in an article published in Pravda. This was going to result in destruction of millions of lives.

### June 22, 1930
The Seventh Convention of the disunited Communist Party of the U.S.A. convenes in New York. The unity still was lacking even after this convention.

### June 26 – July 14, 1930
The Sixteenth Congress of the C.P.S.U. convenes, Stalin admits that the Soviets were willing to accept the advice of the West in technology.

### July 21, 1930
Maxim M. Litvinov becomes the Soviet Commissar for Foreign Affairs, succeeding Chicherin.

### September 14, 1930
The Nazis receive 107 seats in the German Reichstag through the election. Germany was approaching its crucial hour.

### October 22, 1930
Norwegian Communists experience a setback in the election; they receive only 20,000 votes.

### November 1930
The Communist Party is established at Iceland.

Chiang Kai-shek sent some 100,000 troops to chase Mao Tse-tung; Chiang's commander Lu Ti-p'ing and his army were repulsed by Mao's forces.

### November 11, 1930
Finland, a democratic country, restricts the activities of the Communists.

### November 20, 1930
N. I. Bukharin recants and admits his mistakes in a written statement addressed to the Central Committee of the C.P.S.U. This is another victory for Stalin.

### December 17–21, 1930
Stalin forces Alexei Rykov, a veteran Bolshevik, out of the Party and the government where Rykov was the President of the Soviet of People's Commissars, the same position that was held before by Lenin.

### December 19, 1930
V. Molotov (born in 1890) is appointed President of the Council of People's Commissars (equivalent to the premier).

### February – May, 1931
The Kuomitang general Ho Ying-chin led an unsuccessful military expedition against Mao Tse-tung's Communist base.

### February 2, 1931
Stalin's speech on the goals of Soviet industrialization. A great deal of projects were undertaken with the slave labor.

### March 4, 1931
M. Gandhi, the leader of the Indian National Congress, a great believer in non-violence, ends his civil disobedience campaign. He was a devout Hindu, a pacifist who was also influenced with Christianity and Judaism. Under his leadership the Indian masses were striving for independence.

### March 7, 1931
The Communists of Czechoslovakia hold their Sixth Congress.

### March 8 – 17, 1931
The Sixth Congress of the Soviets of U.S.S.R. takes place.

### March 8, 1931
U.S.S.R. and Turkey agree on naval reduction in the Black Sea.

**March 21, 1931**
Austro-German customs union is announced. France, Italy and Czechoslovakia protest as they are afraid of a possible *Anschluss*.

**April 14, 1931**
A revolution breaks out in Spain after a decade of political instability. King Alfonso XIII flees the country. Spain became a republic.

**June 15, 1931**
Poland and U.S.S.R. conclude a Treaty of Friendship and Commerce.

**Summer of 1931**
Chiang Kai-shek's 300,000 troops—trained by Nazi, General Wetzell—destroyed a number of Communist bases in West Hupeh and Hupeh-Hunan. Offensive against Mao failed.

**June 23, 1931**
Stalin anounces in his speech: sliding wage scale, piece work pay, and special bonuses to skilled workers, in order to increase the industrial production.

**June 24, 1931**
U.S.S.R. and Afghanistan sign neutrality pact.

**August 11, 1931**
Canadian authorities raid the headquarters of the Communist Party in Toronto. Six leading Communists were arrested and sentenced to long prison terms while the C.P. was declared illegal.

**September 3, 1931**
Germany and Austria renounce the customs union. Both countries are in a desperate economic situation.

**September 7 – December 1, 1931**
The Second India Conference is held in London and attended by Mahatma Gandhi.

**September 13, 1931**
The Austrian rightist military organization *Heimwehr* undertakes unsuccessful coup. The Social Democrats and the Christian Socials struggle for power.

**September 18, 1931**
The Mukden incident results in Japanese attack on Manchuria, a northern Chinese province. The long armed struggle between China—torn with internal

dissent for decades—and Japan was only beginning. Within five months Japan conquered Manchuria.

**October 20, 1931**
The Law for Protection of the Republic is proclaimed in Spain. The republican government was introducing many political and social reforms.

**November 7, 1931**
A Chinese Soviet Republic with Mao as its President is proclaimed in Kiangsi Province; its center was in Juichin. The Communists control about 30 million people in these regions. Their Red Army grew to more than 350,000.

**December 9, 1931**
A republican constitution is promulgated in Spain. Alcala Zamora becomes its President. Spain is undergoing a serious internal crisis as a result of the growing struggle between the Right and Left. Catalan nationalism was another serious problem.

**1932**
The year marks the end of the First and the beginning of the Second Five-Year Plan. There was great famine in the Soviet Union. Many historians maintain that the famine was created by the Soviet regime to break the resistance of the peasants, and in Ukraine, of a whole nation. According to some sources, between ten and eleven million people died from starvation during 1931–1933.

**January 21, 1932**
Finland and U.S.S.R. conclude a Treaty of Nonaggression and Pacific Settlement of Disputes.

**January 25, 1932**
Poland and U.S.S.R. conclude such a pact.

**January 30 – February 4, 1932**
The Seventeenth Conference of the C.P.S.U. is held; it discusses the results of the First and sets goals for the Second Five Year Plan.

**February 5, 1932**
Latvia and U.S.S.R. sign a Non-aggression pact.

**March 3, 1932**
A nationalist revolt takes place in Finland.

**March 9, 1932**
After taking Harbin (on February 5) the Japanese

install the Chinese ex-emperor Pu Yi as the President of the puppet state of Manchukuo (Manchuria).

**April 10, 1932**

Hindenburg is re-elected President of Germany.

**April 24, 1932**

The Nazis win elections in Prussia, Wuertemberg and Hamburg.

**May 1 and 8, 1932**

The leftist parties win majority in French elections.

**May 4, 1932**

Estonia and U.S.S.R. sign a Non-aggression Pact.

**May 20, 1932**

Engelbert Dollfuss, the leader of the Catholic political party (Christian Socials), becomes the Chancellor of Austria and introduces an authoritarian rule.

**June 6–18, 1932**

After a revolution in China the Socialist Government was established.

**June 29, 1932**

U.S.S.R. concludes Non-aggression Pact with China.

While trying to build external security by such non-aggression pacts, the Soviets continue to build their heavy industry. Many Western engineers work in the Soviet Union. There was a great deal of German-Russian military collaboration. As Germany could not have an air force, according to the Treaty of Versailles, the German pilots were trained in the Soviet Union.

**July 7 – 29, 1932**

These are the critical days during the Bonus March on Washington. The Communists exploit the plight of the army veterans for their own goals.

**July 31, 1932**

A war breaks out between Bolivia and Paraguay.

In German elections the Communists win over 5,250,000 votes; the Nazis receive some 13,750,000. Plagued by economic depression Germans vote for two extremist parties.

**September 14, 1932**

A military coup takes place in Chile.

**November 8, 1932**

Norman Thomas (born in Marion, Ohio in 1884 and an active Socialist since 1917) polls 884,781 votes in the Presidential election. The Communist candidate W. Z. Foster receives 102,991 votes. An ordained Presbyterian minister Thomas had always been more of a Christian than Marxist Socialist. Unsuccessfully running for various offices on several occasions Thomas was quite different from Eugene Debs and in 1960's he became outspoken in protesting our involvement in Vietnam.

**November 8, 1932**

Franklin D. Roosevelt wins the election. The Democratic Party scored a significant victory partly because of the promise of the New Deal. The country suffers from joblessness and there were many difficulties to be solved by the incoming administration.

**November 29, 1932**

France and U.S.S.R. conclude a Non-aggression Pact. During the 1930's France was suffering from political instability, frequent changes of government, economic crisis, and the rise of extremist ideologies.

**December 9, 1932**

The Japanese armies invade the Chinese Province of Jehol.

**December 18, 1932**

E. Bernstein, the leading German Socialist, dies in Berlin.

**1933**

Purges undertaken by Stalinist leadership eliminate about 1,000,000 members from the C.P.S.U. The Party was seething with discontent. In Ukraine—where in the recent past nationalist tendencies were fostered—the Russian Communists now undertake a policy of Russification. Stalin is now undisputed dictator, having disposed of former main collaborators.

**January 2, 1933**

American troops evacuate Nicaragua in Central America.

**January 2–12, 1933**

Left revolt rages in Spain; the country is drifting into chaos.

**January 12, 1933**
The Secretary General of the French Communist Party, Maurice Thorez, pays a visit to the German Communists in Berlin. He returned the visit of the German Communist leader Ernst Thaelmann.

**January 24, 1933**
Stalin sends P. Postyshev (of half Russian and half Tunguz descent) as his plenipotentiary to pacify Ukraine and destroy all signs of Ukrainian nationalism. Having purged the Ukrainian local government and party, Postyshev became known as the "Hangman of the Ukraine."

**January 28, 1933**
Fall of the Schleicher ministry in Germany causes a serious crisis.

**January 30, 1933**
Hindenburg appoints Adolf Hitler as Chancellor of Germany. This is great victory for the Nazi Party, a crossroads in the modern history of Germany.

The Nazi take-over was a great shock especially to the French Communist Party. Numerous German Communists flee Germany and find refuge in France and other foreign countries. Hitler's victory was also turning point in the activities of the Comintern which now embarked on the strategy of collaboration with all parties opposed to Fascism.

**February 23 – March 12, 1933**
The Japanese occupy China north of the Great Wall.

**February 27, 1933**
Reichstag fire, set by Nazis. Hitler blames the Communists. He now starts to persecute them.

**March 4, 1933**
F. D. Roosevelt is inaugurated as the thirty-second President of the United States. The Communists opposed the New Deal.

**March 5, 1933**
In German elections the Nazis win 44 per cent of votes, while the Nationalists poll 8 per cent. This coalition has a small majority over all other parties. Legally Hitler still does not possess absolute power.

**March 6, 1933**
The Greek general Nicholas Plastiras with parts of the army undertakes a coup against the government of E.

Venizelos. The coup fails. Greece is undergoing many troubles and fails to secure internal stability.

**March 7, 1933**
Chancellor Dollfuss suspends parliamentary rule in Austria.

**March 23, 1933**
Securing the "Enabling Law" Hitler is consolidating his power and liquidating the opposition.

**March 27, 1933**
Japan, busy with expanding the "Empire of the Rising Sun" on the Asiatic continent, leaves the League of Nations.

**April 16 – July 1, 1933**
Britain imposes embargo on all Soviet imports.

**May 2, 1933**
Hitler abolishes the German trade unions.

**May 5, 1933**
Germany and the Soviets prolong the treaties of 1926 and 1929.

**May 28, 1933**
The Nazis win the election in the Free City of Danzig that is administered by the League of Nations.

**June 16, 1933**
The Roosevelt administration passes the National Industrial Recovery Act, one of many during the New Deal to bring the country out of depression.

**July 3, 1933**
The protocol of the London International Conference defining aggressor in international relations is signed by: Afghanistan, Estonia, Latvia, Persia, Poland, Rumania, the U.S.S.R. and joined later by Czechoslovakia and Yugoslavia.

**July 14, 1933**
German parties other than Nazis are forbidden by Hitler's regime. Thousands of his opponents are leaving country; many are arrested. Hitler's dictatorship is in full swing.

**October 1933**
Over 900,000 Chinese Nationalist troops—of which 500,000 are under the personal leadership of Chiang Kai-shek—undertake offensive against Mao's Kiangsi

Soviet Republic. Subsequently about a million people were killed or starved to death during the long siege.

### October 14, 1933
Germany leaves the League of Nations.

### October 16, 1933
The Labor Party wins the Norwegian election.

### November 12, 1933
In Nazi-controlled election Hitler receives 95 per cent of votes.

### November 16, 1933
America establishes diplomatic relations with the Soviet Union. This is considered a considerable success of the Russian diplomacy.

### November 19, 1933
Rightist parties win Spanish election. Chaotic conditions continued in Spain.

### December 23, 1933
The Reichstag Fire trial is ended. One of the defendants, the Bulgarian Communist Georgi Dimitrov, accused the Nazis of setting the fire. In view of the world wide publicity and excellent showing of Dimitrov, the Nazis experienced a propaganda fiasco. Dimitrov was acquitted and permitted to go to Russia. The feeble-minded Dutch Communist M. van der Lubbe was sentenced to death.

### December 30, 1933
The members of the Fascist Iron Guard assassinate the Rumanian Liberal Premier Duca.

### 1934
The rise of Hitler, strength of Italian Fascism, the weakness of the French C.P., disintegration of the Balkan Communist parties—all contribute to a general weakness of international Communism. Stalin's continued purges reduce the Communist membership in the Mother Country of Communism. The Soviet industrialization and enslavement of the peasants went on. The C.P.S.U. became more centralized and bureaucratized. After many experiments the Soviets undertook many ideological changes. The Popular Front became a necessity.

The year of 1934 thus marks beginning of a new phase in tactics and activities of world Communism.

### January 1934
The Second All China Soviet Congress discussed the fate of Mao's Kiangsi Republic. Mao appeals for help to save the republic; however, the Fifth Congress of the Chinese Communist Central Committee rejected Mao's appeal. Soon after this preparations were undertaken for the Long March which will involve some 100,000 soldiers and many civilians.

### January 26 – February 10, 1934
The meeting of the Seventeenth Congress of the C.P.S.U. On the 26th Stalin reported on "Growing Tensions in the Political Situation in the Capitalist Countries." The Second Five-Year Plan was approved.

### January 26, 1934
Nazi Germany and Poland conclude a Non-aggression Pact for ten years.

### February 1 – 16, 1934
Civil war rages in Austria. The Social Democrats revolt against the dictatorial government of E. Dollfuss. Fighting was severe in Vienna where fighting Socialists were subdued with government's artillery. Thousands of Socialists were arrested; many fled abroad. The massacre of Socialists discredited the Catholic political regime in Austria. Dollfuss continued to rule as a dictator.

### February 6 – 9, 1934
Huge demonstrations and fighting, organized by left Socialists and Communists, overthrew the government of M. Daladier. France moves toward Popular Front regimes.

### February 9, 1934
The Balkan Pact is signed; its members are: Rumania, Greece, Yugoslavia, and Turkey.

### February 12, 1934
Communist-controlled labor unions of France undertake a huge strike. It was supported also by the Socialists who now make a united front with the Communists, as directed by the Comintern.

### February 16, 1934
Anglo-Russian trade agreement is concluded.

### March 1934
Cuban Communists staged a strike against the government of Ramon Grau San Martin.

**March 16, 1934**
The Protocols of Rome are signed between Italy, Austria, and Hungary. Mussolini gives his firm support to the instable regimes of Austria and Hungary.

**March 24, 1934**
America declares Philippines independent after 1945.

**April 2 – 8, 1934**
The Eighth National Convention of the C.P.U.S.A. meets in Cleveland, Ohio. Its Resolution denounces the New Deal as a "program of fascization."

**April 7, 1934**
Finland and the Soviet Union sign a Non-aggression Pact for ten years.

**April 16, 1934**
The Soviet Union establishes as the highest distinction and decoration the title of Hero of the Soviet Union.

**May 16, 1934**
The Soviet Council of the People's Commissars and the Central Committee of the C.P.S.U. issue decree "On the Teaching of Civic History." This is the new Stalinist conception of history as "politics projected into the past." It is to be patriotic and to stress the Russian heroes of the past which were slighted by the late Soviet historian M. N. Pokrovsky. Stalin denounced him as *"too dogmatic."* Thus—after his death (in 1932) Pokrovsky was "purged." The new history will be a synthesis of national and Marxist views.

**May 19, 1934**
Military circles in Bulgaria revolt and abolish all political parties. They proceeded to suppress the nationalist Internal Macedonian Revolutionary Organization. Communism is now almost non-existent in Bulgaria.

**June 9, 1934**
Soviet-Czechoslovak relations are resumed.

An article in the *Pravda* indicates the new trends in the Soviet historiography: to praise the heroes of the Russian past and thus boost the Russian patriotism.

**June 14 – 15, 1934**
Mussolini and Hitler meet in Venice.

**June 30, 1934**
In a bloody purge Hitler eliminates the influence of the military Nazi *Sturm Abteilungen* (S.A.). Hundreds of Nazi and non-Nazi opponents of Hitler were massacred, including Captain Ernst Roehm.

**July 25, 1934**
During a short abortive Nazi uprising in Austria Chancellor Dollfuss is assassinated by Nazis. The revolt is suppressed and the new Chancellor is Kurt Schuschnigg of the Catholic political party.

**August 2, 1934**
President Hindenburg of Germany dies. Hitler now becomes the Leader (Fuehrer) of the German Reich. Germany rearms and many military preparations worry the Soviets.

**August 6, 1934**
After the release from prison of the Indian Communist leader Joshi, the C.P. of India is reactivated.

**August 17, 1934**
The Italian leftists form a secret front against Fascism.

**September 5, 1934**
Susumu Okano, the Communist leader, reveals in an article in the *Communist International* that the Japanese C.P. is badly split and in chaotic conditions.

**September 6, 1934**
The American Communist leader, Earl Browder reports to the Central Committee of the C.P.U.S.A. on the efforts to create a "United Front" in America.

**September 14, 1934**
The Baltic Entente is organized between Estonia, Latvia, and Lithuania. Its purpose is to resist the rising threat of the Soviet Union.

**September 18, 1934**
The Soviet Union becomes a member of the League of Nations. In this weakened international organization, the Soviets will play a significant role.

**October 1934**
A civil war broke out in Spain. The leftist elements: the Socialists, Communists, and Anarchists, took control of the province of Asturias. The troops of the rightist government eventually smashed the revolt.

*Kirov, assassinated in 1934* — Keystone

Over 1,300 people were killed; some 30,000 were arrested. This was a rehearsal for the civil war that will break out two years later.

### October 9, 1934
The king-dictator of Yugoslavia, Alexander, and the French Foreign Minister Louis Barthou are assassinated in Marseilles by Macedonian and Croatian revolutionaries. This broke the backbone of the dictatorship in Yugoslavia. Prince Paul takes over as regent. The leadership of the C.P. was still abroad. Tito had served a five-year prison term. Many leading Communists were still in prison.

### October 16, 1934
The Long March of the Chinese Communists starts under the leadership of Mao. Some 100,000 Red Army soldiers leave Yutu by night to start the long trek that will last a year and cover some 8,000 miles.

### Early November 1934
Mao's Red Army, fighting off enemy attacks, reached the Hunan-Kiangsi border.

### December 1, 1934
Serge Kirov, a close collaborator of Stalin and the head of the Leningrad Party organization, is assassinated by Communist Nikolayev. This triggers a new wave of purges by Stalin in which many thousands of old Bolsheviks and Red Army officers were liquidated.

### December 25, 1934
The Fourth Conference of the C.P. of Yugoslavia is held in Ljubljana, Slovenia. Tito was elected to the Central Committee and the Politburo. A few days later Tito leaves for Vienna on his way to Moscow.

### 1935
This year is marked by the definite new strategy on the part of the Comintern—the United or Popular Front policy against the rise of Fascism. All Communist parties were ordered by Moscow to follow this new line, which has been also called the Fourth Strategy of World Communism. At the same time Stalin was increasing his personal power by continued purges of his enemies.

### Early January 1935
Josip Broz Tito came to Moscow after fourteen years of absence.

### January 13, 1935
The people of the Saar decide by a plebiscite to rejoin Germany.

### January 16, 1935
The session of the Central Committee of the C.P. of Yugoslavia, meeting in Vienna, recommends Tito as the member of the Balkan Secretariat of the Comintern in Moscow. Here he worked under Georgi Dimitrov and was acquainted with P. Togliatti and W. Pieck. (After a few months in the fall of 1935 he returned to Yugoslavia to help reorganize the C.P.)

### January 15–17, 1935
Zinoviev is tried and sentenced to ten years in prison; Kamenev and some other old Bolsheviks are also sent to prison.

### January 28 – February 6, 1935
The Seventh Congress of the Soviets meets; Stalin controls it completely.

### March 1 – 11, 1935
The republican politician E. Venizelos leads a revolt in Greece that was put down by the government.

*Grigory Zinoviev, Russian politician* – Radio Times

**March 7, 1935**
The Saar region is restored to Germany.

**March 16, 1935**
Germany denounces the Versailles disarmament clauses, reintroduces the conscription and continues serious rearmament. Thus new tensions appeared in Europe. The same month the British Foreign Secretary Anthony Eden visited Moscow.

**March 20, 1935**
The Socialists take over the government of Norway.

**March 23, 1935**
The U.S.S.R. sells the Chinese Eastern Railways (they run through Manchukuo) to the Japanese.

**April 9, 1935**
Nazi Germany and the Soviet Union sign a trade agreement.

**April 21, 1935**
King Boris of Bulgaria abolishes all parties in order to restore the political stability.

**April 23, 1935**
New Polish Constitution comes into force.

**May 1935**
Mao's Red Army entered the Province of Yunnan and undertook the crossing of the Yangtze River.

**May 2, 1935**
France and the Soviet Union sign the Treaty of Mutual Assistance aimed against expansion of Germany.

**May 5, 1935**
The oppositional parties in Yugoslavia score victory in national elections. The leader of the United Opposition is Dr. Vladko Maček, the President of the Croatian Peasant Party, who was released from prison.

**May 12, 1935**
Jozef Pilsudski, the leader of Poland, dies.

**May 16, 1935**
Czechoslovakia and the Soviet Union sign a pact of mutual assistance. The future of Czechoslovakia depends whether both France and the U.S.S.R. would—in case of Hitler's attack—come to defend her.

**May 19, 1935**
In the Czechoslovak election the Nazis are the strongest Sudeten German party.

**June 9 – 10, 1935**
The Plenum of the C.P. of Yugoslavia meets secretly in Split, Croatia and announces its support of the Moscow-directed Popular Front policy.

**June 12, 1935**
Armistice is signed between Bolivia and Paraguay.

**June 23, 1935**
Milan Stojadinović becomes Premier of Yugoslavia. Extremist movements both Left and Right are growing.

**July 13, 1935**
America and the Soviet Union conclude trade agreement.

The Brazilian government under President Getulio Vargas outlaws the Communist-controlled National Liberation Alliance, which was headed by the leading Communist Luiz Carlos Prestes.

**July 25 – August 21, 1935**
The Seventh (and the last) Congress of the Comintern convenes under the leadership of the new Secretary General, Georgi Dimitrov. Comintern now orders—in the name of Stalin—the new tactics for World Communism: the United, or Popular, Front. Communists should collaborate with all enemies of Fascism.

One of the foreign Communists present at some meetings was Josip Broz Tito who was then in Moscow. The Yugoslav C.P. now was ordered by Stalin to take a new line in regard to the nationality question. In view of the Popular Front and threat of Fascism, Stalin now advocates preservation and federalization of Yugoslavia instead of giving different nationalities the right of self-determination and secession.

In his speech before the Seventh Comintern Congress Dimitri Z. Manuilsky (1883-1959) who led the International after 1928 stated that "the first place among the Communist parties of the world, right after the Bolsheviks . . . belongs to that of China," and that eventually the Chinese Red Army will defeat Chiang Kai-shek.

**August 14, 1935**

F. D. Roosevelt signs the Social Security Act.

**August 25, 1935**

The U. S. Government protests the Soviet violation of anti-propaganda pledge in the recognition agreement of November, 1933. The protest was caused by inflamatory statements of the C.P.U.S.A. delegates at the Seventh Congress of the Comintern.

**August 27, 1935**

The Soviet government replies to the U.S. protest, stating it had no control over the affairs of the Communist International.

**August 31, 1935**

Alexei Stakhanov, a Soviet coal miner in the Donets Basin, set a record: in six hours he dug 102 tons of coal. This was fourteen times more than the established quota. This marked the beginning of Stakhanovism as a movement to boost the Soviet industrial production.

**September 15, 1935**

The Nazi Nuremberg Laws outlaw the Jews. Thousands of Jewish intellectuals have left the country fleeing the persecution.

**September 22, 1935**

Restoration of ranks in the Red Army.

**October 2, 1935**

The Italian invasion of Ethiopia (Abyssinia) starts. Mussolini is determined to build an Italian empire in Africa and around the Mediterranean.

**October 20, 1935**

Mao's depleted forces (only about 20,000 of the original 100,000) arrive at Wuch'ichen, on the north Shensi border. This was the end of the Long March. Mao now starts to build up a strong Communist movement. In this base he will stay for the next eleven years.

**October 28, 1935**

After the Populist election victory (on June 9) Greece proclaims the monarchy. On November 3, the people by plebiscite decide for George II.

**November 7, 1935**

The treaties between Turkey and U.S.S.R. are extended for ten years.

**November 9, 1935**

John F. Lewis and other labor leaders within A.F.L. found the Committee for Industrial Organizations (C.I.O.) which attracts a large number of members. In May of 1938, Lewis finally declares—in his strife with A.F.L.'s president William Green — the independent Congress of Industrial Organizations. Later on the C.I.O. was infiltrated by some Communist-controlled groups.

**November 18, 1935**

The League of Nations (with headquarters in Geneva) proclaims economic sanctions against Italy, now engaged in war against another League member—Ethiopia.

**November 27, 1935**

The Labor wins the New Zealand election.

**December 1, 1935**

Chiang Kai-shek is elected President of the Chinese Executive.

**December 4, 1935**

N. Zachariadis becomes Secretary General of the Greek Communist Party at its Fifth Congress.

William Gallacher, the leading Scottish Communist, is elected to the House of Commons.

**December 18, 1935**

Eduard Beneš is elected President of Czechoslovakia.

**December 27, 1935**

Uruguay breaks off diplomatic relations with the Soviet Union.

**1936 – 1938**

This is the era of Stalin's Great Purge, the bloodiest period of purges. It is also called *Yezhovshchina* after N. I. Yezhov, the Commissar of Internal Affairs. The terror ravaged all sectors of the Soviet life. Stalin disposed of all his real and potential enemies. For instance, of 139 members elected by the 17th Party Congress (1934) to the Central Committee, 98 were liquidated. Of the 1,966 delegates attending that Congress, 1,108 were arrested and most of them subsequently liquidated. The Purge removed from the Party ranks some 850,000 members or 36 per cent.

Stalin still had many enemies and opponents within the highest echelons of the C.P. and especially the Red Army. However, the serious purges of the army were not undertaken before 1937.

**1936**
Mao Tse-tung published *The Strategic Problems of China's Revolutionary War.*

The number of organized Communists in the world is estimated at some 3,600,000. The French C.P. has 329,000 members. The Belgian Communists numbered about 8,000. There were some 3,500 Communists in Australia; 20,000 in Sweden; 2,000 in Switzerland; and in China over 40,000 militant members.

**January 16, 1936**
The Spanish leftists establish the Popular Front on the eve of a crucial national election. In the Front the Communists had some 50,000 organized members. The rightist elements, too, establish a coalition.

**February 8, 1936**
Matyas Rakosy, the leader of the C.P. in Hungary, is sentenced to life imprisonment.

**February 16, 1936**
The Spanish elections take place. The Popular Front: Republicans, Socialists, Syndicalists, Communists, Anarchists, Basques, and Catalans win with 265 seats in the parliament. The Rights gets 142, and the Center 66. Azaña was elected the Premier. The stage is set for the civil war.

**March 1, 1936**
Stalin states in an interview with the American journalist Roy Howard that peaceful coexistence is possible between Communism and capitalism.

**March 5, 1936**
The Brazilian authorities arrest Luiz Carlos Prestes, the Communist leader, and sentence him to 16 years in prison.

**March 7, 1936**
Germany renounces the Locarno Pact and reoccupies the demilitarized Rhineland. Hitler gets away with this first aggression.

**March 13, 1936**
Dictator general Metaxas becomes Greek Premier.

**April 1936**
Stalin permitted the formation of special Cossak units in the Red Army.

**April 8, 1936**
Treaty of Mutual Assistance is signed between U.S.S.R. and Outer Mongolia, a country in Asia between Russia and China.

**April 26, 1936**
The Communists receive 1,500,000 votes in the French election. This is a victory of the Popular Front under Leon Blum.

**May 1936**
The political commissar system that had been gradually abandoned after 1924, was again re-introduced by Stalin. In practice it meant that every military order had to be countersigned by a political commissar.

**May 14, 1936**
After a wave of strikes and violence organized by Greek Communists, the government of General John Metaxas, the strong-man of Greece, proceeded to liquidate Communism.

**May 15, 1936**
The Central Lenin Museum opens in Moscow.

**May 21, 1936**
Kurt Schuschnigg, Chancellor of Austria, is made the autocratic leader of the Fatherland Front.

**June 4, 1936**
The Blum ministry in France, an unsuccessful example of the Popular Front, starts its existence.

**July 17, 1936**
The Spanish Civil War begins. General Francisco Franco, supported by the army, the Catholics and the Right coalition starts a revolt against the leftist government in Madrid.

**July 20, 1936**
The Convention of Montreux (Switzerland) is signed by the major powers and Turkey. The Straits of Dardanelles and Bosphorus come again under Turkish sovereignity.

**July 24, 1936**
The Spanish Nationalists organize a Junta of National Defense in Burgos. Franco's forces gain ground.

**August 4, 1936**
Greek parliament (in which also 15 Communist deputies were present) is dissolved; General Metaxas, with the permission of the king, introduces authoritarian rule. Subsequently he arrested thousands of Communists and radicals.

**August 11, 1936**
Chiang Kai-shek enters Canton.

**August 19 – 23, 1936**
In a great public trial, staged by Stalin, sixteen old Bolsheviks including Zinoviev, Kamenev, and Smirnov are tried and shortly afterwards executed.

**September 3, 1936**
"La Passionaria" (Dolores Ibarruri), the famous Spanish revolutionary, address  30,000 Parisians appealing for help to the Spanish Republican forces. The French did respond with considerable aid and many volunteers. The Civil War became a rehearsal and Spain testing ground for the forthcoming world war. Eventually U.S.S.R., and Italy and Germany were involved. They rendered military aid to the Republicans and Nationalists respectively. On the other side thousands of foreign Communists fought on the side of the Republicans (or Loyalists). In the Spanish International Brigades fought also a few hundred Americans (Lincoln Brigade) and Canadians. Josip Broz Tito spent a great deal of 1936–1937 in Paris (where at the time the Central Committee of the Yugoslav C.P. was located) organizing the flow of volunteers that were coming from Yugoslavia. Some 1,300 Yugoslav Communists fought in Spain; 700 were killed in action. Many of those who returned home, became later partisan leaders after 1941 and future generals in the Communist Army.

**Autumn 1936**
At a meeting of the Central Committee of the C.P.S.U. a majority of members voted against Stalin and in favor of Bukharin, who at the time was still a member of the Central Committee but deprived of all political offices. Bukharin and many were opposed to personal dictatorship and methods of Stalin. Among senior officers of the Red Army support for Bukharin was growing and Stalin was aware of that.

**September 26, 1936**
G. G. Yagoda is removed as chief of the N.K.V.D.

(secret police) and succeeded by N. I. Yezhov, a great enemy of Bukharin and a faithful Stalinist. It was Yezhov who undertook Stalin's purges.

**October 1, 1936**
General F. Franco becomes the Chief of the Spanish State.

**October 1, 1936**
U.S.S.R. accedes to the London Naval Convention.

**October 16, 1936**
In a telegram to José Diaz, the Secretary General of the C.P. of Spain, Stalin acclaims the significant role of Spanish Communists in the Civil War. By now the C.P. had already some 300,000 members in Republican territory. All over the world the Communists make a great propaganda drive for the cause of Republican Spain and collect funds, aid, supplies; in addition they send thousands of volunteers for the Republican army. Atrocities were committed on both sides. Hostages were shot. Many Spanish non-Communists fought against Nationalists. Churches, monasteries and convents were burned. Thousands of priests, nuns, and Catholic laymen were killed.

**October 19, 1936**
German Four-Year Plan is promulgated. Germany builds up a strong air force, navy, and army. In less than three years the Nazis will have many motorized units, tank corps and other units with thousands of *Panzers* and vehicles of several kinds. German industry is booming, the armament is developing with full speed, and Hitler's determination for aggression is growing.

**October 20, 1937**
The Norwegian Communists receive only 4,300 votes in the national election.

**November 1, 1936**
Mussolini anounces the Rome-Berlin Axis, an alliance of Nazi Germany and Fascist Italy.

During October 25–27 Hitler and Mussolini concluded agreements by which Hitler also promised to respect the sovereignty of Austria.

**November 3, 1936**
F. D. Roosevelt is re-elected.

**November 7, 1936**
The Central Committee of the C.P.U.S.A. issues a statement commenting Roosevelt's victory and expressing satisfaction that "the American people are uncompromisingly opposed to the forces of reaction and fascism both here and abroad." (There were during these years several pro-Nazi and pro-Fascist organizations and movements among the native Americans and nationality groups.)

**November 18, 1936**
Italy and Germany recognize Franco's Spanish Government.

**November 24, 1936**
Germany and Japan conclude the Anti-Comintern Pact against the Bolshevik activities all over the world. In spite of their internal problems (the anti-Stalin opposition and Purges) the Soviets are now very active in many countries. In November A. Zhdanov the chief of the Leningrad Party organization made a threatening speech against all Baltic states.

**November 25 – December 5, 1936**
The meeting of the Extraordinary Eight All-Union Congress of Soviets takes place in Moscow. On the first day Stalin reads his lengthy "Report to the Eighth Congress of Soviets on Draft Constitution of the U.S.S.R." Stalin also declared that Communism was not yet achieved in the Soviet Union.

**December 1936**
The Chinese Red Army occupies Yenan. It was to become Mao's headquarters for eleven years. He and his army lived here in a city of caves.

**December 5, 1936**
The U.S.S.R. adopts the so-called "Stalin Constitution." Kazakh and Kirghiz Autonomous Republics were transformed into two additional Union Republics.

**December 17, 1936**
Beginning of a purge within the Spanish C.P. Many of the purged were followers of Trotsky, Anarchists and Socialists.

**December 25, 1936**
After his capture by Mao's soldiers Chiang Kai-shek makes an agreement with the Chinese Communists to create a united front against the Japanese invaders.

*Chiang Kai-shek with (6th from left) Marshall Chang Hsyeh-liang, his future captor*  — Radio Times

## 1937

Mao Tse-tung publishes his important study *On Guerilla War*; the next year he issues his study *On the Protracted Conflict*. In all his writings he emphasized the idea that in order to win the civil war as well as the war against the Japanese, the Chinese Communist guerillas had to enjoy the support of the masses of the peasants. As evidenced by later events, these tactics did secure the success of the Chinese Communist Revolution. Mao's teaching influenced subsequently other guerilla warfares in Southeast Asia, Latin America and Africa. Mao, in real Chinese tradition, was also a good poet while his writings on guerilla warfare have become classics in this field.

## January 1937

Bukharin and his principal supporter Rykov are in prison.

As already noted, Bukharin enjoyed support among many high-ranking officers of the Red Army. At this time, still about one-fifth of the officers were veterans of the Civil War, and many of them former officers of the old Imperial Army. Almost all highest commands were occupied by these veterans, who were opposed to Stalin.

## January 20, 1937

F. D. Roosevelt's second inauguration for the President of the United States. The Communist criticism of the New Deal policies subsided during 1937.

## January 23-30, 1937

The Great Purge goes on. In the Moscow trial seventeen leading Bolsheviks are tried, and thirteen sentenced to death. A. Y. Vyshinsky earned his notoriety as public prosecutor. The Purge was now reaching the Red Army and the diplomatic corps.

## January 24, 1937

A Pact of Friendship is signed between Bulgaria and Yugoslavia.

## February 1937

Bukharin and Rykov were expelled from the C.P. Radek was in prison for a long term after the last trial in Moscow.

## February 8, 1937

Spanish Nationalists take Malaga.

## February 15-18, 1937

The Balkan Conference at Athens is joined by a new member, Bulgaria.

## March 3, 1937

In his speech to the Plenum of the Central Committee J. Stalin hints about the forthcoming great purges of the Red Army.

## March 18, 1937

Italian troops are defeated by the Republicans at Brihuega. Franco's attack on Madrid is checked by the "Loyalists" supported by international Communists.

## End of March 1937

By now the Chinese have created a more or less united front against the Japanese. Chiang Kai-shek and the Communists agree to stop their civil war and to unite forces against the Japanese aggression.

## March 16, 1937

In a clash between the French police and Communists six people are killed in Paris.

## April 1, 1937

Indian Constitution, granted by Britain, comes into force. It is opposed by the party of Gandhi — the National Congress — and by the Communists.

## May 1937

The Communists — after stubborn struggle — crush the anti-Communist uprising of the Anarchists in Catalonia, Spain.

## May 1, 1937

F. D. Roosevelt signs U. S. Neutrality Act.

## May 31, 1937

German fleet bombards Republican positions in Almeria, Spain.

## June 12, 1937

Marshal M. N. Tukhachevsky, the Chief of Staff, and seven other Soviet highest-ranking generals are executed after a secret court martial. They were accused by Stalin as collaborators of foreign imperialists and supporters of Trotsky. (In 1956 Tukhachevsky was posthumously exonerated.)

**June 21, 1937**
In spite of Communist support, the leftist government of Leon Blum in France collapses; he is succeeded by the Radical-Socialist cabinet of Chautemps. France finds out that the Popular Front policy really doesn't work out.

**June 21, 1937**
Dolores Ibarruri, Secretary General of the Spanish C. P., hails the efforts of Julio Alvarez del Vayo to unite the Socialists with the Communists. After a year of terrible civil war, Communism in Spain is losing ground.

**July 7, 1937**
The Marco Polo Bridge incident near Peking is an excuse to the Japanese for a new attack against China. This time Japan aims at the conquest of entire China.

**July 17, 1937**
Anglo-Russian and Anglo-German naval agreements are signed.

**August 6, 1937**
The United States and the Soviet Union conclude a trade pact.

**August 8, 1937**
The Japanese forces take Peking.

**August 21, 1937**
China and the Soviet Union sign a Non-Aggression Pact. China is struggling for survival against the Japanese militarism.

**August 26, 1937**
The forces of General Franco take Santander in Spain.

**Late Summer of 1937**
Milan Gorkić, the Secretary General of the C.P. of Yugoslavia, is called to Moscow from the Paris headquarters. He was removed by Stalin and later liquidated in Purges. Stalin named Josip Broz Tito, his faithful follower, as the new Secretary General of the C.P.Y. (In early 1938 Tito returned from Moscow to Yugoslavia to save the C.P. which then numbered less than 1,500 members.)

**September 4, 1937**
Ignaz Reiss, a Soviet secret agent who had decided to quit his services, is found dead near Lausanne, Switzerland. He was executed by Soviet agents.

**September 14, 1937**
Thomas G. Masaryk, the founder of Czechoslovakia and an enemy of Bolshevism, dies.

**October 17, 1937**
Riots break out in Sudetenland; the German population was incited by the Nazi propaganda.

**October 21, 1937**
The Spanish Nationalists take Gijon; the next day they capture Oviedo after heavy fighting.

**November 6, 1937**
Mussolini joins the Anti-Comintern Pact of Germany and Japan.

**November 7, 1937**
The Bolshevik Revolution is twenty years old.

**November 9, 1937**
The Japanese take Shanghai. Thousands of the Chinese civilians perish during this war.

**December 7, 1937**
Georgi Dimitrov, one of the leading men of the Comintern, urges in *International Press Correspondence* all the Communists to support faithfully the Soviet Union.

**December 12, 1937**
The Chinese Nationalists lose Nanking to the Japanese. The Chinese capital was moved to Chungking. The Chinese Communist armies break up into small units and in many provinces lead guerilla warfare, gaining territory from the Japanese.

**December 14, 1937**
All parties are banned in Brazil.

**December 28, 1937**
King Carol of Rumania appoints the Fascist leader Octavian Goga as the new Premier. He was violently anti-Semitic and started to persecute Jews. (Carol will dismiss him in February of 1938.)

**The end of 1937**
Mao's New Fourth Army in China numbered some 40,000 members and was very successful in combatting the Japanese and spreading the Communist influence in China.

**1938**
Hitler increases his aggressive policies. The Soviet Union through the Communist parties and the Popular Front throughout the world tried to check the plans and activities of Italy, Japan and Germany. Increased international tensions will inevitably lead to a new world war.

**1938**
The Polish C.P., suffering long from factionalism, lost most of its leaders in purges. In the same year the party was disbanded by the Comintern.

**January 1938**
Trotsky's followers in America formed the Socialist Workers' Party.

**January 12, 1938**
Opening of the first session of the Supreme Soviet of the U.S.S.R.

**February 13, 1938**
During their meeting at Berchtesgaden, Hitler announces to Chancellor Schuschnigg that he wants to take Austria.

**March 2-15, 1938**
Bukharin, Rykov, Yagoda and several other leading Bolsheviks are tried and sentenced to death by Stalin's court.

**March 4, 1938**
Otto Bauer, the old leader of the Austrian Socialists, dies in exile in Paris.

**March 12, 1938**
Hitler's forces invade and occupy Austria, his homeland. Abandoned by the West, Austria becomes the first victim of the Nazi aggression.

**March 19, 1938**
Mexico expropriates the British and American oil properties.

**March 27, 1938**
The Nationalists invade the Spanish province of Catalonia.

**Mid April 1938**
Whitaker Chambers, who worked for years in Communist underground, breaks away from the Communist Party. His superior was Col. Boris Bykov of the Soviet G.P.U. Chambers revealed later all details of the Soviet espionage and Communist infiltration of governmental offices in Washington in his book *The Witness*.

**May 7, 1938**
Finland, Denmark, Iceland, Norway and Sweden declare strict neutrality.

**May 11, 1938**
Nazi revolt is suppressed in Brazil. Hitler's agents are very active in South American states.

**May 20, 1938**
The Czechs mobilize their military reserves.

**May 27-31, 1938**
The C.P.U.S.A. holds its Tenth National Convention and reaffirms the Popular Front (in America called Democratic) policy. The Communists claim 75,000 members. Earl Browder, the General Secretary of the Party, published in early 1938 his programatic book, *The People's Front*.

**June 1938**
The Communist New Fourth Army started to build southern Kiangsi anti-Japanese base; Communist strongholds and bases of military operations spread in several Chinese provinces. The relations between them and the Nationalists were very bad again.

**June 30, 1938**
Earl Browder, the leading American Communist, admits during an investigation conducted by the State of New York, that American C.P. was connected with the Comintern and followed its directives.

**July 11 – August 10, 1938**
The Soviet troops clash with the Japanese along the borders of Korea, Manchukuo, and Siberia. After severe fighting a truce was established.

**July 25, 1938**
Sent by the British Government, Lord Runciman went to the Sudeten area to see the situation there; his published report favors Nazi claims to the Sudetenland in Czechoslovakia.

**July 31, 1938**
Bulgaria signs a Non-aggression Pact with the Balkan Entente. By now German influence is strong in the Balkans.

**September 5, 1938**
Nazi plot fails in the South American republic of Chile.

**September 15, 1938**
The British Premier Neville Chamberlain meets Hitler at Berchtesgaden. They discuss the crisis in the German area of Czechoslovakia, the Sudetenland. The leader of the Sudeten Germans was Konrad Henlein.

**September 18, 1938**
The British and French present their proposals to the Germans to solve the Czech-German crisis; three days later they urge the Czechs to accept the German terms.

**September 22-23, 1938**
Chamberlain, who thinks he can appease Hitler, meets him at Bad Godesberg.

**September 28, 1938**
As the crisis in Europe increases, the British mobilize their fleet.

**September 29, 1938**
The Munich Agreement is concluded between Germany, Italy, Great Britain and France. Hitler thus receives the Western approval to occupy and annex the strategic Sudeten area in Czech parts of Czechoslovakia. The territory comprised some 10,000 sq. miles and it was inhabited by some 3,500,000 Germans and 800,000 Czechs. As Czechoslovakia lost its natural frontier against Germany, it was now exposed to further German expansion and final conquest. The Soviets were not even consulted during the Munich crisis; they could not help the Czechs because the French had capitulated to Hilter and thus had given up defense of the Czechs. This is the height of appeasement. After Munich, K. Gottwald, the leader of the Czech Communists, left the country for Russia.

**October 1-7, 1938**
The Germans occupy the Sudetenland.

**October 2, 1938**
The Poles occupy the Teschen industrial area in Czechoslovakia that was denied to them after World War I.

**October 5, 1938**
President E. Beneš of Czechoslovakia resigns and leaves for exile. Dr. Emil Hacha assumes the duties of the President.

**Early Autumn of 1938**
The Soviet Marshal V. K. Bluecher is liquidated by Stalin's regime.

**October 8, 1938**
Mao Tse-tung states that his alliance with the Nationalists was permitted by the Comintern.

**October 17, 1938**
K. J. Kautsky, the famous Socialist leader, dies as a poor refugee in Amsterdam. He had fled Austria after the Nazi Invasion.

**October 20, 1938**
The C.P. of Czechoslovakia is outlawed.

**October 21, 1938**
The Japanese invaders enter Canton in China.

**October 24, 1938**
The German foreign minister von Ribbentrop tells the Polish ambassador Lipski in Berlin that Germany wants the return of Danzig and the construction of an extra-territorial traffic route through the Corridor.

**November 1, 1938**
With Hitler's help Hungary is awarded southern Slovakia.

**November 10, 1938**
Mustapha Kema Ata-Turk dies.

**November 11, 1938**
Chiang Kai-shek's secret agents and soldiers kill some 200 members of the Communist New Fourth Army. In their areas the Nationalists were suppressing the Communists.

**November 14, 1938**
The decision of the Central Committee of the C.P.S.U. to organize the Party Propaganda in order to publicize Stalin's *History of the C.P.S.U. – Short Course*. This is his interpretation of the development of Communism in the Soviet Union.

**November 30, 1938**
14 leaders of the Rumanian Fascist Iron Guard are shot.

*Toukhachevski, Commandant in the Red Army* — Radio Times

### December 9-26, 1938
The Eighth Pan-American Conference in Lima, Peru, issues the Declaration of Lima against "all foreign intervention and activity."

### December 1938
N. I. Yezhov, the chief of N.K.V.D. and the administrator of Stalin's Purges, was deposed and succeeded by L. P. Beria. Yezhov disappeared a year later.

### End of 1938
The Great Purge of Stalin was almost complete. At the same time when (by December 27) the Presidium of the Supreme Soviet was introducing the title of the "Hero of Socialist Labor" the U.S.S.R. was deprived through Stalinist terror of many thousands of its best heroes. It is estimated that throughout 1937-1938 some 35,000 officers of the Red Army were liquidated. This was about half of the total officer corps. Among them were three out of five marshals; thirteen out of fifteen army commanders; fifty-seven out of eighty-five corps commanders; a hundred and ten out of a hundred-ninety-five division commanders; two hundred and twenty out of four hundred and six brigade commanders; Stalin also liquidated all 11 Vice-Commissars of War; seventy-five out of eighty members of the Supreme Military Council.

### 1939
This is the year of many great historic events for Europe and the world. Communism found itself at the crossroads, while Europe under Hitler's aggression entered the most tragic period of its history.

American C.P. boasts of some 90,000 members.

### January 3, 1939
The Soviets introduce a new military oath. The armed forces were weakened by the Purges. The Communist Youth Organization (Komsomol) reaches membership of some 9,000,000.

### January 13, 1939
Hungary, as an ally of Hitler, joins the Anti-Comintern Pact.

### January 29, 1939
The Czech Parliament annuls the mandates of all Communist deputies and senators.

### February 10, 1939
The Japanese occupy Hainan in China.

### February 28, 1939
Great Britain recognizes the government of Franco in Spain.

### March 10-21, 1939
The Eighteenth Congress of the C.P.S.U. meets. Stalin laid down some principles of the Soviet foreign policy and stated: "We stand for peace and the strengthening of business relations with all countries." He also promised "peaceful, close and friendly relations with all the neighboring countries which have common frontiers with the U.S.S.R."

### March 15, 1939
The Germans take Bohemia and Moravia and make them a Protectorate; Slovakia declares independence. Carpatho-Ukraine (Ruthenia) also declared independence and is overrun by Hungarian troops.

Under the impact of German expansion the Soviet Government had between April and August extensive talks with the Western powers. However, at the same time there were secret negotiations between the Nazis and the Russians.

### March 20, 1939
The Finnish government rejects the Soviet demands for territory and bases.

### March 22, 1939
Lithuania is forced to give to Germany the German-inhabited Memel Territory, her only access to the Baltic Sea.

### March 23, 1939
Germany imposes on Rumania a treaty which completely subordinated Rumanian economy to the German Reich.

### March 24, 1939
The British government issues guarantee to Poland as German pressure against Poland increases.

### March 25, 1939
Italy gives ultimatum to Albania.

### March 28-30, 1939
Franco's troops take Madrid and Valencia. This is the end of the Spanish Civil War in which about a million people perished on both sides.

*Mikhail Kalinin, President of the USSR* – Radio Times

**March 31 – April 6, 1939**
The Anglo-French guarantee to Poland is signed.

**Beginning of April 1939**
The German army has definite directives for an attack on Poland "at any time from September first 1939 onwards."

**April 7, 1939**
Italian troops invade Albania. King Zog leaves the country. Mussolini, who has aspirations in several Balkan countries, annexes Albania.

Spain joins the Anti-Comintern Pact.

**April 13, 1939**
France and Britain give guarantees to Rumania and Greece against possible German and Italian aggression.

**April 15, 1939**
President Roosevelt makes his "Peace Plea" to Hitler, who rejects it.

**April 16, 1939**
The Soviet government proposes an alliance with Britain and France against German aggression.

**April 28, 1939**
Hitler abrogates the Anglo-German Naval Agreement of 1935 and the German-Polish Treaty of 1934. Stalin comes gradually to the conviction that the Soviet Union, too, should participate in the division of spoils should war break out between the capitalist countries.

**May 3, 1939**
V. Molotov succeeds Litvinov as the new Commissar for Foreign Affairs. The stage is being set for serious German-Soviet talks.

**May 1939**
Renewed frontier clashes between the Soviet and Japanese troops in the Far East.

**May 20, 1939**
Beginning of the secret Nazi-Soviet talks.

**August 11-13, 1939**
P. Togliatti and other leading Italian Communists hold a secret conference in Paris discussing the impending war.

**August 12, 1939**
English and French military missions arrive in Moscow for talks about proposed military convention. On the same day the Soviet representative in Berlin conveys the willingness of the Kremlin to discuss "all questions of mutual interest." Hitler eagerly accepts and presses for an early date of agreement as time was running short to attack Poland this year.

**August 19, 1939**
Soviet trade agreement with Germany is signed.

**August 23, 1939**
Ribbentrop is in Moscow. Germany and the U.S.S.R. conclude a Non-Aggression Pact including a secret clause about the division of the areas of influence in East Europe. The Molotov-Ribbentrop agreement is a great surprise to the world and to all the Communists. The pact presents a drastic change in the Soviet strategy. Stalin needs peace and hopes to gain it by the agreement with the former enemy. Many Communists were shocked, bewildered and confused. The Communist parties all over the world now have to accept a new propaganda line ordered by Moscow.

American Communist leader, Earl Browder, defends the Nazi-Soviet pact, as the American Communists prepare to follow the new party line.

**August 25, 1939**
Anglo-Polish Pact of Mutual Assistance is concluded.

**August 26, 1939**
On the eve of World War II the Serbs and Croatians reach a compromise about Croatian autonomy. The C.P. with Tito at its head is now a well-organized force with thousands of new members. It is getting ready for the outbreak of war.

**August 31, 1939**
In a speech before the Fourth Session of the Supreme Soviet Molotov attempts to justify the Nazi-Soviet Pact. He stated: "History has shown that enmity and war between our country and Germany have been to the detriment of our countries, not to their benefit .... Therefore the interests of the peoples of the Soviet Union and Germany do not lie in mutual enmity. . . . We have always stood for amity between the peoples of the U.S.S.R. and Germany, for the growth and development of friendship between the peoples of the Soviet Union and the German people."

**September 1, 1939**

After last minute efforts to save the peace, in the early hours of the day, the German armed forces attack the republic of Poland — without a formal declaration of war,— and thus start the greatest slaughter of modern times: THE WORLD WAR II. *By making his pact with Hitler, Stalin made this war possible.* Hitler still is hoping that Britain would remain neutral and stay out of the conflict.

**September 3, 1939**

Britain, France, Australia, and New Zealand declare war on Germany.

**September 15, 1939**

The Soviet Union and Japan sign a Neutrality Pact. This will make it possible for Japan to attack the United States in December of 1941. At the same time we were starting to help the Soviets against the Germans.

**September 17, 1939**

The Soviet Red Army invades Poland, at the time when it was sure that Poland was defeated by the Nazis. The Russians take eastern parts of Poland, primarily the Bielorussian and Ukrainian territories.

**September 19, 1939**

The American Communists urge; "Keep America out of the imperialist war!" After June 1941, the line of propaganda will be radically changed.

**September 28, 1939**

Soviet-Nazi Pact of August, 1939, is modified; a new Frontier and Friendship Treaty is concluded between the two states. This is the Fourth Partition of Poland. The Soviet Union receives a territory of 77,620 sq. m. with about 22,000,000 people. German losses in conquest of Poland were: 8,082 killed, 27,278 wounded and 5,029 missing.

**September 29, 1939**

Estonia is forced to sign a pact with the Soviet Union; it leaves the country open to the Russian invasion.

**October 5, 1939**

The U.S.S.R. and Latvia sign a Mutual Assistance Pact.

**October 10, 1939**

The U.S.S.R. and Lithuania sign a Mutual Assistance Pact. Lithuania gets the consolation prize — Vilna

*Risto Ryti, Premier of Finland* — Radio Times

from Poland. Supported by their agreement with the Nazis, the Soviets were now ready to take over the Baltic area.

**October 11, 1939**

President Roosevelt asks the Soviet President Kalinin not to treat Finland too harshly.

**October 13, 1939**

A Resolution of the Political Committee of the C.P.U.S.A. urges America to keep out of the War.

**October 15, 1939**

Trying to save their nationals from the impending Soviet occupation, Germany signs a Protocol with Estonia and Latvia to affect the repatriation of the Germans from the Baltic area.

**October 18, 1939**

President Kallio of Finland addresses a letter — pleading for help — to President Roosevelt and the American people.

**October 19, 1939**

The Anglo-Turkish Treaty is signed.

**October 23, 1939**

The Finnish delegation in Moscow negotiates the future of Finland with the Soviet Government. They resume negotiations on November 3.

**November 1-2, 1939**
Western Ukraine and Western Bielorussia are eagerly accepted into the Soviet Union as constituent parts of the Bielorussian and Ukrainian republics. (These were Polish territories.)

**November 3, 1939**
The United States passes the repeal of the Arms Embargo making it possible to aid the Western Democracies in Europe.

**November 13, 1939**
The Finnish delegation leaves Moscow after unsuccessful negotiations.

**November 24, 1939**
The Japanese sever China from French Indo-China.

**November 26, 1939**
Soviet Foreign Minister Molotov denounces Finland and demands the withdrawal of all Finnish troops from the Soviet frontier.

**November 28, 1939**
Moscow denounces all existing treaties with Finland.

**November 30, 1939**
The Soviets attack Finland without a formal declaration of war. Fourteen Finnish towns are bombarded. Field Marshal Carl Gustav Mannerheim commands Finnish troops in the Winter War with the Soviets.

**December 1, 1939**
The Russians establish a Finnish puppet government under Otto Kuusinen, a former Secretary of the Comintern Executive Committee.

**December 2, 1939**
Finland appeals to the impotent League of Nations, while on the same day President Roosevelt in a press conference calls the Soviet attack on Finland as a "wanton disregard for law."

**December 14, 1939**
The League of Nations expels the U.S.S.R. because of aggression against Finland.

*Finland, Viipuri Harbor* — Radio Times

THE EASTERN FRONT
WORLD WAR II
1939 – 1945

- 1938 Boundaries
- Axis and occupied areas June 22, 1941
- Russian boundary, 1941

FRONT LINES IN RUSSIA
- —·—·— 1941    ＋＋＋＋ 1943
- △△△△ 1942    — — — — 1944
- RUSSIAN AND ALLIED DRIVES, 1941–1945

NORWAY

SWEDEN

DENMARK

BALTIC SEA

ESTONIA

FINLAND
(War with Russia, 1939–1940)
Joined Germans in attack on Russia in 1941

ALLIED SUPPLY LINE FROM U.S. AND BRITAIN

Murmansk

White Sea

Karelia

Archangel

N. Dvina

U S S R

Leningrad

Tikhivin

Dec. '41

Kalinin

Volga

Gorky

Kazan

MOSCOW

Oka

Mozhaisk

Kuibyshev

Riga

LATVIA

LITHUANIA

"Polish Corridor"

Danzig

EAST PRUSSIA

Vilnius

Smolensk

Minsk

BELO-RUSSIA

July '43

Tula

FARTHEST GERMAN ADVANCE 1941–1942

BERLIN

Elbe

Oder

Torgau

RUSSIA

ALLIES April 26, 45

Warsaw

Bialystok

Brest-Litovsk

Orel

Kursk

Voronezh

POLAND

June '44

U K R A I N E

Kiev

Kharkov

Dec. '41

Stalingrad

CZECHO-SLOVAKIA

Lvov

1939

Danube

Dniepropetrovsk

Don

Volga

Vienna

AUSTRIA

1941

Budapest

HUNGARY

1940

1941

Bessarabia

Dnieper

Rostov

Belgrade

RUMANIA

Bucharest

Kerch

Kuban

Novorossiisk

Mozdok

YUGOSLAVIA
(Taken by the Germans, 1941)

Danube

1940

Sofia

Sevastopol

Yalta

BLACK SEA

CAUCASUS MTS.

ITALY

BULGARIA

Batum

Tbilisi

ALBANIA
(To Italy, 1939)

Istanbul

Erevan

T U R K E Y

Ankara

ALLIED SUPPLY LINE FROM PERSIAN GULF

IRAN

GREECE

Izmir

Athens

(Taken by Germans in 1941)

CRETE

Sam¹ H. Bryant

*From: Basil Dmytryshyn, USSR: A Concise History (New York: Charles Scribner's Sons, 1965), p. 221; by permission of the publisher.*

# PART III:

# From World War II to Stalin's Death: 1940-1953

World War II Rages in Europe and Other Parts of the World ■ The Winter War in Finland Is Over ■ Norway, Denmark, Netherlands, Luxembourg, and France Are Conquered by Nazis ■ The Soviets Take Baltic Countries and Bessarabia ■ Trotsky Is Assassinated in Mexico ■ Hitler Attacks Yugoslavia ■ Germany Attacks the Soviet Union and Millions of Soviet Soldiers Surrender ■ The Atlantic Charter ■ Pearl Harbor: We Are at War ■ Germans Fail to Take Moscow ■ Partisan Warfare in Russia and the Balkans ■ Rise of Tito ■ The Allies Land in North Africa; Hitler Loses Stalingrad ■ Casablanca Conference ■ Comintern Is Disbanded ■ Lend-Lease to U.S.S.R. ■ Italy Surrenders ■ The Red Armies Advance ■ Teheran Conference ■ Allies Land in France ■ Warsaw Uprising ■ Red Armies in Central Europe ■ Baltic and Parts of the Balkans Are Under Soviet Control ■ Germans Retreat on All Fronts ■ Sovietization of East Central Europe Begins ■ Americans Reconquer the Pacific ■ Conference at Yalta; Stalin Gets Concessions ■ Soviets in Berlin; End of Hitler and Nazi Germany ■ Stalin Gets Peace on His Terms ■ The A Bomb; Surrender of Japan ■ The Cold War Between the East and West ■ Yugoslavia Becomes Communist ■ Complete Sovietization in East Central Europe ■ Civil War in Greece ■ Cominform Split ■ Victory of Communism in China ■ The Berlin Blockade ■ The Korean War ■ Death of Stalin — the End of an Era ■

*Josif Stalin* – Culver Pictures

These fateful fourteen years were among the most crucial for the existence of the mother country of Communism – the Soviet Union and for the entire international Communism. Reaping the fruits of their alliance with Nazi Germany, the Soviet Union continued its expansion. After taking eastern parts of Poland in September of 1939, in the next year Stalin added parts of Finland, Estonia, Latvia, Lithuania, as well as parts of Rumania.

By the summer of 1941 the rest of Europe was predominantly under German occupation. The surprise attack of Hitler on the Soviet Union in June, 1941 hit the Soviet regime really hard. By the summer of 1942 the most important parts of European U.S.S.R. were under German control. With the massive military and economic aid of the West, and arousing the patriotic spirit of the Russians, Stalin was able to withstand the German aggression. In February of 1943 with the Russian victory of Stalingrad, the new period of the war was inaugu-

rated. At the Conference of Teheran in late 1943 the Allies made first concessions to Stalin that later made it possible for him to achieve considerable gains in post-war East Europe. The Allied victories in late 1942 in North Africa and the establishment of the Second Front in France in June, 1944, considerably aided the Red Army in its Westward march. By April 1945 the Red Army was in Berlin and Vienna. In early May the war was finished in Europe. In the summer of the same year Japan was defeated. Europe was in ruins. Millions of people were killed by war or by the Germans in their camps of extermination.

After additional diplomatic successes in Yalta (early 1945) and in Potsdam (summer of the same year) Stalin was able to consolidate his hold over many peoples and territories in East Central Europe. By 1948 the Sovietization of these nations was completed.

The post-war period in Europe was marked by tragedy of many millions of people. Many nations gradually recovered from the horrors and destructions of the last war. The increasing frictions between the West and the Soviets were prolonged by a Cold War initiated by Stalin who now was at the top of his power. However, in spite of considerable expansion and many victories during and after the war, Communism with the Cominform split of 1948, became divided.

In 1950 the United States became involved in the Korean War trying to halt the invasion of the North Korean and Chinese Communists in the Republic of Korea. During the three years and one month we lost well over 30,000 killed. However, Korea was saved from becoming Communist.

Wherever the Soviets imposed their rule or influence, a gradual anti-Soviet and anti-Russian opposition arose. Even many native Communists in respective countries started to challenge the leadership of the Kremlin. The death of Stalin in March of 1953 was a relief to millions of Russians and non-Russians alike. This was the end of an era. Moscow ceased forever to be the only center of international Communism. Appearing on the scene were now: "National Communism," polycentrism (instead of the previous monolithic Communism), "Many Roads to Socialism," and above all – the rise of the revolutionary Chinese Communist power. After 1953 Communism could never be the same again. And to the surprise of all loyal Communists, Stalin was to be denounced and cursed in the subsequent years by his own disciples in the Soviet Union.

# 1. *To the End of World War II*

## 1940 – 1945
This is one of the most important periods in the history of Communism, the Soviet Union and of many nations that were affected by this crucial time. Many European nations experienced the horrors of a total war; millions of people died; hundreds of cities were destroyed. With Hiroshima the Atomic Age was inaugurated.

This was a crucial period for the Soviet regime; its very existence was threatened for a while after the German attack on the Soviet Union in June of 1941. However, later the tide was reversed and after Stalingrad the Red Army started to advance towards Germany. The war will end with considerable territorial gains for the Russians and the establishment of Communist regimes in the areas between the Baltic and Black Seas.

## January 22, 1940
Earl Browder, General Secretary of the C.P.U.S.A., is sentenced to four years in prison.

## February 10, 1940
U.S.S.R. and Germany renew the trade agreement. Germany obtains a great deal of raw materials from the Soviets.

## March 5, 1940
The Allied Supreme War Council decides to render military aid to the Finns. It is already too late.

## March 12, 1940
The Winter War between Finland and the U.S.S.R. is over. The Finns agree to sign the peace treaty with the Russians after 105 days of fighting.

## March 20, 1940
The Soviets veto the proposed alliance of Scandinavian countries: Finland, Sweden and Norway.

## March 22, 1940
The final peace treaty between the Finns and the Soviets is signed in Moscow. Finland loses about 35,000 sq. miles of territory, primarily in Karelia. It has been estimated that some 25,000 Finns and up to 200,000 Red Army soldiers were killed in the war.

## Spring of 1940
The Russians massacred in the Katyn Forest near Smolensk, White Russia some 15,000 Polish officers who were taken prisoner in September of 1939. (The mass graves will be discovered later by the advancing German army in Russia.)

## March 29, 1940
The so-called People's Government of Finland is dissolved by the Soviets. Otto Kuusinen, an old-time Finnish Bolshevik, was appointed head of the new Karelian Soviet Socialist Republic. All Finns living in occupied territories – 12 per cent of the entire Finnish population – were forced to leave.

## April 9, 1940
In a surprise attack the Germans invade Denmark and Norway. Denmark was occupied without any fight. The Norwegians resisted fiercely.

## April 24, 1940
Under the impact of the German spring offensive, the French Communist leader M. Thorez urges establishment of a new French Government under Communist leadership.

## May 8, 1940
Marshal S.K. Timoshenko replaces Voroshilov as Commissar of Defense.

## May 10, 1940
The German aggression continues. The German army attacks the neutral countries: Netherlands, Belgium and Luxemburg. Their armies resist but can do little against the war machine of the invaders.

**May 10, 1940**

In this historic period of Western Europe, Winston Churchill becomes Premier and forms a British coalition government.

**May 15, 1940**

The Dutch capitulate. The Queen and the government flee to England.

**May 15, 1940**

The Germans penetrate the French front and keep advancing.

**May 28, 1940**

The Belgians surrender to the Germans after desperate struggle. The King is German prisoner.

**May 28, 1940**

The Germans capture Narvik in Norway after heavy fighting with the Norwegians and the British.

**May 30 – June 2, 1940**

The American Communists during their Eleventh National Convention urge for peace and denounce American military preparations. (Note: the Soviet Union is not in the war; the Communists in most countries still advocate peace.)

**May 30 – June 3, 1940**

After a complete military disaster, the British and their allies undertake the evacuation at Dunkirk. Over 300,000 soldiers were rescued and shipped to England.

**June 9, 1940**

Norwegian resistance ends. Norway is occupied by the Germans.

**June 10, 1940**

The British forces are evacuated from Norway.

*Viborg, Finland – January, 1940. Burning wreckage after bombing raid by Russians.* – Radio Times

**June 10, 1940**

Italy declares war on France – that is already almost defeated by the Germans,– and Britain.

**June 12, 1940**

The Soviet ultimatum to Lithuania indicates that Stalin is ready to expand in the Baltic.

**June 14, 1940**

There is chaos in France. Her armed forces are defeated by the Germans. The Nazis occupy Paris.

**June 14, 1940**

Under Soviet pressure Lithuania accepts the Soviet ultimatum.

**June 15, 1940**

Red Army enters Vilna and Kaunas and occupies Lithuania. This is the end of Lithuanian independence.

**June 16, 1940**

The Soviet Union demands a new pro-Soviet government in Estonia.

**June 16, 1940**

Marshal Pétain, an old hero of World War I, becomes French Premier.

**June 16, 1940**

Moscow orders the establishment of a pro-Soviet government in Latvia.

**June 20, 1940**

Latvia yields to the Soviet ultimatum.

**June 22, 1940**

The Estonian government capitulates to Soviet demands.

**June 22, 1940**

Defeated France and victorious Germany conclude armistice. This is one of the greatest tragedies in French history.

**June 23, 1940**

General Charles De Gaulle, who escaped to London, starts the Free French Movement. Many governments in exile are now located in London. Britain is now in a desperate position but she continues to fight alone against the Germans.

**June 26, 1940**

It is obvious from the timing of Soviet moves, that Stalin as an ally of Hitler wants to expand as much as possible. Now Rumania's turn comes up. Stalin gives an ultimatum to the pro-German Rumanian government demanding Bessarabia and North Bukovina. The Germans are already worried by continued Russian aggression. They cannot help the Rumanians and advise them to yield to Soviet demands.

**June 27, 1940**

The Rumanian government accepts Soviet ultimatum and loses two rich provinces to the Russians.

**July 3, 1940**

The British cripple the French fleet at Oran and Mers el-Kabir in North Africa.

**July 4, 1940**

The Italian forces invade Sudan in Africa.

**July 5, 1940**

The French Government in Vichy (unoccupied France) breaks off relations with Britain. Five days later Petain became the chief of the French state controlled by the Germans. All over France resistance is organized against the Germans and the pro-German Vichy Government. Many of the guerilla fighters or partisans (the *maquis*) were Communists, but there were in their ranks all other political groups too.

**July 14, 1940**

The Soviet-controlled "elections" are held in Estonia, Latvia, and Lithuania.

**July 21, 1940**

The pro-Soviet, newly-elected assemblies in these three Baltic countries vote in favor of a union with the U.S.S.R.

**July 30, 1940**

In this presidential election year the National Committee of the C.P.U.S.A. assails in a special statement the policies of the two major American political parties.

**July 31, 1940**

According to the evidence, on this day Hitler decides to undertake the Plan "Barbarossa", namely the attack on the Soviet Union.

**August 2, 1940**
Out of the occupied Rumanian Bessarabia, the Soviets form the Moldavian Soviet Socialist Republic.

**August 3-6, 1940**
The Soviet Government incorporates Latvia, Lithuania and Estonia as three new Soviet Socialist Republics.

**August 4, 1940**
The Italians invade British Somaliland in East Africa.

**August 8 – September 6, 1940**
As Britain fights alone, the German air force conducts attacks against Britain; this is the Battle of Britain which the British won.

**August 17, 1940**
The British evacuate Somaliland.

**August 20, 1940**
Leon Trotsky is assassinated in Mexico City by a Soviet agent.

**August 30, 1940**
Under German pressure, the Rumanian North Transylvania is awarded to Hungary at the Vienna conference.

**September 2, 1940**
Under the directives from Moscow, in conformity with the Nazi-Soviet policy line, the American Communists create the so-called American Peace Mobilization urging America to stay out of European war.

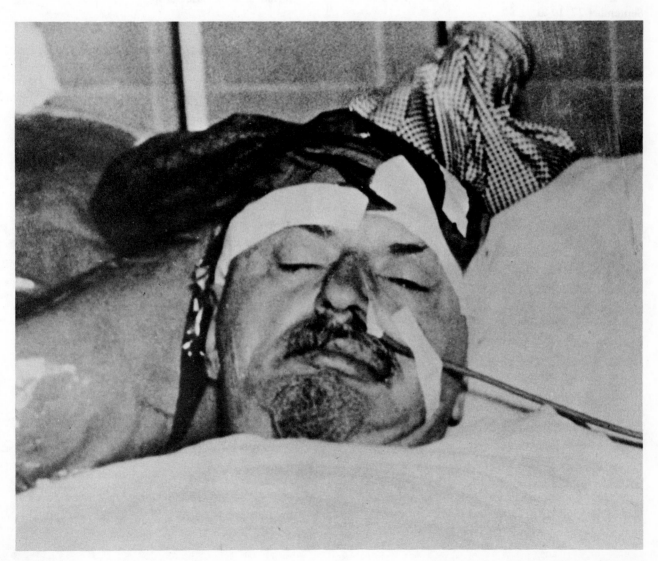

*Leon Trotsky in a Mexican hospital* – Keystone

**September 2, 1940**
In spite of official neutrality, the United States exchange fifty old destroyers for lease of British bases in the West Indies.

**September 6, 1940**
King Carol II of Rumania abdicates. His son Michael takes over. General Antonescu becomes dictator.

**September 7, 1940**
Rumania cedes Southern Dobruja to Bulgaria.

**September 13, 1940**
The Italians invade Egypt.

**September 16, 1940**
The United States introduces compulsory military service.

**September 27, 1940**
Germany, Italy and Japan conclude the Tripartite Pact for the establishment of a "New Order" in the world.

**October 7, 1940**
The Germans put Rumania under strict control; some interpret this as occupation.

**October 11, 1940**
The Finns and Soviets sign a Convention about demilitarization of the Aland Islands that are under Finnish rule and strategically important.

**October 13, 1940**
W. Z. Foster, American Communist leader, in a speech in Chicago urges "peace policy" for America.

**October 18, 1940**
The Burma Road in Asia is reopened by the British.

**October 19-23, 1940**
The Fifth Land Conference of the Communist Party of Yugoslavia, attended by 105 delegates, meets in Zagreb. The C.P.Y. has now some 12,000 members and about 30,000 youth members.

**October 28, 1940**
Italy starts war against Greece. This will turn out as a major military disaster for the Italians.

**October 29, 1940**
British forces land in Greece as allies against the Italians.

**November 5, 1940**
F. D. Roosevelt is re-elected for a third term. The Communist candidate for presidency was Earl Browder.

**November 12, 1940**
Hitler issues directives for the forthcoming attack on the Soviet Union. It was to be in the spring of the next year.

**November 12-14, 1940**
The Soviet Foreign Minister V. Molotov is in Berlin for talks with the German Government. It is certain by now that German and Soviet interests clash in certain areas of East Europe.

**November 14, 1940**
The Germans undertake an air terror raid against Coventry in England.

**November 16-17, 1940**
The C.P.U.S.A. at a special convention revises its constitution and eliminates the phrase "affiliated to the Communist International." Thus it avoided the compliance with the new Voorhis Act that required registration of all agents of a foreign power.

**November 20-25, 1940**
Slovakia, Rumania, and Hungary join the Tripartite Pact.

**November 25, 1940**
The Soviet Union offers Bulgaria a treaty of mutual assistance. The Bulgarians reject the offer.

**November 26, 1940**
The Swiss prohibit the Communist Party.

**December 8, 1940**
The British start their offensive in Libya. It will end on February 8, 1941.

**December 13, 1940**
Hitler gives directives for Operation Marita — to rescue the Italians by attacking Greece in the next spring.

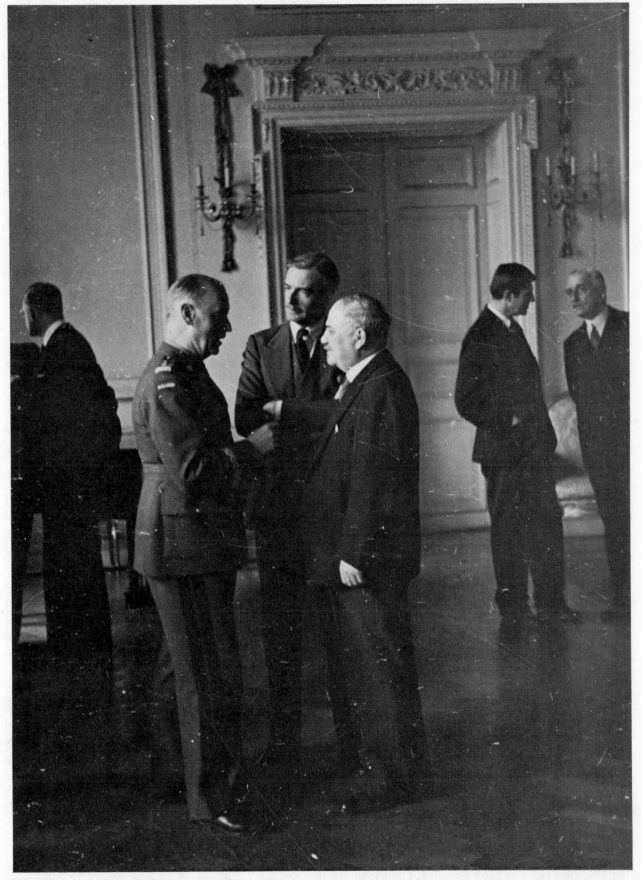

*Ambassador's Luncheon. M. Maisky entertains representatives of Allied Governments at the Soviet Embassy in London. Sikorsky is shown talking to M. Maisky and Mr. Eden, while U.S. Ambassador Winant and Greek Minister Simopoulos talk in the background.*
— Radio Times

**September 9, 1943**
The Allies land at Salerno, Italy.

**September 16, 1943**
The Red Army takes Novorossisk.

**September 17, 1943**
The Red Army takes Bryansk.

**September 25, 1943**
The Soviet armies take Smolensk. They are marching towards Berlin.

**October 4, 1943**
General Von Back-Zelewski is appointed as German Chief of Anti-partisan Combat Units in occupied U.S.S.R. A little later the Germans start a major anti-partisan drive, called "Operation Cottbus". It results in the destruction of some 5,000 civilians and 6,000 partisans. During the six-month period the Germans kill some 500,000 civilians in western parts of the European Soviet Union.

**October 7, 1943**
The Allies take Naples in Italy. The Germans are retreating slowly towards the north of Italy.

In their drive towards Germany, the Red Army crosses the Dnieper River in the Ukraine.

**October 8–9, 1943**
The Germans evacuate the Kuban Region, the homeland of the anti-Russian Cossacks. Some 100,000 Cossacks volunteered their services against the Soviet Government.

**October 13, 1943**
Italy declares war on Germany.

**October 18–30, 1943**
The Conference of Allied Foreign Ministers in Moscow discusses various problems of the war and post-war time. Hull, Eden and Molotov are present.

**October 23, 1943**
Premier Churchill informs President Roosevelt the British have about eighty military missions working with various resistance groups in Eastern Europe.

**November 1943**
The Ukrainian partisans under General T. Chuprynka with various non-Russian representatives form the Anti-Bolshevik Bloc of Nations.

**November 1, 1943**
The three main Allies agree on restoration of Austria after the end of the war.

**November 6, 1943**
The Red Army in heavy fighting takes Kiev.

**November 6, 1943**
On the eve of the anniversary of the Bolshevik Revolution, Stalin issues a statement about the future of Eastern Europe. All peoples will have "the full right and freedom to decide for themselves."

**November 7, 1943**
The Soviet representatives indicate that all territories taken from Poland in 1939 are forever part of the Soviet Union.

**November 21–25, 1943**
The Americans take Tarawa from the Japanese. The MacArthur's forces are closing in on Japan.

**November 22–26, 1943**
On their way to the Teheran Conference, Churchill and Roosevelt meet with Chiang Kai-shek in Cairo, Egypt.

**November 28 – December 1, 1943**
The historic conference at Teheran, Persia, is held between Churchill, Roosevelt and Stalin. The Allies give important concessions to Stalin. He is now more secure — and more bold — after his many victories after Stalingrad. The Allies also decide to give in Yugoslavia military support to the Communist leader Tito, because Mihajlović had collaborated with the Axis. The approximate date of the invasion of Europe is set.

**November 29, 1943**
The Second Session of the Anti-Fascist Council of the National Liberation of Yugoslavia (AVNOJ) meets in Jajce, Bosnia. This is the beginning of the future Communist Government of Yugoslavia. It announced the future federal state with "complete equality of Serbs, Croatians, Slovenians, Macedonians, and Montenegrins."

**December 12, 1943**
President Beneš of the Czechoslovak Government in exile concludes a long-term Treaty of Friendship, Mutual Assistance, and Post-war Cooperation between Czechoslovakia and the U.S.S.R. Benes is

actually paving the way for the Sovietization of his country.

**December 12, 1943**
Earl Browder, the American Communist leader, in a Connecticut speech hails the Teheran Conference as "history's greatest turning point."

**December 14, 1943**
*Izvestia,* the Soviet leading, newspaper, hails in an editorial the Teheran Conference as a guarantee of a "durable peace."

**December 24, 1943**
The American General Eisenhower is appointed the Supreme Allied Commander of the forthcoming invasion of Europe.

**December 31, 1943**
The victorious Russian armies take Zhitomir.

**December 31, 1943**
The Polish Workers Party (the Communists) form a Home National Council. Their leader is B. Bierut who was parachuted by the Russians into Poland in early 1942.

**January 1944**
The Communist-controlled Home National Council in Poland becomes the "Council of National Unity."

**January 4, 1944**
The Red Army crosses the 1939 frontier of Poland.

**January 10, 1944**
The Soviet government declares that the Curzon Line would be the future boundary between Poland and the Soviet Union.

**January 15, 1944**
To this challenge the Polish Government in London responds that America and Britain should mediate in this dispute.

**January 15–February 21, 1944**
The Red Army undertakes an offensive from Leningrad to Pskov.

**January 22, 1944**
The victorious Allies land at Anzio and Nettuno beaches in Italy.

**January 26, 1944**
The Russians reject the Polish suggestion of mediation and consider it as Polish rejection of the proposed boundary line.

**February 1, 1944**
At Stalin's order, the Supreme Soviet decides on the new status of the Soviet Republics: separate armies and diplomatic services. This is only a temporary tactics.

**February 1–May 18, 1944**
The Battle of Montecassino in central Italy. Many thousands Poles died here as British soldiers. The ancient Benedictine place was bombed by the Americans.

**February 4–19, 1944**
The Soviet armies force Germans to give up the upper Dnieper areas.

**February 8–March 13, 1944**
The Russians clear the lower Dnieper area in the Ukraine.

**February 22, 1944**
Premier Churchill in a speech before the House of Commons makes it clear that Poland must make a "compromise in her territory."

**February 23, 1944**
Soviet military mission arrives at Tito's headquarters in Bosnia.

**February 28, 1944**
Soviet armistice terms for Finland are published in Moscow.

**March 4–May 9, 1944**
Successful Soviet Spring offensive develops on the Eastern Front.

**March 7, 1944**
It is reported that the Polish Government has recognized the controversial Curzon Line as a temporary frontier until after the War.

**March 8–21, 1944**
During unsuccessful Finnish-Soviet peace negotiations the Finns reject the Soviet proposals.

**March 10, 1944**
The Greek National Liberation Front, the E.A.M., organizes a Political Committee for National Liberation of Greece.

**March 22, 1944**
The Germans overthrow the government of Admiral N. Horthy in Hungary.

**April 2, 1944**
Russian armies enter Rumania.

**April 8, 1944**
The Red Army reaches the frontier of Czechoslovakia.

**April 10, 1944**
The Red Army liberates Odessa on the southern front.

**May 5, 1944**
The British Foreign Secretary Anthony Eden proposes to the Soviet Ambassador in London, F. Gusev, that Rumania should remain in the Soviet sphere of influence while Greece should remain in the British sphere. This is already the struggle for power in post-war East Europe.

**May 9, 1944**
While talks go on the Soviet armies take Sevastopol in the Crimea.

**May 24, 1944**
The Albanian Communists form the Anti-Fascist Council of National Liberation. The leader is Enver Hoxha. The model for this council is Tito's A.V.N.O.J.

**May 25, 1944**
The Germans make air-borne raid on Tito's headquarters in Bosnia. He barely escapes capture, leaves by plane for Bari and then returns to the Island of Vis. This is now the headquarters of the National Liberation Army of Yugoslavia. Tito has the title of Marshal.

**June 1, 1944**
Ivan Šubašić becomes the Yugoslav Premier in London. Sixteen days later he met with Josip Broz Tito to discuss the future of Yugoslavia. By now the extremist forces of the Serbian chauvinist Draža Mihajlović were disavowed by the British and Americans. Tito and his partisans who were promising a federalistic Yugoslavia for all nationalities were recognized as the sole factor in Yugoslavia.

**June 6, 1944**
*The Allied Forces land in France.* This is one of the greatest operations of World War II. This is finally the Second Front which Stalin needs so badly.

**June 10, 1944**
The Russians start their offensive against Finland.

**June 15–16, 1944**
The Americans start the strategic bombing of the Japanese islands.

**June 20, 1944**
The Russians take Viborg in Finland.

**June 22, 1944**
The Russian offensive starts in German-occupied Bielorussia.

**June 27, 1944**
The Second Bielorussian Congress convenes in Minsk and proclaims the independence of Bielorussia. This German-sponsored move is too late. The country is conquered by the Bolsheviks.

**June 27, 1944**
After establishing a beachhead in Europe, the Allies take Cherbourg in France.

**July 3, 1944**
In their continued drive the Russians take Minsk, the capital of Bielorussia (White Russia).

**July 4, 1944**
A group of Polish Communists under Soviet control establishes the Polish National Council in Lublin. This is the nucleus of the future Polish Communist government.

**July 9, 1944**
The Allies take Caen in western France.

**July 11, 1944**
The Red Army starts its drive against Latvia and Estonia.

**July 13, 1944**
The Russians take Vilna in Lithuania.

**July 14, 1944**
The Russian offensive against Poland begins.

**July 20–August 3, 1944**
The Americans reconquer Guam from the Japanese.

**July 20, 1944**
Anti-Nazi officers – plotting to overthrow Hitler and to surrender to the Allies – attempt through Col. Claus von Stauffenberg to assassinate Hitler. By chance Hitler is saved. The *putsch* in Berlin fails and thousands of plotters are subsequently liquidated by Hitler's henchmen. The historians contend that if the assassination and the revolt would have succeeded the situation in Germany and East Central Europe – in regard to the Soviets – would be quite different.

**July 22, 1944**
The Red Army crosses the Curzon Line into Poland.

**July 26, 1944**
The Soviet Government recognizes the Lublin Committee as the body that will administer the liberated Polish territories. The Lublin Committee is officially known as the Polish Committee of National Liberation.

**July 27, 1944**
The Allies break through the German lines at St.-Lo in France.

**July 28, 1944**
The Bolsheviks take Lvov in Western Ukraine, formerly belonging to Poland.

**August 1, 1944**
Premier S. Mikolajczyk of the Polish Government in London arrives in Moscow for talks on the future of Poland.

**August 1, 1944**
The Polish Home Army under leadership of General Bor-Komorowski starts the historic Warsaw uprising, one of the most magnificent revolts against the Nazi oppression. The Soviet army stops near Warsaw and refuses to help the insurgents. For weeks this heroic revolt goes on without any help from either East or West. The Germans butcher the flower of Polish resistance. Because they all are anti-Communists, the Russians do not want to help them.

**August 11, 1944**
The Allies take Florence in Italy.

**August 12, 1944**
Tito and Churchill meet at Naples.

**August 12, 1944**
Churchill asks Stalin to render aid to Warsaw's fighting men and women. The plea is to no avail. In fact the Russians forbid on August 16 the use of their airfields to the Allied airplanes which were supposed to help Warsaw.

**August 15, 1944**
The Allies land in southern France between Toulon and Cannes.

**August 17, 1944**
The Soviet army reaches the border of East Prussia. The Germans now face the warfare in their own territory, in an area that centuries ago was taken away from the Slavs and Lithuanians. In all East German territories a mass exodus of millions of panic-stricken Germans starts. Millions of Germans – and non-Germans – flee from terror-spreading Russian armies.

**August 18, 1944**
President Roosevelt states at a press conference that the three Allies have reached an agreement on the future of Germany. A week later, on the 25th, the Secretary of State Cordell Hull states that no such agreement was reached.

**August 20, 1944**
The Soviet offensive begins in Rumania.

**August 22, 1944**
Stalin replies to the appeals of both Roosevelt and Churchill in regard to the Warsaw insurgents; Stalin calls them "criminals" because they were anti-Communist.

**August 23, 1944**
The Allies take Marseilles in southern France.

King Michael overthrows dictator General Antonescu and signs the armistice with the Russians. Rumania thus ceases to be German ally and starts to fight on the Russian side. This will cost Rumania: some 350,000 casualties.

**August 25, 1944**
The Allies liberate Paris. De Gaulle returns with his troops.

**August 29, 1944**
The Slovak uprising against the Germans begins. Almost the entire Slovak army goes over to the Russians.

**August 31, 1944**
The Second Ukrainian Soviet Army enters Bucharest, the capital of Rumania.

**September 3, 1944**
The Belgian capital,Brussels, is liberated by the Allies.

**September 4, 1944**
The Finns stop fighting against the Soviet forces.

**September 5, 1944**
After the Bulgarians had already offered to surrender, the U.S.S.R. suddenly declares war on Bulgaria.

**September 9, 1944**
The Soviets announce cessation of hostilities in Bulgaria. Peace negotiations begin. A Fatherland Front government, composed of pro-Soviet elements, is established. After events in Rumania and Bulgaria, the Sovietization of the Balkans is very close to reality.

The Duchy of Luxembourg in West Europe is liberated. The Allies are closing in on Germany from all sides.

**September 10, 1944**
The Finns sign armistice with the Soviet government.

**September 12, 1944**
The American First Army crosses the German frontier. Hitler now has to face war in his own territory.

**September 16, 1944**
The Red Army marches into Sofia, the capital of Bulgaria.

**September 17 – 16, 1944**
The Battle of Arnheim against stubborn German resistance is fought by the British in Netherlands.

**September 18, 1944**
A hundred American airplanes drop supplies over Warsaw. It is already too late.

**September 21, 1944**
Tito flies to Moscow for talks with Stalin.

**September 22, 1944**
The Bolsheviks take Tallin in Estonia.

**September 24, 1944**
British air-borne landing in Greece; Churchill is determined to save Greece from Communism.

**October 3, 1944**
The commandant of insurgent Warsaw, T. Bor-Komorowski sends his last message to the West: "There is no more ammunition. We are exhausted. Help has not arrived and will not come. We must surrender to overwhelming force. Long live independent Poland." The Polish underground army lost some 15,000 killed; over 200,000 civilians perished. German losses were: 10,000 killed; 7,000 missing and 9,000 wounded. This is the end of the ill-fated Warsaw Uprising. Even the Germans were impressed with the courage of the Warsaw defenders; they do not regard them as guerillas but as regular soldiers that have to be treated according to the international Red Cross conventions.

**October 5, 1944**
The Japanese take Foochow, the last seaport in Chinese hands.

**October 6, 1944**
The Russians invade Hungary.

**October 9 – 19, 1944**
Churchill and Eden are in Moscow to discuss with Stalin the complex problem of Poland.

**October 11, 1944**
Tannu Tuva, a Central Asiatic area, is absorbed by the Soviet Union.

**October 13, 1944**
The Red Army takes Riga, the capital of Latvia. Thousands of Latvians are fleeing the country.

**October 14, 1944**
The capital of Greece, Athens, is liberated by the British. The German forces start the evacuation of the Balkans.

**October 15, 1944**
Petsamo in the Arctic region of Finland is captured by the Russians.

**October 17, 1944**
The Greek government in exile with Premier Papandreou returns to Athens.

**October 18, 1944**
The Soviets enter Czechoslovakia.

**October 20, 1944**
The Americans invade the Philippines. General MacArthur keeps his promise: "I shall return."

Enver Hoxha, the Communist leader of Albania and a protegee of Tito, forms a Provisional Communist Government.

Belgrade, the Serbian capital of Yugoslavia, is taken — after severe fighting — by the Red Army and some Communist partisan units.

**October 23, 1944**
The Allies recognize the Provisional Government of Charles DeGaulle. The relations between him and the Allies have not been very happy ones.

Enver Hoxha is officially inaugurated as Premier and the Supreme Commander of Armed Forces in Albania.

Spreading terror and fright the Red soldiers are marching through East Prussia.

**October 25, 1944**
Italy and U.S.A. establish diplomatic relations.

**October 28, 1944**
The Soviet-Bulgarian armistice is signed in Moscow.

**November 1944**
A Communist-controlled National Council for the Carpathian Ukraine in eastern part of Czechoslovakia demands incorporation into the Soviet Union. This is the price the Czechs had to pay for the liberation by the Russians.

**November 1, 1944**
Premier Šubašić of the Yugoslav Government in London and Tito agree on establishing a regency until the future of the monarchy is decided in Yugoslavia.

**November 14, 1944**
General A. A. Vlasov, the former Red Army general who had gone over to the Germans to fight Stalin, founds a Committee for Liberation of Russia in Prague under German sponsorship. The Germans were unable to use many thousands of the anti-Soviet volunteers and it is too late now to turn the tide against the advancing Soviet armies.

**November 29, 1944**
The Albanian Communists take Tirana, the capital of their country.

**December 3, 1944**
In their struggle for power the Greek Communists proclaim general strike. The British commanding general Scobie had ordered on the 1st of December disbandment of all guerilla forces. As the Communists want to overthrow the government in Athens, the British react. A civil war breaks out.

**December 4, 1944**
Albania is free of all German forces.

**December 10, 1944**
The new French government makes a treaty of alliance with the Soviet Union. France is ravaged by the war and in difficult position. The Communists are determined to take advantage of these conditions.

**December 16 – 22, 1944**
The German army launches its last desperate offensive in the West, in the Ardennes, France; it caught Allies by surprise. This is the Battle of the Bulge. After initial success and heavy Allied losses, the Germans were stopped.

**December 25, 1944**
As heavy fighting rages in Greece between the Communists and anti-Communist forces, Winston Churchill visits Athens. The Communist EAM forces are defeated and Greece is temporarily saved from Communism.

**December 30, 1944**
King George of Greece abdicates in London; Archbishop Damaskinos becomes the Regent until the future of the monarchy is decided by the people.

Soviet-controlled Hungary declares war on her former German allies.

**December 31, 1944**

The Soviet troops fight in Budapest, the capital of Hungary.

B. Bierut, the Polish Communist leader, establishes a Polish Committee of National Liberation in Lublin in Eastern Poland.

The year 1944 ends with great Soviet victories all over Eastern Europe. Albania is already completely Communist while other East European governments pretend to have coalition of various parties. The Soviet armies are deep in German territory.

**1945**

This is the crucial year for international Communism and for all those who oppose it.

**January 4 – 5, 1945**

The fighting is finished in Athens. The Communist forces are defeated. This was a major victory for Great Britain and the anti-Communist forces. The E.L.A.S. forces are licking their wounds.

**January 5, 1945**

The Soviet Government gives recognition to the Lublin Provisional Government of Poland. Thus the Russians prepare the way for the Sovietization of Poland.

**January 9, 1945**

The Americans land at Luzon, the Philippine Islands.

**January 17, 1945**

After all delays the Soviet troops enter Warsaw, the capital of Poland. It is mostly in ruins.

**January 18, 1945**

The Lublin Committee ("Government") arrives in Warsaw.

**January 20, 1945**

The Soviets sign armistice with Hungary. The Hungarian government is in Debreczen.

Roosevelt is sworn in for his fourth term as President of the United States.

**February 4 – 13, 1945**

The most important war conference between the Big Three takes place in Yalta, Crimea U.S.S.R. Roose-velt, Churchill and Stalin make decisions about the future of Germany and East Europe. They recognize the provisional government in Poland which will be enlarged by democratic elements from the Polish Government in London. Support was given to Tito in Yugoslavia. A joint statement was issued on the 12th. At Yalta Stalin scored great diplomatic victory. Many historians feel that the West gave too many concessions to Stalin at this conference which disappointed all free Poles, many other peoples, and secured Sovietization of East Europe.

**February 13, 1945**

After a two-month siege, the Soviet troops capture Budapest, the capital of Hungary.

**February 23, 1945**

Neutral Turkey declares war on Germany and Japan.

**February 24, 1945**

The American forces liberate Manila in the Philippines from the Japanese.

**March 4, 1945**

Finland, now on Allied side, declares war on Germany.

**March 6, 1945**

Under Soviet pressure, King Michael of Rumania consents to the establishment of a Communist-controlled government under the premiership of the pro-Soviet politician Peter Groza.

**March 7, 1945**

The Allies cross the Rhine River at Remagen.

**March 12, 1945**

The Russians reward Rumanian Communists by returning Hungarian-held Northern Transylvania to Rumania.

**March 17, 1945**

President E. Beneš and his men reach Moscow on their way home from exile.

**March 30, 1945**

The Soviet troops take Danzig and Kuestrin in the Baltic area.

**April 4, 1945**

E. Beneš reaches Košice in eastern Slovakia, already under the Soviet control.

Sam<sup>l</sup>. H. Bryant

ATLANTIC

OCEAN

UNION OF

SOVIET

Volga

NORWAY

SWEDEN

FINLAND

SOCIALIST

Leningrad

MOSCOW

ESTONIA

REPUBLICS

LATVIA

DENMARK

Kaliningrad

LITHUANIA

Minsk

GREAT
BRITAIN

POLISH
ADMIN.

Danzig

BOUNDARY OF
U.S.S.R. 1938

IRELAND

NETHER-
LANDS

GER.

Berlin

Warsaw

Kiev

Dnieper

Don

London

DEM.

POLAND

Odessa

GERMAN

REPUB.

Prague

Vistula

Yalta

Bonn

BELGIUM

FEDERAL

CZECHOSLOVAKIA

BESSARABIA

BLACK

Paris

REPUBLIC

Vienna

Budapest

SEA

LUXEMBURG

Danube

HUNGARY

RUMANIA

SWITZER-
LAND

AUSTRIA

Bucharest

Istanbul

FRANCE

Belgrade

BULGARIA

TURKEY

YUGOSLAVIA

Sofia

PORTUGAL

ALBANIA

GREECE

Rome

Madrid

SPAIN

MEDITERRANEAN

SEA

**SOVIET TERRITORIAL GAINS IN EUROPE    1939-1949**

USSR in 1938    Soviet satellite states    Acquired by the USSR
1939-1945    Communist
but not Soviet satellites

*From:  Basil Dmytryshyn,* USSR:  A Concise History *(New York:  Charles Scribner's Sons, 1965), p. 239;*
*by permission of the publisher.*

**April 5, 1945**

The new Czechoslovak government is formed and announced in Košice. The Košice Program is adopted. It gives important concessions to the Communists. However, at present four political parties are permitted to function: Social Democrats, Communists, the Czech National Socialists (the party of Beneš), and the Catholic People's Party.

**April 5, 1945**

The U.S.S.R. renounces the neutrality pact with Japan.

**April 9, 1945**

The Allies start a new offensive in Italy.

**April 12, 1945**

Franklin D. Roosevelt dies; the new President is H. S. Truman.

**April 13, 1945**

The Soviet troops are in control of Vienna, the capital of Austria, and of Koenigsberg in East Prussia.

**April 21, 1945**

The Red Army reaches suburbs of Berlin.

**April 21, 1945**

The Polish Provisional Government signs Treaty of Mutual Assistance with the Soviet Union.

**April 22, 1945**

The Provisional Austrian Government is established under Chancellor Dr. Karl Renner, a Socialist. Austria is occupied by: Russians, Americans, British, and the French.

**April 24 – June 26, 1945**

The Conference of the United Nations is held at San Francisco. The Charter of the United Nations is signed by many delegations on June 26.

**April 25, 1945**

American and Soviet troops link up near Torgau on the Elbe River. The Americans neglected the chance to reach Berlin first.

**April 26, 1945**

The Allies take Milan in North Italy.

**April 28, 1945**

B. Mussolini is executed by Italian partisans.

**April 29, 1945**

The German forces surrender in Italy.

**April 29, 1945**

The Allies take Munich in Bavaria and Venice in Italy.

**April 30, 1945**

Adolf Hitler commits suicide in the bunker of the Reich's Chancellery in Berlin.

**May 1, 1945**

Tito's forces take Trieste, a former Italian city, before the Allies could reach it.

**May 2, 1945**

Berlin is captured by the Soviet armies: First Ukrainian and First Bielorussian.

**May 3, 1945**

The British forces take Hamburg, Germany.

**May 3, 1945**

The British take Rangoon in Burma from the Japanese.

**May 5, 1945**

The Germans surrender in North-West Germany, Netherlands, and Denmark.

**May 7, 1945**

At Reims, France General Jodl signs unconditional surrender of all German forces in the name of a Provisional Government under Admiral Doenitz. This is the end of the war in the West and the end of the Third Reich.

**May 8, 1945**

Millions of liberated Europeans celebrate the day of victory over the Nazi tyranny. This is the historical V-E Day.

**May 8, 1945**

Stalin hails the Communist Party of the Soviet Union as the "inspirer and organizer of our victory."

**May 9, 1945**

The final act of German capitulation is ratified under Russian auspices by the heads of the German Army, Navy and Air Force, in the presence of representatives of four leading Allies.

**May 10, 1945**

While American troops are waiting in Pilsen, the Russians take Prague, the capital of Czechoslovakia. Shortly afterwards the U.S. troops under General Patton withdraw from Bohemia and from parts of Austria and Germany. Many thousands of Displaced Persons and refugees are flocking into the American and British zones of occupation. They all flee the Russians.

**May 16, 1945**

The Czechoslovak government with President Beneš returns to Prague.

**May 26, 1945**

Churchill forms a government without the Labor Party.

**End of May 1945**

The American Communists are in serious crisis because of the article by French Communist J. Duclos published in the *Daily Worker* on May 24 in which he denounced deviationism of Earl Browder.

**June 2, 1945**

Under the impact of Duclos' article the American Communists vote for a new party line.

**June 6, 1945**

Bulgarian Communists issue a new electoral law.

**June 9, 1945**

After Allied ultimatum Tito evacuates Trieste.

**June 10, 1945**

In the Peruvian election the Communists win four seats in the parliament.

**June 17 – 20, 1945**

Major Allied ambassadors agree in Moscow on a Polish Government of National Unity.

**June 19, 1945**

Sixteen Polish underground leaders who were arrested by the Russians on March 28, are sentenced to long prison terms. The anti-Communist Poles feel that the Polish cause was given up by the free West.

**June 21, 1945**

The American forces take Okinawa. The victorious war in the Pacific continues with heavy American casualties.

*Maurice Thorez, French Communist Politician* – Radio Times

**June 24, 1945**

The Victory Parade is held in the Red Square in Moscow. By now the Soviet leaders give little, or no credit, to the enormous American war aid that helped to save the Soviet regime in the time of great crisis. The Russians also minimize the American military efforts on all fronts.

**June 25, 1945**

After the return of many leading German Communists from exile in the Soviet Union, the German Communist Party issues a Manifesto in Berlin.

**June 26, 1945**

The U.N. Charter is signed in San Francisco by the delegates of fifty nations.

**June 26, 1945**

The French Communist leader Maurice Thorez addresses the Tenth Congress of the C.P. of France. Thorez is the Secretary General of the Party.

**June 28, 1945**

The Polish government of National Unity is formed in Warsaw. M. Osubka-Morawski, a Socialist, is its Premier; S. Mikolajczyk from the government in exile becomes one of the vice-presidents representing the Peasant Party.

**June 29, 1945**

Soviet and Czechoslovak governments sign an agreement in Moscow: Carpatho-Ruthenia (Ukraine) is transferred to the Soviet Union.

**July 3, 1945**

The new Polish government informs London and Washington that it accepts the Yalta provisions and is ready to hold free and democratic elections.

**July 5, 1945**

America, Britain and France recognize the Polish government in Warsaw and withdraw their recognition from the old Polish government in London.

**July 5, 1945**

The Philippines are liberated by American forces.

**July 10, 1945**

U.S.S.R., Britain and the United States agree on the establishment of an Allied *Komandatura* in Berlin. (France was to join later.)

**July 17 – August 12, 1945**

The last big conference of Britain, America and the Soviet Union, the Conference of Potsdam meets. Churchill, Truman and Stalin discuss various problems regarding the ending of war in the Pacific, the establishment of peace, and the future of Germany. It is agreed that Eastern German territories, beyond the Soviet Zone of occupation, are to be *administered* by Poland and the U.S.S.R. After July 28, Churchill is replaced by the new Premier Clement Attlee. (The Labor Cabinet was formed on the 27th, after the general election in which the Labor received 393 seats and the Conservatives 189 seats in the House of Commons.) The Allied leaders agree on establishing a Council of Foreign Ministers that would meet periodically and work out different solutions regarding many unsolved problems. Provisions were made also for conclusion of peace treaties with: Bulgaria, Hungary, Rumania, Finland, and Italy.

**July 26 – 28, 1945**

The American C.P. is reconstituted, Z. Foster is its chairman.

**August 6, 1945**

*The first atomic bomb is dropped by the Americans on Japan. Hiroshima is destroyed. A new era of history is thus inaugurated.*

**August 6, 1945**

The Soviet Government establishes diplomatic relations with defeated countries of Finland and Rumania.

**August 8, 1945**

The Soviet Union, in agreement with the Potsdam decisions, declares war on Japan.

**August 9, 1945**

Atomic bomb is dropped on Nagasaki in Japan.

**August 14, 1945**

Japan accepts the Allied terms of capitulation and surrenders unconditionally. *This is the end of World War II!*

**August 14, 1945**

Treaty of Friendship is signed between the Soviet Union and China.

**August 16, 1945**

Polish-Soviet treaty is signed; it settled the Eastern frontier and German reparations.

**August 18, 1945**

The U.S. Secretary of State, James F. Byrnes, denounces the violation of democratic processes by the Bulgarian Fatherland Front.

**August 23, 1945**

Stalin announces oocupation of all of Manchuria; five days later the Soviet occupation of the Sakhalin Island is completed.

**August 28 – October 10, 1945**

Mao Tse-tung visits Chungking as the guest of the Nationalist Government under Chiang Kai-shek. By now the Chinese Communists have an army of over 900,000 soldiers and control areas containing some 90 million people.

**September 2, 1945**

Ho Chi Minh proclaims from Hanoi independence of Vietnam.

**September 2, 1945**
A great Allied fleet enters the Tokyo Bay; on the same day on board the battleship *Missouri* the representatives of Japan sign the surrender of Japan. General MacArthur and the representatives of the Allied powers accept on behalf of their respective governments.

America terminates the Lend Lease.

**September 7, 1945**
Igor Gouzenko, an official in the Soviet Embassy in Ottawa, Canada defects and gives the Canadian authorities valuable information on Soviet espionage in Canada.

**September 8, 1945**
General Douglas MacArthur enters Tokyo. As the Supreme Commander of the Allied Powers, he had led the victorious war in the Pacific, and he will undertake in Japan sweeping reforms to create a new political and social order.

**September 9, 1945**
The Japanese forces surrender in China.

**September 10, 1945**
One of the former prominent members of Comintern and now the official representative of the Soviet Ukraine in the United Nations, Dmitri Z. Manuilsky declares in a speech before U.N. that Communists are strong and active in the world. He is considered as the man who coordinates activities of international Communism.

**September 25, 1945**
The Soviet Union establishes diplomatic relations with Hungary.

**September 25 – October, 1945**
The World Federation of Trade Unions – the WFTU— is established in Paris during an international congress. It represents 64 million workers in 52 countries.

**October 1945**
The French Communists have some 550,000 members; in the October national elections some 5 million people vote in favor of the Communists.

**October 3, 1945**
During the meeting of the Council of Foreign Ministers in London serious difficulties arise; Byrnes of U.S.A. and Molotov of U.S.S.R. disagree on many issues.

**October 11, 1945**
The negotiations between the government in Chungking (Nationalists) and the Chinese Communists bring no result.

**October 12, 1945**
Ho Chi Minh wins great majority in the "elections" organized by the Communist-controlled Independence League of Indo-China. The fighting now goes on between the Communists and the French.

**October 20, 1945**
Outer Mongolia votes for independence from China; this Soviet-sponsored plebiscite creates the People's Republic of Mongolia located between China and the U.S.S.R.

**October 20, 1945**
The Allied Council for Austria recognizes the Austrian Provisional Government.

**October 21, 1945**
The Communists win 152 seats in the parliament in the first post-war French national election.

**October 24, 1945**
The Charter of the United Nations comes into force.

**October 25, 1945**
President Beneš puts about 75 per cent of the Czechoslovak industry under state control. This was major victory for Gottwald and his Communists.

**October 30, 1945**
The Communists win some 255,000 votes and 18 seats in the Parliament in Danish elections.

**November 3, 1945**
The Communists receive only seventeen per cent of votes in the Hungarian election. This amounts to about 800,000.

**November 10, 1945**
The Western powers grant provisional recognition to the Albanian Communist government.

**November 15, 1945**
The famous Bulgarian Communist of international fame, Georgi Dimitrov, arrives in Sofia from Moscow. His role is to complete the Sovietization of Bulgaria.

**November 20, 1945**
The trial of the main German war criminals starts at Nuremberg. The International Military Tribunal will work until October 1, 1946.

**November 26, 1945**
Iran (Persia) protests against the presence of the Soviet troops.

**November 29, 1945**
After Communist-controlled elections, Yugoslavia is proclaimed Federative People's Republic. While many thousands of anti-Communists were liquidated, many are in prison.

**December 1945**
The Soviet troops start the final large scale offensive against Ukrainian partisans under T. Chuprynka. N. S. Khrushchev, the First Secretary of the Ukrainian C.P. is in charge of the pacification of the Ukraine.

**December 2, 1945**
The "elections" take place in Albania. 93 per cent of the voters cast ballots in favor of the Communist-controlled Democratic Front.

**December 15 – 26, 1945**
The Council of Foreign Ministers meets in Moscow trying to solve many war-time problems.

*First pictures from interior of Russian zone in Germany. Shown, a scene in Johannstrasse, one of the main thoroughfares of Dresden. The people of Dresden are seen getting on to trains in the midst of chaotic ruins still lying in the street since the 40-minute allied raid which cost the city 100,000 dead.* – Keystone

# 2. *Post-War Period Until the Death of Stalin: January, 1946-March, 1953*

## 1946

Sixty-six Communist Parties throughout the world claim a membership of some 13,000,000 people.

World Communism enters a new era. Everywhere the Soviet Communists advocate the "National Revolutions" and "Wars of Liberation" against Western "Colonialism and Imperialism." Great Britain under the leadership of Churchill won the war, but after 1945 Britain lost her old empire. Communism expands in East Europe and in Asia. In 1946 Albania, Bulgaria, Rumania, and Yugoslavia were under strict Communist control; the coalition governments were still in existence in Czechoslovakia, Hungary, and Poland.

However, after 1945–1946 Communism was losing its monolithic character. Various Communist Parties became more nationalistic. "National Communism" was on the rise. There was an ever increasing opposition on the part of many leading Communists against the exclusive leadership of the Kremlin. With the rise of Communist China, Kremlin will cease to be the "Rome of Communism". Peking will emerge as a new powerful center of international Communism. And additional new centers will emerge.

The new period also witnessed the break-up of the former Grand Alliance. The West was to face first a "Cold" and later even a real "Hot" War waged by Moscow, especially in the Korean conflict. The American Communism, never totally united, was to become an insignificant force in post-war America.

### January 10, 1946
A Political Consultative Conference meets in Chungking but fails to achieve unity between the Chinese Nationalists and Communists.

### January 11, 1946
Albania is officially proclaimed a People's Republic.

### January 14, 1946
The Presidium of the Supreme Soviet ratifies the treaty with Poland about the new eastern frontier.

### January 22, 1946
It is stated that in spite of terrible war losses the population of the Soviet Union is about 193,000,000.

### January 22, 1946
A Kurdish People's Republic, under Soviet initiative, is created in parts of Persia. Its head is Ghazi Mohammed, who has the Soviet backing. Persia is appealing to the United Nations against Soviet interference.

### January 30, 1946
The East German Communist leader, Wilhelm Pieck, appeals to the Soviet authorities to be more conciliatory towards the Germans.

F.P.R. Yugoslavia adopts a new constitution modeled after that of Stalin's Constitution of 1936.

### February 5, 1946
America and Britain recognize the Rumanian government that is Communist-dominated.

### February 22, 1946
The U.S. Government in a sharp note to Sofia protests the Sovietization of Bulgaria. Thousands of anti-Communists have been liquidated.

### February 27, 1946
The Mongolian People's Republic in Asia between the U.S.S.R. and China concludes a Treaty of Friendship and Mutual Assistance with the U.S.S.R.

**February 27, 1946**
The Mongolian People's Republic in Asia between the U.S.S.R. and China concludes a Treaty of Friendship and Mutual Assistance with the U.S.S.R.

**March 1, 1946**
The American authorities reveal that the Soviet Union has asked for a billion dollar loan.

**March 5, 1946**
Winston Churchill in his "Iron Curtain" speech at Fulton, Mo. warns the free world about the Soviet threat to the West. An *Iron Curtain* has been drawn by the Russians between Stettin in the Baltic and Trieste in the Adriatic.

**March 6, 1946**
The Soviet troops intervene against the government troops in Iran. This is a very serious crisis.

**March 9, 1946**
The Soviets give a very sharp reply to the American note on Bulgaria. (To be near to the Straits, it is vital for the Russians to have Bulgaria under their control.)

**March 15, 1946**
Enver Hoxha proclaims a new Communist government in Albania.

**March 15, 1946**
The Soviet Council of People's Commissars now becomes the Council of Ministers of the U.S.S.R.

**March 17, 1946**
The forced union of the Ukrainian Catholic (Uniate) Church with the Russian Orthodox Church is announced by the Soviet authorities. Monsignor Joseph Slipy and thousands of Ukrainian priests are sent to prison because of their opposition to the reunion.

**March 31, 1946**
The newly-formed Bulgarian government under Communist Control is formed.

**April 4, 1946**
The British refuse to send diplomatic representatives to Communist Albania.

**April 5, 1946**
The Soviets declare that by an agreement with the Iranian government there is no reason for the U.N. to discuss the Iranian crisis.

**April 14, 1946**
The U.S.S.R. concludes very favorable trade agreements with Poland and Czechoslovakia.

**April 18, 1946**
The Assembly of the League of Nations meets for the last time in Geneva, Switzerland.

**April 20, 1946**
The Austrian C.P. holds its Thirteenth Conference in Vienna and claims to have 132,000 members. Most of them are in the Soviet Zone of Occupation.

**April 21, 1946**
The Socialists are forced to merge with the Communists in East Germany; their new party is called the Socialist Unity Party—the S.E.P.

**April 25, 1946**
By foregoing further Finnish reparation deliveries, the Russians are easing the relations with Finland.

The reports indicate a severe civil war in China. At the same time some Americans like Gen. Marshall speak that the problem of China is merely an "agrarian revolution."

**May 26, 1946**
In the Czechoslovak elections, the Communists win about 2,700,000 votes of the 7,000,000 votes cast. The Communist Klement Gottwald forms a new coalition government with Communists in key positions.

**May 27, 1946**
President Tito of Yugoslavia arrives in Moscow for important talks with Stalin.

**June 1946**
The Soviet Government announces that Crimean Tartar and Chechen-Ingush Autonomous Socialist Soviet Republics are dissolved and that the population is being deported on account of the alleged collaboration with the Germans. This is practice of genocide.

**June 3, 1946**
Michael I. Kalinin, the Chairman of the Supreme Soviet, dies.

**June 6, 1946**
Soviet Russia restores diplomatic relations with Argentina in South America.

**June 14, 1946**
The Russians sign the frontier treaty with the Afghanistan government.

**June 30, 1946**
The truce brought about by U.S. General Marshall mission in China expires; the Third Revolutionary Civil War Starts.

**July 1, 1946**
The Council of Foreign Ministers meeting at Paris solves the Italian-Yugoslav dispute on Trieste. Yugoslavia gives up the city except its neighboring territories. A corridor will connect Trieste with Italy.

**July 12, 1946**
The Bulgarian government sentences to death the peasant leader G. M. Dimitrov, who found asylum in the American legation.

**July 29 – October 15, 1946**
The delegates from the 21 nations participate in the peace treaty negotiations in Paris. They finally conclude peace treaties with Italy, Rumania, Finland, and Bulgaria all which fought on the German side.

**August 1, 1946**
General A. A. Vlasov and eleven of his leading collaborators are hanged in Moscow. The Americans delivered them to the Russians.

**August 19, 1946**
Two U.S. airplanes are shot down by Yugoslav authorities. Five Americans were killed. After a U.S. 48-hours ultimatum the dispute is settled.

**August 21, 1946**
Andrei A. Zhdanov announces a new strict "Party Line" in Soviet cultural activities. This is the beginning of "Zhdanovshchina."

**August 23, 1946**
The Ukrainian Communist Party organization is rehauled after the war. Nikita S. Khrushchev attacks the Ukrainian nationalism of the party leaders.

*Left to Right.   John Hynd, M.P. (Chancellor of Lancaster), Wilhelm Pieck, leader of the Communist Party (He wanted a Policy for Germany),   and Otto Grotewohl, leader of the Social Democrats*
*— Radio Times*

**September 1, 1946**
The Greek plebiscite returns King George II to his throne.

**September 7, 1946**
The Bulgarian Communist leader Georgi Dimitrov announces that Bulgaria must be a Communist state.

**September 8, 1946**
Bulgarians vote for a republic; King Simeon and the Coburg dynasty are deposed.

**September 12, 1946**
U.S. Secretary of Commerce Henry A. Wallace publicly attacks Truman's administration for its policy against the U.S.S.R. Soon afterwards he was fired.

**September 15, 1946**
Bulgaria is proclaimed a "People's Republic." Its peasantry cares little about Communism.

**September 17, 1946**
Stalin declares that "demilitarization and democratization" of Germany is one of the most important guarantees of a "sound and lasting peace."

**September 18, 1946**
The Yugoslav authorities arrest the Archbishop of Zagreb and Metropolitan of Croatia Alojzije Stepinac on trumped-up charges. The Catholic Church is persecuted. Many of its priests have been murdered or arrested. The West defends Stepinac as an enemy of all dictatorship and a friend of Jews and Orthodox.

**September 20 – 22, 1946**
The Third Congress of the American Slavs convenes at Manhattan Center in New York. The delegates include the Soviet General Gundorov. Twelve Communist countries are represented here and the featured speaker is Mrs. Tsola Dragoicheva, the Bulgarian leading Communist. (The last such Congress was held on September 23–24, 1944 in Pittsburgh.) These congresses are extremely pro-Soviet and Pro-Communist.

**September 24, 1946**
Stalin declares in an interview with the British press that he wants to maintain "friendly competition" with the Western Democracies. The Soviets want to cover up the oncoming "Cold War" against the West.

The Russian Communists, traditionally eager to gain the control of the Turkish Straits, declare they want the change of the Montreux Convention. Turkey firmly rejects this challenge.

**September 28, 1946**
King George II returns from England to Greece.

**October 1, 1946**
The Nuremberg International Tribunal sentences the leading Nazis; twelve are to be hanged.

**October 9, 1946**
The U.S. note to the Kremlin states that America is siding with Turkey on the international status of the Straits; it rejects the proposed Soviet defense of the Straits.

**October 10, 1946**
Archbishop A. Stepinac is sentenced in Zagreb by a Communist court to sixteen years in prison.

**October 20, 1946**
The Communists receive only 20 per cent of the vote in Berlin's municipal elections.

G. M. Malenkov, member of the Presidium of the Supreme Soviet, is appointed Deputy Chairman of the Council of Ministers.

**October 22, 1946**
The British announce that two of their destroyers were seriously damaged by Albanian mines in the Channel of Corfu and that forty of British sailors lost their lives.

**November 4 – December 12, 1946**
The Council of Foreign Ministers meets in New York and solves very few world problems.

**November 8, 1946**
The United States withdraws its diplomatic representatives from Albania.

**November 18, 1946**
Marshal I. S. Konev, of World War II fame, is appointed Commander-in-Chief of the Soviet Armed Forces replacing Marshal Zhukov.

**November 19, 1946**
Communist-controlled elections are held in Rumania. From some 7,800,000 votes the Communists and their allies poll more than 5,300,000.

**November 27, 1946**
Dr. Eugene Varga, director of the Soviet Institute for World Economics and World Politics, "predicts" in *Pravda* an American economic crisis.

**December 18, 1946**
Violent fighting breaks out in French Indo-China between the French and Vietnam rebel forces.

The Chinese Communist general. Chou En-lai in Yenan predicts final Communist victory in China.

**December 31, 1946**
In an article in *Culture and Life (Kultura y Zhizn)* the Soviets claim "single-handed victory" in World War II.

**1947**
According to the official Communist claims, there are approximately 18,000,000 organized Communists in the world.

**January 1, 1947**
Poland introduces a Three Year Plan for the reconstruction of the devastated country.

**January 10, 1947**
Stalin receives Lord Montgomery.

**January 19, 1947**
In the Polish elections, under Communist terror, the Communist Bloc wins 394 seats of 444. America protests this violation of previous treaties: Yalta and Potsdam. Molotov defends Poland which is under full Soviet and Communist control.

**January 25, 1947**
Peace treaties are signed in Paris with Italy, Rumania, Finland, Bulgaria, and Hungary.

**February 23, 1947**
Bela Kovacs, an Hungarian anti-Communist politician is arrested by the Communists.

**February 26, 1947**
It is stated that there are 6,000,000 C.P. members in the Soviet Union; Italy has second place with some 2,200,000; France is third with 1,300,000.

**March 6, 1947**
The U.S. Government protests against Soviet and Communist policies in Hungary.

Poland and U.S.S.R. conclude extensive trade and financial agreements.

**March 10 – April 24, 1947**
The Council of Foreign Ministers (Four Powers) meets in Moscow. The tensions between America and the Soviet Union are steadily rising.

**March 12, 1947**
Reflecting these tensions is also the announcement on this day of the "Truman Doctrine" to halt the expansion of Communism in Greece and Turkey. President Truman requests Congress to grant huge military and economic aid to the two countries (which are also very important for our military strategy).

**March 25, 1947**
The U.S. State Department publishes some undisclosed stipulations of the treaties of Teheran, Yalta, and Potsdam.

**April 13, 1947**
Independent India and the United States establish diplomatic relations.

**April 18, 1947**
Msgr. Josef Tiso, the former President of Slovakia (1939-1945), is executed in Bratislava. President Beneš rejected pleas for clemency.

**May 20, 1947**
Radio Tirana announces discovery of an anti-Communist plot. There are purges in the Albanian C.P.

**May 22, 1947**
President Truman signs Greek-Turkish aid bill.

**May 26, 1947**
The Supreme Soviet decrees abolishment of capital punishment. For crimes hitherto punishable by death, the penalty will be 25 years in prison. (In January 1950 the death penalty was reinstated.)

**May 31, 1947**
The Sovietization of Hungary is complete. The anti-Communist Premier Ferencz Nagy was abroad and forced to resign.

**June 5, 1947**
U.S. Secretary of State George Marshall speaking at Harvard University suggests a massive plan to aid

Europe. This will become known as the Marshall Plan or the European Recovery Act.

**June 15, 1947**
The Russians reject the American demand to investigate the overthrow of the Nagy coalition government in Hungary.

**June 16, 1947**
*Pravda* denounces the Marshall Plan as an American device to control Europe.

**June 30, 1947**
The U.N.R.R.A. ceases its activities; it had helped many nations after the war and saved many millions of people from starvation.

**July 9, 1947**
A force of several thousand Greek Communist guerillas enters Greece from Albania and takes positions in the mountains of northern Greece. The Greek government takes action against them.

Stalin tells the Czech leaders not to accept the American invitation to go to Paris to participate in the Conference on European Recovery. (Originally on the 4th of July the Czechoslovak Council of Ministers had accepted the invitation.) Premier Gottwald and Foreign Minister J. Masaryk came from Moscow and thus under Soviet pressure the Czechs had to refuse the benefits of the Marshall Plan.

**July 12, 1947**
Representatives of sixteen European countries meet in Paris to discuss the Marshall Plan. The U.S.S.R. refuses to participate.

**July 20 – August 17, 1947**
Communist-sponsored First World Youth Festival meets in Prague. Propaganda slogans denounce war, colonialism and "Western Imperialism."

**August 15, 1947**
India becomes independent.

**August 16, 1947**
Nikola Petkov, the leader of the Bulgarian Agrarian Party, is sentenced to death on trumped-up charges and subsequently executed. The Bulgarian Communists thus got rid of a powerful enemy. Thousands of anti-Communists have been liquidated or imprisoned.

The Communist General Markos (Vafiades) establishes a "Free Government" in the mountains of Greece.

**August 31, 1947**
The C.P. of Hungary receives a majority in the Communist-style elections. The Communists have 1,112,000 votes.

**September 21 – 28, 1947**
The Communist Information Bureau—Cominform—is founded during a secret conclave in Poland. Main reports were given by A. A. Zhdanov and W. Gomulka. The purpose of the Bureau is to coordinate the activities of the Communist Parties. The headquarters will be in Belgrade. The members are C.P. of France, Italy, Poland, Czechoslovakia, Hungary, Rumania, Bulgaria, and the Soviet Union.

**September 27, 1947**
The Czechoslovak Social Democratic Party merges—under pressure—with the C.P.

**October 5, 1947**
The Soviets officially announce the formation of the Cominform.

**October 9, 1947**
The Rumanian Socialists merge with the Communists.

**October 22, 1947**
*Pravda* publishes Zhdanov's article on the formation of the Cominform. Zhdanov is a member of the Politburo and a secretary of the Central Committee of the C.P.S.U.

**November 25 – December 15, 1947**
The Fifth Session of the Council of Foreign Ministers is held in London.

**December 4, 1947**
Bulgaria adopts a Communist Constitution.

**December 10, 1947**
Czechs and Soviets sign a 5-year trade agreement.

**December 29, 1947**
H. A. Wallace, the editor of the *New Republic* and the founder of the Progressive Citizens of America, announces he would run for presidency on a third-party ticket. Observers predict he would poll from

*General Marshall* – Keystone

5,000,000 to 8,000,000 votes in 1948 elections. Wallace is very popular among various leftist organizations.

**December 30, 1947**
The monarchy is overthrown in Rumania. King Michael, unable to get the support of the West, is forced to abdicate. Rumania becomes a "People's Republic."

**1948**
The Polish Workers' Party (the Communists) numbers 820,000 members. There are some 700,000 Communists in Hungary.

**January 1, 1948**
The Benelux Customs Union is formed; this is the beginning of the European federation under democratic leadership.

The Cominform denounces the American plans in Europe, especially the Marshall Plan which is rebuilding and saving Western Europe. While denouncing the American policies as imperialistic, the U.S.S.R. treats her own "Satellites" in Europe as colonies and exploits them in more than one way. The Russian hegemony is particularly detested by Yugoslav Communists who feel they had won the victory without Russian help.

**January 7, 1948**
Anglo-Soviet trade agreement is made public.

**January 16, 1948**
Bulgarian Premier Georgi Dimitrov, the Rumanian Premier Petru Groza and his foreign minister Ana Pauker, conclude a treaty of alliance and friendship.

**January 17, 1948**
The U.N. Balkan Committee accuses Albania of aiding the Greek Communist partisans.

**January 21, 1948**
Mikhail Suslov, the Soviet propaganda chief, denounces—during the observance of the 24th anniversary of Lenin's death—the "American imperialists and their junior English partners."

**January 25, 1948**
Nikita S. Khrushchev, secretary of the Ukrainian C.P., calls for merciless suppression of the Ukrainian nationalists.

**January 26, 1948**
Poland and the Soviet Union conclude a five-year trade agreement.

**January 28, 1948**
*Pravda* denounces the plan of Georgi Dimitrov for a Balkan federation. Stalin feels that such a federation would resist his schemes in the Balkans. Tito and Dimitrov work together and here lies one of the reasons for disagreement between Moscow and Tito.

**February 4, 1948**
Rumania and the Soviet Union sign a treaty of friendship and mutual cooperation. Rumania is a docile Soviet "Satellite."

**February 10, 1948**
Stalin warns Yugoslavia and Bulgaria against their plans for a Balkan federation.

**February 16, 1948**
A North Korean "Democratic People's Republic" is formed under Soviet sponsorship.

**February 18, 1948**
Hungary and the Soviet Union conclude a mutual defense pact.

**February 19, 1948**
Valerian Zorin, the Soviet Deputy Foreign Minister, arrives in Prague to supervise the Communist take-over.

**February 21 – 24, 1948**
The Rumanian Workers' Party (Communists) holds its First Congress.

**February 22, 1948**
Marshal Nikolai A. Bulganin speaking at the celebration of the 30th anniversary of the founding of the Red Army warns that the Soviet Union would be ready against any threats from "Western Imperialists." In the same spirit the *Izvestia* on the same day praises the "single-handed" Soviet victory in World War II.

**February 25, 1948**
The Communists take over the government in Czechoslovakia. Under pressure, Beneš calls Gottwald to form a new cabinet. The Communists have 12 leading posts, Jan Masaryk remains minister for foreign affairs. This is the last coalition government overthrown by the C.P. in East Europe.

**February 26, 1948**
The governments of America, Britain and France denounce in a joint statement the Communist coup in Prague.

**March 8, 1948**
The Hungarian Social Democratic Party joins the C.P.

**March 13, 1948**
The Austrian Chancellor L. Figl states that the Communists are too weak to overthrow his government. Austria is occupied by the four war-time Allies. The C.P. has most of its members in the Soviet Zone of occupation.

**March 17, 1948**
Speaking before a joint session of the Congress, President Truman charges that "the Soviet Union and its agents have destroyed the independence and democratic character of a whole series of nations in eastern and central Europe."

**March 18, 1948**
Bulgaria and the U.S.S.R. conclude a 20-years mutual defense pact.

Polish Socialists merge with the Communists.

**March 23, 1948**
A.A. Gromyko, the Soviet Deputy Foreign Minister, denounces the U.N. proposal to investigate the Communist coup in Prague.

**March 28, 1948**
In Rumanian elections the Communist-controlled People's Democratic Front gets over 90 per cent of 7,700,000 votes cast.

**April 6, 1948**
Finland and the U.S.S.R. sign a 10-year mutual defense and friendship treaty.

**April 19, 1948**
Communist-organized riots break out in Bogota, the capital of Colombia, to disrupt the Ninth Conference of the American States. Participating in the riots was the young Cuban revolutionary Fidel Castro.

The Greek government estimates that the Communist partisans have lost some 10,000 men, but still their strength increased from 12,000 to about 30,000.

**April 16, 1948**
The Greek government undertakes a spring offensive against Communist forces which are supported by Albania, Bulgaria and Yugoslavia.

**April 23, 1948**
Czechoslovakia and Bulgaria conclude a pact of mutual defense.

**May 1, 1948**
Cominform denounces the American aid to Greece.

**May 9, 1948**
Czechoslovakia adopts new constitution modeled after that of the U.S.S.R.

**May 10, 1948**
Jan Masaryk is found dead; the official statement maintains he committed suicide, while the Western press suspects murder by Communists.

**May 11, 1948**
Henry Wallace, former Vice-President of the United States, Secretary of Agriculture under Roosevelt and Truman's Secretary of Commerce sends an open letter to Stalin offering proposals for improving the American-Soviet relations. Stalin replies on May 17. Wallace thinks that Stalin's letter is "a most important document."

**May 20, 1948**
British Foreign Secretary, Ernest Bevin declares Soviet Government could end the Greek Civil War by "the lift of a finger" and thus ease world tensions.

**May 29, 1948**
Bulgaria and Poland conclude a 20-year treaty of friendship and mutual assistance.

**May 31, 1948**
In Czechoslovak elections the Communists win 89 per cent of the entire vote.

**June 7, 1948**
President E. Beneš of Czechoslovakia resigns his office.

**June 12, 1948**
The Hungarian Communists open their Fourth Party Congress. On the 14th they officially announce, and complete, the merger of the Social Democratic Party with the C.P.

**June 14, 1948**
The Communist leader Klement Gottwald becomes President of Czechoslovakia.

**June 16, 1948**
Hungarian parliament adopts a bill nationalizing all Catholic schools.

**June 17, 1948**
It is announced that the Czechoslovak C.P. numbers 1,750,000 members.

**June 19, 1948**
The Soviet blockade of Berlin starts and develops into a general blockade between eastern and western zones. This is a serious test of Western strength in the "Cold War".

*U.S. Secretary of State George Marshall and Foreign Minister Ernest Bevin* – Radio Times

**June 24, 1948**
The Communist East European foreign ministers meet to discuss the German question. While they are meeting in Warsaw, the Americans and British fly in many tons of food and fuel to help West Berlin.

**June 28, 1948**
The Czech Communist newspaper *Rude Pravo* announces in a 3,000-word statement issued officially by Cominform that Yugoslav Communist Party was expelled from membership in Cominform. The causes of this break between Moscow and Tito were many. Tito and his C.P.Y. were shocked by this expulsion. They defended themselves against charges of deviationism. The C.P.Y. strive for reconciliation, but Stalin rejected it. Stalin's decision to expell the C.P.Y. in the long run contributed to disunity of international Communism. The "Schism" of Belgrade will have lasting effects on many C.P.

**July 1948**
The Central Committee of the Albanian C.P. in a series of statements condemns the Yugoslav Communists as "traitors" and "Trotskyites."

**July 1 – 2, 1948**
The Communist-controlled Popular Democratic Union of Finland is defeated in the elections; the strongest party are the Agrarians. Finland is far from being a Soviet "Satellite."

**July 3, 1948**
By now eight other Communist parties rebuke and denounce Tito and his party.

Cominform headquarters move from Belgrade to Bucharest.

**July 14, 1948**
Attempted assassination of P. Togliatti takes place in Italy.

**July 21 – 28, 1948**
The Fifth Congress of the Yugoslav C.P., the first in twenty years, convenes in Belgrade in the midst of the crisis with Cominform. Over 2,300 delegates represent some 468,000 party members. The Congress produces the new program and statutes of the C.P. Tito and the leading Yugoslav Communists reject the accusations of the Cominform. Despite of the challenge by "Cominformists" within the C.P.Y. Tito maintains strong control of the party. Thousands of pro-Cominform Communists are sent to prison.

**August 1, 1948**
Elizabeth Bentley, a former Communist, reveals in one of hearings before the House Committee on Un-American Activities details on Communist activities in Washington.

**August 8, 1948**
T. D. Lysenko, President of the Lenin All-Union Academy of Agricultural Sciences, denounces Mendelian laws of genetics as an "alien bourgeois biology." Environment is more important than heredity maintain Soviet scholars.

**August 8 – 14, 1948**
The Communist-sponsored International Youth Conference is held in Warsaw. 446 delegates represent 46 different countries, many in Africa and Asia to which the Communists now devote a lot of attention.

**August 19, 1948**
V. M. Molotov denounces the formation of the (South) Korean Democratic Republic supported by America.

The Greek government announces significant victories in the war against Communist guerillas.

**August 20, 1948**
The U.N. Balkan Committee condemns the Albanian, Bulgarian and Yugoslav aid to Greek Communist partisans.

**August 29 – September 3, 1948**
The C.P. of Finland holds its Eighth Congress.

**August 31, 1948**
Andrei A. Zhdanov, the acknowledged leader of Cominform, dies suddenly under mysterious conditions at the age of 52. Zhdanov was at the height of his power. He was a virtual dictator of literature and arts in the Soviet Union.

**September 3, 1948**
E. Beneš is dead and mourned by millions of his countrymen.

**September 5, 1948**
There is an open split in the Polish C.P. Vice-Premier and the Secretary General of the Party Wladislaw Gomulka is dismissed as party secretary because he sided with Tito. The new Party secretary is B. Bierut.

**September 19, 1948**

The Russians announce withdrawal of their troops from North Korea.

**September 25, 1948**

A. Y. Vyshinsky, the Soviet Deputy Foreign Minister, states in the U.N. Assembly that America and the West plan an attack on the Soviet Union.

**September 26, 1948**

Purges of pro-Titoist elements are reported in the Albanian C.P.

Henry A. Wallace addresses the American Slav Congress. The congress endorses him for the presidency on the Progressive Party ticket. (In May of 1948 the American Slav Congress was branded by U.S. authorities as "a Moscow-inspired and directed federation of Communist-dominated organizations.")

**October 1, 1948**

The Communists celebrate the tenth anniversary of Stalin's book, *Short Course of the History of the C.P.S.U.*

**October 3, 1948**

The Rumanian Catholic Church of Byzantine Rite (the Uniates) with a membership of some 1,300,000 is forced to sever ties with the Vatican and to join the Rumanian Orthodox Church.

**October 15 – 16, 1948**

The People's Republic of North Korea is recognized by the U.S.S.R. and several other Communist states.

**October 15, 1948**

The war between the Chinese Communists and Chiang Kai-shek is raging. As Chinchow falls Chiang loses about 100,000 men.

**October 18, 1948**

The Russians begin arming the East German People's Police (Volkspolizei, Vopos); by now some 200,000 Communists are armed.

**October 30, 1948**

Yugoslavia claims that some 3,000 Soviet technicians, engineers and skilled people are working in Albania.

*Eduard Beneš* – Radio Times

**November 1, 1948**
Mukden in Manchuria is taken by Chinese Communists. Chiang Kai-shek loses 500,000 men.

**November 2, 1948**
In the most surprising election in American history, Truman is victorious with over 24,000,000 votes. Wallace gets only 1,156,000.

**November 7, 1948**
On the anniversary of the Bolshevik Revolution Molotov "predicts" the doom of Capitalism.

At the Battle of Hwai-Hai the Chinese Nationalists lose some 500,000 soldiers.

**November 11, 1948**
The International Military Tribunal for the Far East sentences seven leading Japanese politicians to death by hanging. (They were executed on December 23, 1948.)

**November 22, 1948**
The American Government accuses Bulgaria for violation of the peace treaties by liquidating all non-Communist parties.

**November 27, 1948**
Matyas Rakosi, Deputy Premier and the Secretary General of the C.P., announces collectivization of agriculture and industry in Hungary.

**December 18 – 26, 1948**
The Bulgarian Workers' Party holds its Fifth Congress in Sofia. It changes its name to the Communist Party of Bulgaria.

**December 24, 1948**
According to Soviet estimates, there are some 23,000,000 organized Communists in the world.

**December 27, 1948**
Joseph Cardinal Mindszenty is arrested in Hungary by the Communists.

**December 31, 1948**
Moscow and Belgrade announce a decrease in trade on account of Cominform dispute.

**January 1, 1949**
Bulgaria starts its First Five-Year Plan.

**January 8, 1949**
The Chinese Nationalists appeal to the Four Powers to mediate between them and Mao Tse-tung.

**January 15, 1949**
The Chinese Communists take Tientsin. While their armies are taking over China, some elements in America call them "agricultural reformers."

**January 17, 1949**
The longest trial in American history starts in the Federal District Court in New York City. The defendants—twelve leading American Communists—are charged with conspiracy to overthrow by force the U.S. Government. (The trial will last until October 14.)

**January 18, 1949**
The Soviet Government rejects Chiang's plea for mediation.

**January 21, 1949**
W. Gomulka is removed as Vice-Premier of Poland.

*Pravda* writes that coexistence between America and the Soviet Union is still possible.

**January 25, 1949**
A Council for Mutual Economic Assistance, the COMECON, of six East European states is organized under the initiative of the Soviet Union. This is a counterpart of the West European Common Market. However, in due time, many East European Communists will complain that their countries are economically exploited by the Russians.

**January 29, 1949**
Moscow denounces the Western European Union, the N.A.T.O. and the Pan-American Union as enemies of the U.S.S.R.

**January 30 – 31, 1949**
Moscow and Washington issue statements regarding a possible meeting of Stalin and Truman. Stalin invites Truman to the Soviet Union. Truman invites Stalin to Washington.

**January 31, 1949**
Peking, the ancient capital of China, is taken by victorious Chinese Communists. Mao boasts that one of the reasons for the tremendous success of his Red Army is the fact that they never kill any prisoners of war. They "re-educate" them.

**February 1, 1949**
M. Rakosi formally proclaims Hungary a "People's Republic."

**February 4, 1949**
The Soviet Politbureau denounces N.A.T.O. as an aggressive alliance against all Communist states.

**February 8, 1949**
In a Communist-style trial, Cardinal Mindszenty, the Primate of Hungary, receives the life sentence.

**February 22, 1949**
Albania joins the COMECON.

**February 22, 1949**
Marshal K. K. Rokossovsky arrives in Warsaw for a visit. On the same day, Marshal N. A. Bulganin, the Soviet Defense Minister, warns the Soviet peoples in a speech of American "aggression."

**March 1, 1949**
Hungary forbids the Zionist movement. In all Communist East European countries there is still a great deal of anti-Semitism.

**March 2, 1949**
The New York Times reports that the Soviet Government rejected British and American proposal to admit an international commission to inspect the labor camps. Millions of people have gone through Stalin's concentration camps.

**March 4, 1969**
Vyshinsky succeeds Molotov as the Minister for Foreign Affairs. He will hold the position until 1953.

**March 5, 1949**
Stalin receives a delegation from North Korea.

**March 19, 1949**
The People's Council in East Germany (under Soviet occupation) approves draft of a Constitution for a "Democratic German Republic."

**March 21, 1949**
The U.S.S.R. accuses Finland of pro-Western orientation.

**March 23, 1949**
Albanian delegation headed by Enver Hoxha, who is a devoted Stalinist, signs a trade agreement in Moscow.

**March 24, 1949**
Marshal A. M. Vasilevsky replaces Bulganin as the new Soviet Minister of Defense.

**April 4, 1949**
The North Atlantic Treaty Organization, the N.A.T.O.—in the making for some time—is founded in Washington. Its purpose is to defend the free European countries against the armed aggression by Communism. The original agreement was signed by: United States, Great Britain, France, Canada, Belgium, the Netherlands, Luxemburg, Italy, Portugal, Denmark, Iceland, and Norway.

**April 9, 1949**
Isolated from the Communist camp, Tito makes overtures to the West. He declares he would like to trade with the West.

**April 23, 1949**
Nanking in China falls to the Communists without struggle. (In May the Communists will return to Shanghai from which they had been expelled in 1927.)

**May 5, 1949**
U.S.S.R., Great Britain and the United States make an agreement about ending the Berlin Blockade on the 12th of May.

**May 8, 1949**
A final draft for a constitution of a West German Federal Republic is adopted in Bonn.

**May 12, 1949**
The Berlin Blockade ends after 328 days. This is an American victory in the "Cold War" with the Soviet Union.

**May 23, 1949**
The Federal Republic of Germany (in West Germany) comes into existence. Its capital is Bonn.

**May 23 — June 20, 1949**
The Sixth Session of the Council of Foreign Ministers meets in Paris.

**May 25 — 29, 1949**
Czechoslovak Communists hold their Ninth Congress.

**June 2, 1949**
Tito protests in Moscow against the Soviet support of

the Cominformists active in overthrowing his regime. Moscow replies it will continue to support these elements.

**June 13, 1949**
General D. MacArthur assails the Soviet Union's role in inciting the disorders in Japan.

**June 16, 1949**
A wholesale purge of the "Titoists" starts in Hungary. Laszlo Rajk, the Minister for Foreign Affairs, is among those arrested.

**June 25, 1949**
Traicho Kostov, an old Communist and Bulgarian Deputy Premier, and ten other leading Communists are arrested as pro-Titoists. Kostov is sentenced to death as "deviationist" and executed December 16, 1949.

**June 28, 1949**
Rumanian Communists arrest the last two of five Roman Catholic bishops.

**July 21, 1949**
Georgi Dimitrov, the Communist Premier of Bulgaria, dies in Moscow, reportedly of diabetes.

**July 13, 1949**
Pope Pius XII in an official statement forbids all Catholics to join the Communist Party under penalty of excommunication.

**July 20, 1949**
The Soviets protest Italy's joining the N.A.T.O. as a violation of the peace treaties.

**July 31, 1949**
Moscow concludes a trade agreement with the still existing Manchuria.

**August 7, 1949**
Hungary adopts a new Constitution modeled after that of the Soviet Union.

**August 23, 1949**
Enver Hoxha, the Communist leader of Albania, charges Yugoslavia wanted to annex Albania and make it its seventh republic.

**September 8, 1949**
American Export-Import Bank grants $20 million loan to Yugoslavia.

**September 21, 1949**
Six hundred members of the People's Political Consultative Conference meet in Peiping (Peking). They produce three basic documents of the Chinese People's Republic: the Common Program; the Organic Law of the Central People's Government; and the Organic Law of the People's Political Consultative Conference. Madame Sun Yet-sen was one of the participants.

**September 24, 1949**
Laszlo Rajk and four other leading Hungarian Communists are sentenced to death and subsequently executed as anti-Stalinists.

**September 24, 1949**
It is learned in the West that an atomic explosion took place in the Soviet Union.

**September 29, 1949**
The Soviet Union cancels the Mutual Aid and Friendship Treaty with Yugoslavia. The Soviets and their docile "Satellites" put a lot of pressure on Yugoslavia, one of the reasons why America wants to help Tito to keep him "independent of Moscow."

**October 1, 1949**
Mao establishes the "People's Republic of China"; this is a great victory for Communism. Mao is the Chairman of Communist China.

**October 7, 1949**
The Soviet Union is the first state to recognize Communist China.

The German Democratic Republic, East Germany, becomes a Soviet "Satellite". A large contingent of Soviet troops remains there. All East European countries are opposed to unification of Germany.

**October 14, 1949**
After a long trial (since January 17) in New York City's Federal District Court, the jury finds all 12 Communists guilty as charged. Ten of them receive sentence to five years in prison and fines of $10,000 each.

The Chinese Red Army takes the important city of Canton in Southern China.

**October 17, 1949**
The Soviet Union establishes diplomatic relations with East Germany.

**October 17, 1949**
The Greek Civil War ends with a decisive defeat of the Communists. By now Tito refused to aid the Greek Communist partisans, a factor that helped to determine their defeat. This is a victory for America and the "Truman Doctrine." For all practical purposes Greece is saved from Communism.

**November 3, 1949**
By easing ban on shipments to Yugoslavia, America makes it possible to render aid to Communist Yugoslavia.

**November 6, 1949**
G. M. Malenkov stresses the "Peace" propaganda theme in his report to the Moscow Party members celebrating the 32nd anniversary of the Bolshevik Revolution.

**November 7, 1949**
Marshal K. K. Rokossovsky becomes a Polish citizen, Polish Minister of Defense, and a Marshal of the Polish Army. This is the high point of the Polish subjugation to Moscow.

**November 12, 1949**
Yugoslavia breaks off the Friendship Pact with Albania.

**November 14, 1949**
In radical purges of the Polish C.P. Gomulka is expelled from the Party and imprisoned as "Titoist."

**December 16, 1949**
Mao Tse-tung, President of Communist China, arrives in Moscow. He is warmly received by Stalin and other Soviet leaders.

**December 18, 1949**
N. S. Khrushchev becomes the Secretary of the Central Committee of the C.P.S.U.

**December 21, 1949**
Stalin celebrates his 70th birthday in presence of many foreign dignitaries including Mao Tse-tung.
Malenkov declares in *Pravda* that Communism and Capitalism can coexist.

**December 30, 1949**
The Moscow radio speaks of great unemployment in America and predicts "death of Capitalism."

**January 7, 1950**
The Soviet army paper, the *Red Star,* attacks Truman's the State of the Union Message.

**January 11, 1950**
Albania decides to erect a great monument to Stalin in Tirana.

**January 12, 1950**
The U.S.S.R. restores the capital punishment for "serious crimes."

**January 21, 1950**
Alger Hiss, an accused Communist high official in the State Department, is convicted of perjury on the evidence produced by Whitaker Chambers, a former Soviet agent. There were wholesale investigations of many employees of the U.S. Government and a real "Red Scare" swept the country when the accusations were raised that the Anglo-American Soviet agents betrayed atomic secrets to the Soviets.

**January 24, 1950**
The Soviet Union recognizes the new independent state of Indonesia.

**January 31, 1950**
The Soviet Union recognizes Ho Chi Minh's Democratic Republic of Vietnam. France protests the recognition.

**February 1, 1950**
Vulko Chervenkov, former Vice Premier and Secretary General of the Bulgarian C.P., becomes the Premier of Bulgaria.

The U.S. Air Force Secretary W. Stuart Symington, states the Soviets and their "Satellites" have "the world's largest ground army, air force, and undersea fleet."

**February 3, 1950**
The Communist Vietnamese government receives recognition from the East European Communist governments.

Dr. Klaus Fuchs, the top British atomic scientist, is arrested in London as a Soviet spy.

**February 14, 1950**
Soviet Union and Mao's China conclude a 30-year friendship and mutual assistance pact. The Soviet troops are evacuating Port Arthur. Both sides guarantee the independence of Mongolian Republic.

**February 16, 1950**
The Secretary of State Dean Acheson calls for "total diplomacy" to win the Cold War.

**February 16, 1950**
The Rumanian C.P. reports the purge of some 180,000 members, about 18 per cent of the total membership.

**February 20, 1950**
In the midst of the Second Red Scare in America, Senator Joseph R. McCarthy renews his charge that 57 Communists work for the State Department. There were accusations that during the war and after it many leftist elements had infiltrated all departments of the U.S. Government. As a result of this trend the FBI makes some 14,000 full-scale investigations of doubtful cases; over 2,000 employees resign; and 212 are dismissed. It is obvious from the evidence that the most important Communist cell in Washington during the New Deal era was the so-called "Ware Group" of which A. Hiss was a member. McCarthy also accused Owen Lattimore of the Johns Hopkins University in Baltimore, an expert on the Far East, as the head of "the espionage ring in the State Department." The FBI cleared him of this charge.

**February 21, 1950**
America breaks off diplomatic relations with Communist Bulgaria.

**February 21, 1950**
In the purges of the Bulgarian C.P. the strict Stalinists eliminate V. Chervenkov and many other followers of the late Georgi Dimitrov.

**February 24, 1950**
Dean Acheson, American Secretary of State, states that Bulgaria, Rumania and Hungary "cut the people of Eastern Europe off from the free world and deprived them of all hope."

**March 1, 1950**
Dr. Klaus Fuchs receives a 14-year sentence in London for passing atomic secrets to Russia. He had collaborators in America.

**March 5, 1950**
Lieutenant General Taras Chuprynka, the commander of the Ukrainian Insurgent Army (the U.P.A.), is killed in a surprise attack by the Soviet Security Police in the Western Ukraine. The highest number of the U.P.A. membership was about 200,000.

**March 10, 1950**
Patriarch Alexei of the Russian Orthodox Church, now in good relations with the Soviet government, appeals to all Orthodox Church leaders to join in the "defense of peace." All Orthodox Churches in Eastern Europe collaborate with the Communist regime.

**March 14, 1950**
The foreign minister of Czechoslovakia, Vladimir Clementis, an old-time Communist, is replaced in office by Vice Premier, Viliam Siroky. Both are Slovaks. The unsolved question of the Czech-Slovak relations is one of the main problems in Czechoslovakia. The Slovaks feel that they are oppressed by Prague centralism. The Slovaks are also staunchly Catholic and oppose the persecution of the Catholic Church.

**March 16, 1950**
Czechoslovakia breaks off diplomatic relations with the Vatican.

**April 14, 1950**
The Italian C.P. under the dynamic leadership of Palmiro Togliatti claims a membership of some 2,532,000. His right hand is L. Longo, a former veteran of the Spanish Civil War and educated in the Soviet Union for his important role as successor of Togliatti.

**April 22, 1950**
Vatican reports that between 800,000 and 1,000,000 Lithuanians, Latvians and Estonians have been deported by the Russians into the interior of the Soviet Union.

**April 22, 1950**
The United States pledges its firm resistance to any Communist attempt to seize West Berlin.

**May 10, 1950**
Eugene Varga, the leading Soviet economist, predicts again in the *Pravda* a serious economic crisis in America. At the same time all Communist countries are having such crises.

**May 11, 1950**
The Polish Communists elect Marshal K. K. Rokossovsky to their Politbureau.

**May 24, 1950**
The Soviets publish statistics on their press publications. The daily newspaper circulation is 33.5 million with 7,700 dailies. Both *Pravda* and *Izvestia* claim a daily circulation of more than a million each.

Clementis is denounced by the Czech Communists as a "bourgeois nationalist deviationist."

**May 29, 1950**
The Albanian C.P. wins 98 per cent of the total vote in the national election.

**May 31, 1950**
Tito declares in a speech he would remain neutral between the East and the West.

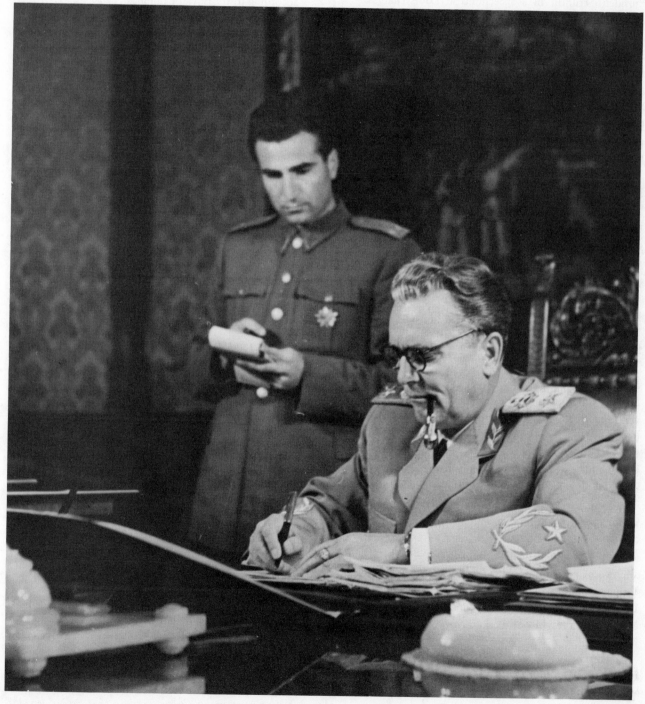

*Josip Tito working at a desk in his private villa situated outside Belgrade.  On the left is secretary Lieut-Colonal Branco Vucinich who is deputy-commander of the Marshal's personal guard.* — Radio Times

**June 6, 1950**
Poland and East Germany conclude an agreement recognizing the Oder-Neisse Line as a definitive boundary between Poland and Germany.

**June 8, 1950**
Rumania launches its First Five Year Plan.

**June 10, 1950**
President Truman in a speech in St. Louis charges that the Russians prepare for war.

**June 23, 1950**
East Germany and Czechoslovakia agree on the final settlement of the Sudeten Problem. Over 3,000,000 Sudeten Germans had already been expelled to *West* Germany where they were incorporated into the economy. The West German government has a different view on the same problem.

**June 25, 1950**
The Cold War becomes a real "hot" war. At 5 a.m. the North Korean Communist troops begin invasion of South Korea. The U.S. troops are completely surprised. The U.N. declare this attack a breach of peace. The invasion of South Korea was prepared by the North Korean Communist leader Kim Il Sung, the organizer of the so-called Fatherland Unification Democratic Front. The invasion has been prepared for at least a year.

**June 26, 1950**
President Truman orders American military intervention in Korea. All Communist countries then denounce the Americans as "aggressors" in this war. In the serious conflict the Russians did not lose one single soldier. China will get involved and the Americans will eventually lose over 33,000 killed soldiers. The Korean War marks a landmark in our relations with International Communism.

After the beginning of this agonizing war – for which we were not quite ready – Kim Il Sung, the Communist boss of N. Korea, became the Supreme Commander of the "Korean People's Liberation Army" and a Marshal of the Red Army.

**July 5, 1950**
Msgr. G. P. O'Hara, Bishop of Savannah, the last Vatican diplomat behind the Iron Curtain (at this time) is expelled from Rumania. Everywhere the Communists are persecuting the Catholic Church, Judaism and Islam as a threat to their regime.

**July 7, 1950**
Premier E. Hoxha of Albania also assumes the offices of the Ministries of Foreign Affairs and Defense.

**July 12–21, 1950**
Czechoslovakia reorganizes army and the penal codes according to the Soviet examples.

**July 17, 1950**
Julius Rosenberg is arrested as a Soviet spy. (Before him Harry Gold was arrested for the same reason on May 23, 1950; he pleaded guilty on July 20. On June 16, 1950 David Greenglass was arrested and indicted on July 6.) Rosenberg is indicted on August 17. His wife Ethel is arrested on August 11, 1950 and indicted on August 17.

**July 24, 1950**
The Third Party Congress of the East German Socialist Unity Party (Communists) is held in East Berlin.

**July 27, 1950**
The Communist forces that swept down the Korean Peninsula are within fifty miles of Pusan.

**August 1, 1950**
The first 35 American military advisers arrive in South Vietnam.

**August 1, 1950**
Stalin stresses in a statement the need for a "stronger Russia" to prevent being crushed by a "capitalist encirclement."

**August 8, 1950**
The Russian Orthodox Church leaders issue a world-wide appeal for preventing the "war preparations."

**August 17, 1950**
Indonesia, a former colony of Netherlands, that first declared independence under the Japanese occupation during World War II, declares its final independence under President Sukarno. This country is a highly potential ground for Communism.

**August 22, 1950**
Jacob A. Malik, the Soviet representative at the U.N., accuses the United States as aggressor in Korea.

**August 24, 1950**
Russian Orthodox Church and the Presidium of the Soviet Academy appeal to the U.N. Security Council to "stop aggression in Korea." They urge withdrawal of all foreign troops. (As of July 8, the Commander of all U.N. Forces in Korea was General Douglas MacArthur. The war is now in a critical stage. On August 18 the Communist drive on Pusan was finally stopped.)

**August 25, 1950**
The report by the U.S. House Foreign Affairs Committee stresses the expansion of the Soviet Union. By 1950 the Soviet domination had extended to *13,415,700 sq. miles (including 8,591,700 sq. m. of the U.S.S.R.), or about 25 per cent of the world's land and 32 per cent of its people.*

**September 12–19, 1950**
The Conference of Western Foreign Ministers, held in New York, agrees to rearm West Germany to strengthen the defense of Western Europe against the Soviet threat.

**September 14, 1950**
Plans for improvements in communications and irrigation of the Soviet Union are made public.

**September 18, 1950**
The U.S. Department of Defense releases a report — after extensive hearings — about the Katyn Forest Massacres. It charges that some 11,000 Polish army officers were massacred by the Soviet authorities near Smolensk.

**September 25, 1950**
The Americans are in Seoul, South Korea. The Communist forces are defeated.

**September 29, 1950**
The German Democratic Republic (East Germany) joins the COMECON.

**October 4–5, 1950**
Greece and Turkey accept invitation to join the N.A.T.O. They will become members in 1952.

**October 7, 1950**
The U.N. forces in Korea cross the 38th parallel and invade Communist North Korea.

**October 11–12, 1950**
The U.N. Balkan Committee charges that Poland and Albania still support the Greek Communist partisans.

**October 20–21, 1950**
The conference of East European foreign ministers convenes in Prague and denounces remilitarization of West Germany. Molotov represents the U.S.S.R.

**November 3, 1950**
Moscow note denounces remilitarization of West Germany and demands that the Council of Foreign Ministers meet to discuss the future of Germany.

**November 6, 1950**
Marshal Bulganin boasts in a speech of Soviet achievements in atomic energy.

**November 6, 1950**
General MacArthur reports the Chinese Communist intervention in Korea.

**November 15, 1950**
Harry Gold reveals that for eleven years he had spied for the Russians. He and seven other spies had been arrested by American authorities.

**December 3, 1950**
Chancellor Konrad Adenauer of West Germany warns America that the Soviet Union wants to conquer Europe.

**December 16, 1950**
President Truman warns of Communist imperialism in Europe and Asia.

**December 29, 1950**
President Truman signs aid bill for Yugoslavia; Tito will receive $38 million from the funds of the Marshall Plan.

**December 31, 1950**
Vatican claims that the Czechoslovak authorities had arrested over 1,000 Catholic priests.

**December 31, 1950**
Karl Renner, the Socialist President of Austria, is dead.

**January 2, 1951**
The Russians state they possess the atomic bomb. The armament race is increasing.

**January 15, 1951**
Negotiations with the Soviets about their debts through the Lend Lease are reopened in Washington. (The Russians had received well over 11 billion dollars worth of Lend Lease during the last war.)

**January 26, 1951**
America bans the import of the Soviet crab meat on grounds that it is produced by "forced, convict, and indentured labor."

**January 31, 1951**
The Soviet Government requests an indefinite postponement of the Lend-Lease settlement negotiations.

**February 3–4, 1951**
Leaders of the Scandinavian Communist Parties (Denmark, Norway, Sweden, and Finland) meet in Helsinki. Communism was never a serious threat to the Scandinavian area.

**February 4, 1951**
The Soviet war hero, Marshal Ivan Koniev, is reported as the commander of the armies in the "Satellite" area.

**February 7, 1951**
The U.S. Secretary of State Dean Acheson reports military buildup in the Soviet-dominated East Europe.

America demands that the Soviet Government return 672 Lend-Lease naval and merchant ships given to the Russians during the last war. The U.S. Government asks only $800 million dollars to settle the overdue Lend-Lease account of at least eleven billion dollars.

**February 16, 1951**
The American Jewish Labor Committee reports continued persecutions of Jews in all East European countries.

**February 16, 1951**
Stalin declares: war is not inevitable, but it may become inevitable. He accuses the Western powers as those who want a war.

**February 27, 1951**
V. Clementis, former Czechoslovak Foreign Minister, is arrested for "espionage." It is reported that 169,544 C.P. members in Czechoslovakia were purged during the last year.

**March 1, 1951**
J. Edgar Hoover, director of the F.B.I., declares that, American Communists have gone underground.

**March 9, 1951**
A Communist plot is reported in El Salvador, a tiny Central American republic. Guatemala in the same area is a strong Communist revolutionary ground.

**March 12, 1951**
The U.S.S.R. passes a law against the war propaganda.

**March 19, 1951**
Stalin pledges aid to North Korea.

**March 30, 1951**
The Premier Arnold Veimar is dismissed by the local Communist government in Estonia.

**April 5, 1951**
Atomic spies Julius and Ethel Rosenberg are sentenced to death in New York as Soviet spies. They had delivered to the Soviets top American atomic secrets at the end of the war.

**April 6, 1951**
The official Soviet Tass Agency reports there are no Soviet troops in Manchuria.

**April 7, 1951**
The Foreign Ministers of the 21 American republics, meeting in Washington, D.C., issue the "Declaration of Washington" denouncing Communism in the Americas.

**April 8, 1951**
Reports from Vienna indicate that political prisoners from the "Satellite" countries are being deported to the Soviet Union.

**April 16, 1951**
Moscow declares that the last Five Year Plan was reached nine months ahead of time and that the industrial production is 48 per cent higher than in 1940.

**April 22, 1951**
Sweden and the U.S.S.R. make a trade agreement.

**April 28, 1951**

The leader of the Turkestanians, Usman Batur, who was fighting both the Russians and the Chinese from 1940 to 1951 is hanged by the Chinese Communists in Urumtchi.

**April 28, 1951**

America proposes that the Lend-Lease dispute be transferred to a three-member international arbitration board.

**May 1, 1951**

There are major purges in the Estonian C.P. The main reason: the Estonian nationalism.

**May 3, 1951**

Moscow announces a new 20-year loan of 30 billion rubles at 4 per cent interest to be used for the reconstruction of the country.

**May 7–8, 1951**

America, Britain, and Communist China receive notes from the Soviet Union suggesting a conference of foreign ministers to be summoned in June or July to draft the Japanese peace Treaty. All nations who were at war with Japan should participate.

**May 8, 1951**

The Rumanian Communists celebrate the thirtieth anniversary of their party.

**May 21, 1951**

Reports indicate major purges in the C.P. of Lithuania and Moldavia (former Bessarabia).

**May 22, 1951**

Poland and the U.S.S.R. sign a frontier agreement involving an exchange of territories and a mutual transfer of population.

*Marshal Ivan Koniev with Austrian President K. Renner at a Four Power dinner in Vienna, 1947* – Radio Times

**May 27, 1951**

The Chinese Communists announce the "peaceful liberation" of Tibet, a country that traditionally belonged to China. This is the end of this theocratic state with Dalai Lama.

**June 9, 1951**

The Soviets claim they were inventors of the first airplane.

**June 10, 1951**

The Soviet Union declares that the peace treaty with Japan should be based on the Yalta Agreement.

**June 18, 1951**

There are reports that America is supplying even military aid to Communist Yugoslavia.

**June 23, 1951**

Y.A. Malik, the Soviet delegate to the U.N., proposes a Korean settlement (of course on Soviet terms).

**June 28, 1951**

A. A. Gromyko, the Soviet Foreign Minister, and the American Ambassador in Moscow, Admiral Kirk, agree on armistice in Korea.

**June 28, 1951**

The successor of Cardinal J. Mindszenty of Hungary, the Archbishop Josef Froesz, is sentenced to fifteen years by the Communists.

**July 4, 1951**

In an Independence Day speech, President Truman warns America of continued Communist threat.

**July 6, 1951**

The U.S. State Department again demands from the Soviets the return of 672 Lend-Lease ships and a settlement of the outstanding Lend-Lease debts by an arbitration commission. We never received that money back and the Soviet history books completely forgot there ever was any Lend Lease.

**July 13, 1951**

The *Pravda* with firm words announces drive against perennial Ukrainian nationalism.

**July 14, 1951**

The "Voice of America" radio broadcasts to the Soviet Peoples an American declaration of friendship for the peoples of the U.S.S.R. It is to little avail.

**July 26, 1951**

The Soviet U.N. delegate Malik denies his country wants to export revolution.

**July 29, 1951**

It is reported that the Soviet Russians had deported or liquidated seven minority groups for alleged collaboration with the Germans during the last war. The list includes: the Volga Germans, the Crimean Tartars, the Chechens, Ingush, Kalmucks, Karachais, and the Volga Bulgarians.

**August 3, 1951**

The Catholic Church in Albania is forced to cut off all ties with the Vatican. Some ten per cent of Albanians are Catholic.

**August 5–19, 1951**

The Third World Youth Festival is held in East Berlin under Communist auspices.

**August 12, 1951**

The Soviet Union accepts the invitation to attend the Japanese Treaty Conference in San Francisco. On the 16th America informs the Soviets that the conference is meant exclusively for the conclusion and the signing of the final text of the peace treaty and not for the negotiations of the terms.

**August 22, 1951**

At the resumed Lend-Lease negotiations, the Soviet delegate stated that his country was willing to give only few concessions.

**September 7, 1951**

Rudolf Slansky, secretary general of the Czechoslovak C.P., is removed from his position.

**September 8, 1951**

Gromyko denounces the Japanese Peace Treaty signed by 48 non-Communist nations at San Francisco Conference.

**September 10, 1951**

Foreign ministers of America, Britain and France meet in Washington for a two-day conference to discuss the Soviet policies and the future of Germany.

**September 13, 1951**

The East German Socialist Unity Party (Communist) estimates membership at 1,600,000.

**October 3, 1951**
Washington reports another atomic explosion in the Soviet Union.

**October 24, 1951**
America proclaims end of state of war with Germany.

The *New York Times* reports from Vienna serious economic crises in the "Satellite" countries.

**November 3, 1951**
The Soviet Union denounces Turkey for joining the N.A.T.O. which is interpreted as a step against the U.S.S.R.

**November 13, 1951**
The United Nations reject Soviet-sponsored proposal to admit Communist China as a new member. After he lost the mainland, Chiang established his Nationalist Government at the Island of Formosa; his government is a member of the U.N.

**November 14, 1951**
President Tito and the American Ambassador in Belgrade, George V. Allen, sign an agreement by which Yugoslavia would receive American arms under Mutual Security Program.

**December 7, 1951**
President Gottwald of Czechoslovakia denounces R. Slansky as a "Titoist."

**December 28, 1951**
Maxim Litvinov dies.

**January of 1952**
Ernesto Guevara (23 years old) leaves for one of his extensive Latin American trips to get acquainted with the poor. He is a student of medicine at the University of Buenos Aires.

**January 25, 1952**
The East European Communist press denounces America as a threat to the peace in the Balkans.

**January 30, 1952**
The American press reports on the Soviet suppression of the Moslems in Central Asia.

**February 5, 1952**
The Bulgarian legal system is adapted to the Soviet model.

**February 15, 1952**
The Cominform press praises the "National Liberation Movement" in Malaya.

**March 1, 1952**
A. A. Fuentes, a leftist, becomes the new President of Guatemala and the country moves into Communist anarchy.

**March 6, 1952**
The 1952 Soviet Budget is estimated at 508,800 million rubles; military expenditures amount to 113,800 million.

**March 10, 1952**
Fulgencio Batista takes control of Cuba and becomes dictator.

**March 21, 1952**
The U.S.S.R. breaks off diplomatic relations with the Cuban government as Batista's regime puts strict control on Soviet diplomats. The Soviet Embassy in Havana has been for years principal center for organizing Communist activities in Latin America.

The Communist press attacks Eisenhower's visit to Turkey and Greece.

**March 23, 1952**
The Yugoslav authorities convict 22 Albanians as spies and terrorists.

**March 24, 1952**
It is reported that the Soviets control the Albanian army. Soviet naval bases are being established in Albania.

**April 1, 1952**
Stalin states that peaceful coexistence is possible.

**April 11, 1952**
The Cominform organ *For a Lasting Peace* repeatedly charges Americans as war criminals in Korea. The entire Communist press raises false charges about American use of germ warfare.

**April 25, 1952**
Intelligence reveals that East German Communists had purged some 150,000 Party members.

**April 30, 1952**
President Tito, in spite of Western aid, rejects membership in the N.A.T.O.

**May 1, 1952**

President Wilhelm Pieck of East Germany in a speech during the traditional May Day celebration warns against rearmament of West Germany.

**May 3, 1952**

It is reported that some 300,000 people are in Czech concentration camps.

**May 14, 1952**

Under Soviet suggestion, East Germany rejects the unification of Germany as proposed by the Western powers.

**May 22, 1952**

The Soviet Union protests against American military aid to Iran.

**June 3, 1952**

Anna Pauker, the Vice Premier and the Rumanian Foreign Minister, is dropped from the Politbureau and purged.

**June 16, 1952**

The U.N. special Committee on Forced Labor begins hearings on the extent of slave labor in Communist countries.

**June 17, 1952**

The Baltic exile sources report the Soviets had deported some 1,500,000 people from Estonia, Latvia and Lithuania.

**June 23–28, 1952**

The Ambassador of the U.S.A. in Moscow, George Kennan, reports very extensive Soviet anti-American propaganda.

**July 2, 1952**

A special House Committee in Washington investigating the Katyn massacres, confirms that the Soviet authorities did liquidate there some 15,000 Polish officers.

**August 1, 1952**

The Communist press lauds opening of the Volga-Don Canal and other Soviet achievements.

**August 2, 1952**

The Soviet C.P. reorganization is proposed. The Politbureau and Orgbureau will be replaced by a single Presidium. A new draft statute defines the C.P. as "a voluntary militant union of Communists."

*George Kennan, U.S.A. Ambassador in Moscow* – Radio Times

**August 17, 1952**

The Soviet and Chinese Communists hold a conference in Moscow. This is the first open conference between the two countries. Chou En-lai, the Premier and Foreign Minister, heads the Chinese delegation.

**August 20, 1952**

Stalin calls the 19th Congress of the C.P.S.U. This is the first Congress since March 1939. Major items on the agenda are: the Party reorganization and the industrialization.

**August 22, 1952**

The C.P. of Yugoslavia reports the membership increased from 468,175 in 1948 to 779,382.

**August 29, 1952**

Finland completes payments of reparations to the Soviet Union; they amount to $570 million.

**September 3, 1952**
The *New York Times* reports that the Soviet Union has 22 divisions numbering 230,000 men in East Germany.

**September 18, 1952**
President Truman announces a State Department publication on forced labor in the U.S.S.R.

**September 26, 1952**
The *Pravda* denounces George F. Kennan, the American Ambassador in the Soviet Union, as an enemy of the U.S.S.R. The Soviets ask for immediate recall of Mr. Kennan who on September 19 complained about isolation of Western diplomats.

**October 1952**
Ernesto Guevara returns to Argentina after a short visit in the United States and a long trip through Latin America.

**October 2, 1952**
The Soviets protest against Denmark's joining the N.A.T.O.

**October 3, 1952**
The Soviets announce the publication of Stalin's *Economic Problems of Socialism in the U.S.S.R.* The previous day Stalin published in the *Bolshevik* an article predicting the war between the Capitalist countries and the U.S.S.R.

**October 5, 1952**
V. Molotov opens the 19th Congress of the C.P.S.U. He stresses necessity of peace. G. M. Malenkov, the Secretary of the Central Committee of the C.P.S.U., delivers the main report to this Congress.

**October 6, 1952**
The Chinese Communists start their biggest offensive on the Korean Front.

**October 11, 1952**
Milovan Djilas, one of the leading Yugoslav Communists, criticizes Stalin's economic theses.

In the meantime the 19th Congress of the C.P.S.U. introduces many organizational changes. It founds the Presidium of the Central Committee, and it launches a new Five-Year Plan. Stalin is named the Chairman of the Presidium and the first member of the Secretariat. New Statutes are also adopted.

**November 2–7, 1952**
The C.P. of Yugoslavia meets at its Sixth Congress in Zagreb, the capital of Croatia. It is reorganized under a new name: the League of Communists of Yugoslavia It also admits the failure of agricultural collectivization.

**November 4, 1952**
General D.D. Eisenhower is elected the 34th President of the United States.

**November 5, 1952**
America demands return of 186 Lend-Lease ships from the Russians and again insists to settle the outstanding Lend-Lease obligations on the part of the Soviet Government.

**November 27, 1952**
The Czechoslovak government condemns eleven former top Communists (including both Slansky and Clementis) to death. All of them were liquidated because they were against Stalin and challenged the Russian leadership of World Communism. (They were also called "Titoists.")

**December 6, 1952**
The *Pravda* reports that Soviet trade with the "Satellites" has increased threefold. What the paper does not report is the fact that the Soviet Union squeezes out of East European countries about a billion dollars profit a year by charging them discriminatory prices.

**December 12–20, 1952**
The Communists hold the so-called "Peace Congress" in Vienna.

**December 17, 1952**
The Yugoslav government breaks off diplomatic relations with the Vatican because the Pope has elevated the imprisoned Croatian Archbishop A. Stepinac to the rank of a Cardinal.

**January 13, 1953**
The Soviet State Security organs arrest a number of physicians, including nine Jewish doctors, who had allegedly plotted against lives of Stalin and some Soviet leaders. The Jewish doctors are accused as American spies.

**January 31, 1953**
*Pravda* publishes the list of the accused spies.

**February 12, 1953**
The Soviet Union severs diplomatic relations with the state of Israel.

**February 20, 1953**
The *Red Star* declares that the struggle against Zionism has nothing to do with anti-Semitism.

The Cominform denounces Zionism as an "agency of American imperialism."

**February 22, 1953**
In the Austrian elections the Communists receive out of 4,319,000 votes only 228,000.

**February 28, 1953**
The Balkan Pact (treaty of friendship) is signed between Greece, Turkey, and Yugoslavia in Ankara for five years.

**March of 1953**
E. Guevara receives his doctorate in medicine at the University of Buenos Aires.

**March 1, 1953**
Stalin suffers a stroke.

**March 4, 1953**
Official announcement admits that Stalin is gravely ill.

**March 5, 1953**
Joseph Stalin, long-time dictator of the Soviet Union, dies at the age of 73 at 9:30 p.m. *This is the end of an era.*

**March 6, 1953**
On the morning of this day the Moscow radio announces the death of Stalin.

*From:* Basil Dmytryshyn, USSR: A Concise History *(New York: Charles Scribner's Sons, 1965),*   p. 189; by permission *of the publisher.*

# PART IV:

# After Stalin:
# Communist Polycentrisim:
# 1953-1968

The Collective Leadership in U.S.S.R. ■ The Thaw ■ The First Upheavals in East Europe Against the Communist Rule: the East German Revolt ■ The Fall of Beria ■ The Fall of Malenkov and the Emergence of N. S. Khrushchev ■ The Case of Milovan Djilas ■ Eisenhower's "Domino Theory" ■ The End of French Rule in Indo-China and the Geneva Conference ■ The Emergence of South Vietnam and Beginning of Our Fateful Involvement There ■ The Rapprochement Between the U.S.S.R. and Yugoslavia ■ The Emergence of Fidel Castro in Cuba ■ The "De-Stalinization" in the Soviet Union ■ The Polish and Hungarian Revolts After the Soviet Twentieth Party Congress ■ The Rehabilitation of the Anti-Stalinists ■ The *Sputnik* Inaugurates a New Era ■ The Emerging Disunity of International Communism ■ The Chinese "Great Leap Forward" ■ U.S. Intervention in Lebanon ■ The Case of Writer Pasternak ■ The Victory of Castro and Guevara ■ The Rise of Independent African States ■ The Twenty-First Soviet Party Congress ■ Tibet Falls Victim to Red China ■ Mr. "K." in America ■ U-2 Incident ■ The Summits Fail to Bring Results ■ The Thousand Days of J.F.K. ■ The 1960 Communist Summit in Moscow ■ Rumania Wants to Be Free of Russian Domination ■ The Cuban Threat Is Removed ■ The "Wall of Shame" in Berlin ■ The Twenty-Second Congress of the C.P.S.U. ■ The Sino-Soviet Split ■ The COMECON ■ China Attacks India ■ Tito in America ■ The Vietnamese Question Becomes a Nightmare ■ The Fall of Khrushchev ■ The Emergence of Brezhnev and Kosygin ■ President Johnson and Vietnam ■ The Twenty-Third Soviet Party Congress ■ The Soviet Occupation of Czechoslovakia ■ Federalization of Czechoslovakia ■ Genocide in Nigeria ■ Apollo 8 ■ 1969—a Very Eventful Year ■ Sino-Soviet Struggle Continues ■ Richard M. Nixon Elected President ■ Arab-Israeli Conflict ■ Complete Destruction of Liberalism in Czechoslovakia ■ The Rise of Gustav Husak ■ NATO's Twentieth Anniversary ■ Campus Revolt in America ■ New Era in France ■ The Communist Summit in Moscow ■ The Vietnam Controversy ■ Mission of Apollo 11 ■ The Moon Is Conquered—the World Rejoices ■ Nixon in Bucharest ■ August Riots in Prague ■ Death of Ho ■ The Chicago Trial ■ Moratorium Days ■ The Plight of Latin America ■ SALT Meetings ■ Japan's Rise ■ 1970 as a Revolutionary Year ■ Events Indicate a Turbulent Decade ■ Our Losses in Vietnam ■ W. Germany and Austria Go Socialist ■ Violence at Kent State and All Over the Country ■ Our Continued Withdrawal from Vietnam ■ Centenary of Lenin's Birth ■ The Expansion of War in Indochina ■ Riots in Europe ■

*Nikita S. Khrushchev* — Keystone

With the death of Stalin a new era in the history of international Communist movement emerged. For all practical purposes monolithic Communism ceased to exist. Already a few weeks after the dictator's demise a powerful anti-Communist and anti-Russian revolt broke out in East Germany. The tremors of this remained felt for the next few years: in 1956 significant revolts shook up Poland and Hungary. By now N. S. Khrushchev was emerging as the new leader of the Soviet Empire. In 1955 he patched up his differences with Tito. Many former anti-Stalinists in East Europe were exonerated. A more relaxed atmosphere was felt in the Soviet Union where millions of Stalin's victims demanded reforms and liberalization. All over Eastern Europe, too, there was new hope and emergence of "different roads to Socialism." And in Asia Red China was emerging as a new powerful center of Communism. The Chinese strictly adhered to the old Stalinist tenets. Mao and his collaborators thought that coexistence between Capitalism and

Communism was impossible and that war with capitalist countries is inevitable.

At the Twentieth Party Congress in February of 1956 Khrushchev attacked Stalin and the cult of personality thus shattering the confidence of the Chinese and many old-time Communists. In Yugoslavia, Milovan Djilas, the No. 2 Communist revolted against the strict dogmatism, in fact against basic ideas of Communism and was duly arrested and imprisoned. By 1958 Khrushchev was the Premier of his country. He continued downgrading his former master, Stalin. At about the same time Cuba came under the domination of Castro's revolutionary rule. Communism showed up only 90 odd miles off the U.S. coast.

In the meantime Stalin was completely degraded, China became more militant as the "true center" of Marxism-Stalinism, Albania became the Chinese beachhead in Europe, and Communist influences spread in Asia and Africa. Khrushchev became the busiest Communist salesman in the world. He came to America and to the United Nations. During the continued struggle with the Chinese Khrushchev was sacrificed by the Kremlin leadership in order to accomplish a reconciliation with Peking. He was ousted but the reconciliation was not accomplished.

New centers of Communism emerged in Peking, Belgrade, Warsaw, Bucharest. The word "Satellite" became obsolete. In the view of the Sino-Soviet struggle most of the East European countries succeeded in becoming at least partly independent of Moscow. Nationalism appeared — paradoxically as a very powerful force among all Communists who - by virtue of the old Marxist doctrine - were supposed to be internationalists. Many new states have emerged in Africa, Asia and other parts of the world. In most of them after initial tries, Communism has failed.

In 1967 Svetlana, Stalin's own daughter sought asylum in — the United States. And in 1968 Czechoslovakia, one of the foremost former faithful "Satellites" became a liberal Communist state, only to be crushed by the Soviet intervention in August of 1968. There is a flux and a constant change all over the Communist world. Things have changed after Stalin's death, but Communism still remains basically a revolutionary doctrine. Its most outspoken representative is now Red China. And while Che Guevara dies a martyr's death in air-thin heights of Bolivia, his slogans are shouted by thousands of the rebellious students at the barricades of Paris in early 1968. They were repeated during the upheavals of 1969 and early 1970.

# 1. *From 1953 Until the Revolts of 1956*

**March 6, 1953**
The C.P.S.U. and the Soviet Government are reorganized. There is a five-member Presidium of the Council of Ministers. Georgi Malenkov succeeds Stalin as Chairman of the Council of Ministers and the first member of the Secretariat. The Deputy Chairmen are: Beria, Molotov, Bulganin, and Kaganovich. Molotov takes over foreign affairs. The dreaded Beria takes Internal Affairs and the State Security. Khrushchev is listed after Malenkov in the Secretariat. Voroshilov becomes the Chairman of the Presidium of the Supreme Soviet. Vyshinsky is a permanent representative at the U.N.

**March 9, 1953**
Malenkov in his speech at Stalin's funeral stresses the peaceful coexistence.

**March 10, 1953**
Yugoslavia receives the first shipment of the American jet military airplanes. Many Americans criticize the American armament of Communist Yugoslavia.

**March 14, 1953**
The Czechoslovak President Gottwald dies of natural causes after attending Stalin's funeral.

The Soviet Secretariat is reduced in size. G. Malenkov is removed from this body; it makes it easier for Khrushchev to rise to power.

**March 20, 1953**
Khrushchev takes Malenkov's post in the Secretariat as Secretary General.

**March 21, 1953**
The Czechoslovak Parliament elects the Premier Antonin Zapotocki as the President of Czechoslovakia, Gottwald's successor.

**March 27, 1953**
Sweeping amnesty for criminal and political prisoners is granted in the Soviet Union. This is the beginning of the "Thaw."

**April 1, 1953**
The retail prices are lowered in the U.S.S.R. This is a concession to the population. The "Thaw" continues. The Soviet peoples are awakening from the nightmare of Stalinism.

**April 3, 1953**
The Jewish doctors in the Soviet Union are released from prison and exonerated.

**April 9, 1953**
Sweden signs a trade agreement in Moscow.

**April 16, 1953**
Administrative changes and anti-Stalinist purges are announced in many Soviet republics.

**April 29, 1953**
A Sino-Indian treaty is signed in Tibet.

**May 27, 1953**
The *Komunist* calls for collegiality in Party leadership, denounces the old "cult of personality" and espouses the "role of the masses."

**June 5, 1953**
Disorders and riots break out in the Czech city of Pilsen and other industrial centers. At least six workers were killed by the Communist police.

*Imre Nagy, President of the Council of Ministers* – Keystone

**June 8, 1953**
The Soviet Union requests the re-establishment of diplomatic relations with Yugoslavia.

**June 11, 1953**
The Soviet Foreign Ministry expresses its desire to settle many problems with Turkey; notably the Straits and the territorial disputes.

**June 13 – 15, 1953**
The Slovak C.P. holds its Tenth Congress in the Slovak capital Bratislava.

**June 14, 1953**
Yugoslavia and the Soviet Union resume diplomatic relations.

**June 17, 1953**
The first anti-Communist and anti-Russian revolt breaks out in East Germany. Strikes and riots take place in East Berlin. The revolt is crushed by the Soviet troops. The master of the situation is W. Ulbricht, an old Stalinist.

**June 19, 1953**
Shortly after 8:00 p.m. Julius and Ethel Rosenberg, sentenced to death as Soviet spies, are executed at Sing Sing Prison, Ossining, New York.

**June 26, 1953**
L. P. Beria, an old friend of Stalin is arrested and denounced as a "foul enemy of the Party;" the new leaders also denounce him as an "international imperialist agent" a phrase very familiar during Stalin's (and Beria's) Purges.

**July 4, 1953**
In Hungary M. Rakosi is replaced by Imre Nagy as Premier. This means the relaxation of the Stalinist regime. All over East Europe there is now a relaxation of the strict Stalinist Communist regimes.

**July 12, 1953**
The Soviet authorities end the martial law regime in East Germany.

**July 16 – 18, 1953**
It is announced that many high officials are being removed in Soviet Republics.

**July 19, 1953**
The Turks reply to the Soviets they will not change the status of the Straits (Dardanelles and Bosphorus). The Montreux Convention is still valid. The Soviet note gives up all Soviet claims on Turkish territory.

Moscow re-establishes diplomatic relations with Israel.

**July 26, 1953**
The young Cuban lawyer, Dr. Fidel Castro, leads a suicidal attack on Moncada army barracks near Santiago, Cuba with 165 followers. This inaugurates the rise of Castro's "26th of July Movement." Castro is arrested, sentenced after brilliant self-defense and sent to prison. He becomes idol of the Cuban revolutionaries.

**July 27, 1953**
The Korean Armistice is signed. The war in Korea lasted three years and thirty-two days. About 34,000 American soldiers, many U.N. members of the 15 nations, and some one million of South Korean civilians and soldiers were killed in this war that still has not been ended.

**August 1, 1953**
Vorkuta Camp massacre committed by the Soviets.

**August 8, 1953**
Malenkov admits serious agricultural deficiencies and announces a "new course" in the Soviet economic policy. Increased food and consumer production is promised.

**August 12, 1953**
The Soviets are reported to explode the first hydrogen bomb.

**August 16, 1953**
The Soviets propose re-unification of Germany to the Western Powers holding a German peace conference. The West German Chancellor K. Adenauer rejects the Soviet proposal.

**August 18, 1953**
A Soviet-Egyptian trade agreement is signed.

**August 20, 1953**
Moscow officially admits the explosion of the hydrogen bomb.

**August 23, 1953**
The Soviet-East-German agreement is signed. The Russians give Communist Germans various concessions in order to boost their regime.

**August 29, 1953**
The *New York Times* reports that Khrushchev has gained in his struggle for power.

The Finnish Communists celebrate the 35th anniversary of the founding of their Party.

**September 3, 1953**
Iran and the Soviet Union sign a trade agreement.

**September 12, 1953**
Khrushchev is officially confirmed as the First Secretary of the C.P.S.U. (As evident from these entries, the sources are a little bit confusing.)

**September 15, 1953**
Mao Tse-tung expresses gratitude for all Soviet aid.

**September 21, 1953**
The first Yugoslav ambassador since the Cominform break arrives in Moscow.

*Fidel Castro interrogated by Batista police after his capture on July 26, 1953* – Keystone

**October 23, 1953**
Soviet government orders "sharply-increased" consumer goods production.

**October 27, 1953**
The Soviets sign trade agreement with Italy.

**November 2, 1953**
M. Rakosi, the former Premier, becomes the First Secretary of the Hungarian Workers' (Communist) Party.

**November 12, 1953**
The Cominform states that the World Communist movement has more than 25 million card-carrying members.

**November 18, 1953**
The Soviet government urges Finland to adopt a "practical policy" towards the U.S.S.R.

**November 24, 1953**
The *Pravda* calls for a closer cooperation between the Soviet Government and America.

**December 2, 1953**
India concludes a five-year trade agreement with Moscow.

**December 3, 1953**
Israel and the U.S.S.R. sign a profitable trade agreement.

**December 9, 1953**
The Soviets reject President Eisenhower's proposal at the United Nations for an atomic pool.

**December 14, 1953**
The American intelligence reveals that the Communists of Guatemala seek influence in several Latin American countries. (In Colombia a guerilla warfare rages in rural areas and results in killing of many thousands of people.)

**December 15, 1953**
The Soviets declare that Beria will be tried for "high treason."

**December 21, 1953**
Yugoslavia and Albania resume diplomatic relations.

*Milovan Djilas* – Keystone

**December 23, 1953**
Lavrenti Beria, the former chief of the Soviet secret police, and six accomplices are sentenced to death and executed.

**December 26, 1953**
J. F. Dulles, the U.S. Secretary of State, denounces Soviet policies in East Europe.

**December 27, 1953**
Milovan Djilas, one of the top Communists in Yugoslavia (a Montenegrin), is elected the President of the National Assembly. He is also the Vice President of the Republic. On the same day he publishes an article criticizing the red bureaucracy in Yugoslavia.

**January of 1954**
E. Guevara arrives in Guatemala City. Later he receives temporary asylum in the Argentine Embassy and then goes to Mexico.

**January 1, 1954**
*Nova Misao* (The New Thought), a Communist Yugoslav periodical, whose editor is M. Djilas, publishes his highly critical article "The Anatomy of a Moral" denouncing the Communist practices. There is a reaction against Djilas' liberal ideas.

**January 14, 1954**
The U.S.S.R. rejects any idea of a German election under supervision of neutral foreign observers.

**January 17, 1954**
At a two-day session of the Central Committee of the League of Communists of Yugoslavia, Tito and his collaborators reject Djilas' ideas as expressed in his writings. He is expelled from the Central Committee and relieved of all his official duties. (A few weeks later in April, Djilas will quit his old membership in the Party.)

**January 24, 1954**
The Communist China concludes a trade agreement with the Soviet Union.

**January 25 – February 18, 1954**
The Four Powers Conference takes place in Berlin.

**February 28, 1954**
By a special agreement, the Soviets assume large developments in Afghanistan.

**March 13, 1954**
Malenkov acknowledges that another world war would mean "the destruction of world civilization"; he calls for "economic competition with the capitalist world."

Ho Chi Minh, the Vietnamese Communist leader, starts with his well organized forces the battle for Dien Bien Phu. Within five days the French garrison was effectively sealed off from the world.

The Committee for (Soviet) State Security (K.G.B.), under chairmanship of Ivan Serov, is formed to succeed the former Ministry of State Security which was headed by Beria.

**March 19, 1954**
The Crimea is incorporated into the Ukrainian Republic.

**March 20, 1954**
General Paul Ely, the French Chief of Staff, informs President Eisenhower that the French in Dien Bien Phu could be saved only through American intervention. After a long debate the U.S. Government decides not to intervene in the Vietnamese war; this was then known as French Indo China.

**March 26, 1954**
The Soviets decide to return to America 38 small naval vessels obtained from the Lend-Lease aid.

**March 28, 1954**
The Soviet Government decrees increased grain production through cultivation of virgin and fallow lands. (The program is expanded on August 17, 1954; it will prove a big failure.)

**April 7, 1954**
President Eisenhower refers to the "Domino Theory." "You have a row of dominoes set up, and you knocked over the first one; and what would happen to the last one was the certainty that it would go over very quickly." Many years afterwards this theory was cited in regard to the Vietnam War and the American policy in South East Asia.

*Ho Chi Minh* – Keystone

**April-26, 1954**

The Geneva Conference on Korea and Indo China opens. It was agreed upon at the Berlin Foreign Ministers Conference. The French were now worn out by a 9-year war. Nine countries were represented: America, Great Britain, France, the Soviet Union, Red China, Laos, Cambodia, South Vietnam, and North Vietnam. (The conference will meet until July 21.)

The Supreme Soviet reduces direct military expenditures for 1954 by 9 per cent compared with 1953.

**April 27, 1954**

The Supreme Soviet elects Malenkov as the Chairman of the Council of Ministers.

**May 8, 1954**

The French stronghold, Dien Bien Phu is overwhelmed by the Communist Vietnamese forces. The French casualties including prisoners are about 12,000. This means the end of French rule in Southeast Asia.

**May 27, 1954**

A Soviet cruiser and two destroyers, after properly notifying the Turkish authorities — according to the Montreux Convention — pass through the Straits on their way to Albania. The Soviets use the Albanian Adriatic bases as their stronghold in the Mediterranean.

**June 16, 1954**

Emperor Bao Dai in South Vietnam asks Ngo Dinh Diem to form a new government.

**June 19, 1954**

Diem becomes dictator of South Vietnam.

**July 7, 1954**

An independent government is established in Saigon by Diem.

**July 12, 1954**

School reform is promulgated in the Soviet Union. There is stress in sciences. Uniforms for boys and girls are introduced.

**July 17, 1954**

Finland and the Soviet Union agree on a 5-year Trade Agreement.

*President Diem presents to the press the new members of his government* — Keystone

**July 21, 1954**

The Geneva Conference results in a truce agreement. Vietnam is partitioned. Laos and Cambodia are neutralized. Thus North Vietnam is established, a new Communist state in Asia, a new success for Communism. The French are out of Asia. The second document, the so-called Final Declaration, consists of 13 points. The most important called for a general election in July of 1956. (The present day conflict in Vietnam is an outgrowth of the Geneva Conference.)

At the signing of the Geneva Agreement the total French losses were 172,000. The Vietnamese losses were at least three times as high; among them were 250,000 South Vietnamese civilians who perished.

**July 21, 1954**

E. Hoxha relinquishes his position as Premier of Albania; he is succeeded by tough Stalinist Mehmet Shehu.

**July 22, 1954**

N. Riumin, former Soviet Deputy Minister of State Security, responsible for the arrest of the doctors under Stalin (January 1953) is found guilty of falsifying the evidence and sentenced to death. The "De-Stalinization" continues.

**August 1, 1954**

The All-Union Agricultural Exhibition opens in Moscow.

**August 9, 1954**

Greece, Turkey, and Yugoslavia sign a 20-year military alliance.

**September 20, 1954**

After long preparations and discussions, the new Communist Chinese Constitution is adopted in Peiping (former Peking).

**September 28 – October 3, 1954**

A Nine-Power Conference meets in London to discuss the sovereignty of West Germany and her rearmament. The powers feel there is no strong Europe without a strong Germany. West Germany is now a fully-fledged ally of the Western Democracies.

**October 5, 1954**

Italy, Yugoslavia, America, and Britain solve the problem of Trieste. The city and a corridor connecting it with Italy, go to Italy.

*Andre Vyshinsky, Minister of Foreign Affairs* – Keystone

**October 12, 1954**

By a special agreement with China the Russians give up Port Arthur and all special privileges in China.

**October 23, 1954**

President Eisenhower pledges American aid to South Vietnam's Premier Ngo Dinh Diem.

**November 22, 1954**

B. P. Vyshinsky, the Soviet delegate at the U.N., dies in New York. (He was responsible during the Purges for thousands of death sentences.)

**December 2, 1954**

The Soviet-Iranian boundary agreement is signed.

**December 15 – 26, 1954**

The Second All-Union Writers' Congress in the Soviet Union reaffirms the principle of party-mindedness. The ideas of revolt are by now evident in the writings of the post-Stalin Soviet writers.

**December 24, 1954**

Victor Abakumov, former high-ranking chief in the Ministry of State Security, and three of his collaborators are sentenced to death as accomplices of Beria.

**January 5, 1955**
The Soviet Union and Yugoslavia sign the first formal trade agreement since 1948.

**January 7, 1955**
N. S. Khrushchev stresses priority of heavy industry.

**January 25, 1955**
The Plenum of the Central Committee of the C.P.S.U. starts its six-day meeting. A decree ends the state of war with Germany. Khrushchev attacks Malenkov's "New Course" policy.

**February 2, 1955**
The Soviet Government signs an agreement with India to build there a large steel plant at Bhilai.

**February 3, 1955**
Khrushchev as the First Party Secretary declares again that the development of heavy industry is more than vital. This means that consumers' goods are going to be neglected. The Soviet citizens, deprived of many necessities, do not like this program.

**February 8, 1955**
Malenkov resigns as Chairman of the Council of Ministers. On Khrushchev's recommendation Bulganin succeeds Malenkov. Khrushchev's rise to power thus continues.

**February 9, 1955**
Marshal G. K. Zhukov succeeds Bulganin as Minister of Defense.

**March 10, 1955**
A Soviet edict grants more initiative to collective farms. They become decentralized.

**April 18 – 24, 1955**
Red China is the participant and the co-signer of the Final Communiqué of the Bandung's Conference of the Afro-Asian States.

**May 5, 1955**
The West German Federal Republic becomes a completely sovereign state as the 1954 Paris Agreement goes into effect.

**May 10, 1955**
The Soviet Union submits broad arms reduction plan to the London Disarmament Conference.

**May 11, 1955**
A Soviet-sponsored conference opens in Warsaw. Present are delegates of Albania, Bulgaria, Czechoslovakia, E. Germany, Hungary, Poland, and Rumania.

*The Soviet-Yugoslav conference in Belgrade. Left to Right Khrushchev, Tito and Bulganin* – Keystone

**May 14, 1955**

The Warsaw Pact of the above states is signed. This is the Soviet answer to the N.A.T.O. and to rearmament of Germany.

**May 15, 1955**

The Austrian State Treaty is signed by the U.S.S.R., Britain, United States, and France. Austria becomes a neutral and completely sovereign state. The Russians must now leave Austria.

**May 15, 1955**

Fidel Castro who was imprisoned by the Batista regime is released from jail.

**May 26 – June 2, 1955**

Khrushchev, Bulganin and Mikoyan arrive in Belgrade to affect reconciliation with Josip Broz Tito. In his speech Khrushchev refers to "many roads to Socialism" thus admitting the polycentrism of Communism.

**June 2, 1955**

Tito and Bulganin sign a joint declaration of friendship and cooperation.

**June 25, 1955**

Bulganin during his visit in Asia signs a treaty of friendship with J. Nehru in India.

**July 4 – 12, 1955**

The Plenum of the Central Committee of the C.P.S.U. convenes. Kirichenko and Suslov are promoted to the Presidium. Industrialization and agriculture are important topics. The Twentieth Party Congress is convoked.

**July 18 – 21, 1955**

At Geneva a Summit Conference is held between heads of the United States, Britain, France and the Soviet Union. Bulganin and Khrushchev represent the Soviet Union. They discuss many major problems and tensions.

*Left to Right in front row – Mr. Khrushchev, Marshal Zhudov, Marshal Bulganin and Mr. Molotov in Geneva –* Radio Times

**January 9, 1960**
The C.P.S.U. issues decree on propaganda tasks.

**January 14, 1960**
Khrushchev reveals that the strength of Soviet armed forces is 3,600,000 and announces planned reduction of 1,200,000.

**February 10, 1960**
Khrushchev leaves for a visit to India, Burma, Indonesia, and Afghanistann. He is wooing the "Non-Aligned" nations.

**February 14, 1960**
The Soviet government announces a five-year sugar purchase agreement with Cuba, after Mikoyan returned from Cuba. This is considerable help to Castro's regime.

**February 21, 1960**
The U.S.S.R. announces it will establish a Peoples' Friendship University in Moscow primarily for African, Asian and Latin American students. (This too will help to spread the Soviet and Communist influence.)

**February 22, 1960**
President Eisenhower leaves for a two-week trip in Latin America.

**May 1, 1960**
The Soviet authorities shoot down an American U-2 plane over Soviet territory. (Such planes are used for gathering intelligence.)

**May 4, 1960**
Following the U-2 incident a Plenum of the Central Committee of the C.P.S.U. is convoked. F. R. Kozlov is named a Secretary of the C.C. while Kosygin, Podgorny, and Polyansky are promoted to full Presidium membership.

**May 5-7, 1960**
The Supreme Soviet approves phased elimination of income tax, revaluation of the ruble, and reduction of the workday. L. Brezhnev replaces Voroshilov as the Chairman of the Presidium of the Supreme Soviet.

**May 14, 1960**
Sino-Cuban Friendship Society is founded in Havana. Castro's regime becomes more and more Communist.

**May 14–19, 1960**
Khrushchev is in Paris for summit talks with Western leaders. He breaks off talks on May 17 when his demands on American reconnaissance flights are not met.

**May 20 and June 15, 1960**
Soviet notes to Japan warn against ratification of a Security Pact with the U.S.

**June 15, 1960**
The *New York Times* reports: Anna Pauker, one of the former leading Rumanian Communists, died in Bucharest.

**June 22, 1960**
Khrushchev meets leaders of twelve Communist Parties in a closed session in Rumania.

**June 24, 1960**
The representatives of twelve Communist states sign in Bucharest a statement supporting the Soviet position in the controversy with China.

**June 30, 1960**
Khrushchev arrives in Vienna for an eight-day official visit. Austria is a neutral state.

**July of 1960**
The twelve-years long fighting with the Communist guerillas in Malaya ends with British victory.

**July 15, 1960**
Khrushchev threatens direct Soviet intervention if "aggression" against the newly independent Congo continues.

**July 16, 1960**
The Plenum of the Central Committee of the C.P.S.U. emphasizes introduction of new technology. Kozlov gives a secret report on the meeting in Bucharest.

**July 20, 1960**
E. Che Guevara publishes his book *On Guerilla Warfare*. One of the main rules emphasized here is that guerillas cannot succeed unless they gain support of the native population.

**August 12, 1960**
Western reports indicate that Soviet technicians and experts are leaving China as split grows.

**August 16–28, 1960**
The foreign ministers of the Organization of American States (O.A.S.) meeting in San José, Costa Rica, invoke strong measures against the Dominican government of General R. L. Trujillo, a long-time dictator. They also censure Cuba for receiving Soviet military aid.

**August 19, 1960**
F. G. Powers, the pilot of the American U-2 plane, shot down in the Soviet Union, is sentenced to ten years in prison by a Soviet court.

**September 5–10, 1960**
At the Third Congress of the Communist-dominated Lao Dong Party in Hanoi, a United Front is formed to overthrow the South Vietnamese government in Saigon.

**September 7, 1960**
The Soviets promulgate a new code of military discipline which indicates the strict control of the Party over the armed forces.

Wilhelm Pieck, the Communist premier of East Germany, dies of natural causes. Walter Ulbricht, an old Stalinist and extremely unpopular, becomes his successor. He is the First Secretary of the Party and the First Chairman of the State Council (premier).

**September 9, 1960**
Khrushchev sails for America aboard a Polish ship. He is accompanied by most of East European Communist leaders and wants to attend the U.N. Assembly that opens on September 20. America watches an unique sight in New York: the largest gathering of the world Communist leaders under auspices of the United Nations. Castro too joins them. The New York police are busy for days securing the safety of the fifteen dictators and curbing thousands of angry anti-Communist demonstrators.

**September 13, 1960**
The U.S. Congress authorizes the erection of a statue of the great Ukrainian national poet Taras Shevchenko in Washington, D.C.

**September 17, 1960**
The Emergency Assembly of the U.N. discusses the serious Congo crisis; the discussions go on for days.

**September 19–October 13, 1960**
Khrushchev and other Communist leaders, including Tito of Yugoslavia, attend the U.N. sessions.

**September 22, 1960**
Tito addresses the U.N. Assembly as a "neutralist" and appeals for peace.

**September 23, 1960**
Khrushchev addresses the U.N. and angrily calls for change in the U.N. Secretariat and denounces "colonialism."

**September 28, 1960**
Tito and Khrushchev meet in New York. Tito also met briefly President Eisenhower in New York, but does not receive an invitation to Washington. The anti-Communist demonstrators make the sojourn of Communist leaders in New York a frustrating experience.

**September 29, 1960**
Khrushchev interrupts rudely Macmillan's speech in the U.N. Assembly and pounds his shoe on the table.

**November 6–30, 1960**
A very important Communist summit conference is held in Moscow. Eighty-one Communist Parties are represented. Most of them denounce the Chinese and support the Soviet. Enver Hoxha of Albania furiously attacked Khruschev and left the conference. The Sino-Soviet split is now wide open. Khrushchev realizes that he has lost Albania and China has gained it.

**November 11, 1960**
A trade agreement is signed between Rumania and the Soviet Union promising Rumania 500 million dollars' worth of raw materials, machinery and equipment.

**November 16, 1960**
President Eisenhower orders American naval units to patrol Central American waters to bar any attack by pro-Castro rebel forces on Guatemala and Nicaragua.

**December 6, 1960**
The leaders of 81 C.P. assembled in Moscow issue a lengthy manifesto on strategy and goals of World Communism.

**December 20, 1960**
The National Liberation Front for South Vietnam is officially organized. It issues a ten-point Manifesto.

**December 26, 1960**
Shortly after his return from New York, Tito delivers an anti-American speech in Belgrade.

**December 31, 1960**
President Eisenhower warns, through our State Department, that America "would take the most serious view of any intervention in Laos by the Chinese Communists or Viet Minh (North Vietnam) armed forces or others in support of the Communist Pathet Lao, who are in rebellion against the Royal Laotian government."

**January 3, 1961**
The United States severs diplomatic and commercial relations with Cuba. Thousands of Cuban refugees are coming to America.

**January 6, 1961**
Khrushchev endorses in a speech to Party functionaries "liberation wars and popular uprisings." At the same time many in the West brand him as the head of the greatest colonial empire in existence. He also ex-

plains the Manifesto of December 6, stressing especially "the world Socialist system" and desire for peace.

**January 6, 1961**
Indonesia and the Soviet Union sign an arms agreement. President Sukarno of Indonesia, along with Nehru, Nasser, and Tito, is one of the leading "neutralists" in the world.

Soviet ruble is revaluated domestically on 10:1 basis.

**January 10–18, 1961**
During the Plenum of the Central Committee Khrushchev defends his agricultural policies which so far have failed to bring good results.

**January 20, 1961**
John F. Kennedy is inaugurated as the 35th President of the United States. In his inaugural address, he urges against "the common enemies of man: tyranny, poverty, disease, and war itself." He also emphasizes "quest for peace."

*John F. Kennedy Inauguration* – Culver Pictures

**January 23, 1961**

The Red Chinese authorities admit great agricultural failures. Millions of Chinese are starving. This is but one of the results of the "Great Leap Forward."

**January 29, 1961**

The Hanoi radio states officially that North Vietnam has recognized the National Liberation Front of South Vietnam. As N.L.F. pledges destruction of the government in Saigon, this is bound to result in more bloodshed and continued war in which America will eventually be involved.

**February 9–19, 1961**

Soviet President L. I. Brezhnev tours Morocco, Guinea, and Ghana. This is the first trip to Africa by a top Soviet leader. Soviets are trying to get a foothold among the newly emerging African nations.

**February 12, 1961**

The deposed premier of Congo, Patrice Lumumba, is murdered in Katanga. A wild reaction follows in the Communist world where Lumumba had reputation as a pro-Communist. The Communists hail him as a martyr. A Lumumba University exists today in Moscow.

**February 13, 1961**

President Tito sails for Africa to visit Ghana, Togo, Liberia, Guniea, Morocco, Tunisia, and Egypt.

**February 13–20, 1961**

The Albanian Communists hold their Fourth Congress.

**March 23, 1961**

In a nationally televised news conference, President Kennedy states American position on Laos; he is opposed to any Communist aggression.

**April 3, 1961**

The U.S. Department of State charges in a special 36-page pamphlet that Cuba is a Communist outpost in the Western hemisphere.

**April 12, 1961**

The Soviets put man in space. Yuri Gagarin, the Russian astronaut, successfully orbits the earth and returns safely. He is hailed as a hero by the Soviet leadership and the peoples.

**April 17, 1961**

The Bay of Pigs invasion of Cuba begins; about 1,400 American-supported Cuban exiles land in an attempt to overthrow Castro.

**April 20, 1961**

It is clear by now that the invasion of Cuba is a disaster. As the American prestige suffers greatly, President Kennedy assumes publicly full responsibility for the fiasco and states on the same day: "We do not intend to abandon Cuba to the Communists."

**April 26, 1961**

The Soviet government cancels all aid to Albania.

**May 5, 1961**

President Kennedy tells a news conference that the use of American military forces in South Vietnam is being considered.

**May 5, 1961**

The Soviet Union decrees death penalty for "economic crimes."

**May 9–24, 1961**

Vice President L. B. Johnson, on his Asian tour, assures several Asiatic nations of continued American aid and support against Communist aggression.

**May 20, 1961**

Khrushchev states that heavy and light industry will grow at equal rates.

**May 30, 1961**

General R. L. Trujillo, the Dominican dictator, is assassinated.

**June 1961**

Soviet statistics estimate the membership of 87 Communist Parties in the world at some 36,000,000. The largest C.P. is that of China with more than 15,000,000 members and candidate members.

**June 3–4, 1961**

Kennedy and Khrushchev meet in Vienna for summit talks. Khrushchev proposes a demilitarized "free city" of Berlin. The Americans cannot accept this.

**June 19, 1961**

The Plenum of the Central Committee of the C.P.S.U. endorses draft of a new Party program and agrees to change the statutes of the Party.

**Summer of 1961**

The number of the American advisers in South Vietnam is increased to 1,362; they will be gradually increased to 16,500 by late 1963.

**July 8, 1961**
Khrushchev announces increase in the Soviet defense budget and suspension of any further demobilization.

**July 25, 1961**
In a nation-wide radio and TV address from the White House, President Kennedy states: "We cannot and will not permit the Communists to drive us out of Berlin."

**July 30, 1961**
The Communist Party of the Soviet Union issues its new program, the first after Lenin. It contains approximately 45,000 words, and it is called "Program for the Building of Communist Society."

**July 31, 1961**
According to reliable reports, some 30,000 Germans had escaped from East Germany during the month of July and found refuge in West Germany. It is a terrible drain of manpower for East German Communist regime.

**August 6–7, 1961**
The Soviet astronaut Gherman S. Titov circles the earth seventeen times.

**August 11, 1961**
To stop the exodus of East Germans, the East German authorities decide to stop the flow of refugees into West Berlin, the main escape gate.

**August 13, 1961**
The East German Communists start erecting the Wall between East and West Berlin. The West tacitly accepts the building of this — as it became known — "Wall of Shame." (The decision of Ulbricht to save this way the East German economy — by cutting completely the escape route to the West — proved very effective.) Many critics maintain that America and the West should not have permitted the erection of the Berlin Wall, and that the lack of Western firm intervention was a serious mistake.

**August 19, 1961**
Soviet Ambassador Shikin leaves Albania.

**August 31, 1961**
The Soviet Union announces its decision to resume testing of nuclear weapons. America then follows suit.

**September 1–6, 1961**
Representatives of 25 "non-aligned" and "neutral" nations meet in Belgrade for an international conference. The Soviets impress the conference by exploding at the same time huge H bombs. Nations denouncing America at the conference had previously received more than $8 billion worth of American economic and military aid. The conference urges the U.S. to continue talks with the Russians.

**September 8, 1961**
The leftist president of Brazil Joao Goulart is inaugurated. He was later accused of being a tool of Communists.

**September 18, 1961**
Dag Hammarskjold, Secretary General of the United Nations for the past eight years, is killed in a plane crash in North Rhodesia while on a mission seeking cease-fire between the U.N. troops and Katangan forces in the Congo.

**September 25, 1961**
President J. F. Kennedy addresses the General Assembly of the U.N. and states that America stands firm on Berlin.

**October 4, 1961**
*Pravda* denounces nationalist tendencies among Lithuanian Communists. It also attacks for the same reason the Estonian C.P.

**October 10, 1961**
West German reports indicate Soviet military buildup in East Germany; "Satellite" armies are massed there for display of military strength.

**October 11, 1961**
President Kennedy pledges American military aid to South Vietnam.

**October 13, 1961**
The U.S. Government reveals it had sold at a very low price 130 jet fighters to Yugoslavia and had trained Yugoslav pilots in America.

**October 16–17, 1961**
The Finnish President Urho K. Kekkonen spends two days in Washington on official visit. President Kennedy stated that the U.S. will observe strict neutrality of Finland.

### October 17–31, 1961

The Twenty-second C.P.S.U. Congress is held in Moscow. Khrushchev attacks Albania. The congress is under the impact of the Sino-Soviet split. Khrushchev also denounces Stalin and the "Anti-Party Group." Chou En-lai defends the Chinese position. Of the 66 foreign C.P. present, 22 refrain from supporting the Soviet stand against the Chinese.

### October 27–28, 1961

American and Soviet tanks face each other in direct confrontation across Berlin sector border. As the "Wall of Shame" in Berlin gets stronger and higher, the flow of East German refugees stops almost completely.

### November 1, 1961

Stalin's body is removed from Lenin's mausoleum and buried near the Kremlin wall as result of Khrushchev's last denouncement of the late dictator.

### November 3, 1961

U Thant, the Burmese Ambassador to the U.N., is elected as the Acting Secretary General of the same.

### November 8, 1961

The Albanian Communists celebrate the twentieth anniversary of the founding of their C.P.

### November 13, 1961

In his speech at Skopje, the capital of Macedonia, Tito denounces Enver Hoxha and the Chinese delegation at the 22nd Soviet Party Congress.

### November 22, 1961

The Canadian Prime Minister Diefenbaker, in a speech to the ethnic groups in Toronto, attacks Soviet imperialism.

### November 24, 1961

President of Finland Kekkonen confers with Khrushchev at Novosibirsk. The Soviets apply new pressures on Finland which wants to be strictly neutral between the East and West.

### November 27, 1961

The Central Committee of the League of Communists of Yugoslavia in its Third Plenum hails the Soviet anti-Chinese stand at the 22nd Party Congress.

*The Twenty-second C.P.S.U. Congress is opened at Moscow* — Keystone

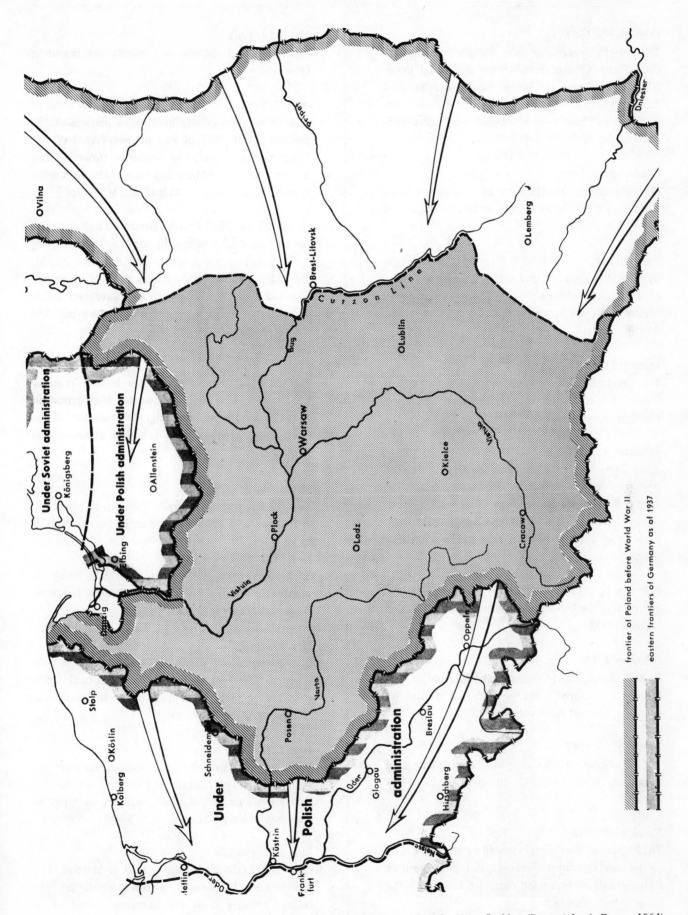

*How Poland was pushed westward. From: The Oder-Neisse Problem (Bonn: Atlantic Forum, 1964).*

**December 3, 1961**

The Soviet Union breaks off diplomatic relations with Communist Albania. It is an unprecedented move. Albania becomes a Chinese beach-head in East Europe. The Soviets lose strategic naval Adriatic bases in Albania. Their submarines and naval units withdraw to the Baltic.

**December 10, 1961**

*Pravda* features an article by the Rumanian Party chief Gheorghe Gheorghiu-Dej endorsing the Soviet stand against China.

**End of 1961**

By now it is apparent that the U.S. Government has definitely decided for a military intervention in South Vietnam. We are becoming directly involved in that Asiatic conflict.

**January 15, 1962**

The Communist-led People's Revolutionary Party is formed in South Vietnam. The National Liberation Front has some 300,000.

**February 4, 1962**

After Cuba was expelled from the Organization of American States, in a huge rally (with one million people present) Castro sponsors "The Second Declaration of Havana". This is his reply to "the submissive conclave of Puenta del Este" that was sponsored by the United States.

**February 7, 1962**

The total of the U.S. military personnel in S. Vietnam reaches 4,000.

**February 8, 1962**

Rudolf Barak, the Czechoslovak Minister of the Interior, is removed from the C.P. and arrested by tough Communist A. Novotny.

**February 10, 1962**

The Americans release Col. Rudolf Abel, a convicted Soviet spy, in exchange for the pilot of U-2 Gary Powers.

**March 5-9, 1962**

The Plenum of the Central Committee of the C.P.S.U. reorganizes agricultural management and approves Khrushchev's anti-grassland campaign to increase the agricultural production.

**March 14, 1962**

Eighteen-nation disarmament conference begins in Geneva.

**April 7, 1962**

The Cuban Communist authorities sentence 1,179 prisoners of the Bay of Pigs invasion (April 17–19, 1961) to thirty years imprisonment. However, they were permitted to obtain their freedom on paying the fines. (This is actually blackmail that we accept.)

(On April 14, 1962 Castro releases 60 sick prisoners for a pledged $2.5 million by the U.S. The remaining 1,113 prisoners are returned on December 23–24, 1962; President Kennedy awaits them in Miami and promises that the Cuban flag will wave over a free Cuba. In exchange for these prisoners we pay $58 million in food and medicine.)

**April 17, 1962**

Milovan Djilas, one of the former leading Yugoslav Communists, who had been released from prison on parole, is arrested again in Belgrade on account of the forthcoming publication of his book *Conversations With Stalin.*

**May 6, 1962**

Tito in a major speech in Split, Dalmatia admits many difficulties with economy and nationality questions.

**May 18, 1962**

Khrushchev pays visit to Sofia, Bulgaria lining up support against the Chinese. Some leading Bulgarian Communists side with Mao.

**May 25, 1962**

*Conversations With Stalin* by Milovan Djilas is published in New York by Harcourt. In this book Djilas condemns Soviet Communism and calls Stalin the greatest murderer in history.

**June 1, 1962**

Soviet government orders price increase for meat and butter and lowers draft registration age to 17. Demonstrations against price increases are reported from several Soviet cities.

**June 6-7, 1962**

The COMECON conference is held in Moscow. The Soviets want Rumania to remain primarily an agricultural country while the Rumanians want to industrialize the country. This causes opposition on the part of the Rumanian leadership which now starts to look more to the West for economic assistance and thus Rumania slowly moves away from the Soviet control. Rumania also exploits the Soviet difficulties with China and wants to be a mediator between the two Communist giants while asserting her own independence.

## July 1, 1962
After seven years of fighting truce in Algeria is signed.

## July 9, 1962
Secretary of State Dean Rusk defends American aid to Tito and Gomulka, as the House begins discussion on foreign aid bill. The main purpose of this aid is to make both Poland and Yugoslavia independent of Moscow, said Mr. Rusk.

## July 11, 1962
The Soviets admit shooting down an American RB-47 plane.

## July 22, 1962
As a result of Tito's speech in Split, the Plenum of the League of Communists of Yugoslavia discusses in Belgrade the economic reform.

## July 26, 1962
It is reported that Moscow began increased shipments of military aid and technical and military personnel to Cuba. Castro's country is turning into an aggressive arsenal for a possible attack on the United States.

## August 1962
Khrushchev's article in the Communist journal *Problems of Peace and Socialism* denounces the European Common Market and urges greater economic integration of the Communist bloc in East Europe. Many East European Communists are complaining that their countries are economically exploited by the Russians and detest the compulsory aid to Castro. (According to some reports, throughout the years the Russians were able to squeeze out of the "Satellites" a billion dollars' profit by overcharging them for many goods and using various means of discrimination.)

## August 12–16, 1962
The Soviet astronauts Nikolayev and Popovich successfully complete orbital flights.

## September 22, 1962
The Soviets indefinitely postpone the income tax reduction.

## October 20, 1962
Serious fighting breaks out between India and China on the Himalayan front.

## October 21, 1962
*Pravda* publishes E. Yevtushenko's poem "Stalin's Heirs." There is now a lot of criticism of Stalin's era in the Soviet literature. Millions of people who could not forget their experience in the concentration camps are very outspoken in denouncing Stalin and the cult of personality. Many of the critical voices are actually anti-Communist. Khrushchev does not want to tolerate this and sooner or later many Soviet writers are in trouble with authorities.

## October 21, 1962
The Soviet President L. Brezhnev, during his visit in Yugoslavia, delivers a significant speech in Gornji Milanovac, Serbia.

## October 22, 1962
*We are on the brink of the war:* the Cuban missile crisis begins; on this historic day President John F. Kennedy charges Russia has been turning Cuba into an offensive base. Russia put missile sites and jet bombers on the island. He also announced the American "quarantine" of Cuba to halt all Soviet ships carrying offensive weapons. He demanded immediate dismantling of all offensive weapons, threatened further action by America, if necessary, appealed to the Cubans to rise against Communist tyranny; and finally warned the Soviet Government: "Any hostile move anywhere in the world . . . will be met by whatever action is needed."

## October 28, 1962
Khrushchev agrees to American demand for removal of Soviet offensive missiles from Cuba. Thus a very serious crisis was averted.

## November 1962
Solzhenitsyn's novel *One Day in the Life of Ivan Denisovich* is published in the Soviet Union. It describes concentration camp in Siberia under Stalin.

## November 5–14, 1962
The Congress of the Bulgarian C.P. supports the Soviets in the split with China.

*Adlai E. Stevenson* — Culver Pictures

## November 19–23, 1962

The Plenum of the Central Committee of the C.P.S.U. reorganizes industrial and agricultural management and changes the organizational structure of the party apparatus. Party — State Control Committee is reestablished.

## November 20–24, 1962

The Hungarian C.P. Congress endorses the Soviet position in the Sino-Soviet split.

## November 25, 1962

Adlai E. Stevenson, the U.S. Ambassador to the U.N., addresses a letter to the President of the U.N. General Assembly castigating the Russians for oppressing many nationalities.

## December 3, 1962

As the Cuban missile crisis is over, the American authorities declare that the Russians have begun withdrawal of their offensive weapons from Cuba, including the IL-28 jet bombers. The whole crisis was a humiliation for the Soviets. During the crisis some 2,800 American citizens were evacuated from the U.S. Guantamano base.

## December 3–21, 1962

Tito pays a friendly visit to the Soviet Union. On December 13 he is given the unique honor for a foreign Communist visitor — to address the session of the Supreme Soviet. He stresses unity with the Soviet Union.

## December 4–8, 1962

The C.P. of Czechoslovakia (A. Novotny is Party Secretary and the President of the Republic) holds its Congress and of course — as an obedient "Satellite"- supports the Soviets against the Chinese.

## December 17, 1962

The Soviet Party leadership meets with their leading intellectuals and rejects the "peaceful coexistence with bourgeois art."

## December 17, 1962

The Communist Party of the United States is convicted by a Federal jury in Washington for criminally failing to register with governmental agencies as an agent of the Soviet Union.

## December 20, 1962

The Hungarian question is removed from the agenda of the U.N. whose Assembly resolves that "the position of the United Nations representative on Hungary need no longer to be continued."

## December 21, 1962

Castro agrees to release to the U.S. the remaining 1,113 prisoners of the Bay of Pigs invasion in exchange for medical supplies worth some $53,000,000. (Although many object to this as blackmail, the Americans will agree to this exchange.)

## December 30, 1962

The Chinese charge Indians with continued war aggression. The first published reports reveal that the Indians had over 4,000 casualties, including 322 killed. The Indian neutrality policy toward China thus did not pay off. The Red Chinese kept some Indian territories and continued to claim additional areas in the Himalayas. Altogether they aspire to some 51,000 sq. m.

## End of 1962

According to official reports, during this year the Cuban-trained insurgents had committed subversive activities against several Latin American countries.

**January 1, 1963**
The Chinese *People's Daily* again attacks Khrushchev and especially the "revisionist" Tito.

**January 2, 1963**
The American death toll in South Vietnam is 30 by now.

**January 14, 1963**
The Soviet shipment of MIG-21 planes to India indicates the Soviet eagerness to support India in her border conflict with the Red Chinese.

**January 15, 1963**
Fidel Castro appeals to the Congress of Women of America assembled in Havana, to undertake revolutions in their respective countries.

**January 15–21, 1963**
The Communist Party Congress is held in East Berlin. It is attended by Khrushchev; the present anti-Chinese majority interrupts the speech of the Chinese delegate.

**January 26, 1963**
*Pravda* denounces the American celebration of the Ukrainian Independence Day on January 22.

**February 6, 1963**
The Soviet Union denounces the Franco-German treaty as a "war treaty."

**February 8, 1963**
The pro-Soviet Iraqui government of Premier Abdul Karim Kassim is overthrown in a bloody revolt. He is killed.

**February 9, 1963**
The Soviet authorities announce they have released from many-years imprisonment the 71-year old Ukrainian Metropolitan of the Catholic Church of Byzantine Rite, Archbishop Josef Slipy. He goes to Rome to become a Cardinal there.

**February 15, 1963**
At the COMECON meeting in Moscow, the Rumanian delegation refuses the Soviet demands that Rumania should stop building heavy industry and concentrate on agriculture.

**February 22, 1963**
Soviet Defense Minister Malinovsky warns that any attack on Cuba would provoke World War III.

**February 27, 1963**
Khrushchev indicates budget shifting in favor of military expenditures.

**March 7, 1963**
Pope John XXIII receives Alexei Adzhubei, Khrushchev's son-in-law and the editor of the *Izvestia.*

**March 18, 1963**
President Kennedy arrives in Costa Rica, a Central American country, for a meeting with Central American presidents.

**March 28, 1963**
Rumania reestablishes diplomatic relations with Albania in open defiance of the Soviet attitude. Rumania is becoming more independent.

**March 30, 1963**
The American Government bans all Cuban exile raids against Castro. Many thousands of Cubans are now living in America and they belong to a large number of political organizations.

**April 7, 1963**
After long discussions, Yugoslavia adopts a new Constitution, the third within seventeen years. The new name of the state is the *Socialist* Federative Republic of Yugoslavia.

**April 8, 1963**
Radio Bucharest announces conclusion of a Sino-Rumanian trade treaty.

**April 18, 1963**
Dr. José Miro Cardona, the President of the Cuban Revolutionary Council in America, issues a 6,500-words statement denouncing President J.F. Kennedy for not keeping his promise on liberation of Cuba. Cardona resigned as the President of the Council. In 1963, there are about 300 Cuban exile groups legally registered in Miami, Florida where the great majority of Cuban exiles are congregated. Cardona's Cuban Revolutionary Council comprises sixteen major organizations.

**April 24, 1963**
It is reported that George F. Kennan, the American Ambassador in Yugoslavia and a friend of President Tito, is going to resign his position because of his protest against American decision to cut drastically aid to Tito.

*José Miro Cardona* – Keystone

**April 27, 1963**
Premier Castro arrives in the Soviet Union for an official visit. He is awarded the highest Soviet decoration.

**May 9, 1963**
The U.S. Senate Preparedness Subcommittee issues a lengthy statement on the presence of at least 17,500 Soviet citizens, including 5,000 combat troops, in Cuba.

**May 11, 1963**
Oleg V. Penkovsky, a former Soviet intelligence official, who had spied for the West, is sentenced to death and subsequently shot. His associate–a Britisher, G. M. Wynne – receives an eight-year sentence.

**May 24, 1963**
One of the top Soviet leaders Nikolai V. Podgorny leads a delegation to Rumania to discuss important matters.

**June 3, 1963**
Pope John XXIII, who had initiated a movement of reforms within the Catholic Church, dies in Rome. His successor (elected on June 19) is Paul VI (Giovanni B. Montini); he continued reforms, conducted Vatican II Council, and also made many contacts with the Communist world.

**June 3, 1963**
Castro returns from his 37-day trip to the Soviet Union.

**June 5, 1963**
The Organization of American States issues a report on Communist subversive activities in Latin America. Cuba serves as a base and the principal target is Venezuela.

**June 12, 1963**
The Rumanians announce an agreement with Yugoslavia for the construction of a gigantic hydro-electric power plant at Iron Gates on the Danube River.

**June 14, 1963**
The *Open Letter* of the C.P. of China, addressed to the C.P.S.U., lists 25 "crucial questions" for discussion. Seven such letters were exchanged in bitter dispute. The Chinese attack the Russians as traitors to Marxism-Leninism and collaborators with the "Western imperialists."

**June 26, 1963**
President Kennedy is enthusiastically received in West Berlin. He saw the Wall. In a historic speech he uses the phrase: "Ich bin ein Berliner..." He returns to Washington on July 3.

**June 29, 1963**
The First Secretaries of East European Communist Parties meet in East Berlin on the occasion of Ulbricht's birthday.

**July 5 – 20, 1963**
Sino-Soviet talks in Moscow fail to remove the split. The rift is widening and has its repercussions in many Communist Parties.

**August 5, 1963**
The United States, the Soviet Union and Britain sign an Atom Test Ban Treaty. All but underground tests are discontinued. Dean Rusk represents the U.S. in this special ceremony in the Kremlin.

**August 20, 1963**
Khrushchev arrives in Yugoslavia for a 15-day visit.

**August 28, 1963**
The "March on Washington" is held. Over 200,000 people demonstrate for civil rights.

**August 30, 1963**
The "Hot Line" is opened between the White House and the Kremlin to serve as instant communication, especially in times of crisis.

**September 2, 1963**
President Kennedy states his views on South Vietnam and assails the South Vietnamese President Ngo Dinh Diem for his "persecution of the Buddhists." (Diem is a Catholic and Kennedy's speech will contribute to the overthrow of Diem.)

**September 12, 1963**
President Kennedy states at a press conference he does not believe that an American invasion of Cuba "is in the interest of this country."

**September 17 – 23, 1963**
The Fifth International Congress of the Slavists is held in Sofia, Bulgaria. The Slavs on both sides of the Curtain celebrate 1,100th anniversary of the beginning of missionary activities of Sts. Cyril and Methodius among the Slavs. Many scholars from America and the West are present in Sofia.

**September 22, 1963**
A party and government shakeup takes place in Czechoslovakia. Premier V. Siroky is succeeded by Jozef Lenart, a Slovak. There are six Slovaks and twenty-two Czechs in the new cabinet. There is still old antagonism between the Czechs and Slovaks.

**September 23, 1963**
W. Ulbricht of East Germany comes for a visit to Poland. The relations between the East German and Polish Communists are cool in spite of the fact that Germans had consented to the loss of East German territories to Poland.

**September 26, 1963**
Yugoslavia and the Soviet Union conclude a significant trade agreement amounting to $220 million.

**September 27, 1963**
Khrushchev openly admits poor harvest in the Soviet Union.

**October 4, 1963**
As Tito is touring Latin America, the *Time* magazine reports that Tito's visit in Brazil is a "diplomatic disaster."

**October 9, 1963**
Canada announces sale of 250,000 tons of wheat to Communist Bulgaria. All Communist countries produce too little wheat. (Bread is still the most important part of the East European diet.)

**October 10 – 18, 1963**
Soviet Marshal Rodion Malinovsky and some 200 high-ranking Red Army officers visit Poland.

**October 16, 1963**
Tito arrives in the United States for a 10-day visit.

**October 17, 1963**
In spite of many protests and objections, President Kennedy receives President Tito in the White House. Tito's visit in Washington lasted only five hours. The White House was picketed by demonstrators. Fearing further demonstrations, Tito cancels his visit to California.

The General Assembly of the U.N. rejects again admission of Red China to its membership.

**October 22, 1963**
Tito addresses the General Assembly of the U.N. pleading for co-existence and peace. Tito's presence in New York causes many wild demonstrations.

**October 25, 1963**
Tito leaves New York aboard an Italian ship.

**November 1 – 2, 1963**
A coup overthrows the government of Ngo Dinh Diem in S. Vietnam. Diem and his brother Nhu are assassinated on the 2nd. The general contention is that the U.S. Government encouraged the overthrow of Diem and thus destroyed a considerably stable regime.

**November 4, 1963**
Canada sells Poland 400,000 tons of wheat.

**November 7, 1963**
At the Kremlin reception on the forty-sixth anniversary of the Revolution, Khrushchev denounces America.

**November 14, 1963**
The U.S. Department of Commerce declares that America is selling 100,000 tons of wheat to Communist Hungary.

**November 22, 1963**
President John F. Kennedy is assassinated in Dallas, Texas. The new President is L. B. Johnson. Kennedy's death is mourned in America and all over the world, including the Communist countries.

**November 25, 1963**
As the entire world and America watch on TV, Kennedy's funeral takes place in the capital. He is buried in Arlington National Cemetery. Present are many chiefs of state, with many Communist dignitaries. First Deputy Premier Anastas Mikoyan represents the Soviet Union.

**November 29, 1963**
President Johnson appoints a special Commission under Chief Justice Earl Warren, to investigate the assassination of President Kennedy.

**November 30, 1963**
Gheorghe Gheorghiu-Dej, the Communist leader of Rumania, arrives in Belgrade for important talks with Tito. Rumanian-Yugoslav relations are very good.

**December 1, 1963**
In spite of Communist terrorism, undertaken by Communist guerillas, the national elections in Venezuela are well attended. The vote indicates that a great majority of the Venezuelans are opposed to Communism.

**December 16 – 20, 1963**
The Foreign Minister of Yugoslavia is in Prague. This is the first visit since 1948 by a top official of Yugoslavia in the Czechoslovak capital.

*President Kennedy's flag draped coffin with honor guard from four armed services, in the East Room of the White House* — Keystone

**December 21 – 22, 1963**

The Plenary Meeting of the C.P. of Slovakia is held in Bratislava. The participants denounce "bourgeois nationalism," which is apparent in the Slovak C.P. One publication attacking dogmatic Marxism in the country is the literary weekly *Kulturny Život*.

**December 31, 1963**

Chou En-lai, the Chinese Premier, arrives in Albania for a ten-day visit. He promises more aid to Albania and in his speeches attacks the Soviet Union.

**End of 1963**

According to official statements, some 15,000 American military instructors and advisers are present in South Vietnam. By now we learn something about guerilla warfare. The Communists of Vietnam follow the old doctrines of Mao Tse-tung on "the Art of War" which is summed up in the following rules:

"The enemy advances, we retreat;
The enemy halts, we harass;
The enemy tires, we attack;
The enemy retreats, we pursue."

Under similar rules and especially those designed by E. Che Guevara the Castroites are waging their guerilla warfare in Latin American countries. There were during 1963 28 major invasions of Castroites in Latin America, principal target still being Venezuela.

**1964**

The Italian C.P. has 1,728,000 members; it controls municipal governments in 1,800 towns, and it has 140 deputies in the parliament.

**January 1, 1964**

The COMECON Bank opens in Moscow.

**January 2 – 5, 1964**

Khrushchev visits Poland.

**January 5, 1964**

After a four-day trial, Ivan Assen Khristov is sentenced to death in Sofia as an agent of the C.I.A.

**January 9, 1964**

Choe En-lai in his speech in Tirana attacks the Soviet Union and praises Albania for its anti-Soviet stand.

**January 10 – 11, 1964**

W. Ulbricht of East Germany visits Moscow.

**January 12, 1964**

Communist-led rebels (many trained in Cuba and China) overthrow the government of Sultan Abdulah at the African Island of Zanzibar. It comes under strong Chinese influence. In several African countries the Chinese are very active.

**February 14, 1964**

Speaking to the Central Committee of the C.P.S.U. Khrushchev bitterly denounces the Chinese for spreading disunity among the Communists.

**February 15 – 18, 1964**

Todor Zhivkov, the Communist Premier of Bulgaria, and a high level Communist delegation visit Moscow. Bulgaria is still a faithful "Satellite" of Moscow.

**February 21, 1964**

Hungarian Communist delegation led by J. Kadar arrives in Moscow to pledge allegiance to Khrushchev in his struggle with China. Hungary is an obedient follower of the Soviets.

**February 25, 1964**

Secretary D. Rusk explains in a speech why America supports some Communist states like Poland and Yugoslavia. For years many critics of our foreign policy have deplored aid to any totalitarian country.

**March 6, 1964**

Bulgaria and West Germany sign a trade agreement. Bonn is dealing with many Communist and non-Communist countries. West German industry and entire economy are booming and the Germans are importing many foreign workers. Among them are thousands from Yugoslavia.

**March 16, 1964**

Rumanian Premier Maurer returns from a two-week visit in Red China.

**March 31 – April 1, 1964**

Joao Goulart, the Brazilian leftist President, is overthrown by a military anti-Communist coup.

**March 31, 1964**

Khrushchev arrives in Hungary. In his speeches he ridicules the strict dogmatic Chinese Communists and says it is better to be less dogmatic and have goulash (a good Hungarian dish) in the stomach.

**April 2, 1964**

Dimitar Ganev, the Bulgarian head of state, dies at the age of 65. His successor is Georgi Traykov.

**April 3, 1964**

*Pravda* announces that V. M. Molotov, G. M. Malenkov, and L. M. Kaganovich—all old Bolshe-viks—were expelled from the C.P. as "anti-Party Group."

**April 13, 1964**

W. Gomulka of Poland arrives in Moscow for talks with the Soviet leaders.

**April 15, 1964**

The Plenum of the Central Committee of the Ruma-nian C.P. starts its week-long meeting. It stresses the Rumanian role as mediator between the Soviets and the Chinese and denounces the Soviet attempts to dominate the economy of the East European states.

**April 26, 1964**

Subsequently the Rumanian C.P. publishes a state-ment on the problems of World Communism and stresses the "Polycentrism" of the international Com-munist movement.

**April 28, 1964**

It is made public that Yugoslavia will receive 240,000 tons of American wheat.

**May 11, 1964**

The Algerian leader Ben Bella, known for his leftist leanings, comes to Prague for a visit.

**May 18, 1964**

A high-level Rumanian delegation headed by Deputy Premier G. Gaston-Marin arrives in Washington. Talks end on June 1. The two countries agree to raise their legations to the rank of embassies and conclude several economic and cultural agreements.

**May 21, 1964**

Adlai E. Stevenson, the U.S. Ambassador to the U.N., states in his address to the Security Council that "the United States cannot stand by while South east Asia is overrun by armed aggression."

**May 25, 1964**

Khrushchev returns home after a 16-day visit to Egypt. Nasser is getting ample Soviet military and economic aid.

*M. Gheorge Gheorghiu-Dej, Roumanian president* – Keystone

**May 30, 1964**

The Moscow radio denounces Rumanian cooperation with the West.

**June 1 – 8, 1964**

Playing the role of a neutralist leader, President Tito visits Finland.

**June 8, 1964**

On his return from Finland, Tito meets Khrushchev in Leningrad. According to some reports, Khrushchev asked Tito to urge the Rumanians not to be too radical in their anti-Soviet policies.

**June 12, 1964**

East Germany and the U.S.S.R. conclude a Treaty of Friendship, Mutual Assistance, and Cooperation.

**June 12, 1964**

President Johnson and the visiting West German Chancellor Ludwig Erhard state that Germany should be reunited. Poland, Czechoslovakia and all Com-munist states in East Europe would never agree with this idea.

*Tage Erlander, Swedish Prime Minister* – Keystone

**June 16 – 21, 1964**
Khrushchev visits Denmark.

**June 22 – 27, 1964**
Khrushchev visits neutral Sweden to gain popularity for the Soviet Union. Everywhere he goes he is met by anti-Soviet demonstrators.

**June 25, 1964**
Tito comes to Warsaw for an eight-day visit of Poland.

**June 27, 1964**
Robert F. Kennedy arrives in Poland for a three-day private visit and is enthusiastically greated by the Polish people. (There are 5,000,000 Americans of Polish descent and America is very popular in the country of their ancestors.)

**June 27, 1964**
The monument to the Ukrainian national poet Taras Shevchenko is unveiled in Washington. Former Presi-

dent Eisenhower is the main speaker. Present are some 100,000 American and Canadian Ukrainians.

**June 29 – July 4, 1964**
Khrushchev is in Norway.

**June 30, 1964**
According to the official reports, the membership of the League of Communists of Yugoslavia is 1,080,000. The Yugoslav Communists complain that too few young people and workers are in the Party.

**July of 1964**
General William C. Westmoreland becomes the commander of the U.S. military advisers—and later all armed forces—in S. Vietnam. The number of American "advisers" is now 23,000. After Diem's death the situation is getting worse. There is chaos and desertion in the South Vietnamese army. (It was also disclosed in many reports that Buddhists were not persecuted by Diem, that they collaborated with the Viet Cong, and that S. Vietnam does not have a Buddhist majority.)

**July 8, 1964**
Official reports indicate our losses in S. Vietnam are already 1,387; of these 152 were killed in action. Officially, we are still not fighting.

**July 9, 1964**
A Bulgarian-Greek agreement removes some tensions between these two Balkan countries.

**July 13, 1964**
The Western press reports that Tito is urging both Rumanians and Poles not to press too hard on Moscow.

**July 19, 1964**
Yugoslavia and West Germany conclude economic agreements beneficial to both countries. Paradoxically they have no diplomatic relations; thousands of citzens of Yugoslavia (mostly Croatians)—unemployed at home – find employment in West Germany.

**August 2 – 4, 1964**
The American destroyers *Maddox* and *Turner* are attacked by the North Vietnamese in the Gulf of Tonkin. We decide to retaliate. *This is the watershed of our involvement in S. Vietnam.* The long nightmare is only beginning.

**August 7, 1964**

The U.S. Congress approves a Southeast Asia resolution (Res. 1145) giving the President power to "take all necessary measures to repel any armed attack against the forces of the United States and to prevent further aggression."

**August 11, 1964**

Bulgarian Minister of Agriculture, Marin Gachkov, arrives in Washington for a three-week visit.

**August 22, 1964**

Palmiro Togliatti, the Italian Communist leader, dies in Crimea during his visit in the Soviet Union. He was 71 years old. Three days later he was buried in Italy and was succeeded by L. Longo, a skilled Communist revolutionary.

**September 1, 1964**

The foreign ministers of Bulgaria, Hungary and Poland meet with Khrushchev in Prague.

**September 7, 1964**

G. Gheorghiu-Dej and Tito attend the inaugural festivities of the great construction work at the Iron Gates (Danube River).

**September 10 – 14, 1964**

Tito is in Budapest.

**September 11, 1964**

*Pravda* officially comments on the hundredth anniversary of the founding of the First International.

**September 15, 1964**

The Vatican and Hungary reach a limited agreement on the status of the Catholic Church in Hungary.

**September 17, 1964**

Tito states that Yugoslavia is going to participate in the COMECON.

**September 21 – 26, 1964**

The Czechoslovak President Antonyn Novotny visits Yugoslavia.

**September 21, 1964**

Otto Grotewohl, the Communist Premier of East Germany, dies of natural causes.

**September 27, 1964**

The Warren Commission issues its 888-page printed *Report* on the death of President Kennedy. The Report has been criticized for its credibility.

**October 5, 1964**

Rumors in the Western press reveal that Rumanians had demanded from the Russians return of the former Rumanian province of Bessarabia.

**October 5 – 11, 1964**

Forty-seven "neutralist" nations are gathered in Cairo for a conference.

**October 14, 1964**

A Plenum of the Central Committee of the C.P.S.U. is held in Moscow while Khrushchev is vacationing in Crimea. The C.C. deposes Khrushchev. The official announcement states that the C.C. granted Khrushchev's "request" to be relieved of his duties "in connection with his advanced age and worsened health condition." Leonid I. Brezhnev is the new First Secretary of the party. The new Chairman of the Council of Ministers, elected the following day by the Presidium of the Supreme Soviet, is Alexei A. Kosygin.

This is the end of Khrushchev's rule. (He was arrested in Crimea and brought back to Moscow and then dispatched into retirement in a secluded place near Moscow.) *The end of Khrushchev's era* and the way he was ousted from power came as a surprise to many Communist leaders abroad. Speculations on the reason for ouster indicate that the Soviet leaders by removing him wanted to appease the Chinese and thus settle differences with them. As it later turned out, the rift between Moscow and Red China still continued.

**October 14 – 17, 1964**

Cuban President Dorticos Torrado is in the Soviet Union on an official visit.

**October 15, 1964**

The British Labor Party wins in the parliamentary elections thus ending thirteen years of the Conservatives' rule. The new Prime Minister is Harold Wilson.

**October 17, 1964**
*Pravda*'s editorial "The Immutable Leninist General Line" expresses the policy of the new Soviet leadership after ouster of Khrushchev.

The Soviet press reports the first Chinese atomic explosion.

The Hungarian Communists issue official statement commenting the downfall of Khrushchev.

**October 18, 1964**
Speaking to a Communist rally in Milan, the new Italian Communist leader—successor of Togliatti—Luigi Longo states; "The way in which Comrade Khrushchev has been replaced leaves us worried and bewildered."

The East German Communists in their official statement on Khrushchev's ouster express shock and surprise.

**October 19, 1964**
The leadership of the Czechoslovak C.P. expresses "surprise and emotion" about ouster of Khrushchev.

**October 23, 1964**
The official Yugoslav comments indicate that Tito and his comrades were dismayed and surprised by Khrushchev's ouster.

**October 27, 1964**
The Italian C.P. delegation arrives in Moscow to find out what is going on in the Kremlin.

**November 3, 1964**
Lyndon B. Johnson wins in the American elections by biggest popular vote margin in the history of America. He and his administration inherit a lot of world problems in regard to World Communism. The biggest problem is that of S. Vietnam.

**November 5 – 13, 1964**
The Chinese delegation under Chou En-lai is in Moscow to participate in the celebration of the forty-seventh anniversary of the Revolution. But the split still continues.

**November 7, 1964**
All Communist representatives, except the Albanians, are in Moscow to celebrate the anniversary of the Revolution.

**November 14, 1964**
Soviet reports indicate that further talks with the Chinese produced no results. The Chinese are still adamant in their stand.

**November 16, 1964**
The Plenum of the Central Committee of the C.P.S.U. discards the party reorganization of 1962 and makes important changes in the party leadership.

**December 7 – 13, 1964**
The important Eighth Congress of Yugoslav Communists takes place in Belgrade. There are many difficulties within the Party and in the country: economic troubles and the nationality question. As various republics (notably: Croatia, Slovenia and Macedonia) indicate opposition to Belgrade centralism, Tito tries desperately to preserve his "Brotherhood and Unity" policy. (The great paradox in Yugoslavia and in all Communist East European countries is the rise of fierce nationalism.)

**December 11, 1964**
Ernesto "Che" Guevara, the Cuban Minister of Industry and a professional revolutionary, addresses the General Assembly of the U.N.

**December 17, 1964**
President Johnson in his first address to the United Nations states: "The United States of America wants to see the cold war end."

**December 19, 1964**
A. N. Shelepin heads a Soviet delegation to the United Arab Republic (Egypt). The Arabs are getting Soviet weapons to attack Israel.

**End of 1964**
An eventful year, marked by the ouster of N. S. Khrushchev, comes to its end. Obviously, there are now "many roads to Communism." Moscow is but one of the centers of International Communism. China has asserted its role as at least an equal partner in leadership of World Communism. The "Satellites" tend to be less and less patronized by Moscow. The Communists all around the world are perplexed and insecure in their ideological adherences. The Communist Parties are by now divided between those which side with Moscow and those that follow Mao Tse-tung.

# 3. After Ouster of N. S. Khrushchev: 1964-1967

**January 1, 1965**
Soviet Premier A. N. Kosygin, in an interview with the Japanese paper *Asaki*, pledges Soviet support to an "active policy of peace and relaxation of international tension."

This issue — and the issue for February — of the Belgrade literary monthly *Delo* publishes a report by a young Yugoslav writer (born of Russian exile parents) Mihajlo Mihajlov — "Moscow Summer" — describing the author's impressions of the visit in the Soviet Union. He is very critical of the Soviet regime and denounces their concentration camps. The Soviet Embassy in Belgrade reacts immediately. Thus Mihajlov controversy began.

**January 4, 1965**
President Johnson in his State of the Union message announces "the beginning of the road to the Great Society."

**January 6, 1965**
The *Izvestia* criticizes Johnson's speech.

**January 7, 1965**
The U.S. report indicates that 365 Americans had been killed in Vietnam.

**January 9, 1965**
Anti-American riots break out in the Canal Zone of Panama.

**January 19, 1965**
The leaders of all Soviet-bloc countries gather in Warsaw for a meeting with the Soviet Premier Kosygin and Party chief Brezhnev. The occasion is the session of the Warsaw Pact Political Consultative Committee.

**January 20, 1965**
President Johnson is inaugurated for his first full term. Hubert Horatio Humphrey is the new Vice President; he has good experience in foreign affairs.

**January 24, 1965**
Sir Winston Churchill dies in London at the age of 90. He popularized the term "The Iron Curtain", was distrusted by Stalin and was the first Western statesman who sensed the dangerous impact of Communism.

**January 25, 1965**
France recognizes Red China.

**January 27 — 29, 1965**
The C.P. of Czechoslovakia adopts the economic reform.

**January 29 — 31, 1965**
Brezhnev and Podgorny (now President of the U.S.S.R.) hold a three-day secret conclave in Budapest.

**January 30, 1965**
Frol Kozlov, one of the Soviet leaders, dies. He is buried with honors in the Kremlin Wall on February 2.

**February 6 — 10, 1965**
Kosygin — heading a Soviet delegation — visits North Vietnam and promises more military aid.

**February 7, 1965**
Eight Americans are killed and sixty-two wounded by Viet Cong in S. Vietnam. President Johnson promptly orders American retaliatory air strikes against North Vietnam. We are more involved in the war.

**February 10, 1965**
Premier Kosygin stops at Peking on his return from Hanoi.

**February 11 – 14, 1965**
Kosygin visits North Korea.

**February 16, 1965**
The Albanian delegate in the U.N., Halim Budo, charges that the U.N. is dominated by America and the Soviet Union.

**February 17, 1965**
President Johnson declares America is determined to defend South Vietnam against Communist aggression.

**February 22, 1965**
Soviet-Cypriot trade agreement is signed in Nicosia, Cyprus.

**February 27, 1965**
The U.S. Department of State releases a White Paper: *Aggression from the North*: The Record of North Vietnam's Campaign to Conquer South Vietnam.

**February 28, 1965**
The U.S. introduces continuous air attacks against North Vietnam in an effort to stop the infiltration of S. Vietnam and to force a negotiated settlement with Hanoi.

**March 1 – 8, 1965**
A meeting of the eighteen Communist Parties in Moscow fails to solve many problems of the World Communism and to reestablish the unity of Communism.

**March 4, 1965**
In a note to our Ambassador Kohler in Moscow, the Soviet government protests our bombing of North Vietnam.

**March 12, 1965**
The Chinese demonstrate in front of the Soviet embassy in Peking.

**March 14, 1965**
Ernesto "Che" Guevara returns to Cuba after a three-month visit of Red China, Asia, and Africa.

**March 19, 1965**
G. Gheorghiu-Dej, the Communist leader of Rumania, dies of natural causes at the age of 64.

*Ernesto "Che" Guevera* – Keystone

**March 22, 1965**
Nicolae Ceaucescu becomes the First Secretary of the Rumanian C.P. Two days later, Chivu Stoica becomes the President of the State Council, while the new Premier is G. Maurer.

**March 24 – 26, 1965**
L. Brezhnev gives report on agricultural reforms to a Plenum of the C.C. of the C.P.S.U.

**April 4 – 8, 1965**
Brezhnev and Kosygin visit Poland.

**April 8, 1965**
The new Soviet-Polish Treaty of Friendship, Cooperation and Mutual Aid is signed in Warsaw.

**April 16, 1965**
During his visit to Algiers, Tito in his speech bitterly attacks America (from which he had received $2.5 billion of aid). The American Ambassador leaves the occasion in protest.

**April 17, 1965**
In his speech at Johns Hopkins University, President Johnson announces that America is willing to spend a billion dollars' worth of aid on South east Asia, including North Vietnam.

**April 22 – 25, 1965**
British Foreign Secretary Michael Stewart visits Prague.

**April 24, 1965**
The Hungarian Communist paper *Nepszabadsag* warns that capitalist nations may use trade to divide and weaken the Soviet bloc.

**April 28, 1965**
The U.S. sends troops to revolt-torn Dominican Republic to prevent spread of Communism.

**April 29, 1965**
The official organ of the Yugoslav Communists, *Komunist,* admits that foreign debt of Yugoslavia is about a billion dollars.

**April 30, 1965**
Mihajlo Mihajlov, a professor at the University of Zagreb branch in Zadar (Croatia), is sentenced in Zadar to nine months imprisonment because of his criticism of the Soviet regime in his report, *The Moscow Summer.*

**May 5, 1965**
The first U.S. Army ground unit, comprising 1,200 men of the 173rd Airborn Brigade, arrives in S. Vietnam. More units are following.

**May 7, 1965**
Soviet Premier Kosygin denounces in Moscow speech the "barbaric bombing attacks" by the Americans in N. Vietnam.

**May 9, 1965**
Our military strength in S. Vietnam is: Army – 19,000; Navy – 1,800; Marines – 12,300 and the Air Force – 9,300, a total of 42,000 fighting men.

**May 12 – 19, 1965**
The Indian Premier L. B. Shastri (successor of the late Nehru) visits the Soviet Union.

**May 14, 1965**
Red China reports explosion of its second Atomic bomb.

**June 2 – 8, 1965**
Tito is in Czechoslovakia on official visit. (All Communist leaders like to travel.)

**June 8, 1965**
Tito is in East Berlin to pay a visit to East Germany (German Democratic Republic).

**June 12, 1965**
N. Cao Ky becomes Premier of a weak South Vietnamese government. After Diem's death there are frequent changes of government in S. Vietnam.

**June 16, 1965**
As fighting increases in S. Vietnam, additional 21,000 American troops arrive there.

**June 18, 1965**
Tito arrives in Moscow for a two-week visit.

**June 19, 1965**
The leftist government of the Algerian Premier Ben Bella is overthrown by his former friend Colonel H. Boumedienne who becomes the new head of state. He is less extreme than Ben Bella.

**June 28, 1965**
The American troops in S. Vietnam participate in their first major combat.

**July 1, 1965**
Devaluation of the Yugoslav dinar is announced as part of the economic reform. This is a radical reform in economy and political organization. Many young jobless people are still leaving the country.

**July 10 – 17, 1965**
At the World Peace Congress in Helsinki, Finland, the Soviet and Chinese delegates clash over the Vietnamese question.

**July 12, 1965**
The American casualties in S. Vietnam are: 503 killed and over 3,000 wounded.

**July 19, 1965**
North Vietnam rejects the American peace offer. Hanoi insists America must pull out all troops first. The U.S. resumes bombing of N. Vietnam.

**July 19 – 24, 1965**
The C.P. of Rumania holds its Ninth Congress. Brezhnev is here with a Soviet delegation.

**July 21, 1965**
Kosygin participates in the celebration of the twenty-fifth anniversary of Latvia's incorporation into the U.S.S.R. Mikoyan is in Estonia for the same purpose. Suslov takes part in Lithuanian celebrations. Everybody knows that these are very sad anniversaries for the Baltic nations.

**July 25, 1965**
Gyula Kallai succeeds J. Kadar as Hungarian Premier. Kadar remains the Party chief.

**July 26, 1965**
New economic reforms are officially proclaimed in Yugoslavia.

**July 28, 1965**
President Johnson declares that the U.S. forces in S. Vietnam will be increased to 125,000 within short time. American military power strikes at the Communist N. Vietnam.

**August 11, 1965**
*Pravda* states that the membership of the C.P.S.U. has reached 12,000,000.

The Canadian Wheat Board announces sale of about 5,000,000 tons of wheat to the Soviet Union.

**August 20 – 21, 1965**
The Rumanian National Assembly adopts the new Constitution of the Socialist Republic of Rumania.

**September 3, 1965**
The Rumanian leader N. Ceausescu arrives for talks in Moscow.

**September 6, 1965**
The Czech leader A. Novotny arrives in Moscow for a nine-day visit.

**September 7, 1965**
The Soviet government offers its mediation in the Indian-Pakistan war which is being waged over Kashmir.

**September 11, 1965**
The official communiqué at the end of Ceausescu's visit in Moscow indicates differences between Rumania and the U.S.S.R.

**September 11 – 13, 1965**
L. Brezhnev is Gomulka's guest in Poland.

**September 17, 1965**
W. Ulbricht of E. Germany arrives for a ten-day visit in the Soviet Union.

**September 18, 1965**
An American trade mission arrives in Bucharest for a four-week visit.

**September 21 – 23, 1965**
The 19th session of the COMECON Executive Committee is held in Moscow.

**September 27, 1965**
An important Plenary Meeting of the Central Committee of the C.P.S.U. is held in Moscow. The Party Secretary L. Brezhnev reads his 20,000 words long report on industrial reorganization and failure to bring about reconciliation with the Chinese Communists.

**September 30, 1965**
A Communist-staged revolt breaks out in Indonesia. Among others the Communists kill five anti-Communist generals. The army now reacts fiercely and by October 1 controls the situation. The Communist revolt is smashed and thousands of Communists are either liquidated or arrested. General Suharto becomes the chief of the army. This is the beginning of the end for President Sukarno who was connected with the Communists. *(See Illus. p. 222).*

**October 4, 1965**
Pope Paul VI comes to the United Nations in New York; in his speech to the General Assembly he pleads for world peace.

**October 10, 1965**
The North Korean Communists celebrate the twentieth anniversary of the founding of their party.

**October 11, 1965**
Raul Castro, brother of Fidel, arrives in Moscow for a long visit.

**October 14, 1965**
First anniversary of Khrushchev's fall passes unnoticed in the Soviet Union.

**October 15, 1965**
Brezhnev comes to Prague for a three-day visit.

**October 15 – 11965**
Large demonstrations against American participation in Vietnam are held in several cities between New York and Berkeley.

**October 20, 1965**
A. A. Gromyko, Soviet Foreign Minister, arrives in Havana, Cuba.

**October 21 – 23, 1965**
Warsaw Pact military forces hold maneuvers in East Germany.

**October 25, 1965**
The Secretary General of the U.N., U. Thant, is denounced by the Soviets for his handling of the Kashmir dispute.

**November 15, 1965**
First Secretary Gomulka and Premier Cyrankiewicz of Poland arrive in Belgrade for a five-day visit.

**November 18, 1965**
Thirty-five Polish bishops at the Vatican Council publish their letter addressed to the German bishops inviting them to Poland for celebrations of the Polish Millenium (thousand years of Christianity).

**November 22 – 28, 1965**
Head of the Polish state, Edward Ochab, is in Cairo.

**December 2, 1965**
British Foreign Secretary Michael Stewart ends four days of talks with the Soviet leaders in Moscow.

*INDONESIA,   Djakarta Armed Forces line road outside Army Headquarters during funeral services October 5, 1965 for 6 generals massacred by the communists during the aborted coup of October 1, 1965.   At left, monument was erected to celebrate Indonesia's 20th year as a Republic on August 17. About 10,000 gathered here* – Carol Goldstein, Keystone

**December 5, 1965**
Peking officially announces military aid to North Vietnam.

German bishops reply to the letter of the Polish bishops. They both urge: "Let us try to forget the past tragedies."

**December 8, 1965**
Vatican II Council is ended.

**December 9, 1965**
Anastas Mikoyan, now seventy years old, one of the last old Bolsheviks, is replaced as chief of the Soviet state by Nikolai V. Podgorny (62 years old). Thus the new leadership of the Soviet Union consists of: Brezhnev as Party Secretary, Kosygin as Premier, and Podgorny as head of the state.

President Johnson, in his message to the AFL-CIO Convention in San Francisco, states that America wants peace in South Vietnam.

**December 11 – 14, 1965**
Janos Kadar of Hungary is visiting Moscow.

**December 11 – 16, 1965**
A. Gromyko, Soviet Foreign Minister, visits Czechoslovakia.

**December 15, 1965**
AFL-CIO Convention in San Francisco passes in resolution supporting our policy in S. Vietnam.

**December 24, 1965 – January 31, 1966**
Our bombing raids of North Vietnam are suspended while the U.S. Government tries through various channels to negotiate a settlement with Hanoi.

**December 28, 1965**
In a reply to Pope Paul VI, Ho Chi Minh states that peace in Vietnam can be discussed only after all Americans withdraw from S. Vietnam.

**January 1, 1966**
American losses in Vietnam during 1965 are reported as 1,350 dead and 5,300 wounded. The Viet Cong lost 34,500 dead and 5,700 captured. According to our estimates, the number of fighting Communists in S. Vietnam is about 297,000. Of these 115,000 are main battle force, while over 80,000 are local guerillas.

**January 3 – 13 1966**
The Tri-Continental (Asia, Africa and Latin America) Solidarity Conference meets in Havana, Cuba. There are here altogether delegates from about 100 countries.

**January 9, 1966**
Jesus Maza Paredes, a leftist leader of the Peruvian Armed Forces of National Liberation, who attended the Tri-Continental Conference in Havana states that the aim of his movement is to overthrow the Peruvian government.

**Janaury 12, 1966**
In his State of the Union message, President Johnson speaks of "building bridges to Eastern Europe." He also states our firm stand on Vietnam and promotes his Great Society Program.

**January 13, 1966**
Polish Millenium Celebrations are held in Rome without Cardinal Wyszynski who could not get a Polish visa.

**January 14, 1966**
After return of a Soviet delegation (led by A. N. Shelepin) from Hanoi, the Soviet government declares it will increase its aid to North Vietnam.

**January 14, 1966**
Communist Polish chief Gomulka attacks Polish bishops for their exchange of letters with German bishops.

**January 16, 1966**
The Latin American Solidarity Organization is founded in Havana by the "anti-imperialist" delegates of 27 Latin American countries that were present at the Tri-Continental Conference. The Cubans also found the Afro-Asian-Latin American People's Solidarity Organization.

**January 20, 1966**
President Johnson appeals for peace in Vietnam.

**February 14, 1966**
Two Soviet writers, Andrei Sinyavsky and Yuli Daniel, are sentenced to hard labor for "anti-Soviet propaganda" abroad.

**February 23, 1966**
Vice President H. H. Humphrey returns from a trip to nine Asiatic countries.

The moderate Baath government in Syria is overthrown by a leftist coup.

**February 24, 1966**
Kwame Nkrumah, dictator of Ghana, arrives in Peking and learns that a coup overthrew his government. His fall was disappointment to many Communist leaders.

**February 25, 1966**
Tito in his speech in Belgrade denounces "the class enemy . . . chauvinism, nationalism and nationalist excesses" in Yugoslavia.

**March 2, 1966**
We learn that 215,000 Americans are fighting in Vietnam.

**March 9, 1966**
France announces it will withdraw her forces from the NATO. All NATO bases and its headquarters should be removed from French soil by the end of the year. De Gaulle's policies are puzzling to the Western statesmen.

**March 10 – 11, 1966**
Janos Kadar visits Rumania.

**March 12, 1966**
General Suharto bans the C.P. of Indonesia. He and the military take over. Sukarno is a mere figurehead.

**March 13, 1966**
Vice President Humphrey states on TV that American policy towards China is "containment without necessarily isolation."

**March 23, 1966**
The Chinese C.P. rejects to send any delegates to the forthcoming Twenty-Third Soviet Party Congress.

**March 25 – 27, 1966**
Anti-war demonstrations are held in several American cities; they are repeated on April 10. They receive much publicity in the Communist press of the world.

*Left to right: Gen. Suharto, Sukarno and Dr. Subandrio* – Keystone

**March 29 – April 18, 1966**
The Twenty-Third Congress of the C.P.S.U. convenes in Moscow's new Congress Hall. 4,942 delegates represent 12,471,000 party members. Over seventy Communist Parties of the world are represented by delegations. Brezhnev and Kosygin give extensive reports. The rift in World Communism is still strong.

**April 7, 1966**
The Polish authorities declare they will bar all foreign Catholic visitors from participating in the celebrations of Polish Millenium.

**April 10, 1966**
Chinese Premier Chou En-lai makes a statement on China's policy towards America.

**April 12 – 13, 1966**
The Plenum of the Central Committee of the Rumanian Communists discusses important problems. The C.P. membership is 1,520,000.

**April 18 – 23, 1966**
Tito visits friendly Rumania.

**April 27, 1966**
The Soviet Foreign Minister Gromyko visits Pope Paul VI.

**April 29, 1966**
The Albanian delegation headed by Premier Mehmet Shehu arrives in Peking. It is welcomed by a million cheering Chinese. The visit ends on May 12.

**May – June 1966**
The "Millenium Struggle" between the Catholic Church and the Polish government abounds in incidents, demonstrations, and manifestations.

**May 3, 1966**
At the celebrations in Jasna Gora at the national Czestochowa shrine Cardinal Wyszynski denounces Gomulka for his suppression of the religion. A half a million people cheer the Cardinal.

**May 5, 1966**
U.S. Senator J. W. Fulbright, an outspoken critic of American involvement in Vietnam, criticized our participation in the war. (On many occasions his remarks are cheerfully quoted—and misinterpreted—by international Communist press.)

**May 7, 1966**
N. Ceausescu, the Secretary General of the Rumanian C.P., speaks at the celebrations of the 45th anniversary of the Party and insists on Rumania's "separate road to Socialism." Rumania wants to collaborate "with all countries regardless of social system."

**May 10 – 13, 1966**
Soviet Party chief Brezhnev visits Bucharest to discuss differences with Rumanian Communists.

**May 10 – 18, 1966**
Soviet Premier A. Kosygin visits the United Arab Republic. Nasser is getting considerable Soviet military and economic aid.

**May 12 – 14, 1966**
The Fifteenth Congress of the Slovak C.P. discusses problems of economy and nationalism.

**May 15, 1966**
Ten thousand anti-war demonstrators picket the White House. All such demonstrations receive favorable publicity in Hanoi.

**May 31 – June 4, 1966**
The Thirteenth Congress of the C.P. of Czechoslovakia is held in Prague.

**June 4, 1966**
It is evident from *People's Daily* in Peking that there is struggle for power between aging Mao and his opponents. Mao launches a general attack on intellectuals. China's young Red Guards spread all over the country the "Cultural Revolution." They eliminate Mao's opposition, attack Buddhist tradition and do away with all Western influences. They quote Mao's writings for all occasions.

**June 13, 1966**
Mao introduces numerous educational reforms. There are many signs of anti-Mao resistance and opposition to Red Guard's terror. Agricultural and industrial production lag. The process of deification of Mao goes on and he is hailed as the only true Marxist-Leninist.

**June 13 – 18, 1966**
Soviet Premier Kosygin visits Finland.

**June 24 – 28, 1966**
Chinese Premier Chou En-lai visits Albania again.

**June 25, 1966**
Vatican and Belgrade sign a Protocol on the status of the Catholic Church in Yugoslavia. Both signatories also reestablish diplomatic relations.

**June 29, 1966**
American bombs fall within city limits of Hanoi and Haiphong. This is interpreted as the escalation of the war in Vietnam.

**July 1, 1966**
At the Plenary Session of the Central Committee of the League of Communists of Yugoslavia, held at the Island of Brioni, Tito removes from the Party leadership and from the office of Vice President Aleksandar Ranković. As the chief of the secret police Ranković was the strongest man in the country. Ranković and his Serbian group are opponents of the reforms and liberalization and are considered closer to Moscow than Tito. The friction between various national party groups continues. Nationalism is strong within party ranks. Macedonian, Montenegrin, Slovenian, and Croatian Communists are opposed to the centralistic tendencies of Serbian Communists.

President Charles De Gaulle, who dreams of French great role between the East and West, winds up an eleven-day tour of the Soviet Union.

**July 4 – 6, 1966**
The Political Consultative Committee of the Warsaw Pact meets in Bucharest.

**July 12, 1966**
President Johnson offers amity to China and North Vietnam and tells them: "Victory for your armies is impossible. You cannot drive us out from South Vietnam."

**July 16 – 19, 1966**
British Prime Minister Harold Wilson visits the Soviet capital.

**July 31, 1966**
Major Pedro M. Prieto, a member of the Central Committee of the C.P. of Cuba, speaking to the Fourth Congress of Latin American Students outlines revolutionary plans for Latin America.

**August 1, 1966**
Cardinal Wyszynski in his speech accuses the Polish government of wanting to destroy the Church.

**August 15 – 20, 1966**
The Rumanian Premier Ion Gheorghe Maurer is on a friendly visit in Denmark.

**August 18, 1966**
The Chinese purge goes on. The Defense Minister Lin Piao emerges as top deputy and heir apparent to Mao. The terror of the Red Guards continues. Most European Communist leaders condemn the excesses of the Chinese "Cultural Revolution."

**August 31, 1966**
Yugoslav newspapers admit the past terror and excesses of Ranković's secret police. The Albanian papers publicize the terror of Yugoslav secret police against the Albanians in Yugoslav Kosmet Region (where close to a million Albanians are living).

**September of 1966**
East European Communist press condemns the outrages of the Maoists in China. Reports reveal that little Albania, imitating China, is also undertaking a "Cultural Revolution" of her own. All churches and mosques are closed.

**September 1, 1966**
In a speech during his visit in Cambodia (a former French colony), De Gaulle tells the United States to get out of S. Vietnam.

**September 4, 1966**
In a speech in Murska Sobota, Tito announces a reorganization of his Party "From top to the bottom."

**September 5 – 7, 1966**
Rumanian Foreign Minister Corneliu Manescu visits Rome.

**September 7, 1966**
Official reports admit there are 308,000 Americans and 38,000 South Koreans in S. Vietnam.

**September 15, 1966**
The Czech Communist leader A. Novotny and his host, the Bulgarian Premier Todor Zhivkov, lash the Chinese in their public statement.

**September 15 – 17, 1966**
W. Ulbricht, at a Plenum of East German C.P. Central Committee, denounces Red China and pleads for Communist solidarity.

**September 18 – 24, 1966**
In one week alone 142 Americans are killed in undeclared war in S. Vietnam.

**September 22 – 25, 1966**
Soviet Party chief L. Brezhnev is in Yugoslavia.

**September 26 – October 2, 1966**
W. Ulbricht visits Yugoslavia.

**October 1, 1966**
On the anniversary of the Communist takeover in China Lin Piao, the Defense Minister, bitterly denounces the Soviet Communists.

**October 4, 1966**
The Plenum of the Yugoslav Central Committee reorganizes the structure of the Party. Tito becomes its President (old title: Secretary General); the League of Communists is decentralized.

**October 5, 1966**
At a meeting of the C.P. officials in North Korean capital, Kim Il Sung, the Communist chief of the country, announces forthcoming terror raids against South Korea.

**October 14, 1966**
A British trade exhibition opens in Bucharest in the presence of the British Minister of Trade, W. B. D. Brown.

**October 17 – 22, 1966**
The Soviet Bloc leaders confer in Moscow.

**October 21, 1966**
The North Korean marauders cross demilitarized zone and kill six South Korean soldiers. A few days later North Korean raiders kill a seven-man U.N. patrol in South Korea.

**October 24 – 25, 1966**
On his trip to Asia, President Johnson stops in Manila, Philippines, to confer with our allies (six Asian countries). He also pays a short visit to the U.S. troops in South Vietnam. His seven-day trip ends on November 2.

*President DeGaulle in Moscow standing in car with Premier Kosygin and Podgorny (Nikolai, Soviet President) – Keystone*

**November 7, 1966**
After his disappearance from Cuba in April of 1965, a short stay in the Congo (where he could not get support), and a short secret visit in Cuba earlier this year—Ernesto "Che" Guevara arrives in the Bolivian guerilla camp base. His plan is to spread revolution in Latin America. Eventually he is joined by 20 more Cubans, Castro's best men. As evident later from Guevara's captured *Diary* everything goes wrong from the very beginning. The Bolivian C.P. decides not to support "Che."

**November 12, 1966**
The number of U.S. troops in S. Vietnam is 358,000. So far 4,904 Americans have died in this war.

**November 14 – 19, 1966**
The Bulgarian C.P. holds its Ninth Congress.

**December 1 – 9, 1966**
Soviet Premier Kosygin and Foreign Minister Gromyko pay official visit to France.

**December 5, 1966**
China successfully sets off its fifth nuclear explosion.

**December 18, 1966**
Fidel Castro states at the University of Havana that "the mission of the universities is not to train just technicians, but revolutionary technicians."

**December 20, 1966**
Anti-American demonstrations—because of the war in Vietnam—are staged in several cities of Yugoslavia.

**December 24 – 26, 1966**
Americans observe Christmas truce in S. Vietnam. There are over 60 violations of the truce by the Viet Cong.

**December 30 – 31, 1966**
The United States, Britain, France and the U.N. Secretary U Thant appeal for peace settlement of the war in Vietnam.

**1967**
This is the year when Soviet and all other Communists celebrate the fiftieth anniversary of the Bolshevik Revolution. The Soviet regime is half a century old.

**January 1, 1967**
The U.S. troops in Vietnam number 308,000.

American newspapers report that Milovan Djilas was released from Mitrovica prison after almost five years.

**January 5, 1967**
Our Defense Department states that during 1966 5,008 Americans were killed in Vietnam and 30,093 were wounded. Total American losses since January 1, 1961: 6,664 killed and 37,738 wounded.

**January 19, 1967**
North Korean coastal batteries sink a South Korean patrol craft with 40 crewmen.

**January 21, 1967**
As the "great proletarian cultural revolution" continues in China, clashes are reported from provinces between the Red Guards and workers' militia.

**January 25, 1967**
Students of the University of Puerto Rico demonstrate against "American Imperialism." Stokely Carmichael is one of the speakers.

**January 28, 1967**
Bombs explode in several Yugoslav consulates and embassies in America and Canada.

**January 30, 1967**
The Soviet President N. Podgorny visits Pope Paul VI in the Vatican. This is evidently a new era in relations between the Catholic Church and Communism. There are also many new trends, currents in the Church. There is also a "Catholic Left" arising. After many years of persecution and suppression, the Catholic Church is seeking for a *modus vivendi* with Communist regimes.

**February 6, 1967**
Radio Havana reports on "Guatemala: Five Years Of Armed Struggle." It also calls for continued revolutionary struggle in Colombia. A week later, on the 13th it urges the people of Uruguay to overthrow their government.

**February 6 – 13, 1967**
Kosygin visits Britain.

**February 8, 1967**

Senator Robert F. Kennedy, a newly emerging critic of U.S. foreign policy, states to an University of Chicago audience that the United States must formulate a new policy towards Red China.

**February 20, 1967**

President Sukarno of Indonesia surrenders all executive authority to General Suharto.

**February 23, 1967**

Mao orders Red Guards to stop their terror.

**February 24, 1967**

The Voice of America celebrates its twenty-fifth anniversary. It broadcasts now in 39 languages; many broadcasts are beamed to Communist countries.

**March 4, 1967**

Former Venezuelan Army Captain Elias Manuit Camero, now chief of the Venezuelan Armed Forces of National Liberation's Mission in Havana, announces the "execution" of Dr. Julio Iribarren Borges, an anti-Communist patriot in Venezuela.

**March 14, 1967**

Todor Zhivkov leads a Bulgarian delegation for a visit to Moscow.

**March 15, 1967**

East Germany and Poland sign a twenty-year Treaty of Friendship, Cooperation and Mutual Aid in Warsaw.

**March 17, 1967**

The Croatian weekly *Telegram* publishes a Declaration on the status of the Croatian literary language; it is signed by 19 Croatian scholarly and cultural institutions and 140 leading scholars and writers, many of whom are Communists. The signatories protest against discrimination of the language by various authorities and demand a new amendment in the Constitution that would put Croatian on the equal status with Serbian, Slovenian, and Macedonian. This is more than a linguistic controversy. The movement is suppressed, some expelled from the Party. Miroslav Krleža, the greatest Croatian writer and a Communist for fifty years, quits the party in protest. The biggest problem of Yugoslavia is still the unsolved nationality question.

*Anti-aircraft canon used by the North Vietnamese against American air raids. At right is pictured a woman who also participates in the military.*

Keystone

**March 19 – 25, 1967**
Record U.S. casualties are reported in Vietnam War: 274 killed and 1320 wounded in this week; it brings the American death toll to 8,560. There are already 427,000 Americans fighting in this war.

**March 20 – 21, 1967**
President Johnson meets the Vietnamese leaders at Guam.

**March 21, 1967**
It is disclosed that Ho Chi Minh has turned down President Johnson's peace bid.

A monument is unveiled to the Hungarian Bolshevik Bela Kun on the 48th anniversary of Bolshevik revolt in Hungary.

**March 22, 1967**
We are getting air bases in Thailand and building up tremendous naval bases there. Our bombers use now Thailand too for raids against North Vietnam.

**March 24, 1967**
Former Vice President Richard M. Nixon is in Prague during his East European trip.

**March 28, 1967**
In his speech in Peć (Kosmet Region) Tito attacks the Declaration on the Croatian language; he assails the "anti-party bourgeois elements." The nationalist controversies continue in Yugoslavia.

**March 30, 1967**
Marshal Rodion Malinovsky, the Soviet Defense Minister, dies at the age of 68.

**April 4, 1967**
We have lost up to now 500 planes in our raids against the North Vietnam.

**April 7, 1967**
Gomulka of Poland is in Sofia to sign a friendship treaty with Bulgaria.

**April 15, 1967**
Mass anti-war demonstrations are staged in New York and San Francisco. Martin Luther King participates in New York.

**April 16, 1967**
Polish Premier Cyrankiewicz dedicates the Ausschwitz monument to the memory of the three million Jews and one million Poles who were exterminated there by the Germans during the last war. (This was the death camp of greatest destruction by the Nazis.)

**April 17, 1967**
*Havana Prensa Latina* publishes an article by Che Guevara outlining the struggle against "American Imperialism." Che's whereabouts are unknown.

**April 17 – 21, 1967**
The Seventh Congress of the East German Communists takes place in East Berlin.

**April 19, 1967**
"Der Alte" – the former German Chancellor Konrad Adenauer dies at 91.

Mihajlo Mihajlov, the rebel Yugoslav writer is sentenced to four and a half years in prison for his criticism of the Communism in Yugoslavia. M. Djilas defends Mihajlov in his statements to the American press.

**April 20, 1967**
Jules Régis Debray, the French Communist writer, who spent some time with Guevara in Bolivia is arrested by Bolivian authorities.

**April 21, 1967**
The Greek army overthrows the civilian government for alleged pro-Communist tendencies.

Svetlana Stalin-Alliluyeva, the daughter of J. Stalin, arrives in New York. She receives asylum in America. (Later, in following months she publishes a series of articles and her book, "Twenty Letters to a Friend", in which she described her father and his era.)

**April 22, 1967**
Western press reports that Rumanian C.P. delegates at the East German Party Congress anger many delegates with their dissenting views.

**April 24, 1967**
Indonesia expells two top Chinese diplomats.

*Regis Debray, French writer, philosopher captured with the Bolivian guerillas* – Keystone

The much advertised Conference of European Communist Parties meets in Karlovy Vary, Czechoslovakia. L. Brezhnev is the main speaker. Albania, Rumania, and Yugoslavia are present. Representatives of 24 Communist Parties sign the final communiqué at the end of the two-day conference. Communist unity is not restored.

**April 25, 1967**
President Johnson attends the funeral of Konrad Adenauer in Bonn, West Germany.

**May of 1967**
Our weekly losses in S. Vietnam mount to between 150 and 300. During this month the number of the Americans killed passes 10,000. In early May General Westmoreland returns to the U.S., speaks to the Congress and denounces the anti-war demonstrators.

**May 2 – 5, 1967**
The Austrian Chancellor–Josef Klaus–visits Hungary. This is the first visit by a Western statesman after 1945.

**May 9, 1967**
Rumania celebrates the ninetieth anniversary of its independence.

**May 11 – 15, 1967**
The COMECON meets again in Moscow; several members criticize the Soviet exploitation.

**May 12, 1967**
Brezhnev signs in Sofia, Bulgaria a friendship treaty with the obedient Bulgarians.

Venezuelan authorities capture several Cuban army officers. One of the killed is Antonio Briones Montoto.

**May 16 – 19, 1967**
Elections in Yugoslavia put many new men into top positions. There is rotation in highest Party positions.

**May 16 – 17, 1967**
The Eighth Plenum of the leadership of the C.P. in Poland.

**May 17, 1967**
The Caracas newspaper *Ultimas Noticias* publishes the "Resolution of the Eighth Plenum of the Central Committee of the C.P. of Venezuela." They are Leninists and Castroites advocating guerilla warfare against the Venezuelan government.

**May 18, 1967**
Mika Špiljak, a Croatian Communist, becomes the new Premier and Tito is re-elected as President of Yugoslavia.

**May 22, 1967**
North Korean raiders kill two U.S. soldiers.

**May 22 – 27, 1967**
The Fourth Congress of the Soviet Writers convenes in Moscow. The well-known Soviet writer Alexander Solzhenitsyn – who does not attend it – addresses a letter to the Congress pleading for end of censorship. The letter is published on May 31 in the Paris paper *Le Monde*. There is continued ferment among the Russian and non-Russian writers. Secret trials are held against many for alleged "anti-Soviet propaganda."

Shah Mohammed Riza Pahlevi of Iran visits Czechoslovakia.

**May 25, 1967**
President Tito of Yugoslavia is 75 years old. The question many observers are asking is: what is going to happen after Tito?

**May 27, 1967**
In the week ending on this day, 313 Americans are killed in S. Vietnam. The war is affecting the whole American nation and especially many individual families. In 1967 it costs $20 billion.

Karol Wojtyla, Archbishop of Cracow, is named Cardinal by Pope Paul VI. Now Poland has two Cardinals. As Poland is the only Communist country with over 90 per cent of population (over 30 million) belonging to the R. Catholicism, it has a special meaning to the Vatican. It is also the only country where the native Church is openly defying the Communist regime.

**May 27 – June 5, 1967**
The Warsaw Pact army maneuvers are held in East Germany.

**May 30, 1967**
The Eastern Region of Nigeria in Africa secedes and becomes the independent Republic of Biafra. A terrible civil war breaks out.

**June 5 – 10, 1967**
The Israelis defeat the Arabs in a victorious *Blitz* war. They completely destroy or capture the Soviet-supplied armament: airplanes, tanks, etc. The U.N. Security Council discusses for days the Mid-East crisis. The entire Soviet Bloc supports the Arabs.

**June 9, 1967**
Representatives of European Communist countries meet in Moscow to discuss the Mid-East crisis. Tito is there too. He and other Communists break off diplomatic relations with Israel. They all denounce the "Israeli Aggression" and sign such a declaration. Rumania refuses to sign it.

**June 16, 1967**
The Soviet Premier A. N. Kosygin arrives in New York to plead the Arab cause in the U.N. The Security Council voted down the Soviet proposal to brand the Israelis as aggressors. The Mid-East crisis continues. The Rumanian Premier I. G. Maurer, visiting America during the same crisis, is received by President Johnson in the White House.

**June 21 – 23, 1967**
Soviet President N. V. Podgorny visits Cairo to reassure the Arabs of Soviet friendship and immediate rearmament.

**June 23, 1967**
The Soviet military mission comes to Belgrade. Soviet submarines and warships are reported in Dalmatian ports. The Soviet planes shipping arms to Egypt use Yugoslav airfields on their flights to Africa.

**June 23, 25, 1967**
President Johnson and the Soviet Premier Kosygin meet for fruitless summit talks in Glassboro, New Jersey.

**July 6, 1967**
Reports indicate severe fighting between Nigerian government and the Ibo tribesmen in Biafra. The Nigerians massacred thousands of Ibos, many of whom are Christians.

**July 7, 1967**
General W. C. Westmoreland urges the Defense Secretary, Robert S. McNamara, to provide at least 100,000 soldiers for the war in Vietnam. By now there are some 460,000 Americans fighting in Vietnam. Behind the whole war looms the giant shadow of Communist China. The general states: "We are winning slowly but steadily."

**July 8, 1967**
The Red Chinese instigate the anti-British violence in Hong Kong. Five British policemen are killed by the Chinese agents. More casualties follow the next day.

**July 13, 1967**
The heads of the East European countries—joined by Brezhnev and Kosygin – emerge from a secret two-day meeting on Mid-East crisis. They pledge support to the Arabs while Rumania takes her independent course.

**July 16, 1967**
The North Korean commandos kill three American soldiers in S. Korea.

**August 21, 1967**
Two U.S. Navy jets are shot down by Red Chinese over China.

**September 11 – 14, 1967**
The armed forces of India and the Red Chinese clash in a new flare-up of the border war in the Himalayas.

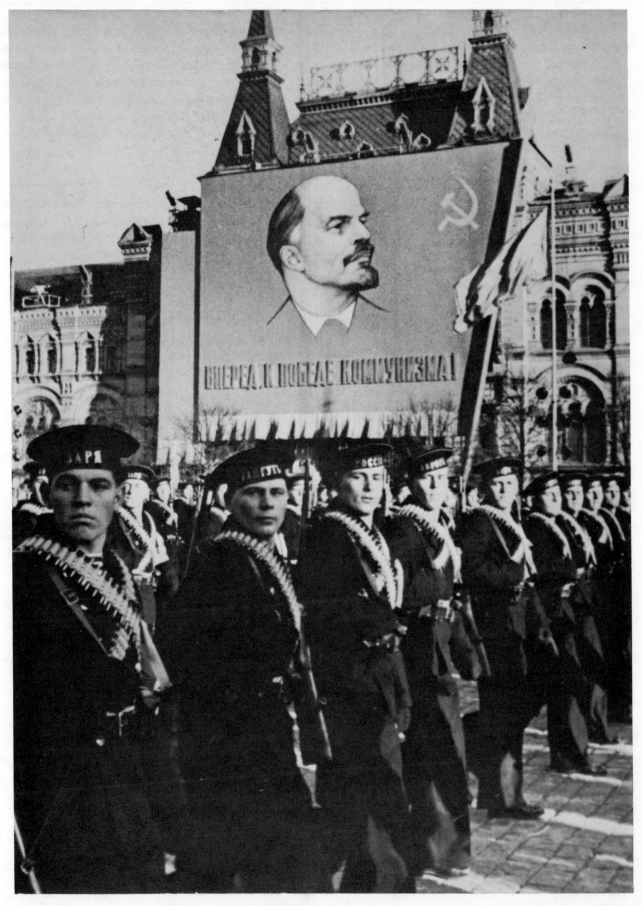

*A parade in Red Square, on the occasion of the 50th anniversary of the Bolshevik Revolution – Keystone*

**September 23, 1967**
Moscow signs with Hanoi (North Vietnam) an aid pact promising more military supplies against the "American Aggressors." Our soldiers are being killed in Vietnam with Russian weapons.

**October 8, 1967**
Ernesto "Che" Guevara, the Argentine-born Cuban revolutionist, is wounded, captured, and then summarily executed by the Bolivian army. This is the weakest and the worst organized army in South America. "Che" perished because he violated all the rules of guerilla warfare he had preached before. He failed because he and his Cuban collaborators did not get the support of the native population. The liquidation of Guevara is a terrible blow to Castro. (Guevara's Bolivian *Diary* will be published in 1968.)

**October 12, 1967**
U.S. Secretary of State Dean Rusk warns that in a few years Red China will be a real threat to America.

**October 21 – 22, 1967**
The anti-war demonstrators stage protest in Washington and in front of the Pentagon.

**October 30, 1967**
Thousands of students demonstrate in Prague. They want continued liberalization of the Communist regime in Czechoslovakia.

**November 2, 1967**
The widow of the late President Kennedy comes to neutralist Cambodia for a six-day visit.

**December 8, 1967**
The Soviet Party chief Leonid Brezhnev arrives in Prague for negotiations with the Czech leaders.

**November 15, 1967**
The Ukrainian journalist and former Communist Youth League official, Vyacheslav M. Chornovil, is sentenced to eighteen months of hard labor in Mordovia because of his protest against persecution of the Ukrainian writers. Later he sent to the Ukrainian authorities his famous "Petition" protesting the treatment by Soviet authorities. His Petition and other related documents were later smuggled out of the country and published as a book, *The Chornovil Papers,* in late summer of 1968 in America and Canada.

**December 8, 1967**
N. Ceausescu, the Secretary General of the Rumanian C.P., is elected as the new Chairman of the Rumanian State Council (the President of the Republic).

**December 13, 1967**
King Constantine of Greece stages an unsuccessful revolt against the generals in power; he is forced to flee to Italy. The strong man in Greece is George Papadopoulos, a former general.

**December 21, 1967**
President Johnson pays a short visit to Australia attending the memorial services for the drowned Australian Premier Harold Holt, who was a good friend of America.

**The end of 1967**
The year marking the fiftieth anniversary of the Bolshevik Revolution contains many worries for the Soviet regime. Moscow is not any more the only center of the International Communism. There is the challenge of Red China, liberalization processes in East Europe, protests of the young breed that grew up under Communism, rise of nationalism, ferment within the Soviet intelligentsia, the American struggle in Vietnam against Communism, and many other facts that do not please the rulers in the Kremlin. Fifty years after the Revolution many millions of people still profess adherence to their respective countries. Communism is desperately disunited.

# 4. The Year 1968–the Year at the Crossroads?

**1968**

This is a very interesting and important year in the history of Communism. It is — judging from many facts — the crossroads and watershed of the World Communism, America, and the entire world. It is also an election year for the Americans burdened with the problems of the War in Vietnam, disorders in our cities, the struggle for civil rights, the revolt of the young masses who soon will compose over fifty per cent of our nation. It is an era of the clash of different ideologies, ferment within Christianity, tensions in the Middle East — and of many other problems whose outcomes are impossible to predict.

In this year too, thousands of young Americans are dying on the battlefronts of Asia. The War in Vietnam is going to cost this fiscal year some $25 billion.

There are presently eighty-nine Communist Parties in existence. Their membership is approximately 46,000,000. Of these, 43,000,000 are in fourteen Communist-dominated countries. The rest of about 3,000,000 Communists are scattered all over the world; of these, eighty per cent belong to the C.P. of Italy, France, Japan, India, and Indonesia. The international Communist movement is still a strong revolutionary force but it is very divided.

**January 1, 1968**

The American press reports that Ho Chi Minh suffers from heart trouble. (He is in his seventies.)

**January 1, 1968**

Hungary's N.E.M. (New Economic Mechanism) starts. It is a drastic, well organized economic reform.

*Aleksandar Dubček* – Keystone

**January 4, 1968**

Aleksandar Dubček, the First Secretary of the Slovak C.P., replaces Antonin Novotny, the hated Stalinist in Czechoslovakia, as the First Secretary of the C.P. of Czechoslovakia. This means a big change in the country.

**January 10 – 13, 1968**

The Yugoslav Premier Mika Špiljak visits Italy and is also received by Pope Paul VI.

**January 10 – 13, 1968**

The Congress of the Communist Youth is held in Sofia, Bulgaria.

**January 11 and 17, 1968**
The Albanian Communists unveil monuments to the 15th century Albanian national hero, George Kastrioti Skanderbeg, the 500th anniversary of whose death is celebrated. (For 24 years he struggled against the Turks and now is called a hero even by the Communists.)

**January 12, 1968**
It is announced that some 400 leading members of the League of Communists of Yugoslavia have been purged. They sabotaged Tito's economic and political reforms.

**January 16, 1968**
Jakob Malik replaces Dr. Nikolai Fedorenko as the Soviet representative in the U.N.

**January 21, 1968**
North Korean commandos try to assassinate the South Korean President Pak. They are either liquidated or caught.

**January 22 – 23, 1968**
At the Conference of the Mediterranean Communist Parties, held in Rome, the Yugoslav Communists condemn "every foreign military presence in the Mediterranean."

**January 23, 1968**
In a cross violation of all international laws, the North Korean Communists capture in international waters the U.S. intelligence ship *Pueblo* with the entire crew of 83.

**January 29 – 30, 1968**
The Czechoslovak Party Secretary A. Dubček visits Moscow to explain his ideas.

**January 29 – 31, 1968**
The Polish Socialist Youth Union, representing about a million members, holds Congress in Warsaw. (The Polish Scouts number some 1,800,000 members.)

**January 29, 1968**
The Cuban Government announces arrest of a group that wanted to overthrow Castro's regime.

**January 29, 1968**
As Yugoslav-Bulgarian controversy about Macedonia flares up; the Yugoslav authorities protest against Bulgarian claims.

**January 30, 1968**
"The Forefathers' Eve" — an anti-Russian play written by the 19th century Polish national poet Adam Mickiewicz — is closed in Warsaw by Polish Communist authorities, a fact that results in demonstrations.

**January 31, 1968**
Bonn (W. Germany) and Belgrade (Yugoslavia) agree to re-establish diplomatic relations that were broken off ten years ago.

The Vietnam Communists strike with some 85,000 troops against the Americans during the Tet (Lunar New Year) truce period. It is an assault of unprecedented violence and ferocity. The Communists attack 40 major cities and 28 of 44 provincial capitals. The campaign will go on for several weeks. The holy city of Hue — the ancient capital — was retaken after 25 days of house to house combat. The casualties are enormous on both sides. This offensive gives initiative to the Communists.

**February 1968**
Various reports indicate strained relations between Castro and Moscow. The Soviet aid is still estimated at about a million dollars a day. It seems that in the Sino-Soviet split Cuba wants to remain neutral.

**February 1, 1968**
The Party boss of Czechoslovakia, Dubček, announces equality for all Czechs and Slovaks. (He is a Slovak.)

**February 2, 1968**
Radio Prague urges: "Bring in the Western Press."

**February 9, 1968**
Heavy fighting is reported between the centralistic government of Nigeria and Biafra, the homeland of some 10,000,000 Ibo tribesmen.

**February 12 – 19, 1968**
The Soviet Foreign Minister Gromyko visits Sofia, Bulgaria.

**February 17, 1968**
543 Americans died in Vietnam in the last week during the Tet Communist offensive.

**February 26 – March 5, 1968**
The consultative conference of the Communist Parties takes place in Budapest; there are 67 parties represented. Of the 14 ruling parties 6 are absent.

**February 29, 1968**

The Rumanian delegation walks out of the Budapest Conference. Again, the Soviets fail to impose the unity of Communism. The big problem now is: the liberal course of Czechoslovakia.

It is stated: Bulgaria is going to introduce compulsory military training.

**March 5, 1968**

The Albanian Communists observe the anniversary of Stalin's death.

**March 7, 1968**

The Albanian Party leader, Enver Hoxha, announces great educational reforms.

**March 8, 1968**

The Albanians announce: there are 2,000,000 Albanians living in the Republic (about a million of them are living in Yugoslavia).

The *Contemporamul* in Bucharest writes; "Let's bring Marxism up to date."

The Polish students demonstrate in the streets of Warsaw. Some 1,200 are arrested immediately.

**March 9, 1968**

The Polish student demonstrators shout in Warsaw: "Long live Czechoslovakia!"

**March 10, 1968**

The Czech students stage demonstrations at the grave of Jan Masaryk at Lany near Prague. (According to the official Communist sources he committed suicide in early 1948.)

Tito, during his week-long visit in Japan, expresses desire for another conference of the "non-aligned" nations.

**March 11, 1968**

The Western intelligence reports: at least 40,000 N. Vietnamese troops are in Laos.

*Visiting Hours.* A U.S. Marine corpsman takes advantage of a lull in the fighting for Hue to dress the shrapnel wound of a man of his company who had been hit in one of the many battles for the ancient Imperial city of Hue – Keystone Tokyo

Thousands of Poles fight the Communist militia in the streets of Warsaw. The students sack the Ministry of Culture.

As the spring comes closer, East Europe is witnessing a historic ferment, a long suppressed revolt of the intellectuals (many of them university professors and writers) and of the young generation that grew up under Communism.

Many published reports indicate that the presence of strong Soviet navy in the Mediterranean is becoming a threat to the American position there.

**March 12, 1968**
Bulgarian National Assembly announces forthcoming Constitution reforms. The Bulgarians also continue their campaign on Macedonia; this month marks the ninetieth anniversary of Bulgaria's liberation from Turkey. The Belgrade and Sofia papers exchange some heated verbal attacks.

**March 13, 1968**
Anti-government student demonstrations are held in Warsaw and eight other cities of Poland.

The main Polish party organ, *Trybuna Ludu,* denounces demonstrators as collaborators of "pro-Zionist circles."

**March 14, 1968**
Colonel-general Vladimir Janko, one of the compromised Stalinists in Czechoslovakia, commits suicide. There follows a wave of suicides by leading men of the old tough regime now being dismantled by Dubček and the liberals.

**March 17, 1968**
Ludvik Vesely, deputy editor-in-chief of the Czech *Literarni Listy* (the leading publication of discontented Czech intellectuals), states in an interview to an Austrian journalist: "Should the Russians march into Czechoslovakia today, possibly the Czechs and Slovaks would return fire . . . ."

**March 19, 1968**
Party chief W. Gomulka in his speech to the Warsaw party activists, blasts the "Zionists" within the party. It is interesting that the Soviets and their strict followers constantly attack some leading party and government officials in both Poland and Czechoslovakia who are of Jewish descent.

**March 22, 1968**
Rumania and Canada sign in Montreal a three-year trade agreement, the first of this kind between the two countries after 1945.

President Antonin Novotny, who was in this office for twelve years, resigns. The first Party Secretary A. Dubček continues his reforms for liberalization of Czechoslovakia. He is giving concessions to Czech intellectuals and to the Slovak anti-centralists.

**March 23, 1968**
Dubček arrives in Dresden, East Germany for talks with Brezhnev, Kosygin and representatives of Poland, East Germany, Hungary, and Bulgaria — all of whom are upset by liberal reforms in Czechoslovakia.

**March 24, 1968**
The Warsaw authorities state that Polish regime had been faced "with an attempted coup . . ."

**March 25, 1968**
Hungarian Premier Jeno Fock and Foreign Minister Janos Peter arrive in Paris for a five-day official visit. De Gaulle's policy aims at building good relations with the Communist Bloc.

**March 26, 1968**
Purge of many Polish professors, writers, and government officials is reported.

**March 30, 1968**
The Czechoslovak National Assembly elects General Ludvik Svoboda (72 years old) as the new President of the Republic.

**March 31, 1968**
Radio Tirana praises the great help of many Chinese experts now present in Albania.

**April of 1968**
Written reports in the American press state that so far the U.S. airplanes have dropped more than 1.5 million tons of bombs on North Vietnam. This is as much as the total dropped on Europe during World War II.

Reports from the Philippines indicate increased activities of Communist guerillas and of the Communist-supported Huks' movement.

**April 1, 1968**
Rumanian Premier I. G. Maurer leads a delegation for a ten-day visit of Finland and Sweden.

**April 3, 1968**
Rumors circulate in Czechoslovakia that Jan Masaryk, the Foreign Minister, was assassinated by "Beria gorillas" in early 1948.

**April 4, 1968**
Oldrich Cernik becomes the new Premier of the liberal Czechoslovak government and forms a new cabinet.

Martin Luther King, the Negro civil rights' leader, is assassinated in Memphis, Tenn. by a sniper. Violence breaks out in several American cities. Washington, D.C. is burning and looted by angry Negro mobs. The Communists all over the world utilize these facts for their propaganda purposes. After April 4, the whole world press and news media are denouncing us as the country of violence and disorders.

The Rumanian Prime Minister Maurer states at a press conference in Helsinki that Finland and Rumania "have similar views on very many problems." Rumania is drifting away from the Soviet-controlled Bloc.

Obedient Hungary duly celebrates the 23rd anniversary of "liberation" by the Soviet troops in World War II.

The Prague *Literarny Listy* urges for real democratization of Czechoslovakia.

**April 5, 1968**
The Central Committee of the Czechoslovak C.P. meets for a five-day session. It issues the historic 24,000 words Action Program on the liberalization of the country and promises equality of all peoples in the republic. A new Presidium is named too.

**April 8 – 10, 1968**
The General Council of World Federation of Trade Unions meets in Moscow representing 77 countries. It gives support to North Vietnam and denounces America.

**April 8, 1968**
Published reports testify to the fact that Nigerian troops under General Y. Gowon are perpetrating wholesale massacres in Biafra where thousands of people are dying of starvation because of the Nigerian blockade.

A. Dubček appoints two non-Communist ministers to the Czechoslovak cabinet.

**April 15, 1968**
After 76 days of siege, the Americans relieve the fortress of Khe San in Vietnam.

**April 16, 1968**
The Czech paper *Rude Pravo* discusses the mysterious death of Jan Masaryk on March 10, 1948 and states "it was a political murder."

**April 16 – 19, 1968**
The Hungarian Patriotic People's Front convenes in Budapest and J. Kadar, the Communist boss, is the main speaker.

**April 18, 1968**
At ceremonies commemorating the 25th anniversary of the Jewish Warsaw Ghetto Uprising, the Polish officials attack Zionism and Israel. They claim the Germans had killed, during World War II, 5,384,000 Poles, of whom a half were of Jewish religion.

The Polish authorities reveal that some 8,400 party members have been purged; among them were many government officials, professors, and writers.

The Czechoslovak National Assembly elects as its chairman Jozef Smrkovsky, a liberal.

**April 19, 1968**
Amnesty is granted to many political prisoners in Czechoslovakia.

The Americans start offensive against A Shau valley in Vietnam where the Communists have huge supplies.

**April 22, 1968**
It is reported we are losing ground in Laos to the Communists; there are some 70,000 North Vietnamese regulars in Laos.

The Albanian party organ *Zeri i Populit* denounces Dubček's policies in Czechoslovakia.

**April 23, 1968**

Representatives of 54 Communist Parties meet in Budapest for a five-day preparatory conference. They agree that on November 25th a summit conference of world's C.P.'s will meet in Moscow. The Czechoslovak leaders at the conference warn the Russians not to interfere with affairs of Czechoslovakia.

**April 26, 1968**

Rumanian Communists denounce the late Gheorghe Cheorghiu Dej as "Rumanian Stalin."

Bulgarian First Party Secretary Todor Zhivkov concludes in Prague a 20-year friendship treaty between Bulgaria and Czechoslovakia.

**April 27, 1968**

Rumanian Party Secretary N. Ceausescu denounces the terroristic regime of the late Gheorghiu-Dej, attacks the "cult of personality" and rehabilitates Lucretiu Patrascanu, one of the C.P. leaders who was murdered by Gheoghiu-Dej's henchmen.

**April 28, 1968**

Tito comes to Moscow for a visit on his return from an Asian trip.

**April 30, 1968**

*Pravda* strikes at "unhealthy trends" in Czechoslovakia.

**End of April 1968**

Marshal Ivan Yakubovsky makes a quick tour of East European capitals (except Bucharest). He is the commander in Chief of the Warsaw Pact military forces.

**May 1, 1968**

The May Day is peacefully marked in the Communist world. The Soviet Defense Minister, Marshal Andrei A. Grechko, states in his speech that United States "is embarking ever more openly on the road of aggression and armed adventure." While in Prague thousands of young people demonstrate for freedom, in Warsaw W. Gomulka sharply denounces "internal and foreign enemies of Socialism in Poland."

Violent student disorders break out in Paris. Many are Maoists and Castroites; disorders will result in a serious political crisis for De Gaulle's regime.

**May 2, 1968**

Walter Ulbricht attacks the Czech "revisionists" in his speech to East Berlin audience on the occasion of the sesquicentennial of Karl Marx' birth.

**May 3, 1968**

The American and North Vietnamese governments agree to negotiate peace in Paris.

**May 4, 1968**

Dubček leads a delegation to Moscow for an unexpected visit to Moscow to defend his liberal reforms.

**May 6 – 7, 1968**

Italian C.P. chief L. Longo visits Prague.

**May 5, 1968**

The 150th anniversary of the birth of Karl Marx is celebrated in Trier, his birth place, and in many other places.

**May 8, 1968**

The Czech authorities release from prison former Minister of the Interior who was sentenced by Novotny regime.

The leaders of C.P.'s of Bulgaria, East Germany, Hungary and Poland arrive in Moscow to discuss the "Czechoslovak crisis." They are upset by Dubček's reforms.

**May 9, 1968**

East German papers report that some U.S. troops are present in Czechoslovakia. Czech authorities promptly deny this.

Polish C.P. organ, *Trybuna Ludu* (Warsaw) denounces Dubček's group as "anti-Socialist."

U.P.I. reports from Warsaw that Soviet troops are moving toward Czechoslovak border.

**May 9 – 10, 1968**

Violent disorders break out with full force in Paris. Barricades are erected in the Latin Quarter. "Che" Guevara's cult is very strong among young French radicals.

**May 10, 1968**

Truce talks begin in Paris between W. Averell Harriman, chief U.S. negotiator, and Xuan Thuy, North Vietnam's top delegate.

**May 11, 1968**

A total of 562 Americans died in Vietnam in the week ending this day.

Polish papers announce the execution of Jerzy Strawam, who was sentenced to death in December, 1967 as an American spy.

**May 13, 1968**

The Soviet Fleet in the Mediterranean is reported to have 40 warships.

General strike breaks out in France. The whole country is paralyzed for many days.

**May 14 – 18, 1968**

French President Gen. C. De Gaulle visits Rumania.

**May 14, 1968**

The Czechoslovak government declares that while maintaining close relations with all Socialist states, it also wants close collaboration with the West.

**May 15, 1968**

Eight deputy premiers of the Communist Bloc attend a meeting of the Council for Mutual Economic Assistance (COMECON) in the Soviet capital.

The Polish Party chief Gomulka arrives in Budapest to renew the 20-year friendship and mutual assistance pact with Hungary.

**May 16, 1968**

Disorders and violence spread in France. Communist-led workers seize some factories. Some students' leaders are reported as pure Anarchists. While the Communists call for overthrow of De Gaulle government, Premier Georges Pompidou states: "The government must defend the republic."

**May 17, 1968**

Soviet Premier Kosygin and Marshal Andrei Grechko arrive in Prague. The Czechoslovak government reluctantly agrees to Warsaw Pact military maneuvers on Czechoslovak soil.

*Boulevard Saint Michel. Student riots transformed the Latin Quarter into a large battleground* – Keystone

American troops give up A Shau offensive as monsoons near. In the preceeding week over 560 Americans were killed in military operations, the highest number so far for a single week in this war.

**May 18, 1968**

With Kosygin present in Prague, some 10,000 Czech students demonstrate against the Soviets and Communism and in favor of democracy. The Russians are infuriated.

**May 20 – 22, 1968**

First Congress of Bulgarian Writers is held in Sofia. Because of the Macedonian controversy, the Yugoslav delegation is absent.

**May 20, 1968**

The United States has some 46,000 troops, also air and naval bases in Thailand.

**May 27 – June 1, 1968**

N. Ceausescu and a high level Rumanian delegation are visiting Yugoslavia.

**May 28, 1968**

President Johnson declares in Paris that while North Vietnamese talk peace in Paris, their military buildup is proceeding at "unprecedented rates."

**May 29 – June 1, 1968**

An important Plenum of the Central Committee of the C.P. of Czechoslovakia decides to convoke an extraordinary Party Congress in September.

**May 30, 1968**

In spite of violent protests, De Gaulle decides to stay in office. A few weeks ago he contributed to shaking up seriously the U.S. dollar; now his Franc is in danger. His answer to the mob is: "I shall not withdraw." (On April 23 and 30 he scored great electoral victory. Then the number of C.P. deputies dropped from 73 to 33 and Left Bloc from 118 to 57.)

As the Americans observe the Memorial Day, remembering the dead of all wars, it is announced that up to now almost 24,000 Americans have died in Vietnam.

**May 31, 1968**

A few Soviet units arrive in Czechoslovakia taking part in announced maneuvers.

**June 1960**

There are about 250,000 Soviet troops in East Germany; about 50,000 in Hungary; and 20,000 in Poland. The Czechoslovak army has some 175,000 (14 divisions).

**Early June of 1968**

The Viet Cong bombard Saigon with mortars; many civilians lose their lives and homes. This terror tactic is very effective.

**June 5, 1968**

Senator Robert F. Kennedy is assassinated in Los Angeles by Sirhan Sirhan, an Arab nationalist. There follows an angry reaction all over the world. The Communist press depicts America as a jungle of violence and lawlessness. As Kennedy advocated peace in Vietnam, he was very popular in Communist countries.

**June 6, 1968**

Soviet tanks are sighted in Czechoslovakia as part of maneuvers by Warsaw Pact.

**June 10, 1968**

It is reported that armed bands trained at Cuba are infiltrating the Portuguese colony of Angola in Africa.

After a week-long strike and demonstrations at the universities of Belgrade and Zagreb (with echoes at the universities of Ljubljana and Sarajevo) President Tito speaks on TV and radio promising to fulfill demands of the students. He acknowledges their grievances.

**June 13, 1968**

The Prague newspapers pay tribute to the late Imre Nagy of Hungary and praise him as a democratic Socialist.

**June 18, 1968**

A delegation of Rumanian scientists arrives in America for a tour of the country; it is headed by Alexandru Birladeanu, the Vice Premier of Rumania.

**Summer of 1968**

Tanzania in East Africa offers the liveliest scene of Communist activities. The Chinese Communists are very busy here. The reports indicate that Tanzania might get Chinese rockets and missiles.

**October 13-19, 1969**
Ceausescu of Rumania visits India. The Rumanians are expanding good relations with many non-Communist countries.

**October 14, 1969**
New Premier of Sweden is Olof Palme, a Socialist and an outspoken critic of America.

**October 15, 1969**
First Moratorium Day is held in Washington, D.C. and across the nation. Hundreds of thousands of opponents of the war in Vietnam are demonstrating mostly peacefully. On most campuses the students cut classes and in many of those that are held professors and students discuss the problem of Vietnam. President Nixon's critics maintain that withdrawal from Vietnam is too slow. By now this is the longest war in U.S. history. These anti-war protests are widely publicized in Communist countries; their news media misinterpret and distort the meaning of this protest.

A. Dubček resigns as Chairman of the Czechoslovak Federal Assembly, his last significant post.

**October 21, 1969**
Socialist leader Willy Brandt becomes Chancellor of W. Germany replacing Kurt G. Kiesinger of the Christian Democratic Union. Brandt's overtures to East Europe will now intensify. West Germany, the most prosperous industrial country on the continent, will be entering the 1970's under a Socialist leadership.

Supreme Revolutionary Council takes power in the East African state of Somalia; it is led by Major General M.S. Bare.

**October 27, 1969**
The C.P. First Secretary G. Husak and the President of Czechoslovak Republic L. Svoboda return from an eight-day trip to the Soviet Union. According to the communique they both "appreciate . . . action of the five fraternal socialist countries" in Czechoslovakia in the summer of 1968.

**October 29, 1969**
The Czech C.P. organ *Rude Pravo,* quoting from the official statement after the Husak-Svoboda trip, writes: "Every communist party is responsible for its activity before the people of its country and bears international responsibility before the countries of the socialist community and the international communist and workers' movement." It is obvious from this that the Czechoslovak C.P. was forced by the Soviet leaders to accept the Russian concept of limited sovereignty of Socialist countries which in practical terms means the Soviet control.

**October 30-31, 1969**
The Foreign Ministers of the Warsaw Pact countries meet in Prague.

**October 30, 1969**
The United States and the Soviet Union submit to the Geneva Disarmament Conference a draft treaty prohibiting nuclear weapons from ocean floor.

**End of October 1969**
There are some 6,500 Soviet technicians and a larger number of military men in Arab countries and South Asia.

For days the East European press has been elated by the fact that Willy Brandt is the new Chancellor of W. Germany.

**November 3, 1969**
President Nixon addresses the nation. He promises to withdraw all U.S. combat forces on a secret timetable and pleads for the support of the "great silent majority."

**November 4-5, 1969**
Student disorders break out at Massachusetts Institute of Technology.

**November 6, 1969**
Famous Soviet writer Alexander Solzhenitsyn is expelled from the Writers' Union. His last two novels — best-sellers in the West — *Cancer Ward* and *The First Circle* are banned in the U.S.S.R. His "Open Letter", very critical of the Soviet oppressive methods, is circulating widely in the Soviet Union. After the defection of the Soviet writer Kuznetsov in August in London, the case of Solzhenitsyn proves again dissatisfaction of the intellectuals in the Soviet Union.

Gamal A. Nasser, the President of the United Arab Republic, states that the Soviets will help to reconquer the lost Arab territories.

**November 10, 1969**
Gov. Rockefeller's 137-page Report on his findings during trips to Latin America is made public. Among other findings are a growing nationalism and an increasing opposition to U.S. influence. One of the conclusions: "All of the American nations are a tempting target for Communist subversion. . . . It is plainly evident that such subversion is a reality today with alarming potential."

The Arab League's Joint Defense Council condemns the United States for assisting Israel.

**November 13-15, 1969**
Huge anti-war demonstrations take place in Washington D.C. (with an estimated crowd of some 250,000), San Francisco and other cities. Many opponents of war contend that President Nixon is moving too slowly and ineffectively to liquidate the war.

**November 13, 1969**
Vice President Spiro Agnew in a speech in Des Moines criticizes television's policies and credibility in reporting news. The Vice President and many of the "Silent Majority" believe that news media are biased and one-sided and that the public is not getting a fair and objective picture of what is taking place in these turbulent times. On the 20th the Vice President singles for attack the newspapers' reporting and editorial policies.

**November 15, 1969**
Fifty-four Iraqi citizens are sentenced to death as American "spies." In the succeeding hangings many of the victims are Jews.

250,000 are marching in Washington, D.C. as part of the second Vietnam Moratorium. Only sporadic violence breaks out.

American and Soviet negotiators arrive on the same day in the capital of Finland, Helsinki for talks on limiting strategic arms (SALT).

**November 16, 1969**
U.S. authorities learn from S. Vietnamese villagers of the alleged killing of unarmed civilians by U.S. troops on March 16, 1968 in Song My. The controversy will drag on for months and result in ugly publicity. Several army officers will face charges. Pictures of the massacred civilians will be published around the world.

**November 17, 1969**
The SALT talks begin in Helsinki in a constructive and optimistic atmosphere.

**November 19, 1969**
American astronauts Charles Conrad and Alan I. Bean land on the moon as participants in the Apollo 12 moon flight that began on the 14th. After a fully successful moon walk, they start the return trip on the next day. Again the world is amazed by the U.S.'s repeated success. The splashdown is on the 24th.

Japanese Premier E. Sato arrives in the White House for official talks. President Nixon promises return of Okinawa to Japan by 1972.

A nation-wide strike hits Italy; it is one in a series.

**November 24, 1969**
The Soviet Writers' Union accuses Solzhenitsyn of being an enemy of the Soviet system. Friends in the West suggest he should leave his country; he refuses the invitation.

Soviet President Nikolai Podgorny signs the Treaty to prevent the spread of nuclear weapons. At the same time President Nixon signs it in Washington. Nineteen more states have to ratify it to make it work.

**December 1, 1969**
The strength of U.S. troops in S. Vietnam drops to 479,500.

**December 3, 1969**
Vice President S. Agnew, in a speech to the states' governors in Washington, D.C., lists these "Ten Commandments of Protest": 1. Thou shalt not allow the opponent to speak; 2. Thou shalt not set forth a program of thine own; 3. Thou shalt not trust anybody over 30; 4. Thou shalt not honor thy father and thy mother; 5. Thou shalt not heed the lessons of history; 6. Thou shalt not write anything longer than a slogan; 7. Thou shalt not present a negotiable demand; 8. Thou shalt not accept any establishment idea; 9. Thou shalt not revere any but totalitarian heroes; 10. Thou shalt not seek forgiveness for thy transgressions; rather thou shalt demand amnesty for them."

**December 4, 1969**
American and Soviet delegates at the SALT meetings agree on the topics of future discussions.

In a police raid in Chicago the Illinois Black Panther leader Fred Hampton is killed together with Mark Clark. As a militant group the Panthers will be making more headlines in the future.

### December 8, 1969
At a news conference President Nixon discusses the Paris peace talks, polarization of the country over the war, and My Lai (Song My) massacre. He also states that dissent will not influence his war policies.

### December 10, 1969
The Saigon authorities state that 1,090,000 S. Vietnamese are under arms. There is more talk on the American side about the "Vietnamization" of the war.

### December 11, 1969
Henry Cabot Lodge resigns as head of the U.S. peace delegation in Paris.

### December 12, 1969
The National Commission on Violence, that was appointed by President Nixon, publishes its report. Of 13 members 6 refuse to sign the report. It discusses civil disobedience, lawlessness, and admits: "Violence in the United States has risen to alarmingly high levels."

A terrorist bomb in Milan, Italy kills at least 13 persons.

### December 13, 1969
It is made known that China has some troops in parts of Laos.

Bulgarian-Yugoslav talks on Macedonia bring no results.

### December 15, 1969
Mr. Nixon announces that 50,000 additional U.S. troops will be withdrawn from Vietnam by April 15, 1970 and cautions against risks evolving from total withdrawl.

Aleksandar Dubček is appointed Ambassador to Turkey.

### December 21, 1969
The Arab Summit starts in Rabat, Morocco. The most important question under discussion is war against Israel. The conference ends in disunity.

### December 28, 1969
The Liberal Democratic Party of Premier Eisaku Sato of Japan wins victory in the elections for the House of Representatives. His government wishes to establish closer contacts with China. Japan is an industrial giant expanding on all world markets. It announces that it wants to overtake the United States by the year 2000.

### January of 1970
After the end of a historic decade another one is starting on a pessimistic note with many unresolved conflicts. This is the beginning of the "Seventies."

Since June of 1969 some 110,000 U.S. combat troops have been brought or ordered home from S. Vietnam. The controversial war seems to be the number one "international headache." Many critics say that the Pentagon's "big war" mentality has been a basic reason for not winning the war in Vietnam. It is not for a conventional war but a *guerilla* war against an enemy who has been highly indoctrinated and well trained for a war in jungle and in such climatic conditions. Having inherited the war from the French whose army and Foreign Legion could not win the war against the tactics of Ho and Giap, the U.S. got trapped in the war.

Areas of conflict continue to be Southeast Asia, Middle East, and Central Asia and the Far East where the Soviets and Chinese are facing each other. China is, and will remain, the main worry of the Soviets. In spite of these tensions the Soviet Union is moving out in the world—especially in the Near and Middle East—as the U.S. is pulling back. There are going to be many new developments in this decade, an eventful and crucial period of human history. There are indications that in presence of the Chinese threat the "Cold War" between the United States and the Soviet Union is – at least temporarily – over. After De Gaulle's departure France will be more cooperative and more realistic. And the future of Europe will depend considerably on how West Germany will get along with the U.S.S.R. and East Europe. Japan's role on the Asian continent is growing. This is a matter of serious concern in Peking.

In the United States there are many problems to be dealt with. Reaction to the war in Southeast Asia, revolutionary trends, campus unrest and violence, crime in the streets, racial and minority problems, polarization of the people, rising inflation and recession, opposition against authority in all its forms, decreasing influence of religion, frustration, worry, fear and restlessness – all these are now part of our scene. The people have suddenly discovered, after so many years, that nature and the very environment in which they live, work and think, is being destroyed; they are running out of clear and fresh air, water, and soil. "Pollution" has at last become a major concern. While some historians, analysts, writers, and politicians—accepting Toynbee's cyclical interpretation of history—are thinking in terms of "rise and fall" of contemporary civilization, many others are more optimistic.

With the beginning of 1970 it is obvious that more than a mere calendar leaf is turning. The entire world is confronted with all kinds of problems, affecting all three large camps: Communist, non-Communist (mostly democratic), and neutral or non-aligned. What happens in this year will likely set the course for the Americas, the Soviet Union, China, and the rest of the world.

**January 1, 1970**
Vice President Agnew stops in Vietnam on his 11-nations Asian trip.

**January 3, 1970**
The Israelis undertake a reprisal raid in Lebanon.

**January 6, 1970**
It is estimated that some 100,000 North Vietnamese have joined their forces in S. Vietnam during 1969.

**January 13, 1970**
Brigadier General Philip Effiong, who had succeeded General Ojukwu as leader of Biafrans, surrenders Biafra after long and hopeless struggle. The head of the Federal Nigerian government in Lagos, Gen. Yakubu Gowon, accepts the surrender and promises good treatment of all Biafrans.

**January 14, 1970**
*Rudo Pravo* attacks A. Dubček; on the 25th Dubček and wife leave Prague for Ankara, Turkey where he will be the Czechoslovak Ambassador.

**January 15, 1970**
Memorial services are held in remembrance of Martin Luther King Jr.

**January 20, 1970**
Albania and China sign new trade and financial agreements.

After two years and 134 previous meetings, ambassadorial talks are renewed between the United States and China in Warsaw.

**January 21, 1970**
The Israelis attack Arab commandos in Jordan. Jordan itself has difficulties with undisciplined guerillas. In weeks to come King Hussein establishes his authority over the guerillas. 12,000 Iraqi troops are also in Jordan but do little in the warfare against Israel.

**January 21-24, 1970**
An additional 44 people are executed by the Iraqi government which is dominated by the revolutionary Baath Party.

**January 22, 1970**
President Nixon gives his first State of the Union address to the Congress. He sees the '70's as "a time of new beginnings" and "a new America" coming. He also announces fight against pollution and crime.

**January 26-29, 1970**
Fighting again breaks out between Honduras and El Salvador.

**January 26-31, 1970**
Students' and workers' demonstrations against the government of President Ferdinand Marcos in Philippines result in many casualties.

**January 26, 1970**
After years of military struggle, the government of Iraq issues general amnesty to the Kurds.

**January 28, 1970**
O. Cernik is removed as Premier of Czechoslovakia and replaced by Lubomir Strougal.

**January 29, 1970**
Aleksander Shelepin, a Politbureau member and one of the Soviet leaders, urges the Soviet people: strengthen the struggle against "absenteeism, loafing and drunkeness." (Drunkeness seems to be a great problem in most countries under Communism. For example, Poland has an estimated 1.5 million alcoholics in a population of 32 million.)

**End of January 1970**
For several months the French Foreign Legion has been active in Chad (former French colony, in the heart of Africa) against Moslem rebels.

According to official figures, the South Vietnamese have lost so far (since 1961) 97,000 combat troops; excluded are the paramilitary units. The enemy has lost 567,000 killed. The South Koreans with 50,000 in the field have had 2,980 dead; Thailand with 11,500 on the front has 196 dead; Australia with 7,500 has 331; Philippines with 1,560 has 8; and New Zealand with 550 participants 22 killed.

Reports in the West indicate that possibly fifty per cent of the members of the C.P. of Czechoslovakia have given up their membership or have been purged by the C.P.

**February 1, 1970**
A trade agreement is concluded between W. Germany and U.S.S.R.

**February 2, 1970**
Heavy fighting is raging between Syrians and Israelis on the Golan Heights.

**February 4, 1970**
President Nixon has sent a letter to Premier A.N. Kosygin in regard to the Middle East, say reports in Washington.

**February 11, 1970**
William P. Rogers, the U.S. Secretary of State, meets with Emperor Haile Selassie in Ethiopia on his tour of ten African countries.

**February 12, 1970**
Seventy Egyptian civilians are killed by Israeli jets.

**February 13-17, 1970**
Communist forces advance in Laos and take Plaine des Jarres.

**February 16, 1970**
The Soviets promise additional military aid to Arab countries.

**February 18, 1970**
Richard M. Nixon sends a 40,000-word message to Congress entitled "United States Foreign Policy for the 1970's." It is an important document which reveals our goals in this decade. The President warns the Russians against increasing tensions in the Middle East. The U.S. will not retreat into isolation; it will negotiate and take new approaches in this new era. While still committed to the basic ideas of freedom, America will not be its sole defender and will not play the role of international policeman.

On the same day one of the most tumultuous trials in the history of American jurisprudence ends in Chicago. It has lasted 21 weeks. Sentenced to 5 years were: David T. Dellinger, 54, a long-time pacifist; Thomas E. Hayden, 29, a founder of S.D.S.; Rennard C. Davis, 29, another founder of S.D.S.; Abbot Hoffman, 31, a leader of the Youth International Party (the Yippies); and Jerry C. Rubin, 31, also a Yippie. William Kunstler was the defense lawyer. Bobby Seale, a leader of Black Panthers was already serving a 4-year sentence for contempt and will be tried separately.

Rioters attach the U.S. Embassy in Manila, Phillippines.

**February 19, 1970**
Random House in New York publishes a 97-page book written by Supreme Court Justice William O. Douglas, *Points of Rebellion*. The book shocks many of the silent majority who start the move to impeach Douglas. It is stated in the book that "violence may be the only effective response" to strong grievances. The author suggests that revolution may be the only answer to oppression.

**February 23, 1970**
French President Georges Pompidou arrives in Washington for an eight-day visit of America.

**February 25, 1970**
Urgent messages from Saigon state that the present deteriorating situation in Laos is of serious concern to the U.S.

**February 26, 1970**
After three days of violence and riots, Governor Ronald Reagan of California orders a state of extreme emergency in Santa Barbara.

**March 1, 1970**
So far some 650,000 refugees have left Cuba which has a population of about 8.2 million.

Calcutta, the second-largest city in India (West Bengal Province) and well known for its poverty and slums, is reported under strong Communist control. The city and the province of 45 million are for all practical purposes under the rule of the "Marxist" branch of the Indian C.P. It is opposed to both Moscow and Peking.

## March 2, 1970
Rhodesia under Prime Minister Ian Smith, a white supremacist, proclaims itself an independent republic. On the 17th the United States closes its consulate in Salisbury. The new state has strong backing of South Africa.

## March 6, 1970
President Nixon issues a statement about Laos. We are intervening but not with ground combat forces.

A house—apparently a "bomb factory"—is blown up in New York City. Two "Weathermen" are killed. Bombings and threats of bombings are reported across the country. On March 17 the government discusses the situation and proposes the necessary legislation.

## March 11, 1970
Iraq grants autonomy to the Kurds.

## March 12-13, 1970
Chief of Cambodia Prince Norodom Sihanouk urges the Vietcong and N. Vietnamese to evacuate his "neutral" state.

## March 12, 1970
The Arabs attack the Israelis on several fronts.

Olof Palme, Premier of Sweden, meets with W. Brandt in Bonn.

## March 15, 1970
EXPO '70 opens near Osaka, Japan. Seventy-seven nations participate in this grandiose world fair, the first of its kind in Asia.

## March 16, 1970
The Tass News Agency publishes the letter of Soviet Premier A. Kosygin urging President Nixon to stop bombing of Laos.

Senator James O. Eastland charges in a Senate speech that there is a direct link between Cuba and spread of terrorism in the U.S.

## March 18, 1970
Prince Sihanouk's regime is overthrown in Pnom Penh, capital of Cambodia by a pro-Western group led by General Lon Nol. The prince is in Peking. The Communists, with 60,000 fighters, control three regions of the country and from their sanctuaries attack the U.S. positions in S. Vietnam. The Cambodian army is weak and poorly armed.

The Security Council of the U.N. condemns white minority rule in Rhodesia.

Increased Communist activity is reported in Laos. The Indo-China war is spreading.

## March 19, 1970
Willi Stoph, Premier of East Germany, and West German Chancellor Willy Brandt meet in Erfurt, East Germany to discuss many mutual problems.

Additional Soviet troops and anti-aircraft missiles are coming to Egypt.

## March 21, 1970
A. Dubček, now Ambassador in Turkey, is suspended by the Czechoslovak C.P.

## March 23, 1970
President Nixon orders troops into New York City to help sort out mail on account of postal strike. The whole country faces a series of long and short strikes.

## March 26, 1970
For the first time in eleven years, a Four Power meeting is held in Berlin to ease the existing tensions.

## March 29, 1970
Violent clashes take place in Belfast, North Ireland.

## March 31, 1970
The last British troops evacuate Libya after 30 years of presence. Rich Libya is a welcome addition to Nasser in his struggle with Israel.

### End of March 1970
Western intelligence reports that the Kremlin team Brezhnev-Kosygin is likely to be changed. Other reports maintain that various signs indicate that Poland is looking towards the West for badly needed economic aid.

**April of 1970**
North Vietnam has some 877,000 armed soldiers, it is supported by some 150,000 Vietcong and Pathet Lao guerillas and ample aid from the Soviets and Chinese.

**April 1, 1970**
This is the twenty-fifth anniversary of the American invasion of Okinawa, the largest amphibious military operation in the Pacific. (49,000 Americans were killed or wounded during three months of fighting.)

The latest Pentagon casualty lists state that 48,292 Americans have died of all causes in Vietnam.

**April 5, 1970**
W. German Ambassador Karl von Spreti, who was kidnapped on March 31 by guerillas in Guatemala, is found dead.

**April 11, 1970**
Yippie leader Jerry Rubin tells a rally of Kent State University students in Ohio: "We've got to break every law and disrupt every institution. We have to invent new laws to break." He calls on his listeners to join a revolution to overthrow the government.

The start of Apollo 13 flight towards the moon. On the 13th the space ship with astronauts James A. Lovell, Fred W. Haise and John L. Swigert is hit by explosion. They start their perilous 205,000 miles return anxiously watched by entire world.

**April 15, 1970**
113,800 Americans have been withdrawn from Vietnam.

**April 16, 1970**
After preliminary meetings in Helsinki, the Strategic Arms Limitation Talks continue in Vienna in neutral Austria.

**April 17, 1970**
Apollo 13 splashdown in the Pacific marks the happy end to a flight that almost ended in tragedy.

**April 20, 1970**
Bruno Kreisky, a Social Democrat, forms the first post-war Socialist government in Austria as result of March 1 general elections.

In a televised speech to the nation, President Nixon announces that 150,000 additional U.S. troops will be pulled out within the next year.

**April 21, 1970**
A state of siege is proclaimed in Colombia.

**April 22, 1970**
This is the hundredth anniversary of the birth of Vladimir I. Ulyanov-Lenin. The centenary of his birth is commemorated and enthusiastically celebrated in the Soviet Union and by Communists all over the world. He was born in Simbirsk, European Russia on April 22, 1870. After the celebrations of the fiftieth anniversary of Lenin's successful Revolution of 1917, this is the most significant celebration in the world Communist movement. To all Communists Lenin symbolizes the essence of this revolutionary age. It was Lenin who predicted that ours will be a century of wars and revolutions.

Yale University students decide to strike; demonstrations and riots will last several weeks.

The "Earth Day" is observed by many thousands of people—professing different ideologies—concerned with the deterioration of the environment.

**April 24, 1970**
China launches its first satellite.

**April 27, 1970**
Chinese submarines have stepped up operations in the Taiwan Strait since the U.S. Seventh Fleet reduced its patrols there.

**April 30, 1970**
President Nixon addresses the nation on his decision to send U.S. troops into Cambodia to destroy the Communist sanctuaries. A nation-wide reaction follows and sparks protests on almost all campuses. The Indo-China war becomes a nightmare of American politics causing additional dissent. Cambodia is threatened by a total collapse. Military strategists firmly believe that in order to secure the pull-out of our troops from Vietnam, it is absolutely necessary to destroy the Communist forces and supplies in Cambodia.

**May of 1970**
More than 50,000 Allied troops are attacking Communist bases in Cambodia. Many bases are destroyed

and great amounts of weapons, ammunition, supplies, and rice are captured. However, the war becomes number one cause of nation-wide unrest and protests all over the country. The nation is in upheaval. During the first two weeks of May violence and protest hit almost all of larger colleges and universities. Mob rule, destruction of property, burning of ROTC and other buildings scares many people who otherwise condone protest and dissent but are opposed to any kind of violence.

300,000 of our troops are still stationed in Europe; cuts are announced for the next year. Middle East is confronted with an all-out war. The war in Southeast Asia is expanded.

**May 1, 1970**
Students rampage through downtown Kent, Ohio.

**May 2-3, 1970**
University of Maryland is scene of serious demonstrations.

**May 2, 1970**
National Guardsmen are sent to Kent State University. The situation is very tense. There are reports that armed Weathermen are on campus.

**May 4, 1970**
After the burning of the ROTC building and continued violence, National Guardsmen kill four Kent State students; two are female and two male, all very young. The "Kent State Massacre" causes immediate spread of protest all over the country.

**May 6, 1970**
During debate in U.S. Senate on the tragedy of Kent State and campus violence, some Senators blame disorders on "hard-core revolutionaries."

**May 7, 1970**
The President has a conference with eight university presidents in the White House.

**May 8, 1970**
Several hundred construction workers attack anti-war protestors in New York's Wall Street. To calm the nation President Nixon promises that our forces will be pulled out from Cambodia by end of June.

**May 9, 1970**
A huge anti-war rally with very little violence is held in Washington near the White House. By now most colleges and universities are closed by strike.

**May 11, 1970**
Between 6,000 and 8,000 Soviet military advisers are believed to be in Egypt.

In racial outbreaks and violence six Negroes are killed by police in Augusta, Georgia.

**May 15, 1970**
Two Negro students are killed by police at Jackson State College in Mississippi.

**May 18, 1970**
To the question whether the revolution has come to the United States, the historian Arthur Schlesinger Jr. gives a reply in an article for the press. He states that the New Left has dreams, not revolutionary plans. For them the revolution is a "life-style" and not an "overreaching conspiracy." He argues the New Leftists have stimulated the national conscience. The causes of dissent should be examined and the words of John F. Kennedy should be remembered: "Those who make peaceful revolution impossible will make violent revolution inevitable."

**May 20, 1970**
The Soviet authorities arrest Andrei Amalrik, the author of *Will the Soviet Union Survive Until 1984?* He is one of the best known Soviet dissidents.

Mao Tse-tung in a rare public appearance attacks the United States and pledges support for "the revolutionary struggle of the American people" against the "fascist rule" in Washington. He denounces U.S. "imperialism in Indo China" and calls on all peoples of the world to oppose American military intervention. According to the New China News Agency Mao warned of the dangers of a new world war: "Revolution is the main trend in the world today."

The Nixon administration, states Mao, "is beset with troubles internally and externally, with utter chaos at home and extreme isolation abroad. The mass movement of protest against U.S. aggression in Cambodia has swept the globe."

**May 22, 1970**

The death toll for the previous week is 217 killed; of these 77 died in Cambodia. Since May 1 166 Americans have been killed in Cambodia; the number of enemy dead is 8,433.

**May 26, 1970**

President Suharto of Indonesia, which is world's fifth largest power, is warmly received in Washington by President Nixon.

**May 28, 1970**

Riots of Maoist students continue in Paris. Disorders, violence, terrorism, and revolts of the young New Leftists take place in France, Italy, and West Germany. While under the impact of events in our own country, our news media tell little about rising revolutionary trends in many parts of Western Europe. Anarchism and bloody clashes are shaking the very foundations of affluent European nations. Disorders, violence, terrorism, and revolts of the young New Leftists take place in France, Italy, and West Germany. While under the impact of events in our own country, our news media tell little about rising revolutionary trends in many parts of Western Europe. Anarchism and bloody clashes are shaking the very foundations of affluent European nations.

*Mr. Gromyko visits the Lenin Exposition in Paris* – Keystone

## *Appendix* 1

# The Communist Countries of the World

| NAME | AREA IN SQ. MILES | POPULATION | CAPITAL |
|---|---|---|---|
| People's Republic of Albania | 11,100 | 2,100,000 | Tirana |
| People's Republic of Bulgaria | 42,729 | 8,500,000 | Sofia |
| People's Republic of China | 3,760,000 | 765,000,000 | Peking |
| Republic of Cuba | 44,218 | 8,100,000 | Havana |
| Czechoslovak Socialist Republic | 49,370 | 14,500,000 | Prague |
| German Democratic Republic | 41,660 | 17,400,000 | E. Berlin |
| Hungarian People's Republic | 35,918 | 10,300,000 | Budapest |
| People's Democratic Republic of Korea | 46,540 | 12,500,000 | Pyongyang |
| Mongolian People's Republic | 592,664 | 1,200,000 | Ulan Bator |
| Polish People's Republic | 120,664 | 32,500,000 | Warsaw |
| The Socialist Republic of Rumania | 92,700 | 20,000,000 | Bucharest |
| Union of Soviet Socialist Republics | 8,647,000 | 237,000,000 | Moscow |
| Democratic Republic of Vietnam | 61,293 | 19,000,000 | Hanoi |
| The Socialist Federative Republic of Yugoslavia | 98,786 | 20,250,000 | Belgrade |
| total | 13,674,642 | 1,168,350,000 | |

Compiled by the author from various sources

Note: Here are the official names of these states. In our usage the German Democratic Republic is better known as East Germany, People's Democratic Republic of Korea as North Korea, and Democratic Republic of Vietnam as North Vietnam.

*Appendix* **2**

## The Communist Parties of the World: 1967

| COUNTRY | MEMBER-SHIP | LEGAL STATUS | SINO-SOVIET DISPUTE |
|---|---|---|---|
| Afghanistan | 175 | | Pro-Soviet |
| Albania | 66,000 | In power | Pro-Chinese |
| Algeria | 1,000 | Proscribed 1963 | Pro-Soviet |
| Argentina | 60,000 | Proscribed 1966 | Pro-Soviet |
| Australia | 5,000 | | Split |
| Austria | 27,500 | | Split |
| Belgium | 12,500 | | Split |
| Berlin, West | 6,000 | | Pro-Soviet |
| Bolivia | 6,000 | Proscribed 1967 | Split |
| Brazil | 20,000 | Proscribed 1947 | Split |
| Bulgaria | 613,000 | In power | Pro-Soviet |
| Cambodia | 100 | | |
| Canada | 2,500 | | Pro-Soviet |
| Ceylon | 1,900 | | Split |
| Chile | 32,500 | | Pro-Soviet |
| China, Communist | 17,000,000 | In power | |
| Colombia | 9,000 | | Split |
| Congo | Negligible | | |
| Costa Rica | 550 | Proscribed 1948 | Pro-Soviet |
| Cuba | 60,000 | In power | Independent |
| Cyprus | 13,000 | | Pro-Soviet |
| Czechoslovakia | 1,689,000 | In power | Pro-Soviet |
| Denmark | 6,000 | | Pro-Soviet |
| Dominican Republic | 1,300 | Proscribed 1947 | |
| Ecuador | 1,500 | Proscribed 1963 | Split |
| El Salvador | 200 | Proscribed 1928 | Pro-Soviet |
| Finland | 49,000 | | Pro-Soviet |
| France | 275,000 | | Split |
| Germany, East | 1,769,000 | In power | Pro-Soviet |
| Germany, West | 7,000 | Proscribed 1956 | Split |
| Greece | 27,000 | Proscribed 1947 | Pro-Soviet |
| Guadeloupe | 1,000 | | Pro-Soviet? |
| Guatemala | 750 | Proscribed 1954 | Pro-Soviet |
| Honduras | 650 | Proscribed 1957 | Pro-Soviet |
| Hungary | 585,000 | In power | Pro-Soviet |
| Iceland | 1,000 | | Pro-Soviet |
| India | 125,000 | | Split |

Source for this Appendix: U.S. Department of State, Bureau of Intelligence and Research, *World Strength of the Communist Party Organizations:* 20th Annual Report, 1968 Edition, pp. 1-8.

| COUNTRY | MEMBER-SHIP | LEGAL STATUS | SINO-SOVIET DISPUTE |
|---|---|---|---|
| Indonesia | 150,000 | Proscribed 1966 | Unknown |
| Iran | 1,000 | Proscribed 1949 | Pro-Soviet |
| Iraq | 2,000 | Proscribed 1960 | Pro-Soviet |
| Ireland | 125 | | Pro-Soviet |
| Israel | 1,600 | | Pro-Soviet |
| Italy | 1,531,000 | | Split |
| Japan | 250,000 | | Independent |
| Jordan | 400 | Proscribed 1957 | Pro-Soviet |
| Korea, North | 1,600,000 | In power | Independent |
| Korea, South | Negligible | Proscribed 1948 | |
| Lebanon | 6,000 | Proscribed 1939 | Split |
| Luxemburg | 500 | | Pro-Soviet |
| Malaysia | 2,000 | Proscribed 1948 | Pro-Chinese |
| Martinique | 700 | | Pro-Soviet |
| Mexico | 5,250 | | Split |
| Mongolia | 48,570 | In power | Pro-Soviet |
| Morocco | 500 | Proscribed 1952 | Neutral |
| Nepal | 8,000 | Proscribed | |
| The Netherlands | 11,500 | | Independent |
| New Zealand | 400 | | Split |
| Nicaragua | 200 | Proscribed 1945 | Pro-Soviet |
| Nigeria | 1,000 | Proscribed 1967 | |
| Norway | 2,500 | | Independent |
| Pakistan | 1,450 | Proscribed 1954 | Neutral |
| Panama | 250 | Proscribed 1953 | Pro-Soviet |
| Paraguay | 5,000 | Proscribed 1936 | Split |
| Peru | 5,000 | Proscribed | Split |
| Philippines | 1,750 | Proscribed 1957 | Neutral |
| Poland | 1,895,000 | In power | Pro-Soviet |
| Portugal | 2,000 | Proscribed | Split |
| Rumania | 1,730,000 | In power | Neutral |
| Singapore | 200 | Proscribed 1948 | Pro-Chinese |
| Spain | 5,000 | Proscribed 1939 | Split |
| Sudan | 7,500 | Proscribed 1965 | Pro-Soviet |
| Sweden | 29,000 | | Independent |
| Switzerland | 4,000 | | Split |
| Syria | 3,000 | Proscribed 1939 | Split |
| Thailand | 1,450 | Proscribed 1952 | Pro-Chinese |
| Tunisia | 100 | Proscribed 1963 | Pro-Soviet |
| Turkey | 1,250 | Proscribed 1925 | Pro-Soviet |
| Union of Soviet Socialist Republics | 12,948,000 | In power | |
| United Kingdom | 32,600 | | Pro-Soviet |
| United States | see Note at the end of Appendix | | |
| Uruguay | 21,000 | | Pro-Soviet |
| Venezuela | 5,000 | Proscribed | Pro-Soviet |

| COUNTRY | MEMBER-SHIP | LEGAL STATUS | SINO-SOVIET DISPUTE |
|---|---|---|---|
| Vietnam, North | 760,000 | In power | Neutral |
| Vietnam, South | No estimate | Proscribed 1956 | Neutral |
| Yugoslavia | 1,046,000 | In power | Independent |

Note: The State Department's official report on world C.P.'s does not list the Communist Party of the U.S.A. Judging from several authoritative sources, there are only about 10,000 to 15,000 C.P. members in our country. The C.P.U.S.A. is far from being united even though this year for the first time after 1940 they have a presidential candidate. However, it should be borne in mind that "there are from ten to twenty times that number of pro-Communists who carry out the orders of the Party members" as Dr. Rodger Swearingen states in his lucid and revealing *The World of Communism* (Boston: Houghton Mifflin Co., 1966), p. 177.

As to the statistics on the previous pages, some comments should be added. In a *revolutionary* organization numbers do not mean much. There were very few Bolsheviks in Russia, only a few thousand, before Lenin took power in Petrograd. A few hundred dedicated revolutionaries may have thousands of sympathizers and "fellow travelers." The fact that in many countries of the world the C.P. has been proscribed does not prevent dedicated Communist activists from giving quite an impact to those countries. We have been used to hearing about Communism in many Arab countries. This list proves that in these countries Communism is actually very weak.

As for Cuba, a revolutionary Communist base for entire Latin America and even for Africa, the C.P. numbers only 60,000 card-carrying Party members. But Cuba is still a Communist country and Ernesto Che Guevara, the top lieutenant of Fidel Castro, was determined to carry the revolution to all Latin American countries. For him it was an ill-fated adventure because the Bolivian peasants did not know about "Yankee Imperialism" and did not care about Guevara's (who was an Argentinian) guerilla warfare. In spite of small "official numbers" of Communists in Latin America, the Communist threat there is still very imminent. The dead Guevara and his legend may be a very powerful weapon for Castro's revolutionaries in that part of our hemisphere.

Contrary to the prevailing beliefs that C.P. of France is very strong, it should be noted that the actual number of Party members is only about 275,000 as indicated on this list. However, the French C.P. has polled recently as high as over 5,000,000 votes! This again proves that the real strength of Communism is not reflected in the figures of the party membership. Many of these numbers are only estimated. They may be higher or lower than indicated here.

The numbers and statistics never prove the whole truth and evidence. The C.P. of Czechoslovakia is listed here as 1,689,000, which for a country of some 14 million is indeed a high percentage. We are witnessing what is happening in Czechoslovakia these days. Many of these Czech and Slovak Communists are enemies of the Russians. Their Communist country has been invaded by five other Communist countries. This proves the existence of a desperate disunity among the Communists.

Just looking at the last left column in this list, the "Sino-Soviet Dispute," one can see how many parties are "Split" on this issue. Here lies the real weakness of this whole revolutionary movement. And if we take into account the parties that are "Independent" and "Neutral" the whole picture for Communism may look even gloomier.

It is with all these reservations in our mind that we should judge the real meaning of these statistics.

Bebel, Ferdinand August, *7, 13, 15, 38*
Belfast, *262*
Belgian Revolt, *6*
Belgian Socialist Party, *17*
Belgrade, *60, 253*
    coup of 1941, *123*
    Neutralists' Conference, *203*
Bella, Ben, *214-220*
Beneficent Socialism, *4*
Beneš, Eduard, *101, 108, 136, 142, 145*
    resigns, *157*
    dies, *158*
Bentley, Elizabeth, *158*
Beran, Josef, *253*
Berchtesgaden, *107*
Beria, Lavrenty P., *110, 124, 178, 180*
Berkman, Alexander, *23*
Berlin, *204, 262*
    Blockade of, *157, 161*
    Wall, *203*
Bernstein, Eduard, *3, 11, 20*
    publishes *Evolutionary Socialism*, *24*
    leader of Independent Socialists, *42*
Bessarabia, *55, 58, 216*
Bevin, Ernest, *157*
Biafra, *232, 246, 249, 260*
Bielorussia, *51, 58, 60, 138*
Bielorussian S.S.R., *271*
Bielorussians, *10*
Bierut, Boleslaw, *137*
Bihać, *132*
Birladeanu, A., *242*
Bismarck, Otto, von, *16, 17, 22*
Black Panthers, *259*
"Black Partition", *17*
Blanc, Louis, *6, 10*
Blanqui, Louis A., *2*
"Bloody Sunday", *28*
"Bloody Week" (Commune), *15*
Bluecher, Vasily K., *108*
Blum, Leon, *102*
Bogota, *156*
Bogrov, Dimitry, *35*
Bohemia, *12*
Bolivia, *91, 249*
*Bolshevik*, *173*
Bolshevik Revolution, *50*
    fiftieth anniversary of, *228*
Bolsheviks, *3, 28, 32*
    final split with Mensheviks, *36*
    Seventh Congress, *56*
Bonaparte, Louis Napoleon, *10*
Bonn, *161*
Bonus March, *94*
Bor-Komorovski, T., *139-140*
Borodin, M., *76*
Bosnia-Herzegovina, *131*
Bosphorus, *102*
Boston police strike, *63*
Boumedienne, H., *220*
Brandt, Willy, *253, 257, 262*
Bratislava, *178, 243*
Brazil, *106, 107, 246, 256*
Bremen, *61*
Breshkovskaya, Catherine, *26*
Brest-Litovsk Treaty, *50-51, 56*

Brezhnev, Leonid I., *202, 207, 216, 219, 227, 231, 234, 253, 255*
Britain, *84*
    Communist Party of, *66*
    Labor Party of, *26, 55, 91, 216*
    Battle of, *121*
British Museum, *11*
Bronstein, Leon D. See *Trotsky.*
Browder, Earl, *107, 118*
Brownson, Orestes A., *4*
Broz, Josip. See *Tito.*
Brussilov, Alexander, *43, 47*
Brzezinsky, Zbigniew, *244*
Budapest, *64, 142, 236*
Budenny, S. M., *66*
Bukharin, N. I., *56, 91, 92*
Bulganin, N. A., *156, 191, 194*
Bulgaria, *17, 26, 38, 63, 122, 266*
    agrarian reforms in, *64-65*
    Boris, King of, *63*
    Communist revolt in, *76*
    suppression of C.P., *82*
    General Workers Union of, *28*
    surrenders, *140*
    Communist Party of, *160, 256*
    Fatherland Front of, *146*
    "People's Republic", *152*
Bulge, Battle of, *141*
Bund, *24, 28*
Burma, *131*
Bykov, Boris, *107*
Byrnes, James F., *146*

Cairo, *136, 216. 250*
Calcutta, *262*
*Call*, *62*
Cambodia, *183, 234, 262, 263-264*
Canada, *211*
Cannon, James P., *89*
Canton (China), *83*
Canton Commune, *88*
Captive Nations Week, *198*
Cardona, José M., *196, 209*
Carmichael, Stokely, *228*
Carnegie Steel, *23*
Carol II, King, *122*
Carpatho-Ukraine, *110, 141, 146*
Carr, Samuel, *80*
Carribean, *198*
Casablanca Conference, *132*
Castro, Fidel, *156, 178, 190, 206, 209, 228, 251*
    released from jail, *185*
    founds "26th of July Movement," *186*
    offensive against Batista, *195*
    enters Havana, *196*
    visits Washington, *196*
    aided by USSR, *199*
    visits USSR, *210*
Castro, Raul, *222*
Catholic Church, *210*
    reforms in, *228*
Ceausescu, Nicolae, *219, 221, 225, 234, 252, 255*
    denounces Gheorghiu-Dej, *240*
    supports Dubček, *244*
Centralia, Wash., *64*
Central Powers, *43*

Cernik, Oldrich, *239, 260*
Chamberlain, Neville, *108*
Chambers, Whittaker, *27, 91, 107, 163*
Chartist Movement, *7*
Chechens, *170*
Cheka, *51*
Chernov, V. M., *26*
Chervenkov, Vulko, *163*
Chiang Kai-shek, *76, 81, 84, 101*
    attacks Shanghai, *86*
    fights Red forces, *93*
    enters Canton, *103*
    captured, *104*
Chicago, *17*
    Democratic Convention, *244*
    Trial, *256, 261*
Chicherin, Georgy, *85*
Chile, *108, 250*
China, *36, 86, 202, 246, 247, 249, 256, 260*
    Civil War in, *54, 159*
    War with Japan *95, 105-106*
    Nationalist-Communist rift, *149, 151*
    People's Political Consultative Conference, *162*
    "People's Republic", *162, 234*
    "Great Leap Forward", *193*
    communes in, *194*
    war with India, *207-208*
    explodes A-bomb, *217*
    "Cultural Revolution", *225-226*
Chinese Communist Party, *70, 251*
    Third Congress, *74*
    denounces Tito, *190;* see also *Sino-Soviet rift.*
Chinese Soviet Republic, *93*
Chkheidze, N. S., *45*
Chornovil, V. M., *234*
Chou En-lai, *78, 153, 172, 213, 217, 225, 256*
Chungking, *106*
Chuprynka, Taras, *132, 148, 164*
Churchill, Winston, *119, 130, 131*
    in Washington, *134*
    in Moscow, *140*
    in Athens, *141*
    "Iron Curtain" speech, *150*
    dies, *218*
Cierna meeting, *243*
C.I.O., *101*
Civil War in Russia, *50*
Classless society, *7*
Class struggle, *7*
Clementis, Vladimir, *164, 168*
"Cold War", *157-158, 161*
Cologne Communist Trial, *11*
Colombia, *180, 228, 246, 249, 263*
COMECON, *160, 192, 206, 221, 249*
Committee on Un-American Activities, *viii*
Communards, *15*
Commune of Paris, *2, 15*
Communist Club of New York, *12*
Communist Correspondence Committees, *8*
Communist Information Bureau (Cominform), *viii, 154, 180*
    moves to Bucharest, *158*
    dissolved, *187*
Communist International (Comintern), *62*
    founding of, *61*
    Second Congress of, *66*
    "Second Strategy" of, *68*

Third Congress of, *70*
"Third Strategy" of, *89*
Balkan Secretariat, *98*
Seventh Congress of, *100*
    dissolved, *134*
Communist Labor Party of America, *63*
Communist League, *8*
*Communist Manifesto, vii, 2, 8, 10*
Communist Party of America, *63*
Communist Party of the Soviet Union (CPSU), *88, 92, 96, 110*
    Nineteenth Congress of, *173*
    Twentieth Congress of, *186*
    Twenty-First Congress of, *196*
    Twenty-Second Congress of, *204*
    Twenty-Third Congress of, *225*
    membership, *153*
    new program of, *202*
    receives Mao's "Open Letters", *210*
Communist Party of the United States (CPUSA), *90, 97*
Communist Propaganda League of America, *60*
*Communist World, 64*
*Conditions of the Working Class in England, 8*
Congo, *200*
Congress of the American Slavs, *152*
Congress of Berlin, *17*
Constituent Assembly, *49-50*
Constitutional Democrats (Kadets), *32*
Coolidge, Calvin, *81*
"Cordon Sanitaire", *88*
Corfu, *76*
Corregidor, *131*
Cossackia, *59*
Cossacks, *45, 56, 136*
Costa Rica, *200*
Council of Foreign Ministers, *146, 152, 153, 154, 161*
Council for Mutual Economic Assistance.
    See *COMECON.*
Council of People's Commissars, *50*
Coventry, *122*
Cracow, *36*
Crete, *124*
Crimea, *51, 58, 129*
Crimean Tartars, *150, 170*
Crimean War, *14*
Croatia, *10, 23, 80, 112, 123, 217*
    uprising in, *126*
    declaration on language, *229-230*
Croatian Peasant Party, *89, 100*
Cuba, *x, 246, 248, 249*
    Bay of Pigs Invasion, *202*
    Communist outpost, *202*
    Missile Crisis, *207-208*
    exiles from, *209*
    Soviet technicians in, *210*
Cuban Revolutionary Council, *209*
Curzon Line, *66, 130, 137*
Cvetković, Dragisa, *123*
Cyprus, *128, 219*
Czech Legion, *58*
Czech National Socialists, *144*
Czechoslovakia, *x, 58, 65, 86, 100, 248, 266*
    Communist coup (1948), *156*
    Communist Party of, *70, 253*
    liberalization, *237-239*
    C.P.'s Action Program, *239*
    crisis in, *243-245*

Czechs, *108, 211, 238*

*Daily Worker, 192*
Dalai Lama, *196*
Dalmatia, *232*
Damaskinos, Archbishop, *141*
Daniel, Yuli, *223*
Danzig, *95, 108*
Dardanelles, *102*
Debray, Jules R., *230, 274*
Debs, Eugene V., *23, 26*
Decembrist Revolt, *4*
Decembrists, *2*
"Declaration of Washington", *168*
De Gaulle, Charles, *120, 141, 226, 227*
    in Rumania, *241*
    loses office, *252*
    reaction to events in Prague, *245*
    defies riots, *242*
De Leon, Daniel, *12, 24*
Denikin, A. I., *64*
Denmark, *118*
Dialectics, *7*
Dialectical Materialism, *7*
Diaz, José, *103*
Diem, Ngo Dinh, *182, 186, 211*
Dien Bien Phu, *181*
Dieppe, *131*
"Different Roads to Socialism", *176*
Dimitrov, Georgi, *18, 71, 81, 96, 147, 155, 162*
Dimitrov, G. M. (Agrarian), *151*
Djilas, Milovan, *126, 173, 180, 251*
    quits C.P.Y., *181*
    publishes *The New Class, 192*
    sentenced to prison, *193*
    publishes *Conversations With Stalin, 206*
    released from prison, *228*
Dmytryshyn, Basil, *115, 127, 149, 276*
Dnieper, *136*
Dobruja, *122*
Dollfuss, Engelbert, *94*
Dominican Republic, *220*
Don Cossacks, *50, 58*
Donets Basin, *101*
Dorpat Peace Treaty, *65*
Douglas, William O., *261*
Dragoitcheva, Tsola, *26, 152*
Dresden, *148*
Dubček, Aleksandar, *235-236, 238, 240, 252, 256, 259, 262*
Duehring, Karl E., *17*
Dukhonin, N. N., *50*
Dulles, John F., *180, 197*
Duma, *32, 34*
Dunkirk, *119*
Dutschke, Rudi, *274*
Dzerzhinsky, Feliks E., *23, 51*
Dzhugashvili, Yossif V. See *Stalin.*

E.A.M., *138*
"Earth Day", *263*
East Berlin Revolt, *178*
East Central Europe, *64*
    Sovietization of, *149*
Easter Rebellion in Ireland, *42*
East Europe, Sovietization of, *142*
East German Revolt, *176*

East Germany, *162, 186, 266*
    refugees from, *203*
    Socialist Unity Party, *166, 170*
    Soviet Troops in, *242*
*Eastern Europe and World Communism, viii*
East Prussia, *139, 144*
Ebert, Friedrich, *82*
Ecuador, *250*
Eden, Anthony, *100, 123, 138*
Egypt, *122, 262*
Eisenhower, Dwight D., *137, 173, 181, 198*
    visits Latin America, *199*
    "Domino Theory" of, *181*
Eisler, Gerhart, *88*
Eisner, Kurt, *61, 62*
El Alamein, *131*
E.L.A.S., *134, 142*
El Salvador, *168*
Emancipation of Labor, *18*
Emergency Quota Immigration Act, *70*
Emerson, Ralph Waldo, *4, 6*
Engels, Friedrich, *2, 4, 7, 8, 20, 23*
    writes *Anti-Duehring, 17*
    writes *Socialism: Scientific and Utopian, 22*
Equal Rights Party, *16*
Erhard, Ludwig, *214*
Estonia, *50, 113*
Estonian Communist Party, *169*
Estonian S.S.R., *271*
Ethiopia, *101, 261*

*Fabian Essays, 25*
Fabian Society, *20, 22*
Famine in Soviet Russia, *70*
Fanon, Frantz, *254*
Far Eastern Republic, *65*
Fascism, *96*
Federal Bureau of Investigation (F.B.I.), *164*
"Fighting Union for the Liberation of the Working
    Class", *24*
Figl, Leopold, *156*
Finland, *32, 45, 50, 55, 124, 172*
    Lapua Movement, *91*
    attacked by Soviets, *114*
    Winter War, *118*
    fights Russians, *130*
    defies Sovietization, *158*
    neutrality of, *204*
Finland Station, *46*
First International, *2, 4, 13, 16*
Fischer, Ernst, *25*
Fiume, *78*
Foch, Ferdinand, *62*
*For a Lasting Peace, 171*
Formosa, *171, 194*
"Forty-Eighters", *11*
Foster, William Z., *9, 18, 35, 64, 77, 81, 122*
Fourier, Charles, *2*
France, *77, 94*
    withdraws from NATO, *224*
    general strike (1968), *241*
Francis Ferdinand, *40*
Francis Joseph, *11, 43*
Franco, Francisco, *102, 104, 110, 255*
French Communist Party, *86, 147*
French General Confederation of Labor, *23*
Fuchs, Klaus, *163, 164*

Fuentes, A. A., *171*
Fullbright, J. W., *225, 251*

Gagarin, Yuri, *202*
Galicia, *41*
Gandhi, Mahatma, *92*
Ganeff, Dimiter, *194, 214*
Gapon, Georgy A., *28*
Gaston-Marin, G., *214*
Gatchina, *50*
"General Jewish Workers' Union." See the *Bund.*
Geneva, *12*
Geneva Agreement (1954), *183*
Geneva Disarmament Conference, *206, 257*
Geneva Summit Conference, *185*
Genoa, *72*
Georgia, *58, 69*
Georgian S.S.R., *251*
German Democratic Republic, *161*
German Empire, *15*
German Federal Republic, *161*
*German-French Annuals, 8*
Germany, *54, 60, 77, 86, 110*
    Anti-Socialist Laws, *17*
    Social Democratic Party of, *22, 40*
    Communist Party of, *61*
    Weimar Constitution, *63*
    Center Party in, *63*
    failure of revolution, *69*
    rearmament, *100, 103*
    Nuremberg Laws, *101*
    occupies Rhineland, *102*
    further aggressions, *108, 112*
    attacks the USSR, *124*
    slave labor in, *130*
Gershuni, G. A., *26*
Ghana, *195*
Gheorghiu-Dej, Gheorghe, *206, 212, 216*
Gheorgiev, K., *82*
Giap, *259*
Gitlow, Benjamin, *81*
Glassboro, N. J., *232*
Goga, Octavian, *106*
Golan Heights, *261*
Gold, Harry, *166*
Goldman, Emma, *64*
*Golos Sotsial-Demokrata, 34*
Gompers, Samuel, *20, 64*
Gomulka, Wladislaw, *30, 154, 158, 188, 192, 214, 253*
    purged, *163*
    attacks Zionism, *238*
Gorkić, Milan, *106*
Gorky, Maxim, *34, 70*
Gosplan, *68*
Gotha, *16*
Gottwald, Klement, *24, 83, 108, 150, 157, 177*
Goulart, Joao, *203, 213*
Gouzenko, Igor, *147*
G.P.U., *71*
Graves, W. S., *59*
Great Purges, *105, 110*
Grechko, Andrei A., *240*
Greece, *58, 98, 101, 253*
    attacked by Italy, *122*
    George II returns to, *152*
    civil war in, *141, 156, 163*
Greek National Liberation Front (EAM), *128*

Greeley, Horace, *13*
Gromyko, Andrei A., *156, 170, 222, 247*
Grotewohl, Otto, *151, 216*
Groza, Peter, *142*
Guadalcanal, *131*
Guam, *130*
Guantanamo Base, *208*
Guatemala, *168, 180, 228, 263*
Guerilla warfare, *105, 274-275*
"guerrillero", *255*
Guesde, Jules, *17, 28*
Guevara, Ernesto "Che", *x, 171, 173-174, 180, 190,*
    *217, 219, 274-275*
    publishes *On Guerilla Warfare, 199*
    in Bolivia, *228*
    killed, *234*
Guyana, *248*
Guzman, J. Arbenz, *186*

Habsburg Empire, *4*
Hacha, Emil, *108*
Haiphong, *226*
Hajek, Jiri, *245*
Hamburg, *76, 144*
Hammarskjold, Dag, *203*
Hankow, *86*
Hanoi, *200, 226*
Hanson, Ole, *61*
Harding, Warren G., *69*
Harriman, W. A., *240*
*Havana Prensa Latina, 230*
Hayden, Thomas, *261*
Haymarket Riots, *20*
Haywood, William S., *30*
H-bomb, *203*
Hegel, Georg W. F., *2, 4*
Hegelians, *7*
Heimwehr, *93*
Heine, Heinrich, *7*
Heinemann, Gustav, *250*
Helsinki, *58, 220*
Henlein, Konrad, *108*
Herter, Christian A., *196*
Herzen, Alexander I., *3, 10, 12, 15*
    *From the Other Shore, 11*
    publishes *Kolokol, 12*
Hess, Moses, *7*
Hillquit, Morris, *27*
Himmler, Heinrich, *126*
Hindenburg, Paul, *41, 82*
Hiroshima, *146*
Hiss, Alger, *91, 163*
Hitler, Adolf, *54, 76, 81, 95, 97, 144*
Ho Chi Minh, *22, 35, 87, 92, 147, 181, 187, 223, 235,*
    *254, 255,*
    as guerilla leader, *255-256*
Homestead Massacre, *23*
Hong Kong, *87, 130*
Hoover, Edgar J., *168*
Hoover, Herbert, *89*
Horthy, Nicholas, *63, 138*
"Hot Line", *211*
Hoxha, Enver, *138, 150, 162, 175*
Hue, *236*
Huks, *238*
Hull, Cordell, *139*
Humphrey, Hubert H., *218, 224*

Hunan, *23*
Hungarian Revolt (1956), *188-189*
Hungarians, *10, 11*
Hungary, *110, 153, 246*
    Soviet Republic in, *61*
Husak, Gustav, *250, 252, 257*
Hyndman, H. M., *18*

Ibarruri, Dolores, *103*
Ibos, *232*
Iceland, Communist Party of, *92*
Immigrants, *11, 35, 64*
    deportation of, *65*
Immigration, *16*
    restriction of, *64*
Independent Labor Party, *25*
Indian Communist Party, *97, 257, 262*
Indian-Pakistani War, *221*
Indo-China, *114, 263*
Indonesia, *163, 166*
    Communist revolt in, *221-222*
Industrial Workers of the World, *30*
Institute for Soviet and East European Studies, *v, vii*
Intelligentsia, *14*
Internal Macedonian Revolutionary Organization, *97*
International Federation of Trade Unions, *63*
International Military Tribunal, *148*
*International Press Correspondence, 106*
International Socialist Bureau, *40*
International Workingmen's Association. See *First International.*
Iran (Persia), *128, 148, 150, 179*
Iraq, *195, 243, 260*
Iron Curtain, *218*
Iron Gates, *216*
Iron Guard, *96, 108*
*Iskra, 27*
Israel, *174, 178, 180, 232, 250, 251, 259*
Italian Communist Party, *73, 213*
Italian Socialist Party, *68*
Italy, *10, 78, 134, 246*
*Izvestia, 30, 165*

Jackson State College, *264*
Japan, *146, 262*
    Communist Party of, *72*
Japanese, *59*
Jaurès, Jean, *26, 28*
Jehol, *94*
Jelačić, Josip, *11*
Jews, *18, 24, 130, 134*
Joffe, Adolf, *76*
John Carroll University, *v, vii*
John XXIII, Pope, *209*
Johnson, Hiram, *61*
Johnson, Lyndon, *202, 212, 214, 217, 218, 231, 242*
    on Great Society, *218*
    on Vietnam, *219, 220, 223*
    trip in Asia, *227*
    in Central America, *243*
Jordan, *251, 260*
"June Days" of 1848, *10*
"July Days" of 1830, *6*

Kadar, Janos, *189, 213, 221, 223, 239*
"Kadets", *50*
Kaganovich, Lazar M., *192, 214*

Kaledin, Aleksey M., *50*
Kalinin, Mikhail I., *73, 111, 150*
Kalmucks, *170*
*Kapital, Das, 3, 10, 14, 16*
Kaplan, Dora, *59*
Karageorgevich, *60, 98*
Karelia, *118*
Karelo-Finnish S.S.R., *188*
Karlovy Vary, *231*
Kashmir, *221*
Kassem, Abdul Karim, *196, 209*
Katanga, *202*
Katyn Forest, *118, 133, 167*
Kautsky, Karl J., *3, 12, 18, 22, 28*
    writes *Theories of Surplus Value, 28*
    joins the Revisionists, *32*
Kazak, S.S.R., *251*
Kazakstan, *74*
Kekkonen, Urho K., *203, 256*
Kemal, Mustapha, *68, 73*
Kennan, George F., *172, 173, 209*
Kennan, George, *20*
Kennedy, John F., *54, 201, 202, 203, 264*
    on Laos, *202*
    addresses U.N., *203*
    and Cuban missile crisis, *207*
    in Berlin, *210*
    denounces Diem regime, *211*
    assassinated, *211*
Kennedy, Robert F., *215, 229, 242, 252*
Kent State University, *263*
    massacre, *264*
Kerala, *198*
Kerch, *130*
Kerensky, Alexander, *20, 40, 45, 47*
Kharkov, *64*
Khruschev, Nikita S., *23, 131, 148, 155, 163, 184, 186, 187, 194, 201, 206, 211, 213*
    First Secretary, *179*
    reconciliation with Tito, *185*
    intervenes in Poland, *188*
    economic reforms, *191*
    in E. Germany, *192*
    in China, *194*
    in Albania, *197*
    visits U.S., *198*
    in Peking, *198*
    Summit in Paris, *199*
    in New York, *200*
    endorses "Liberation Wars", *201*
    denounces the Chinese, *213*
    in Egypt, *214*
    ousted, *216*
    reaction to ouster of, *217-218*
Kiangsi, *95-96*
Kienthal, *42*
Kiev, *128*
Kim Il Sung, *36, 166, 227*
King, Martin Luther, *230, 239, 251, 260*
Kirghiz S.S.R., *251*
Kirov, Sergey M., *84, 98*
Kiesinger, Kurt G., *245*
Knights of Labor, *20*
Kolchak, Alexander V., *60, 64-65*
Komsomol, *60*
Konev, Ivan S., *152, 168*
Korean Communist Party, *82*

Korean Democratic Republic, *158*
Korean People's Liberation Army, *166*
Korean War, *166, 167, 178*
Kornilov Revolt, *48*
Košice Program, *142, 144*
Kosmet Region, *226, 230*
Kostov, Traicho, *162*
Kosygin, Alexei N., *28, 199, 216, 218, 219, 225, 232, 241, 256*
Kovacs, Bela, *153*
Kozlov, Frol R., *191, 218*
Krasnov, Peter N., *58*
Kreisky, Bruno, *263*
Kremlin, *53*
    Communist Summit, *253*
Kriege, Hermann, *8*
Krivitsky, Walter, *91*
Krleža, Miroslav, *229*
Kronstadt, *30, 47, 69*
Kropotkin, Peter, *255*
Krupskaya, Nadezhda, *23, 81*
Kuban, *136*
Kulaks, *90, 92*
Kulturni Zivot, *213*
Kun, Bela, *61, 62, 63, 230*
Kuomitang, *76*
Kurdish People's Republic, *149*
Kurds, *260, 262*
Kuusinen, Otto, *114, 118*
Kuybyshev, *128*
Kuznetsov, Vasily, *245*
Ky, N. Cao, *220*

Labor and Socialist International, *41*
Labor Day, *18*
Laird, Melvin R., *250*
Laos, *183, 237, 239, 247, 259, 261, 262*
"Land and Freedom", *16*
Lassalle, Ferdinand, *2, 4, 10, 12, 13*
Latin America, *210*
    guerilla warfare in, *213*
Latin American Solidarity Organization, *223*
Latvia, *50, 60, 113*
Latvian S.S.R., *271*
Lausanne Treaty, *74*
Lavrov, Peter, *14*
League of Communists of Yugoslavia, *173, 217, 227*
League of Nations, *65, 85, 114, 150*
Lebanon, *194, 247, 252*
"Left Opposition", *85*
Lenart, Jozef, *211*
Lend-Lease, *129, 134, 168*
Lenin, Vladimir, *3, 20, 22, 23, 24, 26*
    writes *Development of Capitalism in Russia*, *24*
    publishes *Iskra*, *27*
    writes *What Is to Be Done?*, *27*
    *One Step Forward, Two Steps Backward*, *28*
    in 1905, *30, 32*
    in W. Europe, *35, 38, 41*
    *Critical Remarks on National Question*, *40*
    publishes *Imperialism, the Highest Stage of Capitalism*, *43*
    returns to Petrograd, *47*
    *State and Revolution*, *47*
    for Revolution, *49*
    rule of, *55-77*
    Testament of, *73, 188*

    death of, *77*
    centenary, *263*
Leningrad, *78, 214*
    siege of, *128, 132*
Lenin University, *84*
Lewis, John F., *101*
*L'Humanité*, *28*
Libya, *122, 255, 262*
Lidice, *131*
Liebknecht, Karl, *15, 35*
Liebknecht, Wilhelm, *4, 10, 14*
Lincoln Brigade, *103*
Lin Piao, *226, 245, 252*
*Literarny Listy*, *239*
*Literary Digest*, *59*
Lithuania, *56, 113, 169*
Lithuanian S.S.R., *271*
Little Entente, *66*
Litvinov, Maksim, *90, 129*
Litvinov Protocol, *90*
Liu Shao-chi, *195, 245*
Ljubljana, *35, 194*
Locarno, *83*
Lodge, Henry C., *245, 255, 259*
London International Conference, *95*
Longo, Luigi, *26, 217, 249*
Lublin, *138, 142*
*Luch*, *36*
Lumumba, Patrice, *202*
Lunik I, *196*
Luxembourg, *140*
Luxemburg, Rosa, *15, 23, 61*
Lvov, G. Prince, *45*
Lysenko, T. D., *158*

McArthur, Douglas, *136, 147, 167*
McArthy, Joseph R., *164*
MacDonald, Ramsey, *77*
McNamara, Robert S., *232*
Macedonia, *38, 80, 193, 194, 217, 245, 259*
Macedonian problem, *236*
Maček, Vladko, *100*
Madrid, *105*
Magnitogorsk, *90*
Malaga, *105*
Malaya, *171, 199*
Malayan Communist Party, *81*
Malenkov, G. M., *152, 163, 177, 184, 214*
Malik, Jacob A., *166, 236*
Malinovsky, Roman, *36, 60*
Malinovsky, Rodion Y., *193, 211*
Manchukuo, *94*
Manchuria, *93, 146*
Manescu, C., *226*
Manila, *142*
Maniu, J., *89*
Mannerheim, G. G., *58, 144*
Manuilsky, Dimitry Z., *100, 147*
Mao Tse-tung, *23, 36, 54, 69, 87, 92, 96, 101, 107, 179, 195, 274*
    on peasants, *84*
    Long March, *96, 98*
    publishes *On Guerilla War*, *105*
    negotiates with Chiang, *146*
    takes Peking, *160*
    in Moscow, *163*
    on world revolution, *264*

Maquis, *120*
"March on Washington" (1963), *211*
March Revolution (Petrograd), *44*
Marco Polo Bridge Incident, *106*
Marcuse, Herbert, *274*
Markos (Vafiades), General, *154*
Marković, Sima, *80, 82*
Marković, Svetozar, *35*
Marshall, George, *153-154, 198*
Marshall Plan, *154*
Martov, Julius, *3, 24*
Marx, Karl, *3, 4, 5, 6-10, 11, 54*
Marxism, historical sources of, *7*
Marxism-Stalinism, *176*
Masaryk, Jan, *154, 156, 237, 239*
Masaryk, Thomas G., *65, 87, 106*
Maurer, Gheorghe, *219, 226, 232*
May Day riots, *62*
May First celebrations, *22, 252*
Mediterranean, *238*
Mein, John G., *244*
Meir, Golda, *256*
*Mein Kampf,* *81*
Memel, *74*
Mensheviks, *3, 28*
Menshikov, M. A., *193*
Menzhinsky, V. R., *87*
Metaxas, John, *102*
Metternich, Prince, *4, 10*
Mexican Communist Party, *123*
Mexico, *82, 246*
Miami, Fla. Cuban groups, *209*
Middle East, *194, 248, 259, 261*
Mihajlov, Mihajlo, *218, 220, 230*
Mihajlović, Draža, *136, 138*
Mikolajczyk, Stanislav, *139*
Mikoyan, Anastas I., *24, 186, 196*
*Militant,* *89*
Military Revolutionary Committee, *50*
Milyukov, Paul N., *45, 46*
Mindszenty, Cardinal Joseph, *160, 161, 189*
Mir, *14, 34*
"Miracle on the Vistula River", *66*
Mirbach, Count von, *59*
Mitchell, Charlene, *243*
Mogilev, *44*
Moldavia, *169*
Moldavian Republic, *55*
Moldavian S.S.R., *121, 271*
Molotov, Vyacheslav, *92, 112, 122, 187, 190, 214*
Molotov-Ribbentrop Agreement, *112*
Mongolia, *147, 266*
Mongolian People's Republic, *70*
Montecassino, *137*
Montenegro, *123*
Montenegrins, *60*
Montgomery, *132*
Montreux Convention, *102, 152*
Moratorium Days, *257, 258*
Moscow, *56*
    battle of, *128*
    C.P.'s Summit in, *200*
Moscow University, *190*
Moslems, *171*
Mukden, *93*
Munich Agreement, *108*
Murmansk, *56*

Mussolini, Benito, *54, 68, 73, 134, 144*

Nagasaki, *146*
Nagy, Imre, *178, 188, 194*
Nanking, *86*
Narodniki. See *Populists.*
Narvik, *119*
Nasser, Gamal A., *195, 257*
National Commission on Violence, *259*
"National Communism", *117, 149*
National Congress of India, *105*
National Labor Union (Baltimore), *14*
National Socialism, *63*
National Workshops (France), *6*
Nazis, *89, 92*
Nazi-Soviet Pact, *112*
Nehru, J., *185, 196*
Netherlands, *140*
*Neue Zeit,* Die, *18*
*New American Cyclopedia,* *13*
New Deal, *94, 95*
New Economic Policy (N.E.P.), *69, 73*
New Left, *264, 274-275*
*New York Communist,* *62*
New York-Moscow air line, *243*
*New York Socialist,* *62*
*New York Times,* *173*
New Zealand, Communist Party of, *68*
Nicaragua, *200*
Nicholas II, Tsar, *23, 45, 59*
Nigeria, *239, 246*
Nihilists, *254*
N.I.R.A., *95*
Nixon, Richard M., *198, 244, 246, 249, 250, 252, 253, 257, 259, 260*
    in Bucharest, *255*
    on Vietnam, *263*
    on Cambodia, *263*
Nkrumah, Kwane, *195, 224*
N.K.V.D., *103*
"Non-Aligned" Nations, *199*
North Atlantic Treaty Organization (NATO), *160, 161, 167, 171, 251*
North Bukovina, *120*
*Northern Star,* *7*
North Korea, *155, 167, 252, 266*
North Rhodesia, *203*
North Vietnam, *202, 219, 230, 266*
Norway, *118*
*Nova Misao,* *180*
Novorossisk, *65*
Novotny, Antonin, *194, 216, 226, 238*
*Novy Mir,* *46*
Nozaka, Sanzo, *23*
Nuclear Weapons, *203*

Ochab, Edward, *222*
Oder-Neisse Line, *166*
Odessa, *138*
O'Hara, G.P., *166*
Okano, Susumu, *97*
Okinawa, *145, 258, 263*
Omsk, *60*
Operation Barbarossa, *123*
Operation Cottbus, *136*
Operation Marita, *122*

Operation Torch, *132*
Oran, *120*
Ordzhonikidze, Sergo, *69*
Organization of American States, *200, 252*
Organization of Ukrainian Nationalists, *124*
Orgburo, *61*
Oriente Province, *190*
Osubka-Morawski, M., *146*
Oumansky, M. *128*
Owen, Robert, *2*

Pacific, *146*
Pakistan, *249, 251*
Palach, Jan, *249*
Palestine Liberation Organization, *249*
Palme, Olof, *257, 262*
Palmer, Mitchel A., *64*
"Palmer Raids", *65*
Panama, *197, 218, 249*
Pan-Slav Congress, *10, 35, 128*
Pan-Slavs, *23*
Pap, Michael S., *v*
Papadopoulos, George, *234*
Paraguay, *91*
*Pariah, 35*
Paredes, J. M., *223*
Paris, *139, 240*
Pasternak, Boris, *195*
Pathet Lao, *198, 249, 250, 263*
Pauker, Anna, *74, 155, 172, 199*
Paul VI, Pope, *210, 221*
Paulus, Friedrich von, *132*
Pearl Harbor, *130*
Peasants, *89*
Peking, *69, 106, 149, 250*
Penkovsky, Oleg V., *210*
*People, 22*
*People's Daily, 194, 225*
"People's Will", *17*
Pepper (Pogany), John, *91*
Peru, *110, 248*
Peshkov, A. M. See *Maksim Gorky.*
Pestel, Paul, *2, 4*
Pétain, Henri P., *120*
Petkov, Nikola, *154*
Petlyura, Simon V., *66, 85*
Petrograd, *44*
Petrograd Soviet, *44, 47*
Petsamo, *141*
Philadelphia, *16*
Philippines, *97, 141, 146, 260, 261*
    Communist guerilla in, *238*
Pieck, Wilhelm, *16, 149, 200*
Pilsen, *145, 177*
Pilsudski, Josef, *14, 22, 66, 73, 85, 100*
Plastiras, N., *95*
Plekhanov, George V., *3, 16-17, 18-19, 40, 50*
Plekhve, V. K., *28*
Podgorny, Nikolai V., *199, 210, 218, 223, 232, 258*
    visits Paul Vi, *228*
Pokrovsky, M. N., *97*
Poland, *60, 107, 113, 145, 153, 188, 225, 238, 239,*
    *266*
Poles, *10*
Polish-German Pact, *96*
Polish Legion, *41*
Polish Millenium, *222-223*

Polish National Council, *138*
Polish Provisional Government, *142*
Polish Revolt of 1830, *6*
Polish Revolt of 1863, *13*
Polish Workers' Party, *130, 155*
Politburo, *61*
Polycentrism of Communism, *viii, 185, 214*
Pompidou, Georges, *241, 254, 261*
Popular Front, *96*
Populism, *14*
Populists, *16*
Port Arthur, *163, 183*
Portsmouth Treaty, *30*
Postyshev, P., *95*
Potsdam Conference, *146*
*Potyemkin, 30*
Powers, G.F., *200, 206*
Poznan, *187*
Prague, *x, 10, 234*
*Pravda, 36, 165*
    attacks Czech leaders, *240, 243*
Presidium, *172*
Prestes, L. C., *25, 102*
Princip, Gavrilo, *40*
Proletarian Party of America, *71*
Proletarians, *10*
Protectorate of Bohemia-Moravia, *110*
Protocols of Rome, *97*
Proudhon, Pierre J., *2, 6*
Provisional Government, *45*
Prussia, *14*
*Pueblo, 236, 246*
Pullman Strike, *23*
Putilov factories, *44*

Quebec, *134*

Rada, *50*
Radek, Karl, *23*
Radetsky, general, *10*
Radić, Stjepan, *89*
Rajk, Laszlo, *162*
Rakosi, Matyas, *22, 63, 160*
Ranković, Aleksander, *226*
Rapallo Treaty, *72*
Rasputin, G. Y., *43*
Reagan, Ronald, *261*
Red Army, *59, 105, 113, 117, 120, 124, 136-137,*
    *139, 140, 141, 144*
    crushes Hungarian Revolt, *189*
Red Guards, *225, 229*
Red Scare in America, *64*
Red Square, *77*
*Red Star, 163*
Reed, John S., *20, 48, 63, 66, 68, 81*
    writes *Ten Days That Shook the World, 48*
Reichstag, *17, 35*
Reichstag Fire Trial, *96*
Renner, Karl, *15, 34, 144, 167, 169*
*Revolution, Die, 11*
*Revolutionary Age, 60*
Revolutions of 1848, *10, 11*
*Rheinische Zeitung, 7*
Rhodesia, *262*
Riga, *62*
Riga Treaty, *69*
Rivera, Primo De, *91*

Rockefeller, Nelson A., *252, 258*
Rodzianko, M., *44*
Roehm, Ernst, *97*
Rogers, William, *252, 261*
Rokossovsky, K. K., *161, 163, 189*
Rome-Berlin Axis, *103*
Rommel, E., *131*
Roosevelt, Franklin D., *54, 94-95, 103, 122, 142, 144*
Root Mission, *47*
Rosenberg, Alfred, *126*
Rosenberg, Ethel, *166*
Rosenberg, Julius, *166*
Rostov, *56*
Rubin, Jerry C., *261*
Ruble, *201*
*Rude Pravo, 158, 250, 257*
Ruge, Arnold, *8*
Rumania, *43, 60, 106, 110, 200, 209, 221, 249, 266*
    Communist Party of, *70*
    monarchy abolished, *155*
    Western orientation, *197*
    and the Sino-Soviet split, *214*
    new constitution, *221*
    independent course, *225, 239*
    threatened by Soviets, *244-245*
Rumanians, *10*
Rumanian Workers' Party (Communists), *156*
Rusk, Dean, *207, 213, 234*
Russia, *3, 10, 14, 42, 49*
    Constituent Assembly, *55*
    Civil War in, *64*
    Committee for Liberation of, *141*
Russian Revolution of 1905, *30-32*
    October Manifesto, *30*
    Duma, *30*
    Peasants' Union, *30*
Russian Orthodox Church, *166, 191*
Russian Revolution of 1917, *44-51, 60*
Russian Social Democratic Labor Party, *25, 28, 32*
Russian Soviet Federated Socialist Republic, *59, 73-74, 251*
Ruthenberg, Charles E., *63, 83*
Rykov, A. I., *50, 92*
Ryti, Risto, *113*

Saar Plebiscite, *98, 100*
Sacco, Nicola, *70*
Sacco and Vanzetti case, *86, 87*
Saigon, *182*
Saint Germain Treaty, *64*
Saint-Simon, Claude H., *2*
Salerno, *136*
SALT, *258, 263*
San Stefano Treaty, *17, 193*
Santiago de Chile, *198*
"Satellites", *155, 162, 173, 203*
Sato, Eisaku, *258, 259*
Sauckel, Fritz, *130*
Schlesinger, Arthur, Jr., *264*
Schuschnigg, Kurt, *97, 102*
Seattle, Wash., *61*
"Second Declaration of Havana", *206*
Second French Empire, *11*
Second Front, *128, 131*
Second International, *22, 26, 28, 34, 35, 36*
Sedan, *15*
Seoul, *167*

Serbia, *35, 40, 124*
Serbians, *10*
Serbs, Croats, and Slovenes, Kingdom of, *60*
Sergius, Patriarch, *134*
Serov, Ivan, *181, 195*
Sevastopol, *131*
"Seventies", *259*
Sèvres Treaty, *68*
Shanghai, *82*
Shastri, L.B., *220*
Shaw, George B., *20*
Shehu, Mehmet, *183, 225*
Shelepin, A. N., *217, 260*
Shepilov, D. T., *187*
Shevchenko, Taras, *200, 215*
Siberia, *59*
Sicily, *134*
Sierra Maestras, *190*
Sihanouk, Norodom, *262*
Sik, Ota, *245, 253*
Sikorsky, Wladyslaw, *130*
Simović, Dušan, *123*
Singapore, *131*
Sino-Cuban Friendship Society, *199*
Sino-Indian Treaty, *177*
Sino-Rumanian Trade Agreement, *209*
Sino-Soviet Split, *190, 199, 200, 204, 221, 248*
Sinyavsky, Andrei, *223*
Siroky, Viliam, *164, 211*
Skanderbeg, G. K., *236*
Skopje, *204*
Skoropadsky, P. P., *58*
Slansky, Rudolf, *170*
Slavs, *10*
Slipy, J., *150, 209*
Slovakia, *110*
    Communist Party of, *178, 213*
Slovak Soviet Republic, *62*
Slovaks, *10, 140, 164, 211, 238*
Slovenia, *80, 126, 217*
Smetona, Anthony, *86*
Smith, Ian, *262*
Smolensk, *124*
Smrkovsky, Jozef, *239*
Smyrna, *72*
Sobranie, *38*
Social Democratic Party of America, *24*
Social Democratic Party of Germany, *17*
Social Democratic Workingmen's Party of Saxony, *14*
"Socialism in One Country", *78*
Socialism, Utopian and Marxian, *vii*
Socialist Labor Party of North America, *17*
Socialist Party of America, *27*
Socialist Party of the United States, *36*
Socialist Revisionism, *vii, 3, 28*
Socialist Revolutionaries, *26, 32*
Socialist Unity Party (E. Germany), *150*
Social Security Act, *101*
Sofia, *211*
Solzhenitsyn, Alexander, *231, 257, 258*
Song My (My Lai), *258, 259*
Sorel, Georges, *23*
Sorge, Friedrich A., *11, 15*
South Brantree, Mass., *70*
South Vietnam, *166, 187, 200, 213, 215, 250, 251, 253*
    U.S. advisers to, *202*

U.S. pledge to, *203*
People's Revolutionary Party of, *206*
U.S. casualties in, *209, 218, 220, 223, 230, 241*
escalation of war, *220-221, 226, 228, 232, 236, 239*
Soviet, *3, 30, 45*
Soviet Bloc, *227*
Soviet Economy, *190*
Soviet Intelligentsia, *234*
Soviet Republics, *271*
*Sozialdemokrat, 18*
Spain, *51, 94, 102,248*
Civil War in, *102-103, 106*
Spartacus Group, *42, 61*
Špiljak, Mika, *231, 235*
Sputnik, *192*
Stakhanov, Alexei, *101*
Stalin, Joseph V., *viii, 17, 27, 30, 32, 34-35, 38, 45, 90, 94, 163*
writes *Marxism and National Question, 36*
Great Purges, *51*
Secretary General, *72*
publishes *The Foundations of Leninism, 78*
denounces Trotsky, *86*
conception of history, *97*
opposition to, *103*
publishes *History of the C.P.S.U.-Short Course, 108*
Supreme Commander, *126*
opposes Balkan Federation, *155*
death of, *174*
denounced by Khrushchev, *204*
Stalingrad Battle, *132*
Stalinism, *88, 177, 191*
Stambuliski, Alexander, *63-64*
Stauffenberg, Claus, *139*
Stephen, Uriah, *17*
Stepinac, Alojzije, *152, 173*
Stettin, *150*
Stevenson, Adlai E., *208, 214*
Stewart, Michael, *220*
Stojadinović, Milan, *100*
Stolypin, P. A., *35*
Stoph, Willi, *262*
St. Petersburg, *28*
Straits, *178*
Students for Democratic Society, (SDS), *252, 261*
Šubašić, Ivan, *138, 141*
Sudeten Germans, *166*
Sudetenland, *106, 107*
Suez, *189, 250, 254*
Suharto, *221, 224, 265*
Sukarno, *201, 224*
Sun Yat-sen, *36, 76, 82*
Supreme Soviet, *199*
Supreme Court, *208*
Suslov, Mikhail, *155, 185*
Svoboda, Ludvik, *238, 244, 246, 257*
Sweden, *168*
Swiss Federation of the Jura, *16*
Sylis, William H., *14*
Syndicalist League of America, *35*
Syria, *124, 224*

Tadjikistan, *74*
Tadjik S.S.R., *91, 251*
Tallin, *81*

Tammersfors, *34*
Tannenberg Battle, *41*
Tannu Tuva, *140*
Tanzania, *242*
Tass Agency, *168*
Tchaikovsky, N.K., *60*
Teheran Conference, *117, 136-137*
*Telegram, 229*
"Ten Commandments of Protest", *258*
Teschen, *108*
Thaelmann, Ernst, *16, 95*
Thailand, *130, 230, 242, 254*
Thant, U, *204, 222, 228*
Third International (Comintern), *42;* see also *Comintern.*
Third Reich, *144*
Thomas, Norman, *94*
Thorez, Maurice, *26, 95, 145*
Thuringia, *76*
Tibet, *170, 196*
Tiflis, *28, 186*
Timoshenko, Semyon K., *118*
Tiso, Josef, *153*
Tito, *23, 41, 98, 100, 103, 131, 140, 171, 189, 192, 198, 208, 214, 219, 220, 250*
Secretary General of C.P.Y., *106*
moves to Belgrade, *123*
expelled from Cominform, *158*
appeals to the West, *161*
neutralism, *165*
receives U.S. aid, *167*
visits U.S.S.R., *187*
in U.N., *200*
visits Africa, *202*
in Latin America, *211*
addresses U.N., *211*
on nationalism, *224*
supports Dubček, *243-244*
"Titoists", *162*
Titov, Gherman S., *203*
Togliatti, Palmiro, *23, 134, 164, 216*
Toilers of the Far East, *71*
Tonkin Gulf, *215*
Torgau, *144*
Torrado, Dorticos, *216*
Trans-Caucasian Federation, *58*
Transcendentalist Movement, *4*
Trans-Siberian Railroad, *58*
Transylvania, *121*
Trianon Treaty, *66*
Tri-Continental Solidarity Conference, *223*
Trieste, *144, 145, 151, 183*
Tripartite Pact, *122*
Triple Alliance, *40*
Triple Entente, *40*
Trotsky (Bronstein), Leon, *3, 17, 30, 32, 40, 46, 87*
founder of the Red Army, *59*
on "Permanent Revolution", *78*
removed as Commissar, *82*
expelled from the Party, *88*
expelled from the U.S.S.R., *90*
assassinated, *121*
Trujillo, R. L., *200, 202*
"Truman Doctrine", *153*
Truman, Harry S., *156, 160*
Tsankov, Alexander, *74*
Tsaritsyn, *58*

Tsarskoe Selo, *50*
Tsederbaum. See *Julius Martov.*
Tukhachevsky, M., *66, 105, 109*
Tunisia, *132*
Turkestanians, *169*
Turkey, *69, 101, 128, 193*
Turkmen S.S.R., *251*

Uganda, *255*
Ukraine, *45, 47, 54, 55*
    defeated by Soviets, *68*
    nationalism in, *95, 151*
Ukrainian Soviet Republic, *60*
Ukrainian S.S.R., *271*
Ukrainians, *10*
Ukrainian writers, *234*
Ulbricht, Walter, *23, 178, 197, 213, 227,256*
Ulster, *246, 256*
Ulyanov, A.I., *20*
Ulyanov, Vladimir Ilich. See *Lenin.*
"Unconditional Surrender", *132*
Uniate Church, *150, 159*
Union of Polish Patriots, *130*
U.P.A. (Ukrainian Insurgent Army), *132, 164*
Union of Soviet Socialist Republics (U.S.S.R.),
    *53, 73, 78, 86, 266*
    collectivization, *90*
    slave labor, *92, 161, 168*
    non-aggression pacts, *92-94*
    famine, *93*
    industrialization, *94*
    "Stalin Constitution", *104*
    in Baltic area, *120-121*
    invasion by Germany, *127*
    partisan warfare, *130*
    defeats Finland, *140*
    area of domination, *167*
    Presidium, *177*
    explodes H-bomb, *179*
    Seven-Year Plan, *195*
United Arab Republic, *217*
United Nations, *131, 144-145, 147, 246*
    Balkan Committee, *158*
    Security Council, *167*
    and Hungarian Revolution, *188-189*
U.N.R.R.A., *154, 273*
United States, *61*
    recognizes U.S.S.R., *96*
    Neutrality Act, *105*
    Communist Party, *119, 124*
    enters W.W.II., *130*
    Un-American Activities, *158*
    Department of State, *170, 219*
    Southeast Asia Resolution, *216*
    anti-war demonstrations, *222, 224, 248, 263-264*
    reaction to Soviet occupation of
        Czechoslovakia, *244*
    foreign aid, *272-273*
    "Foreign Policy for the 1970's", *261*
U. S. Steel strike (1919), *63*
United Toilers of America, *72*
Universal Workingmen's Association (Saxony), *12*
Ussuri River, *250*
U-2 Incident, *199*
Uzbekistan, *74*
Uzbek S.S.R., *271*

Vanzetti, Bartolomeo, *70*
Varga, Eugene, *153*
Vargas, Getulio, *100*
Vasilevsky, A. M., *161*
Vatican, *167, 216, 226*
Vatican II Council, *210, 222*
V - E Day, *144*
Venezuela, *212, 246*
Venice, *97*
Venizelos, E., *95*
Versailles Treaty, *62*
Viborg (Viipuri), *114, 119*
Vichy, *120, 132*
Vienna, *10, 60, 87*
Viet Cong, *218, 242*
Vietminh, *124, 201*
Vietnam, *146, 183, 228, 235, 246, 250, 251, 261*
Vietnam, Democratic Republic of, *163*
Vietnam Peace talks, *240*
Vietnamese Independence League, *123*
Vilna, *66*
Vladivostok, *58*
Vlasov, A. A., *141, 151*
Voice of America, *170, 229*
Voitinsky, Gregory, *70*
Volga-Don Canal, *172*
Volga Germans, *128*
Volkspolizei, *159*
*Volkstribun, 8*
Volyn Guards, *44*
Voorhis Act, *122*
Vorkuta Camp, *179*
Voroshilov, K. Y., *191*
*Vorwaerts, 22*
Vyshinsky, A. Y., *105, 159, 183*

Wallace, Henry A., *152, 154-155, 156, 159*
Wall Street bombing, *63*
War Communism, *55*
Ware Group, *164*
Warren Commission, *212, 216*
Warsaw, *41, 236, 237*
    Ghetto uprising, *134*
    uprising (1944), *139-140*
Warsaw Pact, *185, 218, 251, 257*
    maneuvers in Czechoslovakia, *242*
    troops invade Czechoslovakia, *244-245*
Weathermen, *262*
Webb, Sidney, *20*
Wells, H. G., *25*
West Europe, Common Market of, *160*
West German industry, *213*
West Germany, *172, 253*
Westmoreland, William C., *215, 232*
West Ukraine, *114*
Weydemeyer, Joseph, *11, 12*
Weygand, Maxime, *66*
Whampoa Military Academy, *78*
Wheeler, Earle, *254*
Wilson, Harold, *216, 226*
Wilson, Woodrow, *43, 45, 59, 78*
Witos, W., *85*
Witte, Segei, *30, 31*
*Woodbull and Claflin's Weekly, 16*
Woodstock, N. Y., *70*
*Worker, 72*
Workers' Party of America, *71*

Workingmen's Party of New York, *4*
World Communism, *84, 102, 193, 267-270*
    membership, *202, 235*
        "Program for the Building of Communist
           Society", *203*
    divisions, *217*
    Communist-dominated countries, *266*
*World Communist Movement, viii*
World Federation of Trade Unions, *147*
World War I, *40, 60*
World War II, *113, 115, 116, 118-119, 120*
    Combined Chiefs of Staff, *131*
    North Africa, *134*
    D-Day, *138*
World Youth Festival, *154*
Wrangel, N. N., *65, 68*
Wuhan, *84*
Wyszynski, Stefan, *225-226*

Yagoda, G. G., *103*
Yakubovsky, Ivan, *249*
Yalta Conference, *142*
"Year of the Moon", *248*
Yekaterinburg, *59*
Yevtushenko, E., *207*
Yezhov, N. I., *101*
Yippies, *261*
Young Turks, *35*
Young Workers' League of America, *72*
Yudenich, N. N., *62*

Yugoslavia, *62, 66, 68, 88, 162, 266, 251, 253*
    dictatorship, *90*
    partisans, *126, 141*
    republic, *148*
    Fifth Congress of the C.P.Y., *158*
    Sixth Party Congress, *173*
    armed forces, *198*
    economic reforms, *207, 221*
    new constitution, *209*
    threat by Soviets, *244-246*
    U.S. aid to, *253*
Yunnan, *100*

Zachariadis, N., *101*
Zagreb, *122*
Zakopane, *38*
Zamora, Alcala, *93*
Zanzibar, *213*
Zapotocki, Antonin, *177*
Zasulich, Vera, *17, 18*
*Zeri i Populit, 239*
Zhdanov, A., *104, 151, 158*
Zhivkov, Todor, *213, 254*
Zhukov, G. K., *129, 184, 193*
Zimmerwald Conference, *42*
Zimmerwald Union, *42*
Zinoviev, G., *42, 61*
"Zinoviev Letter", *81*
Zionism, *161, 174*
Zog, Ahmed, *71, 89*
Zorin, Valerian, *156*